California
Real Estate Practice

California
Real Estate Practice

Lowell Anderson
Daniel S. Otto

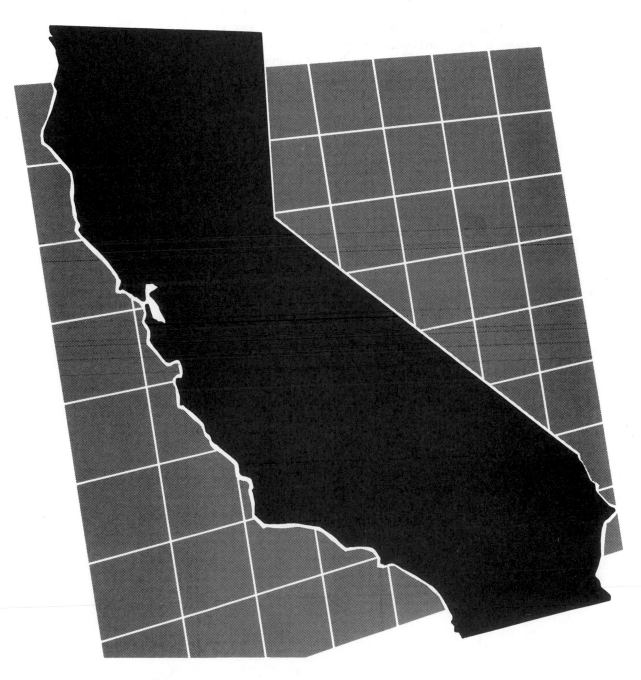

REAL ESTATE EDUCATION COMPANY
a division of Longman Financial Services Institute, Inc.

©1987 by Longman Group USA Inc.

Published by Longman Financial Services Publishing, Inc./Chicago
a Longman Group USA company

Printed in the United States of America.

87 88 89 10 9 8 7 6 5 4 3 2

Library of Congress Cataloging-in-Publication Data

Anderson, Lowell.
    California real estate practice.

    Includes index.
    1. Real estate business--Law and legislation--
California. 2. Real property--California.
I. Otto, Daniel S. II. Title.
KFC446.R3A93 1987   346.79404'37   86-31352
ISBN 0-88462-534-6   347.9406437

Cover Design: Jim Buddenbaum
Illustrations: Michael Arnold

Contents

Chapter 7 **Obtaining and Presenting the Offer   115**

Chapter 10   **Taxation of Real Property Ownership 195**

Chapter 11   **Tax Implications of Home Ownership   215**

Chapter 14　　　　**Organization and Administration of a Real Estate Office 275**

Preface

Every effort has been made by the authors and the publisher to verify the accuracy of the material contained in this textbook and to present the latest changes. The text is to be used in the three-unit or quarter-unit equivalent course in Real Estate Practice. This course fulfills the requirements for the California Real Estate Broker's license or may apply toward the new requirements for the Real Estate Sales license as well as providing three units of the required 24 units needed for a California Real Estate Certificate.

Each chapter is complete with a Chapter Preview, Terms To Look For, Lesson Content, Summary and Review Questions. There also is a separate Test Bank and Practicum that provide additional multiple-choice questions plus exercises that ask students to apply what they have learned. This book also contains the answers to the end-of-chapter questions.

By supplementing the text with the *Real Estate Reference Book,* the *California Real Estate Bulletin,* and the new *California Real Estate Practice Instructor* and *Student Guides,* the instructor can develop a valuable package to use in teaching Real Estate Practices.

The *Real Estate Practice Guides* produced by the Community College Chancellor's Office go hand in hand with the chapters in the text. The guides may be obtained from the Real Estate Education Center at Modesto Junior College. Teachers may obtain the *Instructor's Guide* through their coordinator and students may obtain their copy from college bookstores.

Using the text, the guides, and available publications from the Department of Real Estate, the students can keep abreast of every aspect of the laws and regulations affecting such dynamic and changing subjects as: capital gains treatment for taxes, loan brokerage fees, interest rates, government participation loans, recovery fund amounts, agency relationships, *Easton* liabilities and other vital changes.

Acknowledgments

The authors would like to recognize the support they have received from their fellow coordinators and instructors. This support has been in the form of ideas and worthwhile suggestions, as well as the encouragement to produce a much needed *new* text in this vital and demanding area. To name all who have contributed in some way to the completion of this project would be a monumental task.

We do wish to mention a few whose efforts and assistance have been most helpful:

MARJORIE READ — SAN DIEGO
EVELYN DANIEL — SANTA ANA
LOIS KADOSH — BERKELEY
FRANK BATTINO — OAKLAND
JEAN STROHL — LA MESA
SILAS ELY — SANTA MONICA
CHET PLATT — IRVINE
JOE DECARLO — NEWPORT BEACH
FRANK FOWLER — EL CAMINO
JOHN JURIVICH — REDWOOD CITY
CECELIA HOPKINS — SAN MATEO
GEORGE BAIREY — MODESTO
JERRY WEINSHEINK — C.A.R.
TOM MABRY — DEPARTMENT OF REAL ESTATE

Several forms and illustrations have been provided courtesy of the California Association of REALTORS®, Ticor Title Insurance Company of California, the National Association of REALTORS® and Founders Title Company. In addition, the authors would like to thank William H. Pivar and Jim Londay for permitting us to reprint material from their respective texts, *Classified Secrets* and *List for Success*.

We wish to dedicate the book to our wives and families who have been so understanding and patient with us during the long hours of research and preparation.

1

The Real Estate Brokerage
Business and Regulations

Chapter Preview   This chapter begins by explaining the structure of the California Department of
Real Estate and its duties and responsibilities relating to the California Real Estate
Law. The balance of the chapter is devoted to such subjects as real estate licensing
requirements, the Real Estate Education Fund, the continuing education program,
publications of the real estate department, trade and professional associations and
codes of ethics.

Terms To Look For   **California Code of Ethics**
Code of ethics
Commissioner's regulations
Continuing education
Real Estate Advisory Commission
Real estate broker
Real Estate Commissioner
Real Estate Fund
Realtist
REALTOR®

California Real Estate Law

Before considering the various techniques and methods for the operation of a real estate business, it is necessary to thoroughly understand the *legal* requirements of maintaining a real estate business. The California Real Estate Law, or the licensing law, as it was enacted and is often referred to, is intended to: (1) protect the general public from harm at the hands of dishonest and incompetent agents and (2) protect honest agents from loss of good reputation through adverse publicity and public resentment caused by the unprincipled and unscrupulous agents who occasionally infiltrate the ranks.

Department of Real Estate

The real estate law is administered by the State Department of Real Estate (formerly the Division of Real Estate), which was created by legislative act in 1917. The chief executive of the department is the **Real Estate Commissioner.** The Governor appoints the Commissioner at his or her discretion. To be eligible to serve as Commissioner, a person must have been a real estate broker actively engaged in business in California for five years or must possess related experience associated with real estate activity in California for five years within the past ten years prior to his or her appointment.

 The Department of Real Estate, under the provisions of the real estate law, is responsible for screening, qualifying and testing license applicants; investigating complaints against licensees; regulating some aspects of the sale of subdivisions; regulating certain aspects of syndications, real property securities and nonexempt franchises; and investigating nonlicensees accused of performing acts for which a license is required.

 The Commissioner's mandated responsibility is to determine administrative policy and to enforce the real estate law. Assisting the Commissioner in a consultative capacity is the Real Estate Advisory Commission.

Real Estate Advisory Commission

 The **Real Estate Advisory Commission** is composed of ten members, each appointed by the Commissioner to serve at the Commissioner's pleasure. Six of the members must be real estate brokers, licensed in California, and four are public members. The Commissioner serves as chairman of the commission. Members of the commission, with the exception of the Commissioner, serve without compensation, except that each may receive reimbursement for actual and necessary expenses incurred in the discharge of duties.

The commission must meet at least four times each year to advise the Commissioner on functions and policies of the real estate department—how it may best serve the people of the state and recognize the legitimate needs of the industry that it regulates. The commission makes recommendations it deems beneficial and appropriate for licensees and the general public.

Real Estate Licensing

 A person must be licensed as a real estate salesperson or a **real estate broker** to engage in any real estate transaction in which he or she acts for others for compensation. A real estate transaction is practically any real estate activity, including buying, selling, renting, subdividing, financing and leasing for a fee.

Regular broker and sales licenses are granted for a period of four years. In addition, restricted licenses may be issued by the Commissioner in certain cases where a license has been suspended, revoked or denied after a hearing. At the Commissioner's discretion, the license may be restricted in any one of the following ways:

1. The time period for which the license is issued may be shortened.

2. The candidate may be restricted to working for one particular broker.

3. The licensee may be required to submit certain special reports.

4. The licensee's operations may be restricted to a specific geographic area.

In effect, these restricted licenses are probationary licenses.

A license may be renewed by payment of required fees if renewed before its expiration. After the license expires, it may be renewed, if the licensee is otherwise qualified, within two years of its expiration and after payment of a late renewal fee. The maximum late penalty may not exceed $25. In addition, anyone renewing a license must complete 45 hours of approved continuing education; this will be explained in detail later in the chapter.

Requirements for a Salesperson License After January 1, 1986

To qualify for an original salesperson license, a candidate must:

1. be at least 18 years old;

2. have a reputation for honesty, truthfulness and integrity;

3. pass the qualifying examination provided;

4. make application on a form prescribed by the Commissioner;

5. have successfully completed a three-semester unit (or equivalent quarter course) in real estate principles; and

6. either prior to issuance of the original license or within 18 months after issuance, complete two additional basic real estate courses selected from among the following:

- Real Estate Practice
- Legal Aspects of Real Estate
- Real Estate Appraisal
- Real Estate Finance
- Real Estate Accounting
- Real Estate Economics
- Business Law
- Escrows
- Property Management
- Real Estate Office Administration

 On the first *renewal* of a salesperson license, licensees who have met the foregoing requirements will not be required to complete continuing education requirements (for the first four years), *except* for a minimum three-clock-hour course, in "Ethics."

The license fee for a real estate salesperson is $120 for applicants who have satisfied all of the educational requirements (three courses) prior to the issuance of the license. The fee for those who have not satisfied all of the requirements prior to the issuance of the license is $145.

Requirements for a Broker License After January 1, 1986

A candidate for a real estate broker's license after January 1, 1986, must meet the following qualifications:

1. be at least 18 years of age;

2. have at least two years' full-time experience as a salesperson or equivalent background (such as a B.S. degree from an accredited university) that could be accepted in lieu of the experience requirement at the discretion of the Department of Real Estate;

3. be honest and truthful;

4. pass the qualifying examination;

5. make application on a form prescribed by the Commissioner; and

6. have successfully completed eight statutory three-semester unit (or equivalent quarter) college-level courses. These five courses must be completed:

   - Real Estate Practice
   - Legal Aspects of Real Estate
   - Real Estate Finance
   - Real Estate Appraisal
   - Real Estate Economics or Accounting

In addition, the remaining three courses are to be selected from the following:

- Real Estate Administration
- Advanced Real Estate Appraisal
- Real Estate Principles
- Property Management
- Legal Aspects of Real Estate
- Advanced Finance
- Business Law
- Escrows
- Real Estate Office Administration

The Licensing Examination

The salesperson and broker licensing examinations are designed to test a prospective licensee's practical knowledge. To ensure that the examinations are constructed in such a way as to test a candidate's knowledge of the fundamentals of real estate transactions, five major fields of testing have been established, to which all real estate subject matter is indexed.

 Law—The candidate must demonstrate a reasonable understanding of general real estate law and the license law and its application to real estate transactions. This includes the analysis of listings and deposit receipts.

2. *Matters of Public Control*—The applicant must possess a general understanding of the impact of federal, state and local authority on zoning, subdivision, the power of eminent domain and real estate transactions in general.

3. *Appraisal*—The candidate must demonstrate a knowledge of valuation methods sufficient to serve clients and the general public in a useful and dependable manner.

4. *Finance*—The candidate must possess a general knowledge of available financial sources, procedures, practices and government participation sufficient to assist clients in obtaining and utilizing credit in real estate transactions.[1]

5. In addition, the examination covers the following miscellaneous areas:

   - *Income Taxation*—applied to sale of residences, type of installment sales, capital gains, corporations, real estate investment trusts;

   - *Land Development*—water supply, sewage drainage, streets and community facilities;

   - *Business Ethics*—including familiarity with the Ethics and Professional Conduct Code;

   - *Rentals*—property management;

   - *Escrow*—nature and purpose, requisites, obligations of parties involved in escrow transactions;

   - *Mathematics*—computations required in real estate transactions;

   - *Title Insurance;*

   - *Residential Building Design and Construction;* and

   - *Civil Rights and Discrimination Practices*—in all phases of the real estate industry, including federal and state fair housing laws.

Examination and License Fees

The *California Real Estate Reference Book* lists the license and examination fees for the different types of license examinations. They are:

Real estate broker's license examination fee	$ 50.00
Real estate broker's license (four years)	165.00
Real estate sales license examination fee	25.00
Real estate sales license (four years)	120.00

An applicant who fails to qualify for a license because of lack of experience or inability to pass the examination is not entitled to a refund of the fee paid with the application.

Commissioner's Regulations

The Commissioner is empowered by law to issue **regulations** to aid in the administration and enforcement of the real estate law. These regulations, known as the *Regulations of the Real Estate Commissioner,* have the same force and effect as the

---

[1] *California Department of Real Estate Reference Book,* 1984–1985 edition, p. 37.

law itself and are incorporated as part of the California Administrative Code. Licensees and prospective licensees should have a thorough knowledge of these regulations; at the very least, they should know where this knowledge can be obtained.

 The Commissioner's regulations are public information—they appear in the Department of Real Estate's publication, *Real Estate Law.* In addition, newly enacted regulations are printed in the magazine, *Real Estate,* published by the California Association of REALTORS®. Salespersons and brokers also will find current regulations printed in the *Real Estate Bulletin* of the Department of Real Estate. Figure 1.1 shows an example of these regulations.

Figure 1.1
Regulation 2770
—"Advertising"

Regulation 2770—"Advertising" Advertising of any service for which a license issued under the provisions of the real estate law is required shall not be under the name of the salesperson, unless the name of the employing broker is set forth.

The Education, Research and Recovery Fund

Fifteen percent of a licensee's fees is used for real estate education and research, while five percent is placed in a recovery fund.

Education and Research

Supported and stimulated by the organized real estate industry in 1949, the Real Estate Commissioner recommended the use of a portion of license funds for the development of real estate education and research in California. Augmented by these funds, the development of real estate education in California has been phenomenal. Most of the state's community colleges have full-fledged real estate programs that include the 24 units required to receive the California Real Estate Certificate. An attempt to standardize the courses needed has not been entirely successful, so the requirements for the certificate vary somewhat among the individual community colleges. Figure 1.2 illustrates representative certificate programs offered by community colleges. Most of the community colleges that offer the California Real Estate Certificate provide additional real estate courses that are required for an Associate in Arts or Science Degree in Real Estate and that at the same time fulfill the educational requirements for the broker's license examination.

Through the provisions of the Education and Research Act, the University of California, California State Universities, Extension Universities and private colleges have been able to offer advanced real estate courses and to conduct real estate research projects. The research has studied and reported on such topics as the characteristics of the real estate industry, real estate marketing problems, problems of urbanization, growth trends and other aspects of real estate development in the state. Many of these educational institutions publish periodicals and annotated bibliographies related to the studies of current real estate problems. They welcome inquiries regarding these publications and frequently offer them at little or no cost to those who are interested.

Commissioner's Recovery Fund In 1963 a recovery feature was added to the Education and Research Fund, changing the name to the Education, Research and Recovery Fund. In 1976 the Real Estate Education Research and Recovery Fund became known as the **Real Estate Fund.** In 1983 a separate account in this fund comprising 15 percent of the amount of licensees fees collected was devoted to Education and Research and a separate account comprising five percent of the amount of license fees collected was allocated to the Recovery Account. The recovery portion of the fund is used to underwrite uncollectible court judgments obtained against licensees on the basis of fraud or misrepresentation. If a person is wronged by a licensee's illegal actions and is unable to receive adequate satisfaction from the courts, that person may apply to the Commissioner's Recovery Fund for restitution. The law permits a payment of up to $20,000 to any person who can justify his or her position. If the case involves more than one person, the Recovery Fund will allow up to $100,000 for any one action.

**Figure 1.2
Representative
Certificate
Programs**

THE REAL ESTATE CERTIFICATE

	Real Estate Requirements	Units
Real 11	Real Estate Principles	3
Real 20	Real Estate Finance	3
Real 25	Legal Aspects of Real Estate	3
Real 30	Real Estate Practice	3
Real 31	Real Estate Appraisal	3
Real 60	Real Estate Economics	3
		18

Division Requirements

Any Courses in Accounting	3
Fin 11 or 12 Business Law	3
Minimum Units Required	24

THE REAL ESTATE CERTIFICATE

Completion of eight basic courses, or 24 units.

Required:
1. Real Estate Principles
2. Real Estate Practice
3. Legal Aspects of Real Estate
4. Real Estate Finance
5. Real Estate Appraisal I
6. Real Estate Economics

Suggested Electives:
1. Tax Aspects and Real Estate Exchanges
2. Real Estate Appraisal II
3. Property Management
4. Real Estate Salesmanship
5. Real Estate Practice (Advanced)
6. Escrow Principles
7. Escrow Practice
8. Escrow Problems

Continuing Education

Through Article 10170 of the real estate law, the legislature introduced **continuing education** requirements adopted by the Commissioner and designating certain prerequisites to the renewal of real estate licenses on and after January 1, 1981. To renew a real estate sales or broker's license, the licensee must complete 45 clock hours of instruction in approved educational courses, seminars, conferences or their equivalent during the four-year period preceding the renewal application.

The following statement intended to clarify the education required is contained in Article 10170.4:

> In exercising the authority under this article, the Commissioner shall establish standards which will assure reasonable currency of knowledge as a basis for a level of real estate practice which will provide a high level of consumer protection and service. The standards shall permit a variety of alternatives of subject material to licensees, taking cognizance of specialized areas of practice and alternatives in sources of programs considering availability in area and time.

Note that continuing education offerings will not include courses that are already a part of the regular real estate education program.

Each approved continuing education course must include an examination on the material presented. The Commissioner's main purpose in requiring this examination is to make the continuing education program more meaningful and to assure that those taking the classes will get value from the programs and be present not only in body but also in mind and spirit. Key points in the regulation are as follows:

1. Examinations must be closed book.

2. The minimum number of questions required for each examination are:

   - 25 questions for a three-hour class;

   - 30 questions for a six-hour class;

   - 40 questions for a 12-hour class;

   - 50 questions for a 21-hour class.

3. A grade of 70 percent or better is required for passing.

4. Pass or fail is the rating to be awarded.

5. The time for taking the test is to be part of the approved hours.

6. Students must be present 90 percent of instruction time, excluding examination time.

 The continuing education program has been extended to 1989 by the state legislature. Each applicant now is required to complete a three-hour course in ethics, professional conduct and legal aspects of real estate as part of the 45-hour continuing education requirement every four years.

Real Estate
Endowment Fund California was a pioneer in legislating a system whereby funds contributed by licensees could be used to stimulate real estate education and research. Monies were to be set aside for a fund to be sustained by the use of 25 percent of all license fees.

To assist in the allocation of funds to each educational segment, the Commissioner appointed a California Real Estate Education and Research Advisory Committee (CREERAC). This committee is composed of representatives of industry, state and private universities, community colleges and the Commissioner's staff, as well as representatives of the private sector.

In 1975 a $1.9 million permanent endowment was transferred from the existing fund set up for education and research to the California Community Colleges Board of Governors. This fund, known as the Community Colleges Real Estate Education Advancement Fund, is divided into two parts.

1. $1,500,000—Earnings from this part of the fund are to be used for maintenance, development and improvement of real estate courses and degree specialization and certification programs.

2. $400,000—Earnings from this part of the fund are to be used for maintenance and support of a scholarship program for students enrolled in a real estate career-oriented program.

The $1.9 million endowment amount must remain intact; only the earnings from the fund may be used each year. An endowment fund advisors panel advises the Community College Chancellor on funding activities and reviews and recommends approval of project proposals for the use of the money from individual community colleges or consortiums of several community colleges.

Publications

To assist licensees and to encourage higher ethical, legal and professional standards, the Department of Real Estate formerly produced helpful brochures, publications and guides. These have been curtailed, and at the present time, the department is not printing new publications.

The *Real Estate Reference Book,* published approximately every two years, contains information relating to real estate practice and real estate licensees. It is so comprehensive and complete that it often is referred to as the Bible of the real estate industry in California. This book is supplemented by another, *Real Estate Law,* containing the California Real Estate Law, The Commissioner's Regulations, The Subdivision Map Act and pertinent excerpts from California Codes. These two publications, priced inexpensively, can be obtained through the Department of Real Estate Publications Division and should be on the desk of every salesperson and broker in California.

Surveys indicate that the most widely read real estate publication in the state is the *Real Estate Bulletin.* The department distributes this publication periodically to all salespersons and brokers, keeping them up to date on the latest administrative provisions and current practices in real estate and allied activities.

Through the Department of Real Estate, *Instructor Guides* and *Student Study Guides* were developed a few years ago for use in California community colleges.

The guides were designed to establish uniformity in course offerings and to minimize duplication of courses offered throughout the state. The department produced the following guides, which are used statewide: *Real Estate Principles, Real Estate Practices, Real Estate Finance, Legal Aspects of Real Estate, Real Property Management, Real Estate Office Administration, Real Estate Economics* and *Real Estate Appraisal.* The Department of Real Estate is no longer in the business of providing instructional guides; however, the Community College Chancellor's Office, through endowment funds, has revised and rewritten the following statutory *Instructor* and *Student Course Guides: Real Estate Practices, Real Estate Office Administration, Real Estate Finance, Real Estate Economics* and *Real Estate Property Management.* These guides are available from the new Real Estate Education Center (formerly Real Estate Depository) in Modesto, California. They must be ordered through the Real Estate Coordinator or the person in charge of the real estate program in each community college. Updated revisions of the guides also are being planned for *Real Estate Principles, Real Estate Appraisal* and *Legal Aspects of Real Estate.*

Trade and Professional Organizations

The real estate business has grown rapidly in recent years. With its growth has come the necessity for trade and professional organizations to assist in eliminating unscrupulous competition.

The purpose of these associations is to provide a united effort to eliminate evils and annoyances connected with the business; to promote good fellowship and fair dealing among members; to protect members and the public from irresponsible, unprincipled, or dishonest licensees; to promote the enactment of legislation to protect property rights and interests; and to endeavor to build the stability and dignity of the practice of real estate. [2]

REALTORS®

The National Real Estate Association was formed in 1908 and officially changed its name to the NATIONAL ASSOCIATION OF REALTORS® (NAR) in 1974. The California Real Estate Association, made up of local realty boards, was established on a statewide level. The name was changed to California Association of REALTORS® in 1975. Only members of the NATIONAL ASSOCIATION OF REALTORS® may use the term REALTOR®. Use of this designation without permission is unethical as well as illegal.

The field of real estate includes a number of specialties and a variety of practitioners. To serve their interests, specialized groups have been formed within the NATIONAL ASSOCIATION OF REALTORS®, including:

- American Institute of Real Estate Appraisers (AIREA)
- American Society of Real Estate Counselors (ASREC)
- Farm & Land Institute (FLI)
- Institute of Real Estate Management (IREM)
- International Real Estate Federation—American Chapter (IREF)
- Real Estate Securities & Syndication Institute (RESSI)

- REALTORS® National Marketing Institute (RNMI)
- Society of Industrial REALTORS® (SIR)
- Women's Council of REALTORS® (WCR)

The California Association of REALTORS® (CAR) also has several affiliated divisions, listed below. Membership in CAR is a prerequisite to becoming an affiliate member of any of these groups.

- Graduate, REALTORS® Institute (GRI)
- Industrial Commercial Division (ICD)
- Investment Division
- Property Management Division (PMD)
- Real Estate Certificate Institute (RECI)
- Real Estate Syndication Division (RESD)

A professional organization known as the California Association of Real Estate Teachers (CARET) no longer is affiliated with CAR but has merged with the RECI and now is known as the California Real Estate Education Association. This organization is affiliated with the national Real Estate Educators Association (REEA).

Realtists

Another professional organization, predominantly made up of black real estate brokers, was founded in 1947. This group, the National Association of Real Estate Brokers (NAREB), has given the name **Realtists** to its members. State and local boards of NAREB work for better housing for the communities they serve. Today this organization includes both black and nonblack brokers. Note also that many black brokers are members of the NATIONAL ASSOCIATION OF REALTORS®.

Codes of Ethics

Codes of ethics are, strictly speaking, not legally binding. The principles of conduct set forth in real estate *law* are those that a licensee *must* observe. A code of ethics, in contrast, stipulates conduct that licensees *should* observe.

Code of Ethics of the NATIONAL ASSOCIATION OF REALTORS®

Members of the NATIONAL ASSOCIATION OF REALTORS® subscribe to a **code of ethics**—a set of principles or values setting standards of conduct for its members. Among other things, the Code encourages education and attempts to raise the esteem of licensees in the eyes of their fellow citizens.

California Code of Ethics

In the following words, former Commissioner David Fox expressed California's need for its own code of ethics:

> The most serious problem facing you today is that the public holds real estate agents in low regard. This poor public perception is unwarranted and unjustified. Our challenge is to help consumers better understand and appreciate what a good and professional job we are doing.

The cornerstone of any well-respected profession is a code of ethics for all its members. None has existed for California real estate licensees. Although the California Association of REALTORS® has a fine code, it only applies to a minority of our more than 370,000 brokers and salespersons. It is time for us to fill this void.

After numerous meetings with real estate practitioners statewide, and a full public hearing, I am pleased to announce the adoption of the Code of Ethics and Professional Conduct for all California real estate licensees. . . . I commend it to you and urge you to study the Code carefully, and practice your profession in accordance with its provisions.

I am confident that most of you already honor the basic tenets of this Code in your business lives. I want all consumers to realize this also.

By publicizing our Code, and adhering to it, we will make substantial progress in bettering our public image throughout California. Nothing is more important to the advancement of the real estate profession. [3]

The Ethics and Professional Conduct Code is reproduced at the end of this chapter in Figure 1.3.

[3]*California Department of Real Estate Bulletin*, Summer 1979.

Summary

This chapter has attempted to lay the groundwork for all real estate practices by establishing the legal premise on which these activities are based.

The organization responsible for the administration and interpretation of real estate law is the Department of Real Estate. The chief executive of the department is the Real Estate Commissioner, who looks to the Real Estate Advisory Commission for recommendations deemed appropriate and beneficial to the industry.

The *California Real Estate Law* stipulates the conditions requiring licensing and enumerates the requirements for obtaining a sales or broker's license.

A portion of license fees is placed in the Real Estate Fund to use in the development of real estate education and research and to build a recovery fund to assist in underwriting the payment of otherwise uncollectible court judgments against licensees.

To assist licensees, improve operational standards and provide uniform educational offerings, the Department of Real Estate publishes guides, reference books, bulletins and brochures.

As the industry has expanded, licensees have realized the importance of banding together to control and eliminate unscrupulous competition. This need has resulted in the establishment of local, state and national associations devoted to the betterment of the industry, guided in their operations by strict codes of ethics.

**Figure 1.3
Regulations of
the Real Estate
Commissioner**

REGULATIONS OF THE
REAL ESTATE COMMISSIONER

(Chapter 6, Title 10, California Administrative Code)

Article 11

Ethics and Professional Conduct Code

2785. CODE OF ETHICS AND PROFESSIONAL CONDUCT.

In order to enhance the professionalism of the California real estate industry, and maximize protection for members of the public dealing with real estate licensees, the following standards of professional conduct and business practices are adopted:

(a) **Unlawful Conduct.** Licensees shall not engage in "fraud" or "dishonest dealing" or "conduct which would have warranted the denial of an application for a real estate license" within the meaning of Business and Professions Code Sections 10176 and 10177 including, but not limited to, the following acts and omissions:

(1) Knowingly making a substantial misrepresentation of the likely market value of real property to its owner either for the purpose of securing a listing or for the purpose of acquiring an interest in the property for the licensee's own account.

(2) The statement or implication by a licensee to an owner of real property during listing negotiations that the licensee is precluded by law, regulation or by the rules of any organization, other than the broker firm seeking the listing, from charging less than the commission or fee quoted to the owner by the licensee.

(3) The failure by a licensee acting in the capacity of an agent in a transaction for the sale, lease or exchange of real property to disclose to a prospective purchaser or lessee facts known to the licensee materially affecting the value or desirability of the property, when the licensee has reason to believe that such facts are not known to, nor readily observable by a prospective purchaser or lessee.

(4) When seeking a listing, representation to an owner of the real property that the soliciting licensee has obtained a bona fide written offer to purchase the property, unless at the time of the representation the licensee has possession of a bona fide written offer to purchase.

(5) The willful failure by a listing broker to present or cause to be presented to the owner of the property any offer to purchase received prior to the closing of a sale, unless expressly instructed by the owner not to present such an offer, or unless the offer is patently frivolous.

(6) Presenting competing offers to purchase real property to the owner by the listing broker in such a manner as to induce the owner to accept the offer which will provide the greatest compensation to the listing broker, without regard to the benefits, advantages, and/or disadvantages to the owner.

(7) Knowingly underestimating the probable closing costs in a transaction in a communication to the prospective buyer or seller of real property in order to induce that person to make or to accept an offer to purchase the property.

(8) Failing to explain to the parties or prospective parties to a real estate transaction the meaning and probable significance of a contingency

Source: Chapter 6, Title 10, California Administrative Code

in an offer or contract that the licensee knows or reasonably believes may affect the closing date of the transaction, or the timing of the vacating of the property by the seller or its occupancy by the buyer.

(9) Knowingly making a false or misleading representation to the seller of real property as to the form, amount and/or treatment of a deposit toward purchase of the property made by an offeror.

(10) The refunding by a licensee, when acting as an agent or sub-agent for seller, of all or part of an offeror's purchase money deposit in a real estate sales transaction after the seller has accepted the offer to purchase, unless the licensee has the express permission of the seller to make the refund.

(11) Failing to disclose to the seller of real property in a transaction in which the licensee is acting in the capacity of an agent, the nature and extent of any direct or indirect interest that the licensee expects to acquire as a result of the sale. The prospective purchase of the property by a person related to the licensee by blood or marriage, purchase by an entity in which the licensee has an ownership interest, or purchase by any other person with whom the licensee occupies a special relationship where there is a reasonable probability that the licensee could be indirectly acquiring an interest in the property, shall be disclosed.

(12) A representation made as principal or agent to a prospective purchaser of a promissory note secured by real property with respect to the fair market value of the securing property without a reasonable basis for believing the truth and accuracy of the estimate of fair market value.

(13) Making an addition to or modification of the terms of an instrument previously signed or initialed by a party to a transaction without the knowledge and consent of the party.

(b) Unethical Conduct. In order to maintain a high level of ethics in business practice, real estate licensees should avoid engaging in any of the following activities:

(1) Representing, without a reasonable basis, the nature and/or condition of the interior or exterior features of a property when soliciting an offer.

(2) Failing to respond to reasonable inquiries of a principal as to the status or extent of efforts to market property listed exclusively with the licensee.

(3) Representing as an agent that any specific service is free when, in fact, it is covered by a fee to be charged as part of the transaction.

(4) Failing to disclose to a person when first discussing the purchase of real property, the existence of any direct or indirect ownership interest of the licensee in the property.

(5) Recommending by a salesperson to a party to a real estate transaction that a particular lender or escrow service be used when the salesperson believes his or her broker has a significant beneficial interest in such entity without disclosing this information at the time the recommendation is made.

(6) Claiming to be an expert in an area of specialization in real estate brokerage, e.g., appraisal, property management, industrial siting, etc., if, in fact, the licensee has had no special training, preparation or experience in such area.

(7) Using the term "appraisal" in any advertising of offering for promoting real estate brokerage business to describe a real property evaluation service to be provided by the licensee unless the evaluation process

will involve a written estimate of value based upon the assembling, analyzing and reconciling of facts and value indicators for the real property in question.

(8) Failing to disclose to the appropriate regulatory agency any conduct on the part of a financial institution which reasonably could be construed as a violation of the Housing Financial Discrimination Act of 1977 (anti-redlining)—Part 6 (commencing with Section 35800) of Division 24 of the Health and Safety Code.

(9) Representing to a customer or prospective customer that because the licensee or his or her broker is a member of, or affiliated with, a franchised real estate brokerage entity, that such entity shares substantial responsibility, with the licensee, or his or her broker, for the proper handling of transactions if such is not the case.

(10) Demanding a commission or discount by a licensee purchasing real property for one's own account after an agreement in principle has been reached with the owner as to the terms and conditions of purchase without any reference to price reduction because of the agent's licensed status.

(c) **Beneficial Conduct.**   In the best interests of all licensees and the public they serve, brokers and salespersons are encouraged to pursue the following beneficial business practices:

(1) Measuring success by the quality and benefits rendered to the buyers and sellers in real estate transactions rather than by the amount of compensation realized as a broker or salesperson.

(2) Treating all parties to a transaction honestly.

(3) Promptly reporting to the California Department of Real Estate any apparent violations of the Real Estate Law.

(4) Using care in the preparation of any advertisement to present an accurate picture or message to the reader, viewer, or listener.

(5) Submitting all written offers as a matter of top priority.

(6) Maintaining adequate and complete records of all one's real estate dealings.

(7) Keeping oneself current on factors affecting the real estate market in which the licensee operates as an agent.

(8) Making a full, open, and sincere effort to cooperate with other licensees, unless the principal has instructed the licensee to the contrary.

(9) Attempting to settle disputes with other licensees through mediation or arbitration.

(10) Complying with these standards of professional conduct, and the Code of Ethics of any organized real estate industry group of which the licensee is a member.

Nothing in this regulation is intended to limit, add to or supersede any provision of law relating to the duties and obligations of real estate licensees or the consequences of violations of law. Subdivision (a) lists specific acts and omissions which do violate existing law and are grounds for disciplinary action against a real estate licensee. The conduct guidelines set forth in subdivisions (b) and (c) are not intended as statements of duties imposed by law nor as grounds for disciplinary action by the Department of Real Estate but as guidelines for elevating the professionalism of real estate licensees.

Questions

1. The Real Estate Commissioner is empowered to formulate regulations that:
   a. may be treated as a moral code.
   b. may replace sections of real estate law.
   c. may have the same force and intent as law.
   d. both a and b

2. The Real Estate Recovery Fund is used to supplement unsatisfactory court judgments. This fund is what percent of the total Real Estate Fund?
   a. 15 percent
   b. 5 percent
   c. 10 percent
   d. 20 percent

3. To qualify for the real estate sales examination, a candidate must be:
   a. 21 years of age.
   b. a high school graduate.
   c. a citizen of the United States.
   d. none of the above

4. To belong to the Institute of Real Estate Management, an individual must be:
   a. a qualified applicant.
   b. a member of NAR.
   c. a member of the National Marketing Institute.
   d. both a and b

5. Members of a professional group known as the National Association of Real Estate Brokers use the designation name:
   a. REALTOR®.
   b. Associate Realtor.
   c. Realtist.
   d. RECI.

6. Money for the recovery fund is obtained from:
   a. license fees.
   b. property tax revenues.
   c. assessment taxes.
   d. municipal courts.

7. The designation used by professional appraisers is:
   a. APR.
   b. MAI.
   c. IOA.
   d. CPM.

8. What moral code must be adhered to by California licensees?
   a. NAR Code of Ethics
   b. California Real Estate Law
   c. Commissioner's Code of Ethics
   d. National Code of Ethics

9. Educational requirements for a broker's license:
   a. are optional.
   b. include six required real estate courses.
   c. are determined by the California Association of REALTORS®.
   d. include a course in ethics.

10. The Real Estate Commissioner for the State of California:
    a. holds an elective office.
    b. is appointed by the governor.
    c. is appointed on a yearly basis.
    d. is appointed by the Real Estate Advisory Commission.

11. Instructor's guides are being revised and rewritten in which of the following instructional areas?
    a. Real Estate Practices
    b. Real Estate Economics
    c. Real Estate Office Administration
    d. all of the above

12. One of the Department of Real Estate publications that includes the Commissioner's Regulations and the California Real Estate Law is:
    a. the *Real Estate Reference Book.*
    b. the *Real Estate Bulletin.*
    c. the *Real Estate License Examination Study Manual.*
    d. the *Real Estate Law.*

13. Most of the questions in the examination for a real estate license are related to:

    a. finance.
    b. appraisal.
    c. law.
    d. special fields.

14. The license fees for a California Real Estate Broker's license:

    a. change occasionally.
    b. now are $120.
    c. now are $165.
    d. both a and c

15. In 1975 an endowment fund was set up; $400,000 of this fund was allocated to:

    a. scholarships.
    b. education.
    c. recovery.
    d. research.

16. A new law requires a licensee to complete continuing education offerings:

    a. every two years.
    b. totaling 45 hours every four years.
    c. totaling 24 hours.
    d. including 40 hours every four years.

17. The Real Estate Advisory Commission is composed of:

    a. representatives of CAR.
    b. the Commissioner's deputies.
    c. ten members plus the Commissioner.
    d. real estate brokers only.

18. After January 1, 1986, the following requirements must be met to qualify for a real estate license.

    a. must complete a course in ethics
    b. must have taken a course in Real Estate Principles
    c. must be at least 20 years old
    d. must pay a fee of $125

19. To qualify for the California Real Estate Certificate, a candidate must complete:

    a. eight selected courses.
    b. 24 units of approved college offerings.
    c. a course in legal aspects of real estate.
    d. all of the above

20. To renew a real estate sales license, a licensee is required to:

    a. prove the use of his or her license constantly for four years.
    b. complete at least 45 hours of continuing education.
    c. retake the license examination.
    d. none of the above

2

Planning and Managing for Success

Chapter Preview

There is a lot of truth in the old-time observation that the busiest people get the most accomplished. But it doesn't happen by accident. The "busiest people" don't simply have more energy, and they don't necessarily work any harder than the rest of us. But they do work smarter. In the words of another old adage, "they plan their work, and then they work their plan." In this chapter you learn about important tools, techniques and attitudes that you can use to plan your work—a successful career in real estate—and then work that plan to your benefit.

Terms To Look For

Daily work plan
Enthusiasm
Goal setting
Persistence
Planning
Poise
Sales personality
Self-motivation
Sensitivity
Time management

What Is Planning?   **Planning** is the process of plotting your course of action to reach specified goals and objectives. It is a blueprint of what you intend to accomplish. Add a timetable and you also have a tool to evaluate your performance. A good time-management system rounds out your plan and helps you improve your efficiency and income.

Goal setting   **Goal setting** is a tool for making intelligent decisions. Use the following five principles to help you set your goals effectively:

1. Goals in real estate selling should be exact rather than abstract. For example:

   - *Abstract*—"I will do my best to improve my sales techniques during this week."

   - *Exact*—"I will obtain at least four listings and make one sale during this week."

2. Goals should be in a time frame. Set short- and long-term goals.

3. Goals should be put into writing.

   - It is easier to determine your priorities when your goals are written.

   - Written goals are easier to examine and revise.

4. Goals should be attainable. If your goals are not attainable, you may become discouraged and disappointed.

5. Goals should be adopted only after careful and considerable thought. Think about what you really want and why. Reaching goals can take hard work, so you will probably devote time and energy only to the ones you are really committed to.

Time Management   Sometimes it may seem that no matter how hard you apply yourself and how efficiently you allocate your time, you have more work to do and more people to see than you can handle satisfactorily. **Time management** is part of the solution. As you refine your techniques of self-management, you may expect a release from the pressure of time as your first dividend.

Remember, time is capital. Know what it is worth:

$$\frac{\text{Desired annual earnings}}{\text{1,952 working hours a year (based on 244 working days)}} = \text{Dollar value of one hour}$$

Allowing for other activities and unavoidable delays, you will be fortunate to have 976 hours a year actually to spend with clients or customers. Thus, the dollar value of your time is even greater than the equation above would indicate. To start thinking about how to get the maximum return on your time, ask yourself "How can I raise

1. the number of calls per week?"

2. the number of interviews per call?"

3. the number of presentations given per interview?"

4. the number of closes per presentation?"

5. the number of new prospects per week?"

6. the number of repeat sales?"

7. the dollar value of selling time?"

Attaining Goals

Setting goals is not enough. Attaining them is the point. You have probably set goals for yourself in the past, some of which you met and others of which you did not. If you have written down goals and still find you are having a hard time getting started, try this.

Write down what you will need to do to accomplish a particular goal. This does not have to be done in sequential order. In fact, it may be more useful to apply the following brainstorming technique.

First, write the goal in the center of a piece of paper, like this:

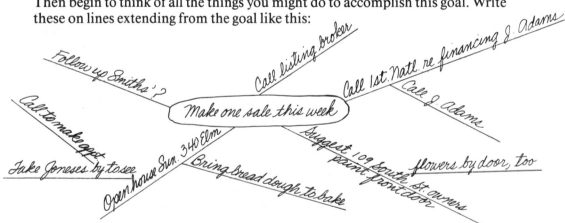

Make one sale this week

Then begin to think of all the things you might do to accomplish this goal. Write these on lines extending from the goal like this:

Then add to these branches other actions you may need to take to make them effective.

As you complete this network of activities, you will begin to see the small steps you can take to reach your goal, and reaching it will seem less overwhelming. As you work on each branch, cross out the activities that you have completed and add others that come to you in the course of completing the first ones.

When you have reached a goal, reward yourself. Take your family out to dinner or read that book you have been meaning to read. Do not plunge into another round of goal setting and activity without first marking your success.

Daily Work Plan

In addition to the activities you set for yourself, you undoubtedly have responsibilities set by others—your boss, your family, your friends. A simple tool for integrating all these and accomplishing more as a result is some form of **daily work plan.**

List everything you want to accomplish. Number the items in order of their importance.

1. Important and urgent
2. Important but not urgent
3. Fillers

1. Important and urgent. These are the things that *must* be done, if not immediately then within a short time. For example, your company may require a status report from you each week. It has to be handed in by 10 A.M. Monday morning, regardless of what else you may have to do. Putting a report like this in the important and urgent category—some time before it is due—ensures that you will get it in on time. One-time events, such as closings, that are to occur at a certain time on a certain day can be noted on your calendar.

2. Important, but not urgent. These items are likely to correspond to your long-range goals, perhaps taking a professional course or working out the bugs in a new approach you have thought up to increase sales. By writing these down, you are more likely to make time to accomplish them—an important step toward making progress in the directions *you* choose. These are activities that no one but you is likely to initiate or make time for.

3. Fillers. These are the time-consuming details of ordinary life—organizing files, making an appointment with the doctor, getting the oil changed in your car. Keep an errand envelope. Every time you think of an errand you need to do, jot it on a slip of paper and stick it in the envelope. Take these out periodically. Some you may not need to do after all. Sort the others by area and organize each trip so that you accomplish several things rather than just one or two. Other fillers, such as phone calls, can be sandwiched between stints of more important work. Sometimes you can organize your files at the same time you are talking on the phone.

The same kind of planning you apply to activities also can be applied to periodicals, letters and just plain clutter. Sort as you go, so that you never handle any paper more than once. Put everything in piles—urgent, pending, reading material. Throw the rest away.

Finally, a good planning habit is to fill out your plan for the next day on the prior night or at the end of your work day. Figure 2.1 is an example of a daily planning sheet that you could adapt to your needs. Then your conscience will let you sleep. You won't have to worry all night about what you are going to do the next day. Your whole day will be organized before you attack it, and you will be ready to get up and take one step at a time. If you accomplish most of the things that you set out to do, you will have put in a good real estate day.

Review and Analysis

Planning must include time to review and analyze goals and the strategies for achieving them. This feedback allows you to make needed adjustments, and there is nothing like the positive motivation of seeing your accomplishments. At the end of the day, set aside time to reflect on the answers to these questions:

1. Did I get my dollar value out of the day's work?
2. When did my enthusiasm falter? What could I have done to bolster it?

Figure 2.1
Daily Planning
Sheet

DAILY PLANNING SHEET

To Be Done Today
(Number in order of
importance)

Phone Calls

_____

_____

_____

_____

_____

_____

_____

_____

_____

_____

_____

_____

_____

_____

_____

_____

Thoughts and Ideas

Correspondence and
Thank-You Notes

_____

_____

_____

_____

_____

_____

_____

_____

_____

_____

_____

_____

_____

_____

_____

_____

_____

_____

Source: Londay, Jim, *List For Success* (Chicago: Real Estate Education Company, 1986), p. 10.

3. What new strong point did I use that I must be sure to use again?

4. Why didn't I get more interviews? What helped me succeed in getting those I did?

5. Why didn't I close more sales? What helped me succeed with those I did close?

The Sales Personality

Personality comes from the Latin word *persona.* In the ancient theater, the *persona* was a mask the actor held over his face so that he could play numerous characters. How your personality is perceived will depend on the extent to which you have developed habits, skills and qualities that interest and serve other people.

Develop a **sales personality.** This is not the stereotypical fast-talking, backslapping, I'll-sell-you-anything, Willy Loman personality. A good salesperson is someone who knows it is not helpful to think of people as "good" or "bad," "smart" or "stupid," but who asks how a given situation should be handled. Effective salespersons strive to grow into creative and mature people with the characteristics that follow.

Attractiveness

Salespersons should look like professionals. They should be well groomed and dressed cleanly, appropriately and in good taste for the occasion.

Poise

Salespersons should have a balanced outlook and be self-possessed. They should be able to handle themselves correctly in any situation.

Open-mindedness

Salespersons should be aware of what is going on, willing to learn from others and not defensive. Salespersons also should be careful to avoid bias or prejudice. These are not only illegal; they are immoral.

Friendliness

Friendly salespersons observe the Golden Rule and employ a sincere smile.

Sincerity

Salespeople should be genuine; they should be what they appear to be. James Russell Lowell once said, "No man can produce great things who is not thoroughly sincere with himself, who would not exchange the finest show for the poorest reality, who does not so love his work that he is not only glad to give himself for it, but finds rather a gain than a sacrifice in the surrender."

Cooperativeness

Salespersons should work with others willingly and contribute to the work of the group.

Courtesy

Salespersons should show politeness and consideration for others. Courtesy is contagious. A courteous person:

• respects other people's time;

• is pleasant to everyone;

- remembers likes and dislikes;

- keeps quiet while customers talk;

- speaks in a low tone of voice; and

- has a reputation for being thoughtful.

Tactfulness and Diplomacy

Salespersons should be able to discern readily the right thing to say or do at the right time. This means working smoothly in difficult situations.

Enthusiasm

Salespeople should be alive in speech and action. Most people are born with enthusiasm, but as they grow older, they often seem to lose it. To be enthusiastic, you must act enthusiastically. If you begin being enthusiastic, the world will give you more help than you ever thought possible.

Honesty

Salespersons should be reliable and trustworthy, persons who can be counted on. Salespeople should be open and aboveboard, upright and honorable. As Shakespeare wrote, "To thine own self be true, and it must follow, as the night the day, thou canst not then be false to any man."

Patience

Salespeople should be calm and self-possessed. This includes being able to wait calmly. Sometimes it helps to think of these paraphrased words: "O Lord, give me the patience to endure the things I cannot change. Give me the courage to change the things I ought to change. And above all, give me the wisdom to know the difference."

Persistence

According to the Economic Laboratory, Inc., the difference between an unsuccessful and a successful salesperson is "hustle." Hustle involves:

- doing something that everyone else is absolutely certain cannot be done;

- getting the order because you got there first or stayed with it after everyone else gave up;

- shoe leather and elbow grease and sweat and missing lunch;

- getting prospects to say Yes after they have said No 20 times;

- doing more for a customer than the other person is doing for him or her; and

- believing in yourself and the business you are in.

Sensitivity

Effective salespersons have keen empathy. They are able to put themselves in another's shoes and take that person's thoughts and feelings into consideration.

Participation

Theodore Roosevelt once said, "Every man owes some of his time to the upbuilding of the industry or profession to which he belongs. There is a destiny that makes us brothers. No one goes his way alone. All we send into the lives of others comes back into our own." Become involved in the problems and needs of your community and your profession.

All these characteristics are important in a real estate salesperson, but the assurance of success requires *work.*

Self-motivation

Not only do people have highs and lows, but the real estate business is fraught with these cycles as well. The inability to cope with the low feelings probably is a key reason why new salespeople leave the business. So, how do you stay motivated and ride out the down times? Some people seem to be natural optimists—seeing the glass as half full instead of half empty. But all of us suffer setbacks. Here are some tips for coping with those down times.

Positive Mental Talk

In our society, the value we place on ourselves and others tends to fluctuate with our success or lack of it. High self-esteem quickly turns to low self-esteem when things do not turn out right. We are likely then to berate ourselves with "should have," "why didn't you," "you're an idiot" and other self-critical talk. One way to counteract this tendency is to separate what you do from what you are.

When the sale falls through or you blow the answer to an objection, heap on the positive affirmations. The next time you find yourself flooding your mind with negative self-talk, *stop.* Then remind yourself of what went well, what you like about yourself and the steps you will take next time to make the situation better.

Creative Visualization

Successful people in all fields, from sports to business, use creative visualization to plan their actions in their minds' eyes. They picture everything in detail—with whom they will be, what everyone will be wearing, the gestures they will make, what will be said. This technique also is a wonderful way to end each day or to motivate yourself when you are down. Instead of picturing the future, you can use the technique to recall some of your best accomplishments. Even more important, it is a tool to help program your success: Visualize your listing and offer presentations before they take place; rerun past presentations and program the way they will turn out in the future.

Meditation

Closely allied with creative visualization, meditation will recharge you during the day and rid you of negative stress. Sit, preferably in a straight-backed chair, close your eyes and breathe deeply. Starting with your feet, tell yourself that each part of your body is relaxing. When you get to your head, try not to concentrate on anything, but let thoughts come and go. End your session with a positive statement and open your eyes at the count of three. For example, "My phone calls during floor time this afternoon will vibrate with my energy and great feelings."

Exercise and Proper Diet

Probably at no other time in history have people been more aware of the relationship between exercise and diet and total fitness. You will increase your effectiveness if you eat a light lunch. A heavy meal makes you sleepy and will dull your mental alertness. Better still, you might want to jump on the bandwagon with those who are replacing lunch with a gym or jazzercize workout.

Beware of overcommitment! Hard work is a necessary ingredient for success in the real estate business. But you can get too much of a good thing. Just as it is necessary to maintain your good health through exercise and proper diet, it is necessary to relax—at least sometimes—to be more effective. Aside from concern for your own personal welfare, consider this: You cannot work at your maximum level of productivity when you are overworked and overtired. You need to be able to work "smart" as well as hard. So turn off the lights, close the door on work and do something else that you enjoy. You will be more effective, more productive and more successful for doing so.

Figure 2.2
Success
Questionnaire

1. *Are you enthusiastic about your work?*
Ralph Waldo Emerson once said, "Nothing great has ever been done without enthusiasm." Study the unusually successful people you know and you will find them imbued with an enthusiasm for their work that is contagious. Not only are they excited about what they are doing, but they also get you excited. Remember the maxim, "Enthusiasm is like a contagious disease—it must be caught and not taught."

2. *How do you overcome objections?*
Numerous spoken questions and objections are being fired at you every day. Do you answer them without hesitation, drawing on your reservoir of knowledge? Do you do so to the satisfaction of the client or prospect? Or is there sometimes a hesitation followed by a garbled description that leaves the client as much in the dark as he or she was before?

3. *Are you self-confident?*
If the client or customer has confidence in you and your company, a sale results naturally. The main factor that determines whether customers will have confidence in your product or service is whether they have confidence in you. Knowledge gives confidence. A thorough knowledge of the property in question and the exact advantages that the customer will receive develops this quality of confidence in you, which shows itself in your personality. Your knowledge gives you assurance, which is a prime factor in assuring others.

4. *Do you have the courage of your convictions?*
"Courage," according to Eddie Rickenbacker, "is doing what you're afraid to do. There can be no courage unless you're scared." Many times we cease to be courageous in the face of the opposition. Shakespeare wrote, "Our doubts are traitors, and make us lose the good we oft might win by fearing to attempt." It is a sad commentary, but we live in an era when rapid change breeds fear. *Conquer fear!* Banish worry, because worry is the interest you pay on trouble before you get it. Keep your fears to yourself and share your courage with others. Remember, fear is only in the mind.

5. *Are your actions and speech in a positive vein?*
A number of years ago there was a popular song with the words "Accentuate the positive—eliminate the negative." How true this is in prospecting. You need to think and act positively.

Those who think *negatively* say, "Business is poor; unemployment rates are more than six percent. That means six percent of the people cannot be considered potential prospects."

Those who think *positively* say, "Business is great; with only six percent unemployment, 94 percent of the people are potential prospects."

However, being positive does not imply that it gives us the right to be dishonest. Remember, we must continually be aware of *Easton* liabilities. (See page 68.) But we can state facts from a positive position without being dishonest.

6. *Are you persistent?*
We admire the bulldog because it hangs on. Its motto is "Never give up." It strains every muscle and gives every ounce of its energy to win. No less do customers admire a salesperson who has developed this quality. No one has respect for a quitter, a person who readily takes no for an answer. Your attitude should be "Thanks for the No. I'm now closer to the Yes" (by the law of averages).

7. *Are you a problem solver?*
Be a problem solver, not a problem seller—problem solvers are people helpers. The basic principles of problem solving are:

- Despite any problem, you can persevere, think and reach a solution.
- Problem solving requires relentless pressure, persistence and determination.
- Act as if the problem were solved. Use the power of positive thinking.
- Remember, you do not sell properties, you sell solutions to people's problems.

8. *Are you willing to fail?*

Perhaps this should be *willing to try,* regardless of the chance of failure. Success cannot be achieved without failure. An old story is a good example of this concept: Robert Bruce, King of Scotland, had just been defeated for the eleventh time by his enemies, the English. He was dejectedly resting by a tree, ready to give up, when he saw a spider persistently trying to spin a web from one limb to another. After 11 times in which the spider failed to reach its goal, it finally succeeded on the twelfth try. Inspired by this incident, Bruce went forth against his enemy for the twelfth time. This time he was victorious, defeating the English at Bannockburn, winning independence for Scotland.

A little closer to our time, the inventor Thomas A. Edison tried 50,000 combinations of elements before he found the right combination and was able to construct a storage battery that worked. Charles Kettering said, "The only time you must not fail is the last time you try." To be a successful salesperson, be willing to try, willing to succeed and willing to fail.

Summary

All of us have read stories about "overnight successes" that in fact were 20 years in the making. It probably will not take you that long to reach a high level of success in real estate, but the idea is the same: The planning and management of your career will be at least as important an ingredient in your success as the actual work involved in attaining that success.

This chapter has shown you various ways that you can increase the likelihood of your success in real estate. To establish your plan—the blueprint for your future performance—you need to set goals. Those goals should have the following characteristics: They should be well-thought-out, concrete and attainable, and they should be in writing for both the short and the long term. The next step is to develop a plan that will enable you to manage your time most efficiently and effectively so that you will be able to reach those goals. A periodic review and assessment of your actual performance also is important. It will help you improve your ability to set goals and to plan your career intelligently. A final key to success is the development of the sales personality, those skills and personal characteristics that increase your chances for success in all sorts of situations. The success questionnaire (see Figure 2.2) at the end of the chapter will help you assess your professional accomplishments and development.

Questions

1. When using the characteristic "tact" in describing a successful salesperson, we mean most nearly:

   a. being wide awake.
   b. doing more than expected.
   c. saying and doing the right thing at the right time.
   d. a person who loves his or her work.

2. The process of plotting your course of action to reach specific goals is called:

   a. evaluating.
   b. timing.
   c. planning.
   d. procrastinating.

3. When setting goals for yourself:

   a. put them in writing.
   b. see that they are easily obtainable.
   c. give them careful and considerable thought.
   d. both a and c

4. If you intend to be successful in the development of a prospecting plan:

   a. do not worry about the time involved.
   b. evaluate your progress.
   c. occasionally revise your plans.
   d. both b and c

5. To increase sales effectiveness, a real estate salesperson should:

   a. relax; Rome wasn't built in a day.
   b. increase the number of calls per week.
   c. increase number of new prospects.   .
   d. both b and c

6. Which of the following suggestions will help overcome selling fears?

   a. Do not consider failure a disgrace.
   b. Set up priorities for the day.
   c. Put plans in writing.
   d. all of the above

7. Enthusiasm is like a disease in what way?

   a. contagious
   b. can be fatal
   c. is dangerous to the salesperson
   d. both a and b

8. Successful salespeople:

   a. are not afraid to fail.
   b. do not hustle.
   c. solve problems.
   d. both a and c

9. It is *always* a good idea to:

   a. never say no to a request; always say yes.
   b. not eat regular meals.
   c. put your job first.
   d. none of the above

10. Time management includes which of the following?

    a. Setting a dollar value on your time
    b. Allowing for possible delays
    c. Having daily work objectives
    d. all of the above

11. The term *empathy* is closely related to which characteristic that is helpful to a salesperson?

    a. Sympathy
    b. Being unprejudiced
    c. Putting oneself in the other person's shoes
    d. Being openminded

3

Prospecting

Chapter Preview This chapter discusses the importance of the salesperson's or broker's attitude toward prospecting. A salesperson with a professional attitude will be a successful prospector. In addition, the chapter introduces a variety of prospecting methods, including their pros and cons. Following this are some suggestions for improved prospecting operations.

The balance of the chapter outlines the steps to be taken in qualifying a prospect. This discussion includes questions to ask and topics to discuss with the prospect.

Terms To Look For **Bird dogs**
Centers of influence
Community services
Door-to-door canvassing
Endless chain
Farming
Geographic farm
Mini-tour
Open house
Prospecting
Psychological commitment
Referral prospects
Social farm
Suspects

Methods of Prospecting

The successful salesperson is always prospecting. **Prospecting** is the art of obtaining clients (sellers) and customers (buyers). A good prospector knows and accepts that different groups of people have varying interests and motivations. People also have substantially different political, social, philosophical and economic views. Prospecting is less a matter of getting listings and sales than it is a matter of developing sources for listings and sales. A licensee's ability to do this is limited only by his or her imagination.

The prospecting methods shown in Figure 3.1 could make you a star. They are the most frequently used methods of uncovering prospects for real estate activities.

Figure 3.1
Prospecting Methods

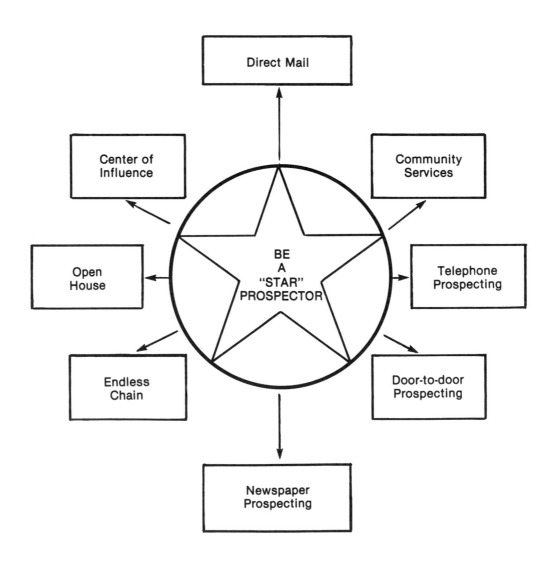

Choosing a Method   The prospecting method that will get the best results will vary according to the situation. The broker or salesperson should choose a method based on:

1. the type of property involved;

2. the period of time planned for;

3. the types of prospects; and

4. neighborhood and property characteristics, including:

   - the property itself—size and shape of the lot, landscaping, number of bedrooms and baths, etc.;

   - income characteristics of the neighborhood;

   - changes taking place, such as a changeover from single-family to multiple-family dwellings; and

   - special advantages of the location—schools, shopping centers, recreation areas, etc.

Direct Mail   With the use of specialized mailing lists and well-planned sales letters or brochures, direct-mail advertising can be an effective way to reach new prospects. Success depends on careful study to discover what type of buyer will be suitable and where such buyers can be found. Evaluate mailing lists carefully to be sure that they contain the targeted people.

One possible mailing list would contain the homeowners who live in the immediate vicinity of your listings. Use a reverse telephone directory, which lists people by address rather than name, to find the names of specific homeowners. Then your mailing can go to an individual rather than to "Occupant."

A letter or postcard to these people might ask them to assist in finding a buyer. The people who get this mailing may have friends or relatives who would like to move into the area; they may wish to purchase the home themselves to use as a rental unit; they may even have contemplated selling their own home. Many real estate offices use what they call a "Would you like to choose your neighbor?" letter, stating that a nearby property is for sale and asking if the homeowner knows of someone in the market for a house. If you use such a format, be sure the letter is written in a personal and sincere manner and is followed later by a phone call.

You may wish to send a notice to neighbors, as a courtesy, to let them know that a house listed in their neighborhood has been sold. This mailing could suggest that they, too, might wish to sell in a rising market. However, avoid any language that may give rise to suspicions that you are engaging in the illegal practice of "blockbusting," the encouragement of panic selling.

Newsletters. Prepare your own newsletter to send to prospects and clients. Such a newsletter can be a valuable public service if it contains articles on such vital subjects as interest rates and tax exemptions and rates. Another feature might be a "Client of the Month." Newsletters also can show pictures of salespersons and brokers. As a public relations gesture, they can advertise church, neighborhood and public functions.

Brochures. Brochures, leaflets and pamphlets also can be used in mailings, particularly if they are clearly identified with your office logo and detail the variety of services that you offer. Possible topics for brochures include the advantages of home ownership, exchanging and selling services, computer services and anything else that will help the prospect remember you when he or she needs your services.

Centers of Influence

One successful method of prospecting is one in which the salesperson or broker cultivates the friendship of influential persons in his or her community or territory. These **centers of influence** can help you obtain prospects by referring people who can use your services. In addition, these influential people can make appointments for you, as well as give information and urge their acquaintances to buy from you. Some of the people who make good centers of influence are:

- prominent club members
- friends
- relatives
- attorneys
- doctors
- ministers, priests, rabbis
- bankers
- public officials
- teachers
- business executives
- people with whom you share a mutual interest, such as a hobby or recreational activity.

The objective of cultivating relationships with centers of influence is to establish genuine friendships whenever possible. Also important is their help in your search for new contacts. Then let your centers of influence know the results of their efforts. This will come naturally if the friendship is genuine, and it encourages the person to keep helping you.

Community Services

Closely akin to the center of influence method is prospecting through local **community service** groups. This method involves making contacts through participation in community activities. This not only can bring in more business but it also can give you personal satisfaction from working for the benefit of others.

Community service organizations recommended for involvement include:

- churches and other houses of worship
- PTA
- educational groups
- college associations
- chambers of commerce

- civic organizations
- service groups
- boys' and girls' clubs
- Boy Scouts and Girl Scouts
- recreational clubs (ski, travel, biking, boating, etc.)
- YMCA and YWCA
- political organizations

Community activities can make many things possible:

1. Opportunities to counsel fellow members in such areas as investments, property management or commercial realty;

2. Constant exposure to referral sources;

3. Constant exposure to other property owners;

4. Personal development by learning and growing through participation; and

5. Development of a more professional image as a real estate licensee.

Your peers will have greater respect for a colleague who participates in community activities. The key is to get involved with people and help fulfill their needs.

Another community resource that should not be overlooked is the people with whom you do non–real estate business. You have to buy food, clothing, gas, personal services and so on. The people who sell things to you should know you are in the real estate business.

However, *beware of overcommitment!* It is important to develop the ability to say no gracefully. If you are not careful you can upset your timetable, and you may also jeopardize your health.

1. Work in only one or two organizations at any one time. Strive for quality, not quantity.

2. Anticipate time-consuming assignments before becoming involved.

3. Do not play personalities for an advantage.

4. Do not play politics.

5. Do not put too much stock in receiving plaques, scrolls, trophies and so on for your services. Accepting honor is fine, but be sure to allow time for business and personal affairs.

To keep aware of what is going on, participate where possible on carefully selected committees. Membership on the following committees has proved to be most helpful to licensees:

- greeter committee
- membership committee
- social or party committee

- "sunshine" (visit the sick, etc.) committee

Be cautious in using membership as a prospecting technique. It is easy to turn members off by being overaggressive. Use, do not abuse, people. When joining a club or association, keep a low profile. It is advisable to do something for the organization before expecting to use the members for referrals.

Open Houses

Although prospecting through the use of **open houses**—the practice of showing listed homes to the public during established hours—is accepted in the industry, many feel its merits can be questioned. Those who question the validity of open houses say that only a small percentage of those who attend an open house can be considered prospects. Every visitor must be greeted and escorted through the property, although few will be bona fide buyers. However, many offices handling high-priced properties will attest to the value of this form of prospecting. Open houses have two purposes:

1. to sell the client's home and

2. to serve as a prospecting tool.

Of those who attend open houses, many will turn out to be good future prospects. Some will be first-time buyers; others may need to sell their present homes before they can buy. The agent holding the open house is developing a prime source of prospective buyers and sellers.

Procedure to follow. If you conduct an open house, remember that those attending must be considered invited guests. They must be treated as if they were personal guests in your own home. You are there to offer a service, so be prepared to do so. The visitor to an open house will have questions that the agent must be prepared to answer. Here are some basic steps to follow when getting ready for an open house.

1. Turn on all lights when you arrive.

2. Tidy or rearrange things as necessary without offending the owner. (Of course, it is best to have an owner leave during an open house.)

3. Arrange for soft music to be played to create a pleasant atmosphere.

4. Present each visitor with a fact and benefit sheet containing:

   - broker's name, address and phone number;

   - financing plans; and

   - features and benefits of the property.

Other tips. One of the best ways of obtaining a list of attendees who may become prospects is to have each person sign a guest register, listing his or her name, address and phone number.

Have an open-house sales kit available. This is to the agent what a hammer and saw are to a carpenter. The kit, shown in Figure 3.2, should contain listing books and contracts, open house and directional signs, flags, deposit receipts, the guest register, a notebook and some scratch paper, a measuring tape, a flashlight, amortization books, maps of the area, a can of household oil, a portable typewriter and wax for repairing squeaky drawers.

The broker holding the open house should be sure to observe all local regulations involving signs and flags, as well as any other pertinent regulations.

Figure 3.2
The Open House
Sales Kit

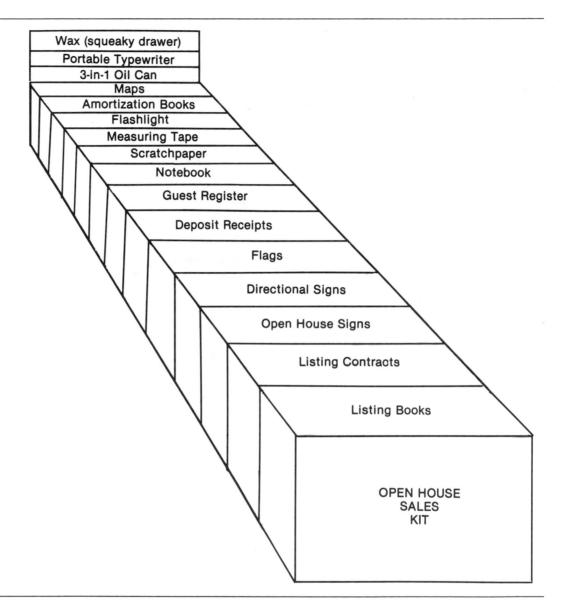

Wax (squeaky drawer)
Portable Typewriter
3-in-1 Oil Can
Maps
Amortization Books
Flashlight
Measuring Tape
Scratchpaper
Notebook
Guest Register
Deposit Receipts
Flags
Directional Signs
Open House Signs
Listing Contracts
Listing Books

OPEN HOUSE
SALES
KIT

Follow-up procedure. Within one week after holding an open house, the agent should follow up by contacting each person whose name appears in the guest register. In the follow-up the agent should thank the person for attending and ascertain if the agent can be of any further service.

This contact can be made by a phone call, a personal contact or a letter or thank-you note with an enclosed reply card. Figure 3.3 shows a sample reply card for such a mailing. This card should be stamped and self-addressed to get the biggest response.

A booklet prepared by the National Institute of Real Estate Brokers contains this statement:

A *Realtor®* should be better informed about the downtown, residential areas, locations of schools and commercial property, zoning laws, and the people of his community than virtually any other business man [sic] in town.

Figure 3.3
Follow-up Reply Card

REPLY CARD

	YES	NO
Are you planning to sell in the future?	☐	☐
Are you planning to buy in the future?	☐	☐
Do you have any need for real estate advice?	☐	☐
Do you have any friends who need real estate advice?	☐	☐
May I call on you in the future?	☐	☐

Newspaper Prospecting

A local newspaper mirrors its community. It can be a fertile source of prospects, yet too few licensees avail themselves of its opportunities. It can be used to uncover leads to prospects with present or future needs for real estate. For-Sale-by-Owner ads (FSBOs), usually found in the classified ad section, often can yield choice prospects. An owner's advertisement says that he or she needs help. However, beware—the competition from other licensees for the listing will be stiff. If you can act in a more professional manner than your competitors do, you stand a better chance of getting the listing. For example, make a *personal visit* to the prospect, after finding his or her name and address in a reverse telephone directory. Do not, however, try too hard to get the listing on the first visit; this will only antagonize the prospect. Aim only to sell yourself and your company on the first visit. Return to close the agreement at a later date.

Other newspaper items to read, observe and act on are:

1. Landlords advertising apartments for rent—they may be in the market for additional property.

2. Garage sales—these often indicate that a house sale soon may follow.

3. Help Wanted ads—these indicate who hires and fires, the kind of people that can make good centers of influence.

4. Birth announcements—wait a month or two to make a personal contact, but immediately send a congratulatory message. Do not forget, a larger family often needs a larger home.

5. Wedding announcements—the young couple soon may need to go house hunting.

6. Miscellaneous articles—filing notices of fictitious business names, abandonment of partnerships, dissolution of businesses, probate hearings and so forth—these activities may signal a need for your services.

Endless Chain

The basis of the **endless chain,** or referral, method of prospecting is to ask every prospect to recommend another prospect. The use of an endless chain results in an amazing number of these **referral prospects.** For example, if you make it a practice to secure the names of two prospects from every person you interview, you would get two names from your first prospect; these two should yield four; these four should provide eight; and so on. This can continue, eventually resulting in thousands who are, at least, suspects. **Suspects** are people whose needs have not been determined yet.

Door-to-Door Canvassing (Farming)

Door-to-door canvassing often is referred to as "**farming** your territory." The term arose because of the similarity between agricultural work and caring for the residents in a real estate area; it takes a lot of preparation and work to reap a harvest. Choose a "farm" in one of the following three areas: where you work, where you live or where you play.

The nature of the farm. Your job is to maintain and develop two farms: a **social farm** and a **geographic farm.** A social farm, as the name implies, refers to the centers of influence, community services and committees referred to previously. Get involved and create your own sphere of interest and influence. Never eat lunch alone or with another real estate salesperson.

A geographic farm should be neither too big nor too small. The ideal size will allow you to return to each house once every three months. About 500 houses is the maximum most licensees can handle. Your job is to become so familiar with what goes on in that area that you become a "walking encyclopedia." You should know when and where:

- new sidewalks and curbs are being installed;
- new street lighting is being installed;
- resurfacing of streets and alleys is taking place;
- new home construction or major remodeling is going on;
- the appearance of a street or block has changed noticeably;
- demolition is taking place;
- For Sale or Sold signs appear;
- listings have been recently sold; and
- listings have expired without a sale.

Procedures. To penetrate your market, you will need to knock on at least 20 doors per day in a four- or five-day week. The major purpose of this is to establish good relationships with the residents of your farm area. You are a specialist, so you must talk with people. Remember, the more contacts, the more suspects, the more prospects, the more sales.

Some licensees have a fear of door-to-door canvassing. What is there to fear? In an average call, you greet the prospect with a smile and a pleasing appearance and are prepared to offer assistance. The proper attitude is one of confidence.

There is no ideal time to call on all prospects. Try one time of the day and monitor the results. Experience shows that it is inadvisable to knock on doors before 9 A.M. or after 6 P.M.

Mentally as well as physically, put on a happy face. The law of averages says that some time during the day or week, someone is going to say that he or she wants to buy or sell. One way to begin is to follow this step-by-step procedure:

1. Introduce yourself.

2. Ask, "Do you mind if I ask you a question?"

3. Ask, "Will you be selling your home within the next six months or two years?"

4. Ask, "Do you know anyone else who might?"

5. Ask, "Would you mind if I did you a favor?" Be prepared to offer a newsletter or notification of any change in interest rates, taxes, market prices and so on.

You may not get through all the steps during the first visit, but keep in mind that you are striving for a **psychological commitment:**

Knowledge → Service → Psychological Commitment → Sale

This type of commitment is an agreement to contract with you eventually; getting it will depend on your ability to control and handle relationships. This requires practice, even to the point of ringing the doorbell and using a canned speech. Do not let the rejections get you down.

Practicing these techniques makes the job easier. The task itself is not really any easier or less involved, but your power and ability will have increased.

If the owners say they want to sell, try to get permission to make a **mini-tour** of the property, either then or later. During this cursory visit, ask such questions as:

1. Where are you moving?

2. When are you planning to move?

3. Why did you purchase this house? (Concentrate on the benefits they bought or need.)

Do not get too technical on the first visit, but be sure to leave your business card so the prospects will remember you.

A good idea is to evaluate the effectiveness of the hours spent. Divide the total earnings by hours worked to get the value of one hour. *Example:* If a $1,000 commission is earned as a result of ten hours of canvassing, each hour was worth $100. To be effective, make your own dollar analysis, rather than relying on other agents for such information.

Telephone Prospecting

You can use the telephone to prospect in many ways. You can use it to answer ad call-ins, follow up on listing agreements, canvass for listings, follow up on personal calls, and make appointments for interviews. It facilitates contact with a maximum number of people in a minimum amount of time.

Why use the telephone? There are numerous advantages in conducting business by phone. A few of them are:

1. It conserves valuable time that might be spent in travel.

2. It preconditions the prospect and paves the way for future sales developments.

3. It provides an easy way to maintain close contact with clients and prospects.

4. It commands attention and, when well used, gets the message across.

5. It helps sift through suspects to get to prospects.

Before using the telephone to set appointments, practice in front of a mirror. Do all you can to improve and polish your voice and manners. Talking with prospects is an opportunity to impress, to sell, to convey an idea. The goal of this effort, either by telephone or in person, is to achieve contact with prospects and customers and give them the most coherent and understandable presentation possible. Thus, when you are prospecting by phone or answering incoming calls, your voice should portray a warm and winning personality. Immediately let your voice characterize you as a vibrant, interesting and alert person.

The major reason for telephone prospecting is to get a face-to-face appointment. Poor telephone techniques interfere with this objective. Not having proper information close at hand and not being completely composed and prepared to give the right answers—and ask the right questions—simply wastes time.

Sometimes you will *receive* phone calls from people who are seeking information, who may be interested in a listed property, who are calling in response to an ad or who are merely curious about some aspect of the business. Keep this idea always in mind: One of those callers might turn out to be an A-1 prospect.

The main points to remember when dealing with incoming phone calls, even those you suspect may turn out to be nonproductive, are:

1. obtain the caller's name;

2. obtain the caller's telephone number; and

3. get an appointment with the caller.

Building a Referral List

Agents must bring some sort of order to their prospect list to avoid getting stuck with a briefcase full of names and little else. To build a list and successfully use referrals, the licensee must:

1. Develop a systematic plan. This includes studying prospects as you talk to them. Ask for leads as soon after contact as feasible and ask the prospects how you may improve your services.

2. Keep track of the results of your methods.

3. Utilize all sources of information, including friends, neighbors, professionals, people in businesses of all kinds and social contacts. Let them all be aware that you are in the real estate business and would appreciate all referrals.

4. Follow up referrals by reporting back to the referrer. Also important: use an appointment book to record referrals for future calls—a person giving a negative response now may still be in the market in the future.

Other Prospecting Methods

In addition to those previously discussed, other prospecting methods include:

1. leads from junior salespeople, often called **bird dogs**—police officers, waiters, barbers, grocers, service station attendants, beauticians and so forth—contacts who often are in a position to point out prospective sellers or buyers;

2. appealing signs, ads and window displays that attract prospects; and

3. the personal observation method—often called the "eyes and ears" system.

Keep a Prospect Card File

A well-organized salesperson keeps a prospect information card file. These index cards, usually 3 × 5 inches or 5 × 8 inches, should contain as much information as you can gather on each prospect. This preserves the information in a systematic way and helps you set up future appointments. The cards usually are indexed by days of the month for future callbacks, thus making an excellent tickler system for follow-up as well.

Prospecting Plan

You will be a more effective prospector if you have a plan. A good plan, such as the one shown as Figure 3.4, establishes goals and objectives and keeps track of results. The essential steps in developing a good prospect plan are:

1. Budget your time to complete your plan. The legal phrase, "Time is of the essence," applies to prospecting. Each person has 24 hours a day to do with as he or she wishes; success depends on how that time is used. To a salesperson or a broker, time is money, so turn *your* time into money. A licensee fights a constant battle against an unseen, unyielding enemy—*time*. You must be diligent enough to make a lot of calls, yet thorough enough to turn calls into sales.

2. Define your area of interest and concentrate your efforts on that area.

3. Identify your prospects.

4. Associate yourself with the right office.

5. Devise a prospecting plan.

6. Execute the plan.

7. Evaluate your progress and revise your plan to attain your goals.

Figure 3.4
A Sample
Prospecting
Plan

The following is a sample plan a salesperson might use when he or she first begins to farm a territory:

1. Identify three centers of influence per month for the next six months and get to know them.
2. Send out one general letter per month to the target area.
3. Knock on 75 doors per month and make 100 phone calls per month.
4. Set up or acquire an appropriate newsletter for the target area and send it out on a monthly basis.
5. Run one newspaper ad every two weeks.

Also, set up a system to track the source of all referrals to identify both the quantity and quality of those referrals. The following will be the criteria for evaluating referrals:

1. Get three prospects and ten suspects per month from an organization.
2. A letter should generate five prospects and five suspects per month.

The salesperson could keep track of the effectiveness of his or her plan by setting goals for each of the prospecting methods used and then recording his or her actual results. He or she might use a form such as the one shown in Figure 3.5 to organize this information.

Qualifying Prospects

A salesperson once remarked, "I went through my prospect list to qualify them and threw all of them out because none were any good." Is that what qualifying means? Webster's dictionary gives this definition of *qualify:* "to reduce from a general to a particular form." In real estate vernacular, qualifying is matching the customer's needs and wants to a particular property.

When you encounter a suspect for the first time, he or she is part of a general mass of humanity. As you get to know the suspect, he or she becomes a separate, valued individual with desires, aims and ambitions. To qualify someone as a *prospect* requires learning everything possible about the person.

The first step in the qualifying procedure is to make a searching analysis of each listing. This includes such questions as:

1. Who desires the property?

2. What type of person qualifies financially?

3. Whose needs would the property serve?

By carefully selecting prospects suited to your listings, you can be assured of finding interested prospective purchasers. Once you have found a prospect, you must qualify him or her by obtaining the following facts. Much of this information can be learned through adroit and tactful questioning and the use of prepared forms. The necessary information is:

1. name and address;

2. business rating;

Figure 3.5
Sample
Prospecting
Summary

METHOD	NUMBER OF CONTACTS/LEADS—GOAL	NUMBER OF CONTACTS/LEADS—ACTUAL
Center of Influence		
Open House		
Newspapers		
Door-to-Door (Farming)		
Telephone		
Community Service		
Direct Mail		
Referrals (Endless Chain)		

3. how long married;

4. earning capacity;

5. hobbies;

6. kind of properties desired;

7. other properties seen;

8. level of devotion to family (by observation);

9. current home ownership status;

10. whether current home is listed;

11. prospect's ability to make final decision; and

12. age and gender of any children.

Knowing the financial ability of a prospect is an important part of qualifying. It is the salesperson's responsibility to find out whether or not the buyer's finances are adequate to make a real estate purchase. These questions may help you obtain such information:

1. What down payment is the person prepared to pay?

2. Is he or she familiar with the price range of homes in the area?

3. Is he or she familiar with current lending policies?

4. If the person rents, how much is he or she paying?

5. Does he or she have the courage to assume a sizable loan?

Because of the importance of financing, it is best to determine the prospect's financial capabilities early. Because you have a threefold obligation—to yourself, to the buyer and to the office—you must handle this aspect of qualifying realistically. This means that you cannot waste valuable time with a prospect who is unable to afford the property. A corollary to this is that the buyer should only be encouraged to purchase property that is priced within his or her ability to pay.

Other information that might be used to qualify a buyer is:

1. price range;

2. reason for buying;

3. use for the house;

4. need for a family room;

5. amount of traveling;

6. educational background;

7. entertainment;

8. friends in the area;

9. transportation needs; and

10. reason for moving.

The salesperson should cover these topics and any others that will help determine if the person is a bona fide prospect. Figure 3.6 summarizes the basics of qualifying.

**Developing a
Proper Attitude
Toward Prospecting**

Prospecting is any method of exposure to people who can buy or sell real estate and, hence, is a major challenge to every licensee. The following questions will help you evaluate your own attitude toward prospecting:

1. Do you consider prospecting a major challenge? Successful real estate selling entails countless hours and considerable expenditure of energy to keep up with a highly competitive market. Your *attitude* is the key to your success.

2. Do you feel the urgency to keep a constant supply of new prospects? It is absolutely necessary to provide a constant supply of customers for yourself, as a real estate licensee. Prospects may be found most anywhere; they are all around you.

3. Do you have a well-organized system to use in prospecting? Because of the many prospect sources available and the necessity of assigning priorities to these sources, advance planning is essential. To get the best results from your prospecting, an effective and well-organized prospecting system is essential.

**Figure 3.6
Qualifying Basics**

The key words in successful qualifying are:

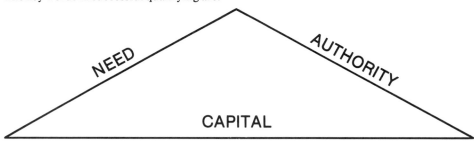

Does the prospect really *need* and want the property? Has he or she the *authority* to make the purchase? Is he or she able to finance the *capital* to make the purchase?

Summary

The principal methods used in *prospecting* include: direct mail, centers of influence, open house, newspaper, endless chain or referral method, door-to-door canvassing (farming) and using the telephone. Door-to-door prospecting, combined with social and geographic *farming,* has proved most helpful in building a bona fide prospect list.

Regardless of the method used, the well-organized salesperson establishes some type of prospect card file for logging future callbacks.

One of the most important jobs of the salesperson or broker is that of *qualifying* prospects. This should focus on the property to be sold. The key elements to be considered are *need, authority* and *capital.*

Not only must the salesperson or broker constantly prospect, but he or she must have the proper attitude toward prospecting. A professional attitude includes: consideration of prospecting as a challenge that needs organizing; enthusiasm for the task; positiveness in speech and action; courageousness; persistence; willingness to fail; and problem-solving and time-management skills. Use the SSS system: See the people; Serve the people; Sell the people.

Questions

1. Customers will have confidence in you if you have a knowledge of:

   a. your competition.
   b. your product or service.
   c. yourself.
   d. all of the above

2. The term *farming* in real estate involves prospecting. Farming is related to which of the following areas?

   a. social farming
   b. agricultural farming
   c. geographic farming
   d. both a and c

3. Which of the following is *not* one of the threefold obligations of a licensee?

   a. obligation to the buyer
   b. obligation to his competitor
   c. obligation to him or herself
   d. obligation to the real estate office

4. Prospecting has added importance for which of the following reasons?

   a. People have varying interests.
   b. People differ in their political, social and economic views.
   c. both a and b
   d. neither a nor b

5. An open house kit should contain which of the following?

   a. deposit receipts
   b. measuring tape
   c. flashlight
   d. all of the above

6. The term *willing to fail* means most nearly:

   a. wants to fail.
   b. willing to try regardless of consequences.
   c. feeling failure is not a disgrace.
   d. both b and c

7. The telephone is used in prospecting for which of the following reasons?

   a. to precondition the prospect
   b. to conserve valuable time
   c. to command attention
   d. all of the above

8. A licensee should constantly be aware of "For sale by owner" signs. They can be a good prospecting source because:

   a. the owner knows more about the property than the licensee.
   b. less time needs to be spent on this prospect.
   c. this prospect probably needs help.
   d. he or she already has a customer.

9. Which of the following words need *not* be avoided in discussing real estate with customers?

   a. rodents
   b. difficulties
   c. overpriced
   d. pleasant

10. Qualifying prospects in real estate means:

    a. matching customer's needs to a particular property.
    b. getting rid of first turndowns.
    c. separating male prospects from female prospects.
    d. determining those who have a college education.

11. Which of the following steps precedes a psychological commitment?

    a. offering a service
    b. gaining knowledge
    c. both a and b
    d. none of the above

12. Which of the following is *not* a method of prospecting?

    a. direct mail
    b. refusing a committee assignment
    c. farming
    d. endless chain

13. The essentials of a good prospecting plan include:

   a. defining an area of interest.
   b. executing the plan.
   c. evaluating progress and revising the plan.
   d. all of the above

14. Community activities make possible:

   a. constant exposure to other property owners.
   b. personal development.
   c. development of a professional image.
   d. all of the above

15. Which of the following is *not* considered a good reason for knowing one's product or service when prospecting?

   a. to overcome objections
   b. to enjoy one's work better
   c. to develop self-confidence
   d. none of the above

16. The endless chain method of prospecting:

   a. is a waste of time.
   b. does not work satisfactorily in real estate.
   c. both a and b
   d. neither a nor b

17. *Social farming* means most nearly:

   a. farming in dress clothes.
   b. accepting committee assignments in the Lions' Club.
   c. belonging to two social clubs.
   d. both b and c

18. Which of these statements most clearly describes direct-mail advertising?

   a. It is not an effective way to reach prospects.
   b. Brochures, letters, leaflets and pamphlets can be used.
   c. It is the most inexpensive type of advertising.
   d. It is impossible to reach selective audiences with direct mail.

19. Telephones are frequently used by brokerage offices to:

   a. answer ad call-ins.
   b. canvass for listings.
   c. make appointments for interviews.
   d. all of the above

20. In real estate prospecting, an open house is:

   a. all doors left open for ventilation purposes.
   b. an invitation to a party.
   c. a method of prospecting.
   d. all of the above

4

Listing Agreements

Chapter Preview   This chapter explains the essential elements of a listing contract. It identifies the basic types of real estate listings—open, exclusive-right-to sell, exclusive agency, net and option—and describes their advantages and disadvantages. The multiple listing service and the techniques of its use also are explored. Having an adequate supply of well-prepared listings is vital in the real estate business. Therefore, many sources of listings are treated in depth. Then the three basic steps in the listing transaction are explained: preparing to take the listing; the listing interview; and servicing the listing.

Terms To Look For   **Bilateral agreement**
Consideration
Contract
Easton **liability**
Exclusive agency listing
Exclusive-right-to-sell listing
Hold harmless clause
Listing agreement
Multiple listing service (MLS)
Net listing
Open listing
Option listing
Safety clause

Essentials of a Listing Agreement	Of all the documents used in the real estate business, none is more important than the listing agreement. This is the instrument that defines the broker's rights and duties. It is the broker's employment contract and gives him or her a right to a commission.
Definition	A **listing agreement,** often called an authorization to sell, is a legally binding contract authorizing a broker to serve as agent for a principal in a real estate activity. Listing contracts may be entered into for the purpose of securing persons to buy, lease or rent property. Generally, though, licensed agents are authorized to find a purchaser for a particular property at a specified price and terms, often within a certain time limit. The agreement spells out the mutual benefits to and obligations of the broker and the seller.
	The agreement is an employment contract to perform a specified action, such as selling the principal's property, for a commission. The broker who fulfills his or her part of the contract is entitled, both legally and morally, to be paid for these efforts.
Elements	Because the listing is a real estate contract, it must include all the essential elements of a **contract,** including competency of parties, lawful object, proper offer and acceptance, and consideration. In addition, a listing agreement should be in writing.
	Oral listings are not illegal, but they are definitely unsound business practice. Even though brokers may use them occasionally, they should be avoided. Oral listings provide the broker with no legal protection whatsoever, because the broker cannot force payment of his or her commission if the seller refuses to pay it.
	The **consideration** in a listing contract is a promise by the broker that he or she will "use diligence in locating a ready, willing and able buyer," in exchange for the seller's promise to pay a commission. This makes a **bilateral agreement,** consisting of a promise (seller to pay commission) given for a promise (broker to use diligence in finding a buyer).
	By its very nature, if executed properly, the contract gives the broker added legal protection, assuring the broker of reimbursement for the time and money spent on fulfilling the contract.
Types of Listing Agreements	There are many variations of the basic listing agreement. Some are for general residential property; others are for special types of property, such as industrial, income, farm or unimproved property. Despite the variations, there are five basic kinds of listings—open listings, exclusive-right-to-sell listings, exclusive agency listings, net listings and option listings. Because the purpose of a listing agreement is to define the relationship between the seller and the broker, some people find it useful to group listings into two kinds of agreements—exclusive and nonexclusive. Figure 4.1 lists the benefits and drawbacks of the five kinds of listings. Figure 4.2 classifies listings according to the relationship between seller and broker.

Open Listings   An **open listing** is a written memorandum signed by the seller authorizing the broker to serve as an agent for the sale of certain property.[1] The seller may give this type of listing to as many brokers as he or she sees fit. The first agent who finds, per the listing terms, a ready, willing and able buyer acceptable to the seller gets the commission. This cancels all other open listings and negates the payment of any other commission. An open listing allows the owner to sell the property himself or herself without being liable to the broker(s) for a commission.

Figure 4.1
Benefits and Drawbacks of Five Types of Listings

Open Listing

1. Customer gets less service.
2. Broker is uncertain that his or her efforts and expenditures will pay off.
3. Client must contact many offices.
4. A conflict of interest arises when client competes with broker.
5. Client can sell his or her own property to save the commission.

Exclusive-Right-to-Sell Listing

1. Broker is encouraged to use resources to promote a sale.
2. Seller has efficiency of communicating with only one office.
3. Client has certainty of knowing to whom the commission will be paid.
4. Because one broker controls the selling process, the most efficient service can be provided.

Exclusive Agency Listing

1. Owner may sell the property without paying a commission.
2. Listing office will receive a commission if any other office sells the property.
3. Broker has less incentive to promote when in competition with the owner.

Net Listing

1. Owner may receive lower income than might be possible.
2. Broker's commission may be larger or smaller than usual.
3. Transaction is subject to legal disclosure provisions.
4. Principal/broker misunderstanding often arises, and ill feeling can cause turmoil among agents within the office.

Option Listing

1. In theory, the listing gives both the broker and seller a high degree of flexibility.
2. In practice, the terms of an option agreement can unfavorably restrict either the broker or the seller.

Figure 4.2
Listing Agreements by Broker/Seller Relationship

Exclusive	Nonexclusive
Exclusive-Right-to-Sell	Open listing
Exclusive Agency	Net Listing (can be exclusive)
Net listing (can be nonexclusive)	
Option	

---

[1]California Department of Real Estate. *Reference Book,* 1984–1985 edition, p. 142.

From the seller's point of view, open listings may appear to provide a wider market than exclusive agreements. However, more sophisticated sellers often conclude that brokers receiving this type of listing are unlikely to give them preferred attention. Sellers soon discover that "what is everybody's business is nobody's business" and that carefully selecting a single competent broker is almost always to their advantage.

From the broker's standpoint, open listings are the least satisfactory because, while advertising and other efforts to sell property are costly, there is no assurance of a commission under an open listing. Consequently, the brokers spend less time, effort and advertising money to sell a property under an open listing.

Exclusive-Right-To-Sell Listing

An **exclusive-right-to-sell listing,** as the name implies, gives a broker the sole right to sell a property. With this type of listing, the broker has the right to receive a commission if the property is sold by anyone—even the owner. Thus, brokers should only take this type of listing if they are willing to spend time and money to find a buyer. The broker is the sole agent and will receive a commission if the property is sold by *anyone* during the term of the listing.

This is the most rewarding type of listing from the standpoint of both property owner and broker. By agreeing to this type of listing, the owner demonstrates complete confidence in the broker and is happy to let the broker complete the entire transaction. The broker will give the exclusive-right-to-sell listing his or her complete and undivided attention. He or she will assign a sizable portion of the advertising budget to such transactions and will endeavor to find a qualified buyer as quickly as possible.

An exclusive listing, by law, must have a definite termination date. Listings should be dated when they are taken and the effective term should be so clearly and definitely set forth that there can be no uncertainty or mistake. An exclusive listing may not contain such wording as "effective until date of sale" or "until cancelled in writing." The California Real Estate Law, Section 10176 (f), states that a licensee is subject to disciplinary action for "claiming, demanding, or receiving a fee, compensation, or commission under any *exclusive* agreement authorizing or employing a licensee to sell, buy or exchange real estate for compensation or commission where such agreement does not contain a *definite, specified date* of final and complete termination [italics added].

Exclusive Agency Listing

An **exclusive agency listing** differs from the exclusive-right-to-sell listing in one major respect—the seller will pay a commission to the listing broker, regardless of which agency makes the sale, but it does not prevent owners from selling their own property. If the owner does sell the property without the broker's efforts, he or she need not pay a commission.

■   **Note:** Because the exclusive agency listing refers to an "agency," rather than a "right to sell," the owner, not being an agent, may personally effect the sale without incurring liability for a commission to the broker holding this type of listing.

Even though the owner may save a commission by making the sale personally, under these conditions he or she cannot expect an all-out effort from the listing broker when the compensation for time and effort are so uncertain. In reality, the owner and the broker are working in competition with one another. If the broker clearly explains this to the owner, the owner will undoubtedly realize the futility of working at odds with his or her agent.

Net Listing

A **net listing** is an agreement in which the commission is not specifically determined in the contract. However, a clause in the agreement states that the owner is asking a certain sum of money from the sale of the property. All expenses, including the broker's commission, are to be covered by any sum the broker is able to obtain in excess of the selling price specified by the seller.

California law requires the broker to disclose in writing to both the seller and the buyer the selling price involved in a net listing. This declaration must be made within one month of the closing of the transaction. In practice, this information may be disclosed by the escrow holder's closing statement.

■ An agent's failure to disclose the selling price under a net listing is cause for revocation or suspension of his or her license.

Net listings are used only sparingly. They are vulnerable to charges of fraud, misrepresentation and other abuses against which the real estate law offers protection.

Many brokers look on net listings as being unfair and consequently avoid using them. For example, the broker might be tempted to persuade the seller to ask for the least possible amount, so that the broker can turn around and sell the property at a much higher price to get a large commission. This type of action is against the broker's duties as an agent. Often speculators will insist on using a net listing because they are only interested in their net profit and have no concern for the broker's commission.

Net listings may be either exclusive or open. They are thus combined with the open, the exclusive agency or the exclusive-right-to-sell listing contracts.

Option Listing

An option is actually a "contract to contract." As such, it cannot be literally termed a listing. However, brokers occasionally resort to the combination of listing and option. An **option-listing** arrangement generally occurs when a broker has a contract to find a buyer and the owner grants the broker an option to purchase the property himself or herself.

A listing broker who has this type of option is forbidden by the law to profit *at the expense of* the owner. If the broker finds a buyer willing to pay more than the option price, and if the broker then exercises his or her option to buy in order to make a greater profit from resale of the property, then the broker must make a full disclosure to the owner. California law covering this is stated as follows:

If a broker employed to sell property is also given an option to purchase the property himself, he occupies the dual status of agent and purchaser and he is not entitled to exercise his option *except* by divesting himself of his obligation as agent by making a full disclosure of any information in his possession as to the prospect of making a sale to another.

In any case, *net* listing with option to purchase by an agent should be avoided. This provision can create serious problems with respect to fiduciary relationships between the seller and the broker.

Figure 4.3
Splitting a
Commission
on an MLS
Listing

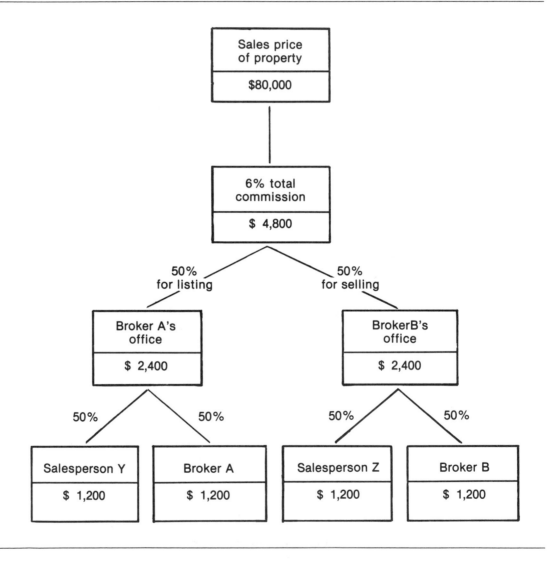

Multiple Listing Service

To provide greater market coverage for their listings, a group of brokers often will conduct a cooperative listing service. The group generally consists of members of a local real estate board. The multiple listing service (MLS) is used most often with an exclusive-right-to-sell listing, but it may be used with other listings as well. A member of the group who takes any listing turns it in to a central bureau, which distributes it to all participants in the service. All members have the right to sell the property. However, they must have the listing broker's permission to advertise or promote it. When a sale is made on an MLS listing, the commission is shared between the listing broker and the broker who found the buyer. Suppose, for example, the MLS commission split was 50/50. The listing broker would get 50 percent of the commission and the broker who found the buyer would get the other 50 percent. Within each agency, the broker would probably also split his or her share of the commission with the salesperson who had actual contact with the seller or buyer. (Only brokers may receive commissions, but they may share them with the salespeople who work for them.) Figure 4.3 illustrates a possible split of the six percent commission on a property that sold for $80,000.

Analysis of the Listing Form

Because the listing agreement is a written contract between the broker and the seller, it must be filled out correctly and signed by the necessary parties. The exact wording in each listing form will vary, depending on the details of the transaction. However, certain basic provisions are part of each listing contract—the form is the same; only the participants, dates, conditions and places are different. The most widely used forms are those provided by the California Association of REALTORS®. Figure 4.4 is the form for an exclusive-right-to-sell listing. The item-by-item analysis in the following paragraphs will refer to this sample form.

Right To Sell: Paragraph 1

Enter here the name of the real estate office or broker receiving the listing. If a salesperson, rather than a broker, takes the listing, the salesperson should write his or her employing broker's name. The salesperson completing the form signs his or her name at the bottom. Note that the words *exclusive* and *irrevocable* make this listing an exclusive right to sell.

After the broker's name, enter the period, including the beginning and the termination dates. Ninety days is a common period; however, if the broker thinks the property will take longer to sell, he or she may ask for more time.

Next, enter the location of the property by city and county, as well as an unmistakable address within the city. Occasionally, in addition to the street address, the location by lot, block and tract, or a metes-and-bounds legal description, may be given.

Terms of Sale: Paragraph 2

The terms of the sale include the price at which the property is being offered. Additional space is provided for stipulating the exact terms the owner requires to sell the property. This includes financial arrangements, such as cash, second trust deeds or loan assumptions.

Personal property. Items of personal property that may be included in the purchase are listed. Misunderstandings often arise as to what personal property the seller intends to include, and listing the items will help alleviate such a problem. Examples of personal property often sold with a residence are major appliances and drapes.

Figure 4.4
Exclusive Authorization
and Right To Sell

EXCLUSIVE AUTHORIZATION AND RIGHT TO SELL
THIS IS INTENDED TO BE A LEGALLY BINDING AGREEMENT — READ IT CAREFULLY.
CALIFORNIA ASSOCIATION OF REALTORS® STANDARD FORM

1. **Right to Sell.** I hereby employ and grant _____
hereinafter called "Agent," the exclusive and irrevocable right commencing on _____ , 19_____ , and expiring at
midnight on _____ , 19_____ , to sell or exchange the real property situated in_____ ,
County of _____ , California described as follows:
_____
_____
_____
_____

2. **Terms of Sale.** The purchase price shall be $_____ , to be paid in the following terms:
_____
_____
_____

(a) The following items of personal property are to be included in the above-stated price:
_____
_____
_____

(b) Agent is hereby authorized to accept and hold on my behalf a deposit upon the purchase price.
(c) Evidence of title to the property shall be in the form of a California Land Title Association Standard Coverage Policy of Title Insurance in
the amount of the selling price to be paid for by _____
(d) I warrant that I am the owner of the property or have the authority to execute this agreement. I hereby authorize a FOR SALE sign to be
placed on my property by Agent. I authorize the Agent named herein to cooperate with sub-agents.

3. **Notice: The amount or rate of real estate commissions is not fixed by law. They are set by each broker individu-
ally and may be negotiable between the seller and broker.**
Compensation to Agent. I hereby agree to compensate Agent as follows:
(a) _____ % of the selling price if the property is sold during the term hereof, or any extension thereof, by Agent,
on the terms herein set forth or any other price and terms I may accept, or through any other person, or by me, or _____ %
of the price shown in 2, if said property is withdrawn from sale, transferred, conveyed, leased without the consent of Agent, or made unmarketable by any voluntary act during the term hereof or any extension thereof.
(b) the compensation provided for in subparagraph (a) above if property is sold, conveyed or otherwise transferred within _____
_____ days after the termination of this authority or any extension thereof to anyone with whom Agent has had negotiations prior to
final termination, provided I have received notice in writing, including the names of the prospective purchasers, before or upon termination of
this agreement or any extension hereof. However, I shall not be obligated to pay the compensation provided for in subparagraph (a) if a valid
listing agreement is entered into during the term of said protection period with another licensed real estate broker and a sale, lease or
exchange of the property is made during the term of said valid listing agreement.

4. If action be instituted to enforce this agreement, the prevailing party shall receive reasonable attorney's fees and costs as fixed by the
Court.

5. In the event of an exchange, permission is hereby given Agent to represent all parties and collect compensation or commissions from
them, provided there is full disclosure to all principals of such agency. Agent is authorized to divide with other agents such compensation or
commissions in any manner acceptable to them.

6. I agree to save and hold Agent harmless from all claims, disputes, litigation, and/or judgments arising from any incorrect information
supplied by me, or from any material fact known by me concerning the property which I fail to disclose.

7. This property is offered in compliance with state and federal anti-discrimination laws.

8. Other provisions:
_____
_____

9. I acknowledge that I have read and understand this Agreement, and that I have received a copy hereof.
Dated _____ , 19_____ _____ , California

Owner_____   Address_____

Owner_____   City. State. Phone_____

10. In consideration of the above, Agent agrees to use diligence in procuring a purchaser.

Agent_____   Address_____ City _____

By_____   Phone_____ Date_____

NO REPRESENTATION IS MADE AS TO THE LEGAL VALIDITY OF ANY PROVISION OR THE ADEQUACY OF ANY PROVISION IN ANY
SPECIFIC TRANSACTION. IF YOU DESIRE LEGAL ADVICE, CONSULT YOUR ATTORNEY.
To order. contact—California Association of Realtors®
525 South Virgil Avenue. Los Angeles. California 90020
Copyright   1978 by California Association of Realtors®
(Revised. 1980)   FORM A-11

Authorization for deposit. Subparagraph 2 (b) authorizes the agent to accept a deposit on behalf of the seller. The deposit never belongs to the broker; it is the property of either the buyer or the seller.

Title insurance. Which party pays for the title insurance policy varies throughout the state. Be sure that this item is properly filled in.

"For Sale" sign and MLS. Subparagraph 2(d) authorizes the broker to place a "For Sale" sign on the property. It also authorizes the broker to cooperate with other real estate licensees as subagents—this is particularly applicable to MLSs. Note, however, that a broker's cooperation with subagents could have legal implications if a subagent places the listing broker in jeopardy where a third party is involved.

Compensation to Agent: Paragraph 3

In an exclusive-right-to-sell listing, the seller agrees that if he or she sells the property before the termination date, withdraws it from the market, leases it or rents it, the broker's commission must still be paid.

Commission rate. Subparagraph 3(a) includes a blank for the commission rate, which is negotiable.

Safety clause. This section includes a **safety clause,** which further protects the broker's commission in the event that the owner sells to a customer who was introduced to the property through the broker's efforts. The clause states that if the listing expires and the property remains unsold, the broker has a mutually agreed–upon period, usually 90 days, during which time he or she may collect a commission. If the property is sold during this grace period by any other broker to anyone with whom the listing broker has had previous dealings, the original broker may still be entitled to a commission. Note that this broker is entitled to a commission *only* if he or she has given the principal in writing the names of customers with whom the broker had negotiated prior to the expiration date of the original listing. However, the owner still reserves the right to give the listing to another authorized broker during the safety clause period, thus negating the original broker's commission.

Court Costs: Paragraph 4

This paragraph reminds the parties to the contract that in the event of a lawsuit, court costs—including attorney's fees—will be added to any judgment the courts may award.

Exchange Agreement: Paragraph 5

This is a reminder that the licensee may not represent more than one principal without the knowledge and consent of each. In an exchange agreement the broker can represent both the buyer and seller if the broker adheres to this law of agency.

Hold Harmless Clause: Paragraph 6

In the **hold harmless clause,** the principal agrees not to hold the agent liable for any damages that may ensue if the information furnished the broker is incorrect or if the principal fails to furnish material information concerning the property.

Compliance with Anti-Discrimination Laws: Paragraph 7

Under this item, the parties are reminded that discrimination with respect to race, creed, color or national origin is in violation of federal and state laws. The parties agree to comply with those laws.

Other Provisions: Paragraph 8

Because each listing differs, space is allowed to include any additional provisions related to the particular property or transaction.

Owner's Signature: Paragraph 9

To be valid, the listing agreement must be dated and signed by the property owner. Section 10142 of the real estate law requires that each person signing a document pertaining to the sale or purchase of real property must be given a copy of the document as soon as it is signed. In California, if the parties are married, both the husband and the wife must sign all documents pertaining to real estate transactions. One can contract, but it takes both to convey.

Agent's Signature: Paragraph 10

The agent—salesperson or broker—signs the agreement. In doing so, the agent fulfills the consideration requirement of the contract by promising to "use diligence in procuring a purchase."

Sources of Listings

To survive in today's highly competitive market, a real estate broker must have a steady flow of listings through the office. Listings are the broker's stock in trade; without them, the broker has nothing to sell.

A well-known broker once said, "The real estate office that suffers the most from competition is usually the one with a low inventory of listings or the one whose shelves are stocked with 'shabby' merchandise or overpriced or unsalable offerings." A marketable listing is one for which the seller has a serious selling motive and has accumulated all the pertinent facts. How can you stock your shelves with marketable listings? As emphasized in the previous chapter, you have to take advantage of every opportunity to prospect for them. This section explores some specific techniques for finding good listings. Some of these are illustrated in Figure 4.5.

"For-Sale-by-Owner" Listings

"For-Sale-by-Owner" signs mean the owner has decided to place his or her home on the market. Because so much is involved in selling a home, this is an opportunity to come to the owner's rescue and convince him or her that now is the best time to turn the sale over to a professional. Put yourself in the owner's shoes, so you can come up with reasons why you can do the best job.

Supermarket bulletin boards are another good source of for-sale-by-owner listings. Again, a seller using this method to advertise his or her property usually knows little about the details of real estate merchandising.

Figure 4.5
Techniques for
Finding Listings

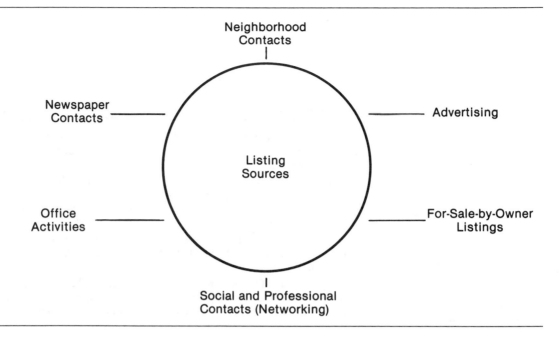

Once you have the name of one of these prospects, how do you turn it into a listing? People trying to sell by themselves may put up some resistance. Figure 4.6 lists some benefits you can cite to convince for-sale-by-owner prospects.

Newspaper Contacts   Your local newspaper is a good source of listings.

1. Know what is for sale in the area and who has the listing.

2. Check daily for notices of marriages, divorces, promotions, births and, most especially, transfer notices. These need your immediate attention.

3. "Furniture for Sale" ads are an excellent tip on someone who may be contemplating a home sale.

Advertising   **Direct mail.** Direct-mail advertising is relatively expensive, but it can bring gratifying results. You can mail cards to likely new suspects—prospective sellers—especially to those in your farm area. Effective wording on such a card might be, "Thinking of selling your home? Do you know what it is worth today? I will be contacting you in a few days and will be glad to give you an evaluation— at no obligation."

Cards should be mailed to specific individuals rather than to "Occupant." They can either be designed by your firm or purchased through companies specializing in real estate sales support. Follow up each mailing with a phone call.

Newspaper ads. Placing a small single advertisement in your local press announcing every new property sold will bring your office attention. A large advertisement placed regularly, listing all of the homes sold by your office over a period of time, will be impressive and also bring results.

Figure 4.6
**Arguments for
Converting a
For-Sale-By-Owner
Prospect**

1. You have but one property to show, yet most real estate today is bought by comparison shopping.

2. Pricing the property accurately is vital, yet how can you determine the proper price? If you price too high, you may waste time and lose prospects.

3. Regardless of the price, you may have to negotiate with buyers. Are you trained to do so to your advantage? What's more, it's easy to allow personalities to enter the picture, and thus lose a good sale. As a broker, I can prevent this and save the sale.

4. The sign "For Sale by Owner" is an invitation to all strangers to drop in on you without screening or qualification.

5. To busy people, time is money. When you are handling the sale, your time is no longer your own. You will be afraid to leave the premises for any period of time for fear of missing a prospect. Going to the grocery store takes your property off the market. Besides, your phone or doorbell may ring at any time, 24 hours a day, seven days a week.

6. Can you compete with the advertising of other properties in the marketplace? As a broker, under contract, I will enlist the services of fellow licensees and give you the advantage of an expanded market.

7. Are you aware of the large number of legal cases that have arisen when owners have endeavored to sell their own property? There are many protective details that must be included in a real property sales transaction that a broker can handle without relative fear of legalities.

8. It is vitally important to arrange for financing. Are you familiar enough with the current home loan market to advise the prospective buyer? Do you have time to leave your job to help the buyer arrange financing? Most jobs require eight hours a day, but selling real estate sometimes takes more. Are you prepared to take a leave of absence from your job for a few months?

Office Activities

Telephoning. Telephone solicitation, if properly used, actually opens more doors and results in more sales than either direct contact or written correspondence. A portion of each day may be devoted to blanketing a certain area by telephone. Such solicitations are known as *cold calls.* The person doing the telephoning should use the reverse telephone directory that lists numbers according to their addresses. This enables the caller to target a specific geographic area.

MLS listings. If the office belongs to an MLS, the salesperson or broker has access to all listings processed by the service. A careful analysis of recently expired listings, with attention to the reasons why a property has not sold, may produce a renewed listing, this time with your firm. Ask yourself, "Why didn't the property sell?" An intelligent approach, attempting to correct the reasons that it did not sell in the first place, may revive an expired listing.

Floor time. Most offices require their salespeople to spend some time, usually called *floor time,* in the office. During this period they may answer telephone calls from potential buyers responding to advertisements placed in the newspaper or from owners interested in selling their property.

Networking

The word *networking* is being used to describe the process of contacting people for the purpose of doing business with them. Close friends and relatives are among the first people a new salesperson should tell about his or her new career. Do not forget about the people with whom you do business, such as your doctor and plumber.

Also talk to neighbors and members of groups you belong to. You can then use your initial contacts to network to others who should be doing business with you.

Personnel managers of key industries also can be extremely helpful to know; transfers of executives and other key personnel provide buying as well as listing customers. The alert licensee, aware that the personnel manager has a responsibility to assist personnel in finding adequate housing and to help transferees dispose of their property, will do everything possible to sell himself or herself and the firm to the personnel manager. Other people you will want to be in touch with are:

1. returning veterans;

2. former clients and customers; and

3. buyers who may need help in selling their current homes.

At some time, just about everyone is interested in real estate. So do not miss an opportunity to let people know you are in the business.

The Listing Transaction

Real estate brokers must pay careful attention to listing details to assure a smooth transaction.

Preparing for the Listing

An old adage about the listing process is that it is "80 percent preparation and 20 percent selling." The amount of time spent on research prior to the first appointment with the prospective seller will vary with each listing. The basic information comes from the competitive market analysis and the customer.

Competitive market analysis. The competitive market analysis often is used as a marketing tool to get an appointment with potential sellers, as well as a base for realistically pricing the property. Accuracy in the competitive market analysis comes from using comparable properties and making sure that data are current and correct.

The objectives of this analysis are to:

1. let the seller respond to marketing facts concerning his or her property;

2. enhance the licensee's credibility by showing that he or she is basing the listing information on market comparison rather than on opinion;

3. allow the seller to analyze his or her market position before pricing the property; and

4. provide the third-party approach to valuation—the market, not the agent, is telling the owner what the property is worth.

Figure 4.7 is a sample form used in preparing a competitive market analysis. The following list suggests sources of data on comparable properties. The information obtained would be entered on a form such as the sample.

1. *Title check*—Check with title insurance company or county recorder to get owner's name, purchase date and purchase price.

Figure 4.7
Competitive Market
Analysis Form

CALIFORNIA ASSOCIATION OF REALTORS® STANDARD FORM

COMPETITIVE MARKET ANALYSIS

PROPERTY ADDRESS _____ DATE _____

PROBABLE MARKETING RANGE $ _____

Information reported herein is based upon published reports or matters of public record.
No representation is made or intended that this information is accurate or complete.
Financing information may not reflect specific loan terms.

The undersigned acknowledge receipt of a copy.

_____ Date _____
_____ Date _____

COMPANY _____
AGENT _____
PHONE _____

CMA-11

To order: contact CALIFORNIA ASSOCIATION OF REALTORS®
525 So. Virgil Avenue, Los Angeles, California 90020
Copyright©(1983) CALIFORNIA ASSOCIATION OF REALTORS®

CRC ® LA

2. *Technical data*—Check with local government agencies for pertinent information of a technical nature, such as improvements made, proposed sewers, possible special assessments, proposed zoning ordinances, tax rate, possible construction of freeways nearby and availability of education. Such information may be found at some of the following agencies:

- building and safety departments;

- city and county planning commissions;

- engineering departments;

- tax assessor's offices;

- division of highways; and

- boards of education.

3. *"Sold" signs*—Check the neighborhood and surrounding area for "Sold" signs. Check on the sale prices and terms of these properties, so that you can better advise your client.

When you have arrived at a selling price, be prepared to forecast the seller's projected net proceeds from the sale (see Figure 4.8).

Customer data. Prior to the listing interview, try to get an idea of the seller's wants and needs. The following questions will help in planning for the meeting with the seller:

1. Have you learned enough about your prospect to have earned the privilege of a call? Use the reverse directory to find neighbors' names and try to find out from them the motivations of the seller.

2. What needs will your prospect most likely want to satisfy?

3. What fact-finding and emotion-finding questions are you going to ask your prospect?

4. Have you made a list of advantages, benefits and solutions to problems that you will offer?

5. Have you anticipated any objections you might receive and prepared rebuttals to them?

6. What closing techniques have you prepared for making your move and asking for the listing?

The Listing Interview   With your preparation and research taken care of, you should be ready to call on your listing prospect. After introducing yourself and your firm, you can make your listing presentation, which, in effect, sells your services to the homeowner. Your presentation should include the steps described in the following paragraphs.

Step 1. Endeavor to determine the seller's motive in selling his or her property. The seller's motive must be strong or else he or she may have difficulty coming to terms with the market. Figure 4.9 shows motives that are considered prime for selling and, when handled expertly, will generally prompt marketable listings.

Figure 4.8
Estimated
Seller's Proceeds

ESTIMATED SELLER'S PROCEEDS
CALIFORNIA ASSOCIATION OF REALTORS® STANDARD FORM

SELLER _____

PROPERTY ADDRESS _____

BROKER _____

This estimate is based on costs associated with _____ financing.   ESTIMATED CLOSING DATE _____
PROJECTED SELLING PRICE $ _____

ENCUMBRANCES
First Trust Deed $ _____
Second Trust Deed _____
Other Encumbrances _____
TOTAL $ _____

PROJECTED GROSS EQUITY $ _____

ESTIMATED COSTS   **ESTIMATED CREDITS**
Escrow $ _____   Prorated Taxes $ _____
Sub Escrow _____   Prorated Insurance _____
Recording _____   Prorated Rents _____
Drawing Deed _____   Impound Accounts _____
Title Insurance _____   Other _____
Transfer Tax _____   Other _____
Notary _____
Pre-Payment Penalty _____
Forwarding or Transfer _____
Reconveyance _____
Interest _____   TOTAL ESTIMATED COSTS $ _____
Discount @ % _____   LESS ESTIMATED CREDITS $ _____
Preparation of Documents _____
Taxes _____
Appraisal _____   NET SELLER'S COSTS $ _____
Structural Pest Control Inspection _____ PURCHASE MONEY NOTE
Structural Pest Control Repairs _____   (if any) _____
FHA-VA or Lender _____   ESTIMATED SELLER'S
Home Warrantee _____   CASH PROCEEDS $ _____
Brokerage _____
Buyer's Fees _____
Miscellaneous Fees _____
TOTAL $ _____

This estimate based upon the above projected selling price, type of financing, and estimated closing dates, has been prepared to assist the seller in computing his costs. Lenders and escrow companies will vary in their charges; therefore, these figures cannot be guaranteed by the broker or his representatives.

I have read the above figures and acknowledge
receipt of a copy of this form.   Presented by: _____

Seller _____ Date _____   Address: _____

_____ Date _____   Phone No.: _____

The estimated seller's proceeds calculated above will vary according to any difference in unpaid loan balances, bonds assessments, other liens, impound account, if any, and any expenses for required repairs. All estimates and information are from sources believed reliable but not guaranteed.

To order, contact—California Association of Realtors®
525 S. Virgil Avenue, Los Angeles, California 90020
Copyright © 1978, California Association of Realtors®   FORM ESP-11

Source: Reprinted by permission, California Association of REALTORS®. Endorsement not implied.

Figure 4.9
Prime Motives
for Listing

Step 2. Ask leading questions in order to get your client talking. To get the client talking, ask such leading questions as:

1. How much are you asking for your home or property?

2. Have you received any offers?

3. How long has your home or property been up for sale?

4. Have you heard of our company?

5. Have you advertised your property?

6. May I see the inside of your house? (when applicable)

7. What are your plans after you sell?

8. Do you have any financial commitments?

After asking questions, be sure to show an interest in the answers and to give your prospect sufficient time to answer. Remember, the ability to be a good listener is just as important as the ability to be a good talker.

Step 3. Review the market data analysis. Go over the competitive market analysis with your client, explaining each item and relating it to the property in question.

Step 4. Explain different methods of financing. The seller should be advised about each method of financing available for his or her property and the possible net from each. Prepare the estimated seller's net sheet (as in Figure 4.7).

Step 5. Anticipate and handle the client's objections. Objections you may have to handle include:

1. Why should we pay you a commission when we can sell it ourselves?
    (Selling real estate is a technical transaction. In the long run, sellers can save
    money by avoiding complicated litigation, loss of time and wasted effort.)

2. We want to think it over.
    (This objection probably means they do not understand or they may fear the
    unknown. Ask them why and volunteer any information desired. Ask them
    what they want to think over and volunteer to discuss it with them. You might
    point out specifically why it will be more profitable for them to make a deci-
    sion now.)

3. We want to buy a new house before we sell.
    (Do not act overanxious. This is an excellent opportunity to suggest an ex-
    change plan. Make them aware of the danger of finding a good deal and then
    having two mortgages to pay until one property is sold.)

4. We have a friend who is a salesperson (or broker).
    (Whatever you do, do not belittle their friend's abilities. Continue to sell your-
    self, your company and the services you are in a position to offer. You may
    stress the fact that you are in a position to be entirely objective in your recom-
    mendations. Would a friend or relative really tell you what is wrong or what the
    problem is? A friend may not want to offend you by doing so. Do they prefer a
    businesslike relationship?)

5. We do not want to sign a written agreement.
    (You might explain the consequences that might arise with oral agreements. An
    agreement in writing protects all parties involved.)

Other objections may be forthcoming. If they do occur, and if you have difficulty in answering them, make a list of them and be prepared with answers for
future transactions.

Step 6. Check for *Easton* liabilities. On May 31, 1984, *Easton v. Strassburger*
changed California real estate practice. Basically, the implication of the ruling in
Easton is that all agents or subagents involved with a listing or sale of real property
are liable for any nondisclosure of known material facts or "reasonably discoverable facts." These "reasonably discoverable facts" constitute ***Easton* liabilities** and
are called "red-flag" items. Some examples of red-flag items are:

*   water-stained ceilings;

*   cracks in walls, ceilings and floors;

*   obvious additions or modifications;

*   unlevel floors; and

*   peeling plaster.

As time goes on, this list will be added to. For listing agents, this means that they
can no longer make a quick, superficial inspection of the property. They now must
make a complete inspection to discover any red-flag items.

■   **Note:** If agents discover any red-flag items, they should never venture an opinion. They should suggest to the seller or buyer that he or she get professional assistance. Also, all disclosures should be in writing.

The agent at times will want to take a shortcut and shortcuts are not recommended. Typical shortcuts include: (1) trying to use a disclaimer to avoid *Easton* liability, (2) using an "as is" clause or (3) paying for a home inspection. A disclaimer is a written statement in which the broker states that he or she is not responsible or liable for his or her acts or failures to act. Generally, the opinion of most attorneys at present is that none of these attempted shortcuts will alleviate the *Easton* liability.

The California Association of REALTORS® has developed these five guidelines to avoid any *Easton* liability:

1. Inquire—Ask the sellers if they have or had any problems (red flags) with the property. If they say Yes, then go into detail: What was the original problem? How extensive was it? If the problem has been solved, when was the problem solved? How was it solved? Is there any warranty? Has there been any recurrence of the problem?

2. Inspect—The listing agent must conduct more than a casual visual inspection of the property. He or she must carefully look for red-flag warning signs.

3. Disclose—The agent must point out any problems (red flags). Remember, do not venture any opinions, but make an inquiry of what caused the problems, using the same line of questioning that was used in step 1.

4. Recommend—Advise the seller or buyer to have an appropriate "professional" inspection. If any homework needs to be done, make sure it gets done. For example, the listing agent notes that the family room appears to be an add-on. He confronts the seller with this and the seller says, "Yes, it was added on after the construction of the home, but there are building permits." It is the listing agent's job to go to the proper authorities and check for building permits. Is it up to code? Has it been "signed off" by the city?

5. Disclose—Disclose the appropriate information to buyer and seller, in writing.[2]

These suggestions for avoiding *Easton* liability are not guarantees. The California Association of REALTORS® is investigating the possibility of developing an "*Easton* Compliance Manual" in conjunction with standard forms for disclosure, as well as a possible buyer/seller checklist (see *California Real Estate,* September 1984, p. 60, for more information).

Step 7. Assist your client in completing the listing form. Complete the listing form with your client, explaining in detail the purpose of each item. Secure the signature of the seller and be sure he or she receives a copy immediately. If sellers are married, get the signature of both spouses. Make sure the homeowner has sufficient

[2]Adapted from *Five Steps To Help Avoid Easton Liability: A Broker's Listing Information Guide and Standard Form,* California Association of REALTORS®, 1984.

equity in the home to pay fees and costs connected with the sale, such as your commission, or verify that the seller will be able to pay fees in cash.

Step 8. Place your sign on the property. Once you get the listing, put your "For Sale" sign on the property. Of course, get the seller's permission first.

Servicing the Listing

To take a listing is not enough; once the contract is signed you must begin servicing your listing. To service a listing means to work with the seller to sell his or her property. Every listing must receive attention and help to build the seller's confidence in you. This will make it much easier if circumstances require you to get price reductions, extensions in terms or any other concessions.

Communication. To service a listing properly, you must communicate. This communication should last all the way through escrow, and even beyond, for good public relations and possible referrals. Communication means that you should:

1. explain all terms of the listing contract and make sure your client understands your marketing procedures;

2. suggest any repairs or improvements you think are necessary;

3. explain all facets of closing and closing costs;

4. discuss open house scheduling;

5. report results of your advertising and send a copy of each ad to your client;

6. report results of property showing, whether done yourself, by your office or by other brokers;

7. inform the seller of any sales in the area affecting the selling price of his or her listing;

8. be prepared to make adjustments in your competitive market analysis; and

9. if need exists, suggest price changes, extensions and renewals.

You can set up communications for price changes or renewals by:

• going to the property every two weeks;

• calling your client weekly at a specific time, such as every Tuesday at 5 P.M.; and

• telling your client everything that has happened in regard to the property.

Servicing checklist. It helps to have a checklist for servicing a listing that reminds you of what needs to be done and when. Figure 4.10 is an example of such a checklist. This checklist is for the first six weeks, and it can be extended if necessary. Although specific activities probably will vary with the circumstances of a particular listing, the checklist shows the basic sequence and kinds of activities involved in servicing most listings.

Exclusive Right To Retain

Common wisdom in the real estate industry says that the seller pays the commission. Legally and technically, the seller *does* pay the sales commission. However, in practice, the seller usually prices the property to cover the amount of the commission plus what he or she wants to receive. First, consider an example of how the buyer pays the commission and the actual cost of not paying it directly to the listing agent. A seller is going to sell a property for $100,000. Negotiations set the commission at six percent, the property is free and clear and other costs are $1,000. The seller's net equity is $93,000 ($100,000 sales price less $6,000 commission less $1,000 other costs). Subtracting three percent for the selling broker would decrease the commission to three percent, or $3,000. Thus, if the selling price were reduced to $97,000, the seller still would net $93,000 ($97,000 sales price less $3,000 commission to listing broker less $1,000 other costs).

Figure 4.10
Checklist for Servicing Real Estate Listings

WEEK	ACTIVITY	ACTION	FOLLOW-UP
1	– Tell seller about caravan scheduling (showings to other brokers) – Save all business cards sheet for brokers	– Discuss sales person's comments with seller – Mail thank you cards – Develop listing information	
2	– Open house	– Discuss home improvements with seller – Double-check accuracy and completeness of listing – Get current financing information	– Analyze results of open house— contact leads
3	– Open house discussion with seller	– Discuss reactions of prospects with seller	– Make suggestions to seller for changes in price, etc., if necessary
4	– Continued sales activity	– Note new listings and sales in the seller's area – Check financing information: FHA/VA	– Discuss possible price reduction with seller – Develop materials to reflect any changes – Consider second open house
5	– Continued sales activity	– Visit the listing – Collect any business cards from other salespersons – Call for reactions – Check property and current financing information	– Consider second open house
6	– Open house	– Discuss preparations – Check on current financing	– Contact prospects for reactions – Discuss reactions with seller

If the selling broker has no commission from the sale, how does he or she get paid? The answer is simple. The money comes from the buyer. The buyer will pay the selling broker a commission (in this example, $3,000). By paying the commission directly to the selling broker, the buyer is actually financing his or her part of the commission. For simplicity, assume the purchaser could buy the property with no money down. If the seller pays all commissions, the buyer will finance $100,000. If the buyer pays his or her share of the commissions, the financed amount would be $97,000. If the buyer financed the property at 13 percent amortized over 30 years, then the $3,000 would cost $33.19 per month in a higher payment; over 30 years it would cost $11,946.19. Some might argue the buyer would be paying off this $3,000 loan in cheaper dollars. This is not the way the buyer will look at it, however, and seldom is the buyer given the opportunity to make the decision. Some day this will go to court, and the real estate industry will be forced to disclose this information.

The exclusive-right-to-retain agreement has been used in the real estate industry for 15 years or more. It has been used by specialists, such as commercial and industrial brokers and exchange brokers. Business opportunity brokers have used their own agreements (called a "send-out sheet"). The first reason these brokers use this type of agreement is to have control over their clients. Having the client sign an exclusive-right-to-retain agreement guarantees the broker a commission no matter who sells the property. Thus, the client will stay with that broker, because he or she will not want to pay two commissions. The second reason for using this agreement is that the broker is now working for the buyer, so the broker can negotiate fully for the buyer. Probably in no other field of endeavor may the same person represent two individuals with conflicting goals, except real estate. This is called *dual agency*. Gradually the use of the exclusive-right-to-retain agreement is growing.

Summary

The *listing agreement* is one of the most important documents used in a real estate transaction. It is a legal, binding contract between the seller and the broker. There are five basic types of listings: *open, exclusive-right-to-sell, exclusive agency, net* and *option.* Each has its advantages and disadvantages. The *multiple listing service* is an association of brokers who pool their listings to secure greater market coverage for their clients. Listing forms are available through the California Association of REALTORS® and other sources. All items on the form must be mutually agreed on by the seller and the broker. The agreement becomes a binding contract when signed by both.

The secret to success for any real estate office is the number of marketable listings it has available. The general sources for securing listings are: neighborhood contacts, "For-Sale-by-Owner" signs, newspaper contacts, advertising ideas, office activities, social and professional contacts and other sources.

In obtaining a listing, three steps are necessary: *preparation* for taking the listing; *taking the listing*; and *servicing* the listing. Taking the listing involves: determining the seller's motives; reviewing market data analysis; developing the seller's net sheet; and anticipating and overcoming objections. The final step in the listing process is servicing the listing. The key to success in this activity is constant communication with sellers, reporting to them the progress on the sale of their property.

Questions

1. When selling your services to a homeowner, your presentation should include:
   a. asking leading questions to get client talking.
   b. reviewing the market data analysis.
   c. anticipating and handling client's objections.
   d. all of the above

2. A broker who holds an exclusive-right-to-sell listing is entitled to a commission if the property is sold by:
   a. himself or herself.
   b. any other broker.
   c. the owner.
   d. any of the above

3. Which of these statements is incorrect?
   a. The commission is specifically determined in the contract.
   b. All expenses are to be covered before a commission is paid.
   c. The owner receives a set amount of money.
   d. The selling price must be disclosed by the broker before close of transaction.

4. An argument that may convince a for-sale-by-owner prospect that he or she should give you a listing is:
   a. you need the money.
   b. the prospect owes it to the industry.
   c. you are better able to help the prospect find financing.
   d. all of the above

5. When using an exclusive-right-to-sell listing, the broker has earned a commission when:
   a. the deed is delivered.
   b. a bona fide offer at acceptable price and terms is produced.
   c. the listing expires.
   d. the escrow closes.

6. Good sources for listings include all of the following *except*:
   a. social and professional contacts.
   b. sales interviews that have not resulted in a sale.
   c. neighborhood contacts.
   d. newspaper ads and articles.

7. A listing agreement is considered a contract. Which type of contract best describes a listing?
   a. unilateral executory contract
   b. bilateral executory contract
   c. an implied contract
   d. express executory contract

8. Under the safety clause, the broker still may get a commission if:
   a. he or she advertises the property.
   b. he or she sells to a customer introduced by his or her efforts.
   c. both a and b
   d. neither a nor b

9. Whenever a net listing is used, California real estate law requires a broker to:
   a. split his or her commission with the owner.
   b. divulge the extent of his or her profit before sale.
   c. supply the owner with the names of all prospects.
   d. none of the above

10. The safety clause in a listing agreement:
    a. extends the period of time under which the broker may receive a commission.
    b. provides proper homeowner's insurance for the seller.
    c. protects the seller when he or she has not submitted material information on the property.
    d. allows the broker the courts' protection.

11. A multiple listing service is most interested in:

 a. open listings.
 b. exclusive agency listings.
 c. net listings.
 d. exclusive-right-to-sell listings.

12. Listings are contracts that permit a licensee to find a buyer for a designated property at an agreed price and usually:

 a. are in writing.
 b. cannot be enforced.
 c. specify a limited time period.
 d. both a and c

13. Consideration in a listing agreement may be:

 a. a promise.
 b. money.
 c. anything of value.
 d. any of the above

14. The key to servicing a listing is:

 a. allowing the principal to change his or her mind.
 b. accepting a reduction in commission if property is not selling.
 c. communicating to the seller your progress in showing the property.
 d. making needed repairs on subject property.

15. If a listing agreement contained a definite termination date, you would assume that it was:

 a. an exclusive-right-to-sell listing.
 b. an option listing.
 c. a verbal listing.
 d. an open listing.

16. Listings often can be optained from:

 I. clients who have read the broker's advertisements for other properties.
 II. clients who have seen the broker's For Sale signs.

 a. I only
 b. II only
 c. both I and II
 d. neither I nor II

17. The employment contract that specifies that the owner can sell the property without paying a commission is known as:

 a. an exclusive-right-to-sell listing.
 b. a net listing.
 c. an exclusive agency listing.
 d. an open listing.

18. The clause in a listing agreement that limits the liability of the licensee is known as the:

 a. limitation clause.
 b. compensation clause.
 c. excuse me clause.
 d. hold harmless clause.

19. Which type of listing can be given to as many licensees as an owner wishes?

 a. net listing
 b. option listing
 c. open listing
 d. exclusive agency listing

20. To get greater market coverage on listings, the licensee would most likely:

 a. use a cooperative listing service.
 b. hire more salespeople.
 c. use a multiple listing service.
 d. both a and c

5

Advertising

Chapter Preview   Advertising surrounds us during all our waking hours. Whether it is the sign on the diner that simply says "Eat," the newspaper with its classified and display ads, the matchbook with its sales message, the advertising letters and pamphlets or the TV or radio message, we are in constant contact with advertising messages of one sort or another.

This chapter points out the importance of laying the groundwork for subsequent sales through the use of the AIDA approach to writing effective advertising. General advertising goals and guidelines are stressed. The most appropriate media for real estate advertising are identified. Each is explored, with special emphasis on the planning and development of classified advertisements.

The importance of adhering to an advertising budget is explained. Suggestions are made for checking and evaluating advertising effectiveness.

The chapter ends with an introduction to the legal implications of advertising real estate. Such regulations are contained in the California Real Estate Law, the Commissioner's regulations and the Truth-in-Lending Act.

Terms To Look For   **AIDA approach**
APR
Attention getters
Classified advertising
Display advertising
FTC
Giveaways
Income dollar
Institutional advertising
Media
Operational advertising
Regulation Z
Right of rescission
Truth-in-Lending Act

| **The AIDA Approach to Advertising** | Advertising can be used for a variety of purposes—to enhance your firm's image, increase market exposure, recruit new agents and educate the public. The most common, and probably most important, reason for advertising is to find ready, willing and able buyers for your listings. All the listings in the world will do you no good unless someone finds a ready, willing and able buyer and makes that elusive sale. |

Why do people buy? For benefits. A particular piece of property offers them shelter. But it also might provide them with other things that are equally important—security, good schools for their children, convenience, prestige and a lot more. The purpose of advertising is to communicate these benefits through the property's features—its price, size, location and so on.

To attract buyers, the ad must be read. To achieve this, most advertising is designed to get the reader's attention, stimulate his or her interest, generate a desire and lead the reader to action. This is commonly referred to as the **AIDA approach,** from an acronym made up of the first letter of each step involved.

1. *Attention*—The first step in any type of advertising is to get the reader's attention. Attention-getters include headlines that use words and word combinations, print and layout that attract prospective buyers and encourage them to read further.

2. *Interest*—The ad should arouse interest in the specific product or service offered. Probably one of the best ways to arouse interest is through curiosity. Curiosity can be stimulated through imagery of the reader using and enjoying the benefits of the product or service.

3. *Desire*—Once the readers' attention is attracted and their interest is aroused, the ad can create desire by appealing to the senses and emotions. At this stage, language must be clear and concise and inspire readers' confidence. Wherever possible, the advertising should try to build mental images and picture the reader as the final recipient of the product or service.

4. *Action*—Finally, your ad should move readers to take action. The advertisement should be directed toward helping readers make a decision, convinced that they really need and want a property. They should be persuaded to take action and buy now.

| **Types of Real Estate Advertising** | Real estate advertising may be divided into two major areas—*institutional* and *operational.* These two categories describe two kinds of goals of real estate advertising. |

Institutional advertising attempts to create a favorable image of the real estate company, the broker and the salesperson. This advertising keeps the company's name in the public eye and tries to inspire trust, confidence and goodwill. Institutional advertising, often done by organized groups having similar interests, manifests pride in and respect for the real estate business. Individual brokers may be required to share some of the costs incurred in this type of advertising.

Operational advertising, also called *specific advertising,* is concerned with immediate results. It is used to describe a particular piece of property, stimulate activity in a specific property or an entire tract of homes and protect the broker against threats of competition.

Advertising Guidelines

There are five basic tenets of advertising.

1. Advertise the right property.
2. Know when to advertise.
3. Choose the right market.
4. Use the proper media.
5. Use correct advertising techniques.

Obviously, a real estate office cannot advertise all its listings, so your advertising strategy has to be based on accomplishing certain objectives. For example, if you are trying to generate a great number of prospects, consider the listings that have the greatest general appeal.

Knowing when to advertise and whom you want to reach are extremely important. You probably would not advertise a home in the northern part of California as featuring a swimming pool if it is the beginning of a cold winter; a fireplace would be a more appropriate feature. Likewise, you would probably avoid advertising an elegant, expensive home in a local newspaper that is distributed primarily to low-income families.

Advertising Media

In selecting the appropriate **media** to use, the advertiser must begin with three basic considerations:

1. the target audience to be reached;
2. the message to be conveyed; and
3. the money available for media purchases.

This means that in addition to determining what to say, the broker must evaluate which medium or combination of media will deliver the maximum number of potential customers for the expenditure the broker can afford.

Because the message cannot contribute toward sales until prospective buyers are exposed to it, the message must be delivered within sight or earshot of such prospects. The delivery function is performed by the various advertising media. Figure 5.1 illustrates the variety of media that are used in the real estate business. Each has its own advantages and disadvantages.

Magazine Advertising

Magazines are an old advertising medium, dating back well over a hundred years. Almost any segment of the population can find magazines that satisfy its desire for enlightenment or entertainment. Magazines hold a distinct advantage in their ability to serve special-interest groups. For example, some magazines appeal to women, others reach high-income families, some specialize in particular interests or hobbies.

**Figure 5.1
Media Used for
Real Estate
Advertising**

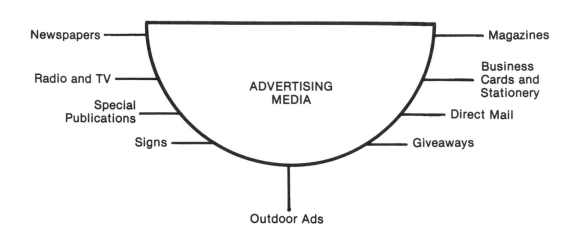

In addition to reaching a selective audience, this medium lends itself to national coverage and often is used institutionally. In addition, it allows high-quality reproduction of colored photographs and often is passed on to other parties, giving it greater circulation. However, magazines are used less frequently than other media in real estate advertising. The reasons for this are the high cost involved and their broad geographic coverage. Other media are better adapted to local coverage.

**Radio and TV
Advertising**

Compared to print media, radio broadcasting is a relatively new advertising medium. The first paid advertisement on radio appeared in 1922. Today radio can reach, at one time or another, nearly 99 percent of the households in the United States. Customers can be reached traveling to and from work, to and from the market, at the beach or in the comfort of their own homes.

Written media can guarantee a certain circulation, but not radio. Each message delivery has only one exposure opportunity. Once it has been delivered, the message is gone for good. Advertising real estate by radio usually involves spot announcements of rather short duration.

Television, the newest of the major media, delivers advertising messages to both the eye and the ear. What is more, it permits the use of motion and color and usually delivers the message in the home. Television advertising, however, is expensive; and because of the cost per client reached, it is used sparingly for real estate advertising. It is used most often by real estate companies and franchisers.

**Business Cards
and Stationery**

Your real estate firm's business cards and stationery should be ambassadors representing the quality of your service and the distinctiveness of your product. Always leave your business card both at each property and with important business contacts. It is a courtesy to the owner (whether at home or not). It also helps to advertise and create good public relations for your office.

The layout of a real estate firm's business card and letterhead should tie in closely with its office signs and should be informative and in good taste.

Special Publications   Various publications produced to reach special groups include school yearbooks, church bulletins, charity event programs and special athletic event programs, as well as house organs and trade papers of various kinds. Real estate advertising in these publications is generally institutional and only occasionally advertises specific property.

Direct Mail   Although direct-mail advertising is rather expensive, it can be an effective way to reach a selective audience. It may be institutional in nature or be designed to promote a new subdivision, an area or even a specific piece of property. A variety of vehicles is used in this method of advertising, including pamphlets, brochures, letters, postcards, booklets, pictures and maps.

Signs Used in Advertising   The design of a licensee's signs should be unique, original, quickly informative and as attractive as possible. The attention-getting value of the signs will be enhanced through the use of color, unique design, an identifiable logo, and type and size of print. Whatever their makeup, signs should be coordinated with any printed material being created for the office.

Giveaways   Most offices include some promotional giveaway items in their advertising budget. These may include note pads, calendars, pencils, directories and pens. Such items promote the company continually to the recipient and can be dispensed through the office, at business and social gatherings, at open houses and during door-to-door canvassing. They are excellent door openers and can be used effectively to get acquainted in a neighborhood.

Outdoor Advertising   Outdoor advertising is used less frequently than other media and depends largely on the size of the town and the availability of advertising billboards. Usually billboards are utilized by larger brokerage offices or chain operations. However, signs may be painted on buildings, fences, bus-stop benches or other places by individual real estate offices as well.

Newspaper Advertising   Newspaper advertising is the oldest advertising medium in the nation and the keystone of the real estate business. Although the first advertisement appeared in the *Boston Newsletter* in 1704, newspapers were rather scarce until 1790. From that point on, the growth was rapid; more than 50 million newspapers are sold each day, and more than 9,000 different papers are published every week.

Newspapers have a degree of audience selectivity. Because of their wide circulation, they may be considered to have extensive coverage. What is more, they have time and place flexibility and are especially important for local advertising. One of the few drawbacks to this form of comparatively inexpensive advertising is that its effective lifespan is short.

Because of their tremendous circulation, newspapers reach all classes of consumers and are considered by most licensees to be the most effective medium for the money. Newspaper advertising is divided into classified and display.

All forms of newspaper advertising are important, but the most common form used in the real estate business is **classified advertising.** Surveys in recent years show that almost 50 percent of all sales made by brokerage firms can be directly traced to classified advertising.

Figure 5.2
Super Attention-Getters

CLEOPATRA'S CANOE

Was pretty splendiferous, but it had nothing on this one. A truly quality executive home in prestigious Sycamore Creek, DANVILLE. 4 spacious bdrms, 2½ baths, huge family rm, gourmet kitchen. TOTAL PRIVACY. $229,500.

Lavish & Luxurious

Elegant shades of browns & blues compliment this lovely 3 bdrm. home with large den and tile fireplace. Formal dining, imported chandelier, upgraded appliances, central vac, tasteful wallpapers throughout. Beautifully landscaped. Pool-size yard lined with rose bushes. SEE TODAY! $97,000.

Lots Of T.L.C.

One of the largest F&Js in Windridge. Very neat with lots of extras, new mini-blinds/paint/wallpaper/hot water heater. Beautiful landscaping and rprivacy fence. Great assumable loan. DON'T MISS IT— $60,900.

C'EST MAGNIFIQUE!

Contemporary executive retreat offering 6 bedrooms, 4 baths. Heated pool & Jacuzzi plus pool house can be viewed from the island kitchen, billard & family rooms. Inviting Atrium, study & sewing room. Solid oak, teak, redwood, cedar & Italian tile are found throughout. 2.2 treed acres in serene area. $469,000.

GINGERBREAD

Beautiful 2-story in Kessler Square built in 1926 features sought-after gingerbread styling reflecting the warmth of an earlier era. Spacious 3 bdrm. home has upstairs WBFP. Natural wood trim in living room and dining room and gleaming hardwood floors throughout. Owners are ready to move. See today!

FLAPPER ERA

Home with updated kitchen and old fashioned front porch and gables. Hardwoods under newish carpet, 7 rooms, 2 baths, 2 fireplaces, and expandable attic. Under $110,000. Open Sunday, call for address.

"Just Listed" STORY BOOK STREET

Lovely 3 bdrm home on beautiful tree-lined street. Lovely living rm, formal dining rm, new kitchen & great brkfst rm. C/H&A. Manicured yard complements spa & gazebo. $129,500.

BE A THIEF

Steal this extraordinary repossessed tri-level w/beautiful POOL. Priced way below market for a quick sale by desperate lender. On private lot w/ magnificent view of surrounding hills. This junior hotel-sized 4 bdrm, 3 full bath boasts decorator drapes & wallpaper, new paint, fireplace-lit family rm & much more. At only $199,950, worth seeing, worth owning. Call about this "must sell" opportunity today.

BACHELOR'S SHOWPLACE

On Buena Vista. 2-2½-den, study, WBFP, pool. Freeform 6-level townhouse with soaring ceilings and 2 private courtyards. Balcony off most rooms. New custom kitchen with tile floor. French doors in abundance overlooking small pool. Fabulous built-ins, security system, wet bar.

Classified Advertisements

Writing classified ads takes imagination. People who read such ads to find a home will thumb through hundreds of them. They will stop and read only those that stand out on an advertising page. Some of the creative features that will catch a reader's eyes are:

- skillfully used white space;
- catchy phrases;
- boldface type;
- large type;
- unusual typefaces;
- interesting layout; and
- vividly descriptive words.

These concepts are illustrated by some sample ads in Figure 5.2. These ads are "super **attention-getters**." Each headline attracts the reader's attention with lively language.

Sometimes *holiday tie-ins* encourage a second look from the prospective buyer. Some of the most common are related to New Year's Day, Valentine's Day, April Fool's Day, the Fourth of July, Thanksgiving and Christmas. *Special day tie-ins* will attract attention when they are used in connection with such special events as income-tax time or Super Bowl season (see Figure 5.3).

**Figure 5.3
Special Day and
Holiday Tie-ins**

> **A VALENTINE**
>
> For both the loves in your life—a beautiful DOCK for your BOAT—and a magnificent waterfront home for your sweetheart!

> **AFTER XMAS SALE**
>
> Price reduced on this under market 4-bedroom home.

> **THE TAX MAN COMETH**
>
> But you needn't worry. You'll be money ahead . . .

> **START THE NEW YEAR**
>
> in a fresh, bright, three-bedroom house.

An unusual type of headline is one that combines words in short, appealing phrases. Using words that rhyme or have a noticeable rhythm or making some play on words grabs attention. Notice the attraction of the headlines in Figure 5.4.

Figure 5.4
Special Wording
Headlines

CUL-DE-SAC CUTIE
$54,500
This darling 4br, 2ba home located in N.H. neighborhood features fresh paint throughout, c-h/a, beamed ceilings & more! Just $2350 down for new FHA or No Down VA!

HOW SUITE IT IS!!!
THE ACADEMY BUILDING
17 Academy Street
Quite simply the best office address around in terms of location, value, & prestige. Just off Broad St between the Public Service & Prudential Headquarters Plazas. Exciting offices avail from 250-4000 sq. ft. We think you're going to like it here!

Welcoming Warmth
Williamsburg style, stunning 2-story 4-3-2 plus study. Grandma size kitchen plus spacious breakfast room. All is sunny and bright. $190's. Call for app't. today.

Solitude Seekers
RUSTIC SETTING ideal for retirement home. Just hillside property. LOG CABIN that has everything. 3 bedrooms, 2 full baths, kitchen has micro-oven, Jenn-Aire grill, Kitchenaide dishwasher, etc. Plush Carpet. 4.8 acres of trees. Two level ranch w/finished bar and family room on lower level. YEAR ROUND SEASONAL PLEASURE with this property. Under $70,000.

SIP & DIP
Executive Home
W/Pool
3/2/2 WBFP. Best of country living with convenience. Elegant custom home with all the amenities, built-in desk & vaulted ceilings.

Some headlines attract because of their use of descriptive words. These are called *"say it with flowers"* headlines (see Figure 5.5). The use of general words, such as *wonderful, big, beautiful, unusual* and *nice,* does nothing to arouse readers' curiosity, nor does it encourage people to read any further. More colorful words will make the advertisement more exciting and noticeable.

Advertising agencies and real estate offices use what are known as "choose a better word" lists. For example, the chart may show alternatives such as these:

Do Not Use	*Do Use*
big	massive, huge, immense, whopping, king-sized
beautiful	lovely, decorative, chic, elegant, lavish, exquisite
nice	superb, ideal, classic, pleasing, crackerjack
unusual	distinctive, spectacular, unprecedented, daring, unmatched
wonderful	extraordinary, super, astounding, miraculous

Some headlines give the impression that the ad was written specifically for the prospect who is reading it. This is accomplished by using the words *you* and *yours,* prominently displayed, as in Figure 5.6.

Figure 5.5
"Say It with
Flowers" Headlines

THE CHARM OF YESTERYEAR—

but updated for todays living! Sought after location near shopping, bus, etc. Old fashioned front porch invites you into living & dining rooms with hardwood floors, fireplace, large country kit. & 3rd bdrm or den. Only $58,900.

UNPARALLELLED

A Westerville location, now priced $10,000 below new replacement costs. Four bedrooms, 2½ bath two story. Outstanding condition. Neutral decor, center hall, traditional. Low $80's.

A TOUCH OF ELEGANCE

A contemporary of extra-ordinary luxury and sophistication. Stately brick walls and iron gates open to lush landscaping surrounding this elegant 5 bedroom 5 bath home. Soaring multi-level ceilings highlight one of a kind offering. This home affords formals, den, study, hugh gourmet kitchen and exquisite master suite with deluxe dressing area. Two separate outdoor entertainment areas-one with an ambiance of Hawaii with secluded Gazebo surrounded by island landscaping. The other with a beautiful heated pool jacuzzi and bathhouse accented by lovely redwood bridge leading to adjacent patio. Many, many extras! Professionally designed and decorated. Offered at $685,000. By appointment only.

HONEYMOONER'S RETREAT $69,500

This darling 2 bdrm home with pool, located in lovely Cottage area, features cozy frplc, spacious fam rm & so much more.

Hide-A-Way Castle

On Lake Tawakoni. 2 Story dream home, 4 bdrm, 2 bath, oversized country kitchen with dining, large living den with WBFP, study, sunroom. Approx. 1½ acres backs up to lake with boathouse, 2 docks, carport, native oak trees, garden space. It's all here. Priced in mid $80's.

FOR THE DISCRIMINATING

Created without compromise is this multi-level Oglesby Group designed 4 Bdrm., 4½ bath contemporary, perched high atop a bluff overlooking scenic creek and Dallas Country Club. Dramatic curved entry features brick floors leading to fully integrated entertaining & Living areas. Living Rm. showcases a panoramic view of natural beauty with floor to ceiling windows. Master suite includes conversation area, WBFP, sunken tub, sauna, & deck to pool area. Outstanding amenities offered are custom designed pool, several levels of decking, 4 WBFPs., custom wall coverings, exterior lighting, & low maintenance landscaping. Truly for the most discriminating. $1,950,000

COLLEGE GREENS BEAUTY

An immaculate 3 bedroom, 2 bath, family room home. Builtins including micro wave, inside utility room and a three car garage. Covered patio with beautiful spa. Must be seen to be appreciated. Only $97,950

2 STORY CASTLE

would compare to a castle w/waterfall, 2 patios, picnic tables, wet bar, RV access. 4 br, 2 ba, 2 frplcs, walk-in pantry, redecorated kitch, So. Lindale. See & buy! $88,990.

Figure 5.6
Use of *You*
and *Yours*

YOU WON'T BELIEVE IT

It really is a mobile home but you would never know from its Colonial clapboard siding or spacious sun filled interior. Set on a quiet paved street in the nicest 5-Star adult park in Sunnydale, the 2 BR and den home features over 1,500 sq. ft. of air conditioned luxurious, carefree comfort. Amenities include 2 full baths, quality appliances, a huge covered deck for relaxation, 2 car carport plus a storage building. Better than new, it's priced to please at only $32,000.

A LOT FOR YOUR FAMILY

On a quiet Cul de Sac walking close to elementary and Jefferson Middle schools, this is a very special site for a happy family. $27,000.

LET YOUR TENANT PAY

For this quality brick duplex on prestigious Washington Circle. Each unit has 3 BR, 1½ baths, stone fireplace, formal dining room, central air and double garage. With $8,000 down, after collecting your rents the total monthly payment is only $376.

CAN YOU AFFORD $300 FOR RENT

If so, you can be the owner of a great 3 BR home on a huge fenced lot in an established Northside family neighborhood. Walking close to schools and shopping, the home boasts a full basement, storage attic, attached garage and a garden that will be the envy of your friends. It's not going to last long so call NOW for details.

Instead of using drab words to describe particular features, advertising agencies recommend other specialized words. Keep in mind, you are not selling a living room, garage, yard or even a view. Rather, you should be selling what each of these features means to the prospect. Ask what they are looking for. In other words, what is the demonstrable difference? Figure 5.7 shows ads that have successfully answered that question.

**Figure 5.7
Demonstrable
Difference
Headlines**

Country Living
This energy efficient home includes 4 bedrooms, 3 bath with fireplaces in den & master. Other amenities include indoor jacuzzi, 6 skylights, 2 heat pumps, 3 ceiling vans, 2 decks, lots of built-ins & much more. All on 2.66 acres with assumable loan plus owner financing. $139,900.

DINNER & SUNSET
from your dinette enjoy a picturesque view of sunset & trees. Custom ranch, 2 BR's, din rm, log burning fireplace, a large summer porch, central air, 2-car garage Lovely landscaped lot in delightful location. $129,900. MUST SETTLE ESTATE! CALL NOW!

TREED LOT WITH STREAM
Outstanding 3 BR ranch, w/2 full baths, liv. rm., din. rm., fam. rm., 2 WBFP's, full bsmt., 2 c. garage, 1st floor lndry. Armstrong floors, extra insulation. 5 years old. Only 15 mins. north of I-270. Take N. Galena Rd. to Kilbourne Rd. and turn right.

OPEN FOR ENTERTAINMENT
Super two-story custom contemporary. Sparkling pool. 4/2/ living den/ dining rm/ fireplace. Two bdrms up, two down. $110,000.

POOL OVERLOOKS WOODS & CREEK
Beautifully terraced lawn, wonderful big rooms, 2 living areas. Walk to Lake Lewisville. Reduced to $149,900. Evenings:

GRAB THE PHONE & CALL ALL YOUR FRIENDS
When you see the 400 sq. ft. family room of this Willow Street ranch home (complete with stand up bar) you'll want to have a get together. Highlighted by birch trees and split rail fencing, this 2 bath beauty also offers you a custom "Krown" kitchen with 9 roomy cabinets and full appliance package. From the plaster walls to the covered patio and large, grassy yard, this immaculate home has much more to offer. At only $64,900, why not inquire today.

EASY OCEAN ACCESS
OPEN TODAY 2-5
12685 Bisc Bay Dr. Isle 5 Keystone's yachtsman paradise, boat slip, lift, dock, minutes to ocean. See the sunrise over miles of Biscayne Bay from a private upper master suite with dressing room + den, 4 family bdrms below, dramatic family room with fireplace, bayview eat-in kitchen, Spanish-style living room, formal dining, 2-car garage, pool, priced to your needs...you must see it!!

Feature	Descriptive word benefits
living room	entertainment-sized, homey, cozy, livable, spacious
dining room	sunny, intimate, perfect for a Thanksgiving dinner
garage	excellent storage, easy to park in, workspace, no-effort doors
yard	fenced, king-sized, parklike, your own garden
view	breathtaking, expansive, romantic, zestful, thrilling

Sometimes the ad writer gets carried away and uses slang expressions and offbeat language. These attract attention, but they must be used with care and caution so as not to demean the property being described or belittle the prospect reading the advertisement (see Figure 5.8).

Figure 5.8
"Goofball" Headings

PIZZAZZ!

De3scribes this beautifully De-signed CONTEMPORARY! 4 bedrooms, Living-Den, Dining, GAMEROOM + POOL/JA-CUZZI—with More Amenities that you dared dreamed of! Lush Landscaping!

AHA!!!!!!!!!!

$99 can get you a sparkling of-fice in a modern, full service bldg. close to freeways, CSU, Playhouse Sq. and Loop bus. Ready to move in or tailored to your requirements..

TOTALLY AWESOME

4213 Southwestern. 2/2 with study, all new inside & out, including kitchen, roof, A/C, & backyard fence. Just some ex-tras: High ceiling in living room, steam shower, wet bar with ice machine, levelors, hardwood floors, new carpet, deck, & much more. $289,500.

BEAM ME UP, SPOCK

High-tech means mastery of the elements exhibited in the quarried marble tile & herring-bone oak parquet. Fine cabin-etry, state-of-the-art appls. Vast expanses of black glass. WBFPs, high ceilings. Deck w/downtown view. $179,500.

If It Were Perfect

...the price would be higher. 4 bdrm., study, game rm., den and pool. 3,150 sq. ft. Priced under appraisal at $114,000.

'SWONDERFUL!

This long & lovely Ranch with 4 BRs, 2 baths, in finest location. 'Sparadise with its lg. DR, lg family rm w/full wall fpl & 2-tiered wood patio, many gla-marous features such as skylight in foyer, spotlighted ceiling in family rm, all on a huge lot. The price 'smarvelous at $217,500.

THE DIRT IS FLYING

Construction is underway on our sen-sational gem of an office bldg. consist-ing of 12,000 sq. ft., one sty (oops, 4,000 ft. just leased--8,000 sq. ft. still avail) This attractive bldg. features a skylit atrium lobby with reflective pool, plen-ty of parking, and great exposure on a prominant Columbia Turnpike corner.

CRACKER BOX

Low priced! Super amenities. Pool, security, hot tub, covered parking. Invest your rent money in this 1-1. $44,500.

A FILET OF A HOME

LEAN Price in Prime location! Sink your teeth into this spacious 3bdrm 3bath home. Featuring formal dining rm, sepa-rate fireplaced family rm and 3car gar. Priced to Move! $129,500. B712

Sometimes, either actually or as a figure of speech, an ad headline will offer a bonus for the buyer. These often are called *giveaway offer* headlines. They contain such words as *rebate, reduced, bonuses* and *affordable,* as well as the word *giveaway* (see Figure 5.9).

**Figure 5.9
Giveaway Offers**

> **JUST REDUCED!**
> Fantastic town-house with 3 spacious bed-rooms . . .

> **WALLET WATCHER
> $39,500**
> Don't let rising housing prices pass you by. This could be your last chance to own a 3 bedroom Cape Cod at a realistic price. A great place with a desired location, 2 car garage, full basement and fenced yard. Make your move now.

> **AFFORDABLE DREAM
> OPEN 1-4**
> Livable, comfortable & cozy describe this Citation blt. home located in So. Natomas area. 3 BR 2 BA situated on lrg corner lot. Many extras & upgrades thruout. FHA, VA & Cal-Vet buyers welcome. Don't miss this opportunity! Asking $75,500.

**Display
Advertisements**

Display advertising may be either institutional or operational in nature. It may combine the two, so that it is used primarily to build goodwill and prestige and keep the name before the public, while at the same time it advertises specific property.

**More Writing
Guidelines**

Ideas to consider when writing classified or display real estate advertisements are:

1. Keep the material direct and to the point.
2. Start with a provocative lead.
3. Do not tell all; leave something to the imagination.
4. Arouse curiosity in your reader.
5. Paint a mental picture.
6. Write as if you were an authority.
7. Do not waste words; they cost money.
8. Put all elements in logical order.
9. Use the words *you* and *yours.*
10. Season your words with enthusiasm.

11. Give the reader the opportunity to reach you.

12. End your ad with sparkle.

News Releases

Newspapers, by their very nature, are always interested in news. However, they quickly detect attempts on the part of real estate brokers to disguise publicity as news. Nevertheless, items frequently published in newspapers deal with the sale, purchase, exchange, modernization or construction of real property.

Whenever possible, a wide-awake licensee should get his or her name or company name before the public in favorable news stories. This is free advertising, and it provides an opportunity for the broker to become better known in the community. Some guidelines for getting a news story accepted by the local press follow.

1. Become acquainted with the news editor and the features editor.

2. Make sure the item is newsworthy and has a broad readership appeal. Examples of such items are:

   - broker's involvement in community affairs, fund-raising campaigns, cultural activities and so on;

   - moving an existing office to a new location or establishment of a new office;

   - announcement of the sale of a particularly well-known property;

   - establishment of a new sales record; and

   - trends that affect the entire community; for example, despite rising interest rates, the broker has worked to create types of financing for all buyers.

3. Articles should be in good taste, well-written and typed double-spaced on the company letterhead.

Advertising Budget

Every *successful* real estate office has developed a system for budgeting its expenses. One of the expenses that must be accounted for is advertising. Advertising is one of the most important steps in the marketing of real property, but it does cost money. Soon after starting in the business, the broker will learn that a certain amount of the firm's income dollar must be allocated to this item to maximize returns.

The division of the company **income dollar** shown in Figure 5.10 was created by the National Association of REALTORS®. Note that it allows for approximately 15 to 21 percent of gross income for advertising, including newspapers, signs and brochures. The amount allocated for advertising may fluctuate from month to month or year to year, depending on such factors as newness of the office, condition of the market and size of the community, as well as the availability of various media.

Figure 5.10
**Company Income
Dollar**

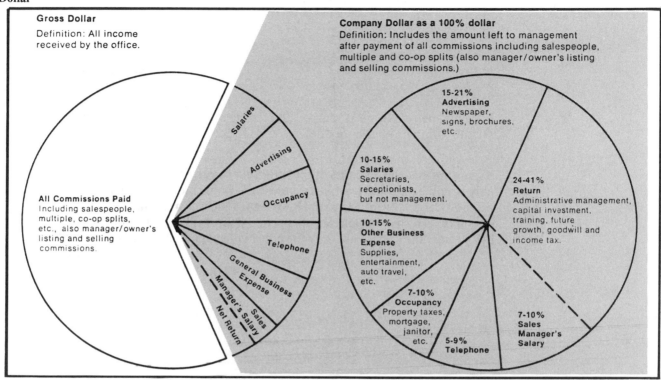

Gross Dollar

Definition: All income
received by the office.

Company Dollar as a 100% dollar

Definition: Includes the amount left to management
after payment of all commissions including salespeople,
multiple and co-op splits (also manager/owner's listing
and selling commissions.)

All Commissions Paid
Including salespeople,
multiple, co-op splits,
etc., also manager/owner's
listing and selling
commissions.

Salaries

Advertising

Occupancy

Telephone

General Business
Expense

Manager's Salary

Sales

Net Return

**15-21%
Advertising**
Newspaper,
signs, brochures,
etc.

**10-15%
Salaries**
Secretaries,
receptionists,
but not management.

**10-15%
Other Business
Expense**
Supplies,
entertainment,
auto travel,
etc.

**24-41%
Return**
Administrative management,
capital investment,
training, future
growth, goodwill and
income tax.

**7-10%
Occupancy**
Property taxes,
mortgage,
janitor,
etc.

**5-9%
Telephone**

**7-10%
Sales
Manager's
Salary**

**Advertising
Effectiveness**

There is an old saying in advertising: "Half of my advertising is worth the money.
The problem is that I don't know *which* half!" Knowing what part of your advertising dollar is producing your sales can be critical to success. You must be able to determine which types of advertising are most effective for you and which produce the most dollars. You can do that by tracking ads and determining the relative cost versus the amount of business they generate.

The key to a good measurement system is simplicity. Whenever you run a newspaper ad or send out a letter or direct-mail piece, put a code on the bottom of the piece. Many real estate organizations use a department number, such as Department Y; a box number; or, in some instances, a designated phone number. Thus, respondents who contact you by asking for Department Y or send a response card to Box 000 have responded to your ad in a particular advertising piece. If possible, try to identify the number of suspects and prospects separately, so you will know the quality as well as the quantity of leads you get. Then determine the cost of each advertisement and the number of leads and sales it produced.

Here is a simple example. Jane Freyman placed two ads in different newspapers for the same period. The ads were identical. She knew that this was important because she wanted to test which publication worked best. If she used different quality ads, one would naturally pull better because it was a better ad, not because the publication was better. She ran the ads at the same time for the same reason. The only difference was that the ad for Paper *A* directed people to ask for Department X, while the ad in Paper B told people to ask for Department Y. There was a difference in the cost of running the ad. Paper A had a circulation of 20,000 and charged $200 for the ad. Paper B had a circulation of 100,000 and charged $1,000. The following are the results that Jane tabulated:

Paper A	Paper B
15 prospects	27 prospects
24 suspects	45 suspects
5 eventual sales	9 eventual sales

Which paper is a more attractive advertising medium? Does she simply want greater numbers of sales or does she want to get more sales more cost-effectively?

Assuming that the amounts of the individual sales were comparable, Paper B probably would be more attractive to Jane if she wants more sales. The ad in Paper B generated more eventual sales. However, if Jane was more interested in cost-effectiveness, she probably would prefer Paper A. The sales numbers were smaller, but so were the costs—not only the cost of the ad, but also the cost per sale:

$$\frac{5 \text{ sales}}{\$200} = \$40 \text{ per sale}$$

$$\frac{9 \text{ sales}}{\$1,000} = \$110 \text{ per sale}$$

Legal Implications of Advertising

Advertising real property is regulated by the California Real Estate Law, the Regulations of the Real Estate Commissioner and the Federal Consumer Protection Act (Truth-in-Lending Act).

California Real Estate Law

Section 10139—"Penalties for Unlicensed Person." This law stipulates that any unlicensed person acting as a licensee who advertises using words indicating that he or she is a broker is subject to a fine not to exceed $500 and/or imprisonment in the county jail for a term not to exceed six months. If the violator is a corporation, it is subject to a fine of $5,000.

Section 10140—"False Advertising." This section states that every officer or employee who knowingly advertises a false statement concerning any land or subdivision is subject to a fine of $1,000 and/or one year's imprisonment. In addition, the licensee may have his or her license suspended or revoked.

Section 10140.5—"Disclosure of Name." Each advertisement published by a licensee that offers to assist in filing applications for the purchase or lease of government land must indicate the name of the broker and the state in which he or she is licensed.

Section 10140.6—"False Advertising." A licensee may not publish in any newspaper, periodical or by mail an ad for any activity for which a real estate license is required that does not contain a designation disclosure that he or she is performing acts for which a license is required.

Section 10235—"Misleading Advertisement." A licensee may not advertise, print, display, publish, distribute, televise or broadcast false or misleading statements regarding rates and terms or conditions for making, purchasing or negotiating loans or real property sales contracts, nor may a licensee permit others to do so.

Section 10236.1—"Inducements." A licensee may not advertise to offer a prospective purchaser, borrower or lender any gift as an inducement for making a loan or purchasing a promissory note secured directly by a lien on real property or a real property sales contract.

Section 10131.7—"Mobile Home Advertising." A licensee is prohibited from engaging in the following activities:

- advertising a mobile home that is not in an established mobile home park;

- failing to withdraw an advertisement of a mobile home within 48 hours of removal from the market;

- advertising or representing a used mobile home as a new one;

- making a false statement that a mobile home is capable of traveling on California highways; and

- falsely advertising that no down payment is required on the sale of a mobile home when in fact one is required.

Regulations of the Real Estate Commissioner

Chapter 1 described how the Commissioner is able to adopt regulations that have the same force and intent as law. Two of these regulations follow.

Article 9, Section 2770—"Advertising." A salesperson may not advertise without identifying the name of his or her employing broker in advertising any service for which a license is required.

Article 9, Section 2770.1—"Advertising, License Designation." Abbreviations such as "bro." or "agt.," referring to "Broker" or "Agent," are deemed sufficient identification in ads to comply with the Business and Professions Code.

These legal references are merely condensations of the actual regulations. Further information may be found in the publications listed in Chapter 1.

Code of Ethics of the NATIONAL ASSOCIATION OF REALTORS®

Even though the Code of Ethics of the NATIONAL ASSOCIATION OF REALTORS® is a moral code and as such is not enforceable by law, the items set forth are observed by most real estate licensees in the state. Professional courtesy and ethics should not stop at those things that have been sanctioned by law. The individual who tries only to stay on the border of the law may at some time step across that border.

Regarding advertising, Article 19 of the Code of Ethics states:

The REALTOR® shall be careful at all times to present a true picture in his advertising and representations to the public. He shall neither advertise without disclosing his name nor permit any person associated with him to use individual names or telephone numbers, unless the person's connection with the REALTOR® is obvious in the advertisement.

The Truth-in-Lending Act The Federal Consumer Credit Protection Act (**Truth-in-Lending Act**) is commonly known as **Regulation Z.** The act, passed on July 1, 1969, protects the real estate customer in the following manner:

1. Lenders must make a full disclosure of all costs to the borrower, expressed in dollar amount and in terms of the Annual Percentage Rate (**APR**). The APR represents the relationship of the total finance charge to the total amount financed or the relative cost of credit as a percentage of the amount financed.

2. Lenders must spell out the total of all costs imposed that a customer must pay directly or indirectly to obtain credit. These financed items include:

   - interest;

   - loan fee;

   - points;

   - credit life insurance premiums;

   - time-price differential;

   - amount paid as discount;

   - service transaction or carrying charges; and

   - finder's fee or similar charge.

3. Borrowers are allowed the **right of rescission** of their credit contract by midnight of the third day after signing, unless the credit is for a first loan to finance the purchase of the borrower's residence; this type of loan carries no right of rescission.

4. The act provides for either criminal or civil liabilities and penalties for the willful violation of any provision of the act.

5. The Federal Trade Commission (**FTC**) is given the responsibility for enforcing the act. If you are in a position where you may be responsible for giving or receiving credit, you should become familiar with the details of the act. The FTC has published a pamphlet, "What You Ought to Know about Truth-in-Lending," that contains the complete text of the law, including sample ads, charts, illustrations and forms. This free publication can be obtained by writing to: Truth-in-Lending, Federal Trade Commission, Box 36005, San Francisco, CA 94102.

Summary

Institutional advertising builds, for the real estate business, the company and its officers and employees, a sound reputation for honesty, integrity and high standards of ethical behavior.

Using attention, interest, desire and action: the *AIDA approach* to real estate advertising develops lists of prospects, buyers and sellers, and stimulates sales on particular properties.

The following *media* are used in the real estate business: magazines, TV and radio, business cards and stationery, signs, giveaways, special publications, direct mail, outdoor ads and newspapers. It is pointed out that *classified ads* in newspapers are the most widely used medium in real estate. Because classified ads are small, the headlines are vitally important; care should be taken in design, word selection and objectives. *Display advertising* and *news releases* giving the licensee neighborhood recognition also are part of the newspaper medium.

Successful licensees will allocate sufficient funds in their operational budget to include advertising expense. The amount will be based on the premise that the amount of money needed to bring the greatest returns is carefully allocated to the media that will best fulfill this charge. The effectiveness of the advertising should be measured and, if necessary, adjusted.

Advertising regulations are contained in the California Real Estate Law, Commissioner's regulations and the *Truth-in-Lending Act.*

Questions

1. Advertising that is used solely to create a favorable image for the real estate company is known as what type of advertising?

   a. company
   b. institutional
   c. operational
   d. reputational

2. Occasionally, outdoor advertising is used. If used:

   a. signs can be painted on buildings.
   b. it depends on size of town.
   c. both a and b
   d. neither a nor b

3. Sometimes advertisements contain "giveaway offers." These can include:

   a. rebates.
   b. financing techniques.
   c. bonuses.
   d. both a and c

4. When using classified advertising:

   a. paint a neutral picture.
   b. start with a provocative lead.
   c. season your words with enthusiasm.
   d. all of the above

5. The AIDA approach to real estate advertising includes which of the following?

   a. interest
   b. attention
   c. desire
   d. all of the above

6. The most frequently used advertising medium in the real estate business is:

   a. TV and radio.
   b. direct mail.
   c. classified ads.
   d. magazines.

7. Which of the following methods is used to place your name before the public without charge?

   a. news releases
   b. cards and stationery
   c. giveaways
   d. direct mail

8. Which of the following headlines is called a "demonstrable difference" headline?

   a. Delightful
   b. Owners Desperate
   c. Garden Galore
   d. Don't Simmer This Summer

9. The basic tenets of advertising include all of these activities *except:*

   a. choosing the right market.
   b. using the proper media.
   c. emphasizing air conditioning in cold weather.
   d. using correct advertising techniques.

10. When designing signs to be used in advertising, care should be taken to include:

    a. type and size of print.
    b. unique design.
    c. use of color.
    d. all of the above

11. In classified advertising, care should be taken to make use of:

    a. catchy phrases.
    b. interesting layout.
    c. sufficient white space.
    d. any or all of the above

12. The basic aims of advertising include all of the following *except:*

    a. create a favorable public image.
    b. arouse public interest.
    c. stimulate sale of properties.
    d. satisfy state requirements.

13. The kind of advertising that usually involves organized groups having similar interests is:

    a. general.
    b. special.
    c. institutional.
    d. operational.

14. The advertising medium that is most effective for reaching a selective audience is:

    a. newspapers.
    b. outdoor ads.
    c. signs.
    d. direct mail.

15. Advertising guidelines include:

    a. choosing the right market.
    b. using the proper media.
    c. knowing when to advertise.
    d. all of the above

16. It is important to select the proper advertising media to use. This decision is most often based on:

    a. the message to be conveyed.
    b. the target audience to be reached.
    c. the cost for media purchase.
    d. all of the above

17. Magazine advertising is not used in real estate advertising as frequently as other media because:

    a. they serve special-interest groups.
    b. of low-quality production of photographs.
    c. both a and b
    d. neither a nor b

18. Almost any type of advertising can be helpful. However, which of the following are less desirable for real estate?

    a. radio advertising
    b. car cards
    c. classified advertising
    d. direct mail

19. The term *Regulation Z* refers to the:

    a. real estate law.
    b. Truth-in-Lending Act.
    c. Commissioner's regulations.
    d. Business and Professions Code.

20. The step in the advertising process that involves appealing to the senses and emotions is called:

    a. getting attention.
    b. stimulating action.
    c. arousing interest.
    d. creating desire.

6

Real Estate Selling and Property Showing

Chapter Preview

Real estate selling differs from other salesmanship in that the salesperson's job is to determine the motivations of *both* the seller and the buyer. Selling property may involve as many as three steps:

1. selling the seller or owner on listing the property;
2. selling the buyer on making an offer for the property; and
3. selling the seller on accepting the offer.

Chapter 4 discussed the techniques used in obtaining a listing. This chapter will be devoted to the other responsibilities of the licensee: salesmanship, in general, and showing the home, in particular. The licensee becomes a negotiator, with the responsibility of bringing about a meeting of minds between the seller and the buyer.

Terms To Look For

Ambiance
Communication
Feature benefits
Goals
Golden rule
Impulsive
Media
Negative motivation
Opinionated
Personality
Persuasion
Preshowing Inspection
Procrastination
Skeptical
Tie-downs

What Is Salesmanship?	A favorite definition of salesmanship says it is "seven Ps in a pod": *Persuade Plenty of People to Purchase Property Pleasurably at a Profit. Plenty of people* indicates that nearly everyone is a customer at some time. *Purchasing property* for live-in purposes or for investment is a decision everyone faces many times. *Pleasurably* has two implications: (1) If the experience is pleasurable for the buyer, he or she will be your best prospect for future sales as well as leads. (2) If the sale is a pleasurable experience for the salesperson, it will encourage increased efforts for future sales. *Profit* is the key to economic life. Everyone expects business people to make a profit; if they do, they will stay in business, if not, they may go bankrupt.

In more formal and traditional terms, salesmanship is the persuasive leadership that influences people to buy or sell goods under circumstances that benefit all parties to the transaction.

Selling Is Persuading	**Persuasion** is the central theme in many descriptions of the selling process:

1. the personal or impersonal process of *persuading* a prospective customer to buy a commodity or service;

2. the art of *persuading* someone to accept or to follow certain ideas, leading them to a desired action; and

3. *persuading* people to want what you have in terms of products, services or ideas.

Unfortunately, the word "persuasion" reminds many people of someone convincing them to buy unnecessary products. You can avoid this problem by understanding that people buy benefits that will satisfy their wants and needs (both conscious and unconscious). Your job is to address the needs and show your customers that satisfying *their* needs is most important to you. The good feelings that result will lead to long-term customer satisfaction and future business.

Selling Is Knowing Your Product	If you are going to sell to satisfy needs and wants, you must know what properties are available and their features. Taking a listing, preparing for a showing, going through the multiple listing service (MLS) books and networking with others are all good opportunities for gathering this information. Knowledge and expertise are becoming even more important as consumers are becoming more sophisticated. Several ways of knowing your product are discussed in the following paragraphs.

Specialize in a market area. Features of properties include those of the community as well as those of specific houses. For example, clients may want to know: Are there good schools nearby? Where is the nearest racquetball court? What are the neighbors like? Because it is difficult to know everything about every community, many salespeople start by specializing in a specific geographic area. Often this market area includes the neighborhoods in which you will do the most business. It will serve you well to get involved in these communities, get to know the neighborhood and keep up with changes.

Promote your firm and yourself. The brokerage firm, you and the services you provide also are a part of the product. Unanswered questions and objections raised in these areas can kill a sale. Early in your relationship with your clients or prospects, you should present information that will establish your credibility and show them that you have the resources to work hard for them. Some agents hand out fact sheets or a résumé. An anecdote about a way in which you and the firm have benefited others may help you establish rapport and provide reassurance if the situation seems appropriate.

Understand standard of care. "There are advantages and disadvantages about this property," said the honest and well-informed real estate agent. "To the north is the gas works, to the east the glue factory, to the south a fish and chips shop, and to the west a sewage farm. These are the disadvantages."

"What are the advantages?" the customer asked.

"You can always tell which way the wind is blowing," was the agent's reply.

As this anecdote illustrates, you often can present disadvantages as advantages. Because it is unlikely that a piece of property will have every feature a client wants, it makes sense to play up the significant features and downplay others. However, you must be meticulous about disclosure issues. You cannot neglect or change the presentation of negative information just because it is (or may be perceived as) a disadvantage. This is because you legally owe each client a high standard of care—a quality of service that a "reasonable, prudent man" would provide. Since the *Easton v. Strassburger* case, many questions have arisen in this area concerning fiduciary responsibilities.

In this vein, there will be times when you are *not* the person who can best serve a particular client. Perhaps he or she is looking for a home that lies outside your market area. Or someone may want a piece of investment property that will involve intricate tax and financing complications. The worst mistake you can make is thinking that you can serve everyone. It is far better to refer people to brokers or other individuals who have the required expertise.

Invest in your education. Education is the best investment that you can make in yourself. As of January 1, 1986, the California Department of Real Estate established the basic educational requirements described in Chapter 1.

Real estate courses serve two purposes: (1) they supply product knowledge for the industry and (2) they provide legal assistance. The trend is definitely toward licensing more knowledgeable and professional salespeople and brokers. Because this is your career, it is in your best interest to choose quality courses (required or not). Turn what you learn into strategies that will work for you.

Education is an ongoing process. As the real estate industry changes, so should your knowledge base. Education and training through in-house programs, association seminars, community colleges, four-year colleges and universities, and private training institutions will ensure that you are up to date.

Selling Is Knowing Your Customer

Your customer is the lifeblood of your business. Your customer does not have to love you, but it is a good idea for you to love your customer. You should always keep in mind how you can best serve him or her.

Customer types. There have been numerous attempts to "pigeonhole" prospects and customers (see Figure 6.1). This can be done if you keep in mind the temperamental fluctuations that might occur. Remember, no customer is a single type; he or she is a composite of several types. Most experienced licensees have seen an individual display more than one temperament during an interview. Some customers put the salesperson on the defensive; some buyers waver; some are irritable, cynical or good humored. Alert salespeople adjust their approaches to the attitudes, temperament and buying needs of each of their customers.

Customer segment specialization. Getting to know a particular customer segment and understanding the needs of people in that segment may be the most worthwhile way to learn about customers. You can choose a segment based on a "people" trend (be sure it is a true trend and not a fad): "yuppies," single parents, extended families or a group with special needs that may not be being met.

An excellent way to find a segment is to go through your old files to see if there is a certain group that you have been serving more than others. When you have identified a customer segment, draw a profile of their demographic and psychological characteristics. Prospecting and after-sale surveys are two avenues for accumulating this kind of information. In analyzing past customers, try to determine why they came to you, how you effectively helped them and the areas in which they felt you were weak. This will help you put together a plan to get more people like them in your customer segment. You also will get more out of your advertising and marketing strategies if these strategies are coordinated around those surveys. Customer segment specialization helps you build a known area of expertise, which will enhance your reputation and result in referrals.

Figure 6.1
Types of
Prospects

	General Strategy to Use
The Silent Prospect—the "Clam"—Does not indicate whether he or she is agreeing or disagreeing	Ask leading questions and be more personal than usual.
The Procrastinator—the "Putter-Offer"—Does not know his or her own mind; has difficulty making up mind	Summarize benefits that prospects will lose if he or she does not act. Be positive, self-assured and dramatic.
The Glad-Hander—Talkative or overenthusiastic	Lead these prospects back into the sale, after letting them talk themselves out!
Argumentative Type—Usually is insincere and tries the salesperson's patience	Sincerity and respect on the salesperson's part will create respect.
Slow or Methodical Type—Appears to weigh every word of the salesperson	Slow down and simplify details. Adjust your tempo to your prospect's.
Skeptical or Suspicious Type—Convinced that every salesperson is trying to "pull the wool over my eyes"	Stay with the facts and be conservative in statements. Allay the prospect's fears.
Overcautious or Timid—Acts as if he or she does not trust the salesperson	Take it slow and easy. Reassure on every point. Use logic, make it simple.
Impulsive—Apt to interrupt presentation before you state all points	Speed up presentation, concentrate only on important points. Omit details when possible.
Opinionated—Ego Type—Overconfident, with strong opinions	Give these prospects "rope" by appealing to their egos. Listen attentively and guide them into changing their minds.

Selling Is Effective Communication

Without effective communication, there is no understanding. Know what you want to say; use listener's language. Do not use fancy words when simple ones will do. Use the "KISS" method (Keep It Simple, Stupid).

Figure 6.2 compares communication in selling with a chain having five links: idea, facts, media, language, receiver. While reviewing these links, remember that "A chain is only as strong as its weakest link."

Figure 6.2
The Communication Chain

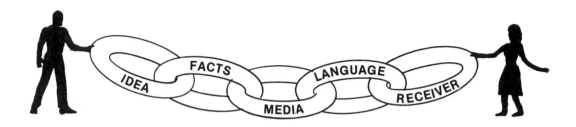

Idea. The most common cause of poor communication is the communicator's own failure to understand the idea he or she wants to express. You must have something to communicate. As a rule, if you are unclear about what you really mean or are lacking essential facts, it is best not to try to communicate your thoughts to others.

Facts. To make the sales message understood, you must provide sufficient facts. Without facts, the person receiving the message cannot form valid conclusions or take effective action. This is illustrated by the story of a temporary post office employee who was told to take a truck and deliver the New York mail. Six hours later the department received a collect telephone call: "I'm out of gas on the New Jersey Turnpike, 11 miles out of New York. Can you wire me some money so I can deliver the mail?" What the boss had forgotten to tell the new employee was, "When we say deliver the New York mail, we mean to drive it two blocks to Union Station and leave it on the train platform."

Media. The choice of a communications medium is extremely important. Should the message be given in person, by phone or by letter? The advantages and disadvantages of the various media should be given careful consideration in each situation. Selling is primarily done through face-to-face communication.

Language. A clear idea, sufficient facts and proper media are of no avail if the communicator uses language that confuses the receiver. Words should be chosen with the utmost care and organized and delivered meaningfully.

Receiver. Words or symbols have different meanings for different people. Assess your receiver before attempting to communicate. Recognition of his or her past experience, mood and temperament, as well as knowledge of the product or service, will make or break the communication chain.

Voice personality. Does your selling voice communicate well? If not, these four guidelines will help you relate to your customer more effectively:

1. Articulate clearly.

2. Sound positive and friendly.

3. Match your customer's speech in volume, speed and tone.

4. Use some of his or her language.

Now rate yourself, using a scale from 1 to 5, and then have someone else rate you. Strive for a rating of 20, or 100 percent.

Listening. In selling, the ability to be a good listener is even more important than the ability to be a good talker. Unfortunately, most people have poor listening skills; they pretend to listen but they do not hear. To add to the problem, the human mind can hear and process around 500 words a minute, yet we speak only about 100 to 150 words a minute. The difference makes it easy to be distracted and allow one's mind to wander. Practice active listening, so you will be sure to hear those words relevant to the customer's needs, problems and solutions.

A good listener listens actively by reinforcing the speaker with words of understanding, repeating what was said (especially when objections arise) and nodding or making some show of approval. Silence also is an excellent tool; when in doubt, the best solution is to keep silent. Discreet silence at the right time often shows an excellent command of language. Also, active listeners do not interrupt or formulate a response when the speaker is talking. Remember that you will not make sales by winning arguments. Speakers need the opportunity to make their points and get unpleasant feelings off their chests. Listen with your eyes as well as with your ears. Keep a relaxed tone while speaking and mean what you say. When you are finished, stop.

Showing Property

As discussed in chapter 2, time is valuable. So when you are ready to show a property, you want to be devoting your time to *qualified* buyers. From your first contact, begin collecting information for a buyer profile, including:

- What are the buyer's intentions?

- What are the buyer's needs and wants?

- What is the buyer's financial capacity?

Qualifying Buyers

Make a tentative commitment. One technique to use in determining if you have a motivated buyer is to offer to make your time the buyer's time and constantly to keep him or her advised. If the buyer agrees to this and agrees to look at the property any time, you have a "warm" prospect.

Make an appointment. Regardless of the method of your original contact, set up a personal interview for the soonest possible time. This interview should most likely be at the buyer's home, where he or she is more relaxed and where you can observe how he or she lives. At this point you can more fully qualify your prospect by asking these follow-up questions:

1. How long have you been looking for a house?

2. Have you been looking with any other brokers?

3. What property appealed to you most?

4. How much can your initial investment be?

5. How much can you pay in monthly payments?

Know the buyer's financial status. You need to know the buyer's financial condition before showing property. If buyers are serious, they will not resent your asking questions. Here are some basic questions that you might ask to assist you in financially qualifying a buyer:

1. Have you owned property previously?

2. Do you own property now?

3. If so, how is it being financed?

4. What is your regular income?

5. Do you have additional income?

6. What type of work do you do and how long have you been employed?

7. Does your spouse work?

8. Do you own other assets?

9. What monthly payments do you plan?

A tool for recording answers to such questions is the Buyer's Confidential Financial Status Form (see Figure 6.3).

Preparation To Show   **Information checklist.** To show property to prospective buyers intelligently, you must make adequate preparation. Five ways of preparing are:

1. Know all available properties in the area.

2. Be able to identify school boundaries.

3. Be cognizant of shopping and recreational facilities in the area.

4. Be familiar with bus schedules.

5. Be aware of any other information about the area that might help prospects make a favorable decision.

Preshowing inspection of property. Make an inspection of the property prior to showing it. Nothing can be more discouraging than being surprised by problems with the property, such as plugged plumbing, an unkept yard or other unknowns. A preshowing inspection will familiarize you with all the facets of the specific property and it will provide a better understanding of the neighborhood in general. Knowledge generates confidence and to the buyer you will appear to be a true professional who can be trusted.

Figure 6.3
Buyer's Confidential
Financial Status Form

BUYER(S) _____

EMPLOYER _____

POSITION _____ YEARS WITH COMPANY _____

SPOUSE'S EMPLOYER _____

POSITION _____ YEARS WITH COMPANY _____

MONTHLY INCOME _____ ADD'L INCOME FROM

OTHER SOURCES _____

MONEY CURRENTLY AVAILABLE FOR A DOWN PAYMENT _____

OTHER ASSETS:

1. _____   3. _____

2. _____   4. _____

OUTSTANDING DEBTS

Credit Card _____   Account # _____

Monthly Payment _____   Total Debt _____

Credit Card _____   Account # _____

Monthly Payment _____   Total Debt _____

HOUSING

CURRENTLY OWN PROPERTY?   YES _____   NO _____

MONTHLY MORTGAGE PAYMENT _____   TYPE OF FINANCING _____

_____

IF NO, ARE YOU RENTING?   YES _____   NO _____   MONTHLY RENT _____

MISCELLANEOUS EXPENSES

1. _____   3. _____

2. _____   4. _____

The seller or owner should accompany you in the preshowing inspection, if possible. The seller's presence will enable you to acquire pertinent facts and ask searching questions. During this time, the seller may decide to assist with financing, change the possession date or disclose little-known facts concerning neighbors. In addition, the seller will feel that you are thorough and a true professional.

Reinspection. You should return to the property for reinspection at a later date because changes can occur in a short period of time. The financing picture may change. Streets may be torn up. The possession date may be delayed. The seller's motivation may change or the seller may decide to finance additional improvements.

Number of homes to show. The number of homes you show a buyer may vary, depending on your experience and the individual buyer's personality. Usually, plan to show no more than five or six. If more are shown, you may clutter up the buyer's mind and wear him or her out. On the other hand, showing too few homes may leave a buyer wanting; he or she may feel cheated and unable to make a satisfactory decision.

Seller involvement. While you do not want sellers around while you are showing a property, there are some ways they can help.

1. Ask the sellers to have the property clean and orderly.

2. Explain that you prefer to show the property to the buyer alone. If the buyer has questions that you cannot answer, you will ask for clarification later. (It is best to establish this when the property is first listed.)

Buyer preparation. Arrange an appointment with the buyer, remembering that the time of day is important. Where possible, avoid heavy periods of traffic. If you are selling to a married buyer, plan to show the property to both husband and wife. If you show the property to one, you are only showing. If you show the property to both, you are *selling.*

Meet the buyers at their home or office. Always drive them to the property in your car. If the children are to be included, bring something to keep them occupied, such as picture books. Because California requires car seats for very young children, you might want to arrange with the buyers to borrow theirs, just to be on the safe side.

Plan your route to sell the neighborhood. Choose the most scenic route, one that includes schools, public parks, golf courses and a shopping center. Adapt your plan to the buyers' motives and desires. Plan to park across the street from the house next door. A house always looks better and bigger from across the street at a line-of-sight angle.

Avoid an anticlimax; show the best property last. Customers will seldom purchase the first property they look at. Remember, you never cease qualifying, so watch reactions and capitalize on your observations. Plan on holding back a few completely different properties as alternates in the event you have misjudged the wants of your customer.

Selling the neighborhood. Because people are buying the neighborhood as much as a specific property, selling the neighborhood cannot be emphasized enough. While driving to the property, endeavor to educate the buyer by discussing only relevant items. If necessary, prepare leading questions. Try to keep the buyers' attention focused on houses of similar price and on the quality of the neighborhood itself. Point out recent sales of comparably priced homes. This increases the buyers' trust in you and establishes a price range in their minds.

A negative motivation technique often works well. This entails warning buyers of any objectionable features. They build these features up in their minds and are relieved when they find that you have exaggerated a bit. Avoid overenthusiasm on specific points; it may backfire. Instead, permit the buyers' discoveries to be new and exciting experiences.

Showing Techniques

Create a favorable ambiance. It is interesting to note that although some buyers are interested in construction and utility, most are attracted by color, glamour, texture and style. They usually buy what they want and what they feel good with. Cater to these feelings by creating a favorable **ambiance**—proper mood and atmosphere. Arrange for soft background music. Have the owner provide fresh flowers in vases. Depending on the weather, either have a fire in the fireplace or the air-conditioning operating. Encourage the buyer to relax and feel at home.

Question, do not tell. The following story illustrates what not to do and what to do in showing property. Mr. and Mrs. Doe are potential real estate buyers. They have decided to go for the traditional Sunday afternoon time-killer, the Sunday drive. As they are touring their town complaining about the traffic, Mrs. Doe's face lights up as she sees a lovely home with lots of little flags flying. It is crisp, modern and obviously open for inspection, so she decides that they will stop and look it over. They walk up to and into the house and are greeted by a real estate salesperson, who puts down a comic book and slowly gets up. The salesperson then proceeds to give this demonstration—a cook's tour.

"This is the living room," the salesperson proclaims with a sweep of the hand. "This is the dining room; notice the roominess. . . . This is the kitchen. These are the kitchen cabinets. This is the oven; it's big and modern." The salesperson continues. "Notice how wide the hall is? Why don't you both look at this bedroom with me? Isn't your husband interested in bedrooms? This is a closet."

By this time the Does have had enough. They remember how much they wanted a chocolate malt and off they go. The salesperson returns to the comic book.

Now imagine the same scene with a different character—a professional salesperson who knows how to communicate, who rises, but waits to let the customers look around the living room for a moment. Then he or she turns to Mrs. Doe and says, "Where in this living room would you place your sofa?" (Do not sell the space, sell the benefits of the space.)

In the kitchen, the salesperson opens a cabinet and says, "What would you put in here, dry groceries or your kitchen china?" Opening the oven, he or she says: "How big a turkey do you think this oven would take?"

True professionals never say, "This is the second bedroom." They always ask, "Whose bedroom will this be?" A professional does not state obvious facts, but sells by asking *who, what, where* or *how* for every room and every feature.

Sell benefits, not just features. A gourmet kitchen is a place to indulge in one's culinary hobby, not to mention a pleasant atmosphere in which to work out tensions. A fireplace contributes to family togetherness and the kindling of romance. A dishwasher is no longer a luxury, but a necessity, given the hectic demands on most people's time. A Jacuzzi and sun deck are status symbols. Sell those features and benefits that are important to the buyer. Listen carefully to uncover what is important to the buyer, as well as probing when appropriate.

Use tie-downs. A good communicator uses **tie-downs.** This method can be used to check out whether a benefit is important as well as build a sense of ownership. No professional salesperson ever makes a positive statement without tying it down:

- This is a spacious room, *isn't it?*

- You really need four bedrooms, *don't you?*

- Your children should be close to school, *shouldn't they?*

- This is the sound investment you've been looking for, *isn't it?*

These words are powerful selling tools: *isn't it, can't it, won't it, don't you, can't you.* Little Yesses easily lead to the big Yes. Sell on minor points.

Invite comparisons. The comparison technique gets buyers involved. Ask such questions as, "Did you like the vanity off the bedroom as it was in the house you just saw or do you prefer this style?" "Will this dining room set off your antique china hutch or can you see it better in the other house?" These questions get the buyers involved in refining what is important to them. Buyers start selling themselves and get prepared to make the big decision by making a lot of little ones.

Additional Showing Tips

Other items that may enhance your presentation are:

1. Occasionally allow the buyers privacy. They may want to feel that they are alone when they discuss personal things.

2. Do not assume that just because you like a feature of the property the buyer will like it as well.

3. Do not resent the presence of a friend of the family. Use the friend as an ally.

4. Always overcome any objections on the scene. If space is an issue, use a tape measure (let the customer measure). Try to settle any questions on the spot.

5. Begin and end the tour of the home in the most beautiful and unique part of the house.

6. The buyers will follow your lead. Whenever you enter a room, they will follow.

7. Involve children. Wherever possible, involve them as helpers.

8. Speak plainly, avoiding technical terms. If people do not understand, they may not ask.

9. Call attention to outstanding features but do not go overboard or you will close the door on the sale of the property.

10. Show the rooms in the most productive order. In a home this is usually hall, living room, dining room, kitchen, bedrooms, attic and last of all to the most attractive rooms on the first floor. This procedure may be varied to suit special cases.

11. If the rooms are small, do not stand in the middle of the room; stand along the side.

12. When possible, the owner should be away during the showing. The buyer will feel more at home rather than feeling like an intruder. If the seller is away, buyers will speak more freely and the agent will be better able to assess their true feelings.

13. The time of day is important. Where possible, avoid heavy traffic periods and choose the most advantageous time in terms of sight, sound and exposure.

| **Rules of Professional Conduct** | The following rules will help you maintain goodwill and a professional manner as you plan for and conduct showings. |

1. If you arrive at a property and notice that someone else is showing it, wait inconspicuously until the other salesperson and his or her clients have left.

2. When showing a home, leave it as you found it. If drapes were closed, see that they are closed when you leave. If inner doors are closed, reclose them when you leave. Double-check all outside doors to see that they are locked. Be sure to replace the key in the lock box where you found it. If dogs, cats or other animals are confined to a given room, yard, garage, etc., see that they do not gain access to other rooms or to the street.

3. Notify the listing office immediately if something seems to be amiss at a property you have shown. Treat all listings as you would want to have your own listing treated.

4. If the listing says "Call first," never take a customer to the door and ask to show the home. If, in showing the property, you decide to show another home and cannot reach a telephone, leave the client in the car while you go to the door and ask the owner for belated permission to show the property. Then abide by the owner's wishes.

5. If a listing indicates that the property is to be shown only during certain hours or gives other information as to particular conditions of showing, do not violate these requests. There must be a reason for them.

6. Leave your business card at each property. It is a courtesy to the owner (whether at home or not). It also helps to advertise your own office. It is a good idea to place the date and the time on the back of the card.

7. Interoffice courtesy requires that when calling another agency for information, you immediately identify yourself and your company.

8. Do not enter a home with a lighted cigarette, pipe or cigar and do not light one while in a home without the permission of the owner.

9. Avoid making uncomplimentary remarks about a house, its condition or its furnishings while in the house. The owner may be in the next room and be embarrassed or hurt by your comments.

Summary

This chapter describes selling real estate as a threefold job: (1) selling the owner on listing the property; (2) selling the buyer on making an offer; and (3) selling the seller on accepting the offer.

The discussion pointed out that selling is a multifaceted activity, including planning, knowing your client and customer, communicating and showing property. Each of these activities was discussed in detail, with techniques for improving relationships with third parties resulting in worthwhile sales.

Questions

1. As a result of the *Easton vs. Strassburger* case:
   a. licensees must be meticulous about disclosure issues.
   b. licensees cannot neglect negative information.
   c. neither a nor b
   d. both a and b

2. There have been numerous attempts to "pigeon-hole" prospects and customers. A licensee, in dealing with customers, should:
   a. remember that customers change personalities.
   b. be aware that customers have only one temperament.
   c. be alert and adjust his or her approach to change.
   d. both a and c

3. Time is valuable when showing property. To save time, it is a good idea to ask the buyer which of the following questions?
   a. What are your intentions?
   b. What is your financial capacity?
   c. What are your needs and wants?
   d. all of the above

4. The financial status of a buyer can be determined by asking all of the following questions *except:*
   a. what is your wife's income?
   b. do you own property now?
   c. what is your annual salary?
   d. do you own other assets?

5. All of the following would be a reason for a reinspection of property *except:*
   a. possession date may be delayed.
   b. seller's motivation may remain the same.
   c. financial picture may change.
   d. streets may be torn up.

6. Buyers' interests will differ. However, most are attracted by the following characteristics:
   a. color
   b. texture
   c. utility
   d. all of the above

7. In showing a home to a prospect, which of the following rules will prevent you from maintaining goodwill?
   a. When showing a home, do not worry about the way you leave it.
   b. Treat all listings as you would have your own listing treated.
   c. Replace the key in the lock box where you found it.
   d. Leave your business card at each property.

8. When showing properties to a prospective customer, a licensee should:
   a. show only those homes he or she likes or is interested in.
   b. show only two homes so that an easy comparison can be made.
   c. usually plan to show no more than five or six homes.
   d. show only those homes the licensee has personally listed.

9. Education is important for licensees. Courses are taken to:
   a. fulfill license requirements.
   b. supply product knowledge.
   c. provide legal assistance.
   d. all of the above

10. Communications often are compared to a chain. Which of the following is not one of the links in the communication chain?
    a. idea
    b. circumstances
    c. facts
    d. receivers

11. You can be assured that you have a "warm" prospect when:

   a. the prospect agrees to look at property.
   b. the prospect takes off his coat.
   c. the prospect argues about financing.
   d. none of the above

12. It is important that care be used in setting up appointments with your client. Which of these would be the *least* important consideration?

   a. Set up as soon as possible.
   b. Where interview is to be held.
   c. Ask leading questions.
   d. All are of importance.

13. Buyer preparation is extremely important. This preparation may consist of these actions:

   a. plan on showing to both husband and wife.
   b. plan to meet buyer in his own home or office.
   c. plan your route to sell the neighborhood.
   d. all of the above

14. "Tie-downs" are powerful selling tools. Which of the following questions would *not* be regarded as a "tie-down"?

   a. Your children should be close to school, shouldn't they?
   b. You don't want spacious rooms, do you?
   c. This is the sound investment you've been looking for, isn't it?
   d. You really could use four bedrooms, couldn't you?

15. Tips to improve your showing techniques include which of the following?

   a. Involve children wherever possible.
   b. Speak plainly and avoid technical terms.
   c. Allow the buyers privacy occasionally.
   d. all of the above

16. All of the following enumerate the attitude the salesperson should have toward his or her customers *except:*

   a. customers are the lifeblood of our business.
   b. customers sometimes are an interruption to our business.
   c. customers are the heart and soul of our business.
   d. it is a good idea for us to love our customers.

17. Being a good listener is important in selling. Many people have poor listening skills because:

   a. they only pretend to listen.
   b. their minds wander.
   c. they are easily distracted by outside noises.
   d. all of the above

18. The licensee should make an inspection of the property prior to showing it. Reasons for doing this are:

   a. to avoid surprises from unexpected problems.
   b. to provide an understanding of the neighborhood in general.
   c. both a and b
   d. neither a nor b

19. Selling the neighborhood can be very helpful. This technique involves:

   a. educating the buyer while driving to the property.
   b. always giving negative motivation by discussing neighborhood problems.
   c. keeping buyer's attention focused on houses of similar price.
   d. both a and c

20. An effective sales technique to be used in making a sale is the "feature benefit analysis." Which of these statements falls in that category?

   a. "Sell the sizzle and not the steak."
   b. This is an excellent fireplace.
   c. The dishwasher will save many hours of your valuable time.
   d. both a and c

7

Obtaining and Presenting the Offer

Chapter Preview   If you are successful in qualifying buyers and showing property, you will have offers
to present to sellers. This chapter discusses the technique of consummating an
offer, including obtaining the offer, overcoming objections, closing the sale, using
deposit receipts, presenting the offer and using the counteroffer.

Terms To Look For   **Acceptance**
Assumptive close
Buying motive
Buying signals
Concede
Counteroffer
Deposit receipt
Emotion
Inducement
Liquidated damages
Liquidity
Needs
Negative motivation
Negotiation
Objections
Offer
Reason
Risk
Security
Senses
Wants

**Obtaining
the Offer**

In striving to obtain an offer to purchase, you will find that each transaction is unique and has its own approach and required motivation. However, some general principles do apply. Understanding why customers buy and the basic steps of transactions will help you prepare for a presentation that will lead to an offer. Four basic steps are illustrated in Figure 7.1 and discussed in the following paragraphs.

**Appeal to Buying
Motives**

Webster's defines *motive* as "that within the individual that incites him to action." Understanding a buyer's **needs** and **wants** is absolutely essential for optimum results. Remember, you are going to be selling the benefits that match those needs and wants. After all, why should an individual buy a home and be responsible for its maintenance, taxes, etc., rather than rent for life? Why should a family skimp and save for a down payment and make monthly payments when they could live in a public housing unit or with relatives?

**Figure 7.1
Steps in
Obtaining
the Offer**

Ownership of real property satisfies several basic needs or **buying motives.**

Survival. The most basic human need is that of survival. If a home has no other amenities than providing shelter, it satisfies the basic human need of survival.

Security. The desire for **security** is a fundamental need that has many applications in the selling process. Every licensee should appeal to it. While many Americans have barely enough money to live on when they retire, the home is a principal financial asset. In times of financial stress, the home is always something to fall back on. People feel secure in their own homes. They do not have to worry about owners asking them to leave because they want their children to live there.

Pride of ownership. Once buyers obtain basic shelter, it is *pride* that impels them to pay considerably more for additional benefits. Healthful exercise can be obtained by work around the home and garden. The do-it-yourself job shown to a relative or friend, the backyard barbecue or the first tomato picked from one's own garden is a source of pride and satisfaction. The creative salesperson establishes pride of ownership immediately by referring to the property being shown as "your beautiful home."

Love of family. Desirable school areas, recreational facilities, shopping conveniences or other factors that may appeal to one member or to all members of the family often will induce the purchase of certain property. Many times one of the foremost factors in the buyer's mind will be how the home can help the family.

Homeowners probably will find themselves taking part in community affairs to a larger extent than renters. They putter around their yards and make repairs and improvements because they are proud of their homes and the security they bring. Children will feel a permanence, too. They form long-term relationships with other children in the neighborhood and they do not have to change schools as often, as children of renters usually do. They will be protected by fenced-in backyards. Special emphasis on love of family as a motivational factor does the buyers a great service.

Health. Motivation arising from health interests is closely allied to the survival instinct and can be a determining factor in a decision to buy. The quality of the environment, air, water, noise level and avoidance of urban congestion often motivate a decision to buy.

Desire for profit or gain. More people have started on the road to financial independence through home ownership than in any other way. Buying a home is an investment for the future because well-located properties usually increase in value. This is called appreciation. The amount of appreciation depends on numerous factors, such as the demand for housing in the area, the supply of homes and the availability of good financing. Historically, property values in California have tended to increase on the average more than three percent a year. In the past few years this percentage has increased substantially. Well-selected real property is an excellent hedge against inflation.

Comfort and convenience. The human drive for comfort and convenience has less influence than the other, previously mentioned factors. However, when basic needs have been fulfilled, these may be considered as an added dimension.

A home is almost always considerably larger than an apartment. Homeowners usually have several bedrooms, a living room, usually two or more bathrooms, a kitchen and maybe a dining room, breakfast room or family room. Do not forget the yard, which probably includes trees, bushes and flowers—and, for convenience, maybe even a patio area and a barbecue. The family can relax in comfort in such surroundings.

Reason versus emotion. *Logic* makes people think, or **reason. Emotion** makes them act. Potential buyers may have decided that a property is logically suited for them, but they do not act because the property does not trigger an emotional response. In most situations, buyers do not buy what they *need,* they buy what they *want.* The successful salesperson probes to find the buyers' desires that, when satisfied, will trigger their motivation to buy.

Negative motivation. The words **negative motivation** apply to knowing what someone does *not* want. There are many things we do not want: pain, hunger, fatigue, worry and strife, just to mention a few. Negative motivation can be more immediate and real to a person than positive motivation. Usually people know what they do not want better than what they do want.

To avoid a fruitless and time-wasting search, the licensee should endeavor to learn buyers' negative motivations as well as the positive ones. Some disadvantages of home ownership are described in Figure 7.2. These are large initial investment, risk, expenses, restricted mobility, a low level of **liquidity** and great responsibility.

Figure 7.2
Disadvantages of
Home Ownership

- **Large Initial Investment:** Normally, buying a home requires a down payment of ten to 20 percent of the purchase price, with the exception of VA and some FHA loans. This means the purchase price of an $80,000 home may require a down payment of between $8,000 and $16,000. In addition, the closing costs will be from $2,000 to $3,000.

- **Risk:** Whenever customers invest money, they risk losing some or all of it. However, well-located properties seldom lose value.

- **Increase in Expenses:** Although the mortgage payments will remain constant in most circumstances, other costs may increase. Property taxes tend to creep upward. Maintenance costs will increase as the home ages. Buyers will have to weigh some of these increased costs against the advantages of ownership, but they should remember that rents may increase, too.

- **Restricted Mobility:** To a degree, people are less mobile once they have bought a home. However, houses can be sold or rented.

- **Lack of Liquidity:** Some say they dislike home ownership because their investment is not liquid. While an investment in a home is not as liquid as having money in the bank, homeowners can use their property as a source of cash. For example, homeowners might consider borrowing on the property by putting a second mortgage on the home. Or they could refinance the first mortgage once sufficient equity has been developed. Or they can rent or sell the property.

- **Greater Responsibility:** An investment in real property has responsibilities. Buyers must properly maintain the property. For example, they may climb a ladder to paint or call a painter and pay the bill. The lawn will need to be watered and cut to protect the investment.

Sensory appeal. People learn about the surrounding world through their **senses,** which include sound, sight, smell, taste and touch. You can enhance your presentation by employing all of the senses as well as emphasizing the benefits that can be appreciated by the various senses.

In appealing to the sense of *sight,* point out the restful and interesting views from the windows, the lush lawns, the lines of the house and the ample wall space. Be careful about going overboard on certain colors; they may be your choice but not the buyer's.

The appeal of *sound* may be either its absence or its presence—perhaps it will be music, man-made or natural, to a buyer's ears. Where possible, call attention to the sound made by the ocean, a lake or a tinkling brook. Also, make buyers aware that machinery in the house, such as the air conditioner, water closet and power switches, operates quietly.

To appeal to the buyer's sense of *smell,* call attention to the fresh air, flower scents or, if possible, the smell of cedar from closets or chests.

The sense of *taste* might be appealed to by testing the flavor of well water, vegetables from the garden or fruit from the trees.

You can appeal to the sense of *touch* by including descriptions of the fine wood paneling, the grain of the wood in the cabinet or the texture of the carpet.

Watch for Buying Signals

In many situations and at various psychological moments during your presentation, the prospect may signal that he or she is ready to buy. These **buying signals** are tip-offs to the salesperson from some action, phrase or expression of the buyer. A buying signal seems to say, "I'm ready to talk terms if you are." The prospect reveals these signals by the spoken word, facial expressions or bodily movements. Even a well-worded objection or an expression of resistance from the prospect can spell "buying signal." These signals are like green lights. After a prospect has exhibited a buying signal, follow up this opportunity with a closing statement.

Buying signals can be divided into three areas: actions, words and facial expressions.

Actions. You are making a presentation and the buyer stays mum. He or she does not even grunt. You start to wonder if you are talking his or her language. Suddenly he or she picks up the deposit receipt and reads a clause or two. Stop your presentation and swing into your close—the buyer is interested. Prospects also are signaling when they return to the upstairs room for a second look.

Words. "Don't you think the price is a little too high?" Is this an objection or a signal? The alert salesperson hears it as a signal, because it shows that the buyer actually is thinking about the purchase. Other possible signals occur if the buyer (1) asks the salesperson to go over the financing details again, (2) inquires about possession time or (3) requests information about closing costs.

Facial expressions. A salesperson who is not watching customers carefully may easily miss facial-expression signals. A signal may be as subtle as a raised eyebrow or a quizzical look. To an experienced salesperson, these expressions could mean, "I'll take it; just ask me."

Overcome Resistance

To obtain the **offer,** be prepared to answer any **objections** raised by the buyer. Buyer resistance will vary with each transaction. Typical objections might include some of the following statements:

- The price is too high.

- The water pressure is too low.

- The rooms are too small.

- The taxes are too high.

- I can't buy until I sell.

- I can't get occupancy soon enough.

- I'll never get my kids in that school.

Human nature being what it is, some salespeople feel they must conquer objections by crushing them decisively. It is an unfortunate truth that many salespeople feel they must treat objections as barriers raised to block them from a goal—the sale or the offer. They see an objection as being in direct conflict with their best interests and therefore fear it and wish to combat it quickly.

Objections are a natural part of any sales routine. They may occur while showing the home or in the buyer's home before signing the offer. Before proceeding, you must determine two things in your own mind: (1) Is it really an objection or just a comment? (2) Is it an objection I can and should do something about?

When objections are real, there are ways to handle them. Five basic steps to be used in meeting objections are shown in Figure 7.3. Carefully following these steps leads to obtaining the offer and closing the sale.

Figure 7.3
Meeting a
Buyer's Objections

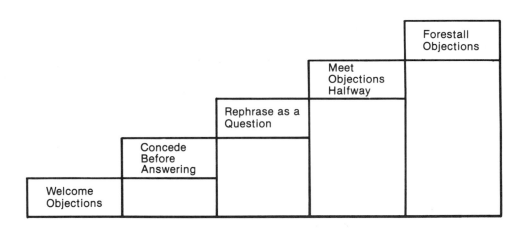

Welcome objections. Welcome objections, do not fear them. Encourage prospects to speak what is on their minds. Objections help pinpoint your talk. They may be a prospect's way of asking for more information. They may throw a light on the prospect's thinking.

Concede before answering. To avoid putting the buyer on the defensive, recognize legitimate concerns. You might make a comment such as, "Your suggestion has much to recommend it" or "I can appreciate your concerns."

Rephrase an objection as a question. The buyer might say, "I don't like tract houses." To which you could reply, "As I understand it then, Mr. Buyer, your *question* is this—'Can I afford a more expensive home in a different neighborhood?'" Try to restate objections as questions. Doing so shows the buyer that you are working together, not as adversaries.

Meet objections halfway. A well-known technique for answering objections is the "Yes-but" technique. This technique meets objections halfway. The objection may be, "This is the smallest bedroom I've ever seen." The licensee could answer, "Yes, Ms. Buyer, you're right, that is a small bedroom, and I imagine it was intended for a small child like your son. Don't you think it would be large enough for him for a couple of years?"

Forestall objections. Your experience tells you to expect certain objections from your prospect. Bring up these potential objections before the prospect does. This is known as forestalling or anticipating the objection. Its effect is to reduce the objection's importance and to show the prospect that you do not fear it.

Answering a question with a question. You must handle questions as well as objections. One way to answer a question from a buyer is to use a "hook." This is the technique of answering a question with a question. It prolongs the sales interview and keeps the buyer in the act. Three examples follow.

- *Question:* Will the sellers take $500 down?
  Wrong Answer: I'm pretty sure they will.
  Using a Hook: Do you want to make a $500 down payment?

- *Question:* Will the sellers consider an offer?
  Wrong Answer: Yes, they've indicated they might listen to an offer.
  Using a Hook: Do you want to make an offer?

- *Question:* Is the stove (refrigerator, drapes, carpeting) included?
  Wrong Answer: I'll ask the seller.
  Using a Hook: Do you want the stove (refrigerator, drapes, carpeting) included?

Attempt a Trial Close　　If a salesperson successfully builds each part of the sale throughout the presentation, the close will come easily. In many cases, the buyer says, "I'm ready to make an offer." There is a psychological moment to close a sale, but it will vary with each transaction. Figure 7.4 shows some signs that help licensees decide when to close.

Attempting a trial close often is called "test and heat." To close any sale and get the buyer's signature on the deposit receipt, do what your great-grandmother did with the old-fashioned flatiron—test and heat. If the customer is not ready to buy, add a little "heat." This means present new evidence or reiterate key sales points and try again.

Figure 7.4
Closing Signs

 Knowing WHEN to close means—

Stalling . . . . . Use the psychological moment to close the sale.

 Alive . . . . Recognize customer buying signals.

 Carefully . . . To utilize the trial close system.

Beginning with the first interview, the salesperson must build for this moment during every phase of the sale because the buyer may make a decision at any time. While all situations and all buyers are different, certain basic closing principles can be set forth:

1. Throughout the sale, use *you* and *yours* or the customer's name.

2. Get agreement throughout the interview.

3. Tell a complete story—in terms of a customer's buying motives. Turn the features into personal benefits and hold some talking points in reserve.

4. Ask for the signature, if it is not volunteered.

5. Watch for buying signals.

Closing Techniques

Six basic closing techniques often are employed: the assumptive close, the positive choice, inducement, fear of loss, narrative and asking for the deposit.

Assumptive close. In an assumptive close, you assume the buyer is going to buy and you complete the deposit receipt form. This close is a natural follow-through when a buyer flashes a buying signal question such as, "Can I get possession by July 1?" Your response should be, "Would you like possession by July 1?" If the buyer asks, "What would the monthly payments be?" ask, "How much would you like to pay each month?"

Positive choice. Give the buyer a choice between two things, rather than between something and nothing. The skillful salesperson never asks the buyer a question that can be answered with a flat No. Here are two examples of positive choice questions:

- Would you prefer FHA-insured financing with a lower down payment and higher monthly payments or conventional financing with a higher down payment and lower monthly payments?

- If the seller will retile the bathroom, which color tile do you prefer, white or pink?

Inducement. If used properly, an **inducement** can be a powerful stimulant to a close. For example:

- If you buy now, I believe we can obtain the lower interest rate. You would like the lower rate, wouldn't you?

- I'm sure we could arrange the closing of escrow so you will not make double payments. You would like to save that money, wouldn't you?

In using this technique, be very careful. If the outcome of the sale hinges on a lower interest rate, a change of tile or an added refrigerator, and you cannot deliver, you may lose the sale. Try to hedge on your commitment by saying that you will do your best to obtain the inducement.

Fear of loss. The fear of loss method, often called the "standing room only" technique, can be effective only if it is based on fact. Buyers have built up an immunity to such statements as, "This is the last house in this plot and the builder doesn't plan on any further development." This technique works only if it is based on facts concerning a personal, immediate and real situation.

Here is an example of a believable fear of loss close, based on researched facts: "This is the last home by this builder available in this tract. All the others are sold. When the new tract is open, the price will be $5,000 higher for the same home. Wouldn't you rather buy now and save that amount?"

Narrative. A narrative close involves the use of a third party as an ally. If you are able to produce third-party verification of the fact you are trying to establish, the buyer is more likely to accept what you say. For example, you could show an article from the evening newspaper that states that interest rates are expected to rise. In this situation, someone else is conveying the information. Or you could say, "Mr. Jones just down the street had a question similar to yours. We were able to find a solution for him. You might want to call him to verify my story."

Ask for the deposit. Many salespeople do an excellent job of making a presentation and even covering all objections, but they are hesitant to ask for the sale. The reason is *fear;* they get a battlefield fear sensation. They fear a rejection, a No answer. Consequently, they overlook asking or are reluctant to ask for the deposit.

Many buyers will buy if they are asked to, but the salesperson rarely asks. Practice and experiment with asking for the deposit. For example, say, "These units do offer an excellent appreciation potential, if you're willing to do some fixup. Why don't you get started on your investment program now? Will you give me your deposit check and let me get your purchase under way?"

Killing a Sale   A positive approach is to ask leading questions, get agreement throughout the sale and then ask for the order. A salesperson who does not use a positive approach may be the loser. The sale also can be killed by these nine mistakes:

1. talking too much;

2. overeagerness to sell;

3. incomplete knowledge;

4. high-pressure tactics;

5. fear complex;

6. criticism of competitors;

7. straying from the subject;

8. negative selling attitude; and

9. argumentative attitude.

The Real Estate Purchase Contract and Receipt for Deposit   "An oral contract is not worth the paper it is written on," said Samuel Goldwyn. The California Statute of Frauds stipulates that all real estate sales contracts must be in writing. An exception to that rule is a lease of real property for one year or less.

When a sale has been consummated and the offer obtained, get everything in writing to avoid costly litigation in the future. Many standard **deposit receipt** forms are used in California, and the buyer's offer can be submitted on any of these. The number of forms has caused a great deal of concern in legal circles and with the California Association of REALTORS® because brokers are seldom attorneys and may be confused by the language employed. As a result, in 1985 the California Association of REALTORS®, in cooperation with the state bar and with the approval of the Department of Real Estate, developed a model form (see Figure 7.5) that is most widely used in California.

Content of the New Form   All of the original form's clauses are included, along with two important additions: (1) a financing addendum and (2) required disclosure statements. Essentially, the form acts as a checklist ensuring a contract that is complete in all respects. When properly completed, the responsible parties comply with the requirements stipulated in the *Easton* case and help both parties avoid entangling legal complications. Any changes should be dated and initialed by the principals to the transaction.

Figure 7.5

REAL ESTATE PURCHASE CONTRACT AND RECEIPT FOR DEPOSIT
(LONG FORM — WITH FINANCING CLAUSES)
THIS IS MORE THAN A RECEIPT FOR MONEY. IT IS INTENDED TO BE A LEGALLY BINDING CONTRACT. READ IT CAREFULLY
CALIFORNIA ASSOCIATION OF REALTORS' (CAR) STANDARD FORM

_____ , California, _____ . 19 _____

Received from _____

herein called Buyer, the sum of _____ Dollars $ _____

evidenced by ☐ cash, ☐ cashier's check ☐ personal check or ☐ _____ , payable to

_____ , to be held uncashed until acceptance of this offer as deposit on account of purchase price of

_____ Dollars $ _____

for the purchase of property, situated in _____ , County of _____ California,

described as follows: _____

1. FINANCING: The obtaining of Buyer's financing is a contingency of this agreement.

A. DEPOSIT upon acceptance, to be deposited into _____ .. $ _____

B. INCREASED DEPOSIT within _____ days of Seller's acceptance to be deposited into _____ .. $ _____

C. BALANCE OF DOWN PAYMENT to be deposited into _____ on or before _____ .. $ _____

D. Buyer to apply, qualify for and obtain a NEW FIRST LOAN in the amount of .... $ _____

payable monthly at approximately $ _____ ☐ or more, including interest at origination not to
exceed _____ %, ☐ fixed rate, ☐ other _____ all due _____ years from date of
origination. Loan fee not to exceed _____ Seller agrees to pay a maximum of _____
FHA/VA discount points. Additional terms _____

E. Buyer ☐ to assume, ☐ to take title subject to an EXISTING FIRST LOAN with an approximate balance of $ _____
in favor of _____ payable monthly at $ _____ including interest
at _____ % ☐ fixed rate, ☐ other _____
Fees not to exceed _____ . Disposition of impound account _____ .
Additional Terms _____

F. Buyer to execute a NOTE SECURED BY a ☐ first, ☐ second, ☐ third DEED OF TRUST in the amount of.. $ _____
IN FAVOR OF SELLER payable monthly at $ _____ ☐ or more, including interest at _____% all due
_____ years from date of origination, ☐ or upon sale or transfer of subject property. A late charge of _____
shall be due on any installment not paid within _____ days of the due date. ☐ Deed of Trust to contain a
request for notice of default or sale for the benefit of Seller. Buyer ☐ will, ☐ will not execute a request for
notice of delinquency. Additional terms _____

G. Buyer ☐ to assume, ☐ to take title subject to an EXISTING SECOND LOAN with an approximate balance of $ _____
in favor of _____ payable monthly at $ _____ including interest
at _____ % ☐ fixed rate, ☐ other _____ . Buyer fees not to exceed _____ .
Additional terms _____

H. Buyer to apply, qualify for and obtain a NEW SECOND LOAN in the amount of .... $ _____
payable monthly at approximately $ _____ ☐ or more, including interest at origination not to exceed
_____ % ☐ fixed rate, ☐ other, _____
_____ , all due _____ years from date or origination. Buyer's loan fee not to exceed _____ .
Additional Terms _____

I. In the event Buyer assumes or takes title subject to an existing loan, Seller shall provide Buyer with
copies of applicable notes and Deeds of Trust. A loan may contain a number of features which affect
the loan, such as interest rate changes, monthly payment changes, balloon payments, etc. Buyer shall
be allowed _____ calendar days after receipt of such copies to notify seller in writing of disapproval.
FAILURE TO SO NOTIFY SELLER SHALL CONCLUSIVELY BE CONSIDERED APPROVAL. Buyer's approval
shall not be unreasonably withheld. Difference in existing loan balances shall be adjusted in ☐ Cash,
☐ Other _____

J. Buyer agrees to act diligently and in good faith to obtain all applicable financing.

K. ADDITIONAL FINANCING TERMS: _____

L. TOTAL PURCHASE PRICE .... $ _____

2. OCCUPANCY: Buyer ☐ does, ☐ does not intend to occupy subject property as Buyer's primary residence.

3. SUPPLEMENTS: The ATTACHED supplements are incorporated herein:
☐ Interim Occupancy Agreement (CAR FORM IOA-11)   ☐ _____
☐ Residential Lease Agreement After Sale (CAR FORM RLAS-11) ☐ _____
☐ VA and FHA Amendments (CAR FORM VA/FHA-11)   ☐ _____

4. ESCROW: Buyer and Seller shall deliver signed instructions to _____ the escrow holder, within
_____ calendar days from Seller's acceptance which shall provide for closing within _____ calendar days from
Seller's acceptance. Escrow fees to be paid as follows: _____ .

Buyer and Seller acknowledge receipt of copy of this page, which constitutes Page 1 of _____ Pages.
Buyer's Initials (_____) (_____)   Seller's Initials (_____) (_____)

OFFICE USE ONLY
Reviewed by Broker or Designee _____
Date _____

To order contact — California Association of Realtors'
525 So. Virgil Ave. Los Angeles, California 90020
Copyright · 1986 California Association of Realtors

REAL ESTATE PURCHASE CONTRACT AND RECEIPT FOR DEPOSIT (DLF-14 PAGE 1)

Source: Reprinted by permission, California Association of REALTORS®. Endorsement not implied.

Subject Property Address _____

5. TITLE: Title is to be free of liens, encumbrances, easements, restrictions, rights and conditions of record or known to Seller, other than the following: (a) Current property taxes, (b) covenants, conditions, restrictions, and public utility easements of record, if any, provided the same do not adversely affect the continued use of the property for the purposes for which it is presently being used, unless reasonably disapproved by Buyer in writing within _____ calendar days of receipt of a current preliminary report furnished at _____ expense, and (c) _____.
Seller shall furnish Buyer at _____ expense a standard California Land Title Association policy issued by _____ Company, showing title vested in Buyer subject only to the above. If Seller is unwilling or unable to eliminate any title matter disapproved by Buyer as above, Buyer may terminate this agreement. If Seller fails to deliver title as above, Buyer may terminate this agreement; in either case, the deposit shall be returned to Buyer.

6. PRORATIONS: Property taxes, premiums on insurance acceptable to Buyer, rents, interest, homeowner's dues, and _____ shall be pro-rated as of (a) the date of recordation of deed; or (b) _____ . Any bond or assessment which is a lien shall be ☐ paid, ☐ assumed by _____. County transfer tax, if any, shall be paid by _____ . The _____ transfer tax or transfer fee shall be paid by_____ .
(Real property taxes will be affected upon transfer of title.)

7. POSSESSION: Possession and occupancy shall be delivered to Buyer, ☐ on close of escrow, or ☐ not later than _____ days after close of escrow, or ☐ _____.

8. VESTING: Unless otherwise designated in the escrow instructions of Buyer, title shall vest as follows: _____

(The manner of taking title may have significant legal and tax consequences. Therefore, give this matter serious consideration.)

9. MULTIPLE LISTING SERVICE: If Broker is a participant of a Board multiple listing service ("MLS"), the Broker is authorized to report the sale, its price, terms, and financing for the information, publication, dissemination, and use of the authorized Board members.

10. LIQUIDATED DAMAGES: If Buyer fails to complete said purchase as herein provided by reason of any default of Buyer, Seller shall be released from obligation to sell the property to Buyer and may proceed against Buyer upon any claim or remedy which he may have in law or equity; provided, however, that by placing their initials here Buyer: ( ) Seller: ( ) agree that Seller shall retain the deposit as liquidated damages. If the described property is a dwelling with no more than four units, one of which the Buyer intends to occupy as his residence, Seller shall retain as liquidated damages the deposit actually paid, or an amount therefrom, not more than 3% of the purchase price and promptly return any excess to Buyer. Buyer and Seller agree to execute a similar liquidated damages provision, such as California Association of Realtors® Receipt for Increased Deposit, (RID-11), for any increased deposits. (Funds deposited in trust accounts or in escrow are not released automatically in the event of a dispute. Release of funds require written agreement of the parties or adjudication.)

11. ARBITRATION: If the only controversy or claim between the parties arises out of or relates to the disposition of the Buyer's deposit, such controversy or claim shall at the election of the parties be decided by arbitration. Such arbitration shall be determined in accordance with the Rules of the American Arbitration Association, and judgment upon the award rendered by the Arbitrator(s) may be entered in any court having jurisdiction thereof. The provisions of Code of Civil Procedure Section 1283.05 shall be applicable to such arbitration.

12. ATTORNEY'S FEES: In any action or proceeding arising out of this agreement, the prevailing party shall be entitled to reasonable attorney's fees and costs.

13. KEYS: Seller shall, when possession is available to Buyer, provide keys to all property locks, and alarms if any.

14. PERSONAL PROPERTY: The following items of personal property, free of liens and without warranty of condition, are included: _____
_____
_____ .

15. FIXTURES: All permanently installed fixtures and fittings that are attached to the property or for which special openings have been made are included in the purchase price, including electrical, light, plumbing and heating fixtures, built-in appliances, screens, awnings, shutters, all window coverings, attached floor coverings, T.V. antennas, air cooler or conditioner, garage door openers and controls, attached fireplace equipment, mailbox, trees and shrubs, and_____ except _____ .

16. STRUCTURAL MODIFICATIONS: Seller shall comply with Civil Code Section 1134.5 by disclosing to Buyer in writing any known structural additions or alterations, or the installation, alteration, repair, or replacement of significant components of the structures upon the property made with or without appropriate permit(s).

17. TAX WITHHOLDING: Under the Foreign Investment in Real Property Tax Act (FIRPTA), IRC 1445, *every* Buyer of U.S. real property *must*, unless an exemption applies, deduct and withhold from Seller's proceeds ten percent (10%) of the gross sales price. The primary exemptions are: No withholding is required if (a) Seller provides Buyer with an affidavit under penalty of perjury, that Seller is not a "foreign person," or (b) Seller provides Buyer with a "qualifying statement" issued by the Internal Revenue Service, or (c) if Buyer purchases real property for use as a residence and the purchase price is $300,000.00 or less and if Buyer or a member of Buyer's family has definite plans to reside at the property for at least 50% of the number of days it is in use during each of the first two twelve-months periods after transfer.
Seller and Buyer agree to execute and deliver as directed, any instrument, affidavit and statement, or to perform any act reasonably necessary to carry out the provisions of FIRPTA and regulations promulgated thereunder.

18. ENTIRE CONTRACT: Time is of the essence. All prior agreements between the parties are incorporated in this agreement which constitutes the entire contract. Its terms are intended by the parties as a final expression of their agreement with respect to such terms as are included herein and may not be contradicted by evidence of any prior agreement or contemporaneous oral agreement. The parties further intend that this agreement constitutes the complete and exclusive statement of its terms and that no extrinsic evidence whatsoever may be introduced in any judicial or arbitration proceeding, if any, involving this agreement.

19. CAPTIONS: The captions in this agreement are for convenience of reference only and are not intended as part of this agreement.

Buyer and Seller acknowledge receipt of copy of this page, which constitutes Page 2 of _____ Pages.
Buyer's Initials (_____) (_____)   Seller's Initials (_____) (_____)

OFFICE USE ONLY
Reviewed by Broker or Designee _____
Date _____

MB-E5-MB/1

REAL ESTATE PURCHASE CONTRACT AND RECEIPT FOR DEPOSIT (DLF-14 PAGE 2)

Subject Property Address _____

20. ADDITIONAL TERMS AND CONDITIONS:

ONLY THE FOLLOWING PARAGRAPHS A THROUGH L WHEN INITIALED BY BOTH BUYER AND SELLER ARE INCORPORATED IN THIS AGREEMENT.

Buyer's Initials _____ Seller's Initials _____

A. PHYSICAL INSPECTION: Within _____ calendar days after Seller's acceptance Buyer shall have the right, at Buyer's expense, to select a licensed contractor(s) or other qualified professional(s), to inspect and investigate the subject property, including but not limited to structural, plumbing, heating, electrical, built-in appliances, roof, soils, foundation mechanical systems, pool, pool heater, pool filter, and air conditioner, if any. Buyer shall keep the subject property free and clear of any liens, indemnify and hold Seller harmless from all liability, claims, demands, damages or costs, and repair all damages to the property arising from the inspections. All claimed defects concerning the condition of the property that adversely affect the continued use of the property for the purposes for which it is presently being used shall be in writing, supported by written reports, if any, and delivered to Seller within _____ calendar days after Seller's acceptance. Buyer shall furnish Seller copies, at no cost, of all reports concerning the property obtained by Buyer. When such reports disclose conditions or information unsatisfactory to the Buyer, which the Seller is unwilling or unable to correct, Buyer may cancel this agreement. Seller shall make the premises available for all inspections. BUYER'S FAILURE TO NOTIFY SELLER SHALL CONCLUSIVELY BE CONSIDERED APPROVAL.

Buyer's Initials _____ Seller's Initials _____

B. GEOLOGICAL INSPECTION: Within _____ calendar days after Seller's acceptance. Buyer shall have the right, at Buyer's expense, to select a qualified professional to make tests, surveys, or other studies of the subject property. Buyer shall keep the subject property free and clear of any liens, indemnify and hold Seller harmless from all liability, claims, demands, damages or costs, and repair all damages to the property arising from the tests, surveys, or studies. All claimed defects concerning the condition of the property that adversely affect the continued use of the property for the purposes for which it is presently being used shall be in writing, supported by written reports if any, and delivered to Seller within _____ calendar days after Seller's acceptance. Buyer shall furnish Seller copies, at no cost, of all reports concerning the property obtained by Buyer. When such reports disclose conditions or information unsatisfactory to the Buyer, which the Seller is unwilling or unable to correct, Buyer may cancel this agreement. Seller shall make the premises available for all inspections. BUYER'S FAILURE TO NOTIFY SELLER SHALL CONCLUSIVELY BE CONSIDERED APPROVAL.

Buyer's Initials _____ Seller's Initials _____

C. CONDITION OF PROPERTY: Seller warrants, through the date possession is made available to Buyer: (1) property and improvements thereon, including landscaping, grounds and pool/spa, if any, shall be maintained in the same condition as upon the date of Seller's acceptance; (2) the roof is free of all known leaks and that water, sewer, plumbing, heating, air conditioning, if any, and electrical systems and all built-in appliances are operative, (3) _____ .

Buyer's Initials _____ Seller's Initials _____

D. SELLER REPRESENTATION: Seller warrants that Seller has no knowledge of any notice of violations of City, County, State, Federal, Building, Zoning, Fire, Health Codes or ordinances, or other governmental regulation filed or issued against the property. This warranty shall be effective until date of close of escrow.

Buyer's Initials _____ Seller's Initials _____

E. PEST CONTROL: Within _____ calendar days from date of Seller's acceptance Seller shall furnish Buyer, at the expense of ☐ Buyer, ☐ Seller, a current written report of an inspection by _____ , a licensed Structural Pest Control Operator, of the main building and all structures of the property, except _____

If no infestation or infection by wood destroying pests or organisms is found, the report shall include a written "Certification" as provided in Business and Professions Code 8519(a) that on the date of inspection "no evidence of active infestation or infection was found."

All work recommended in said report to repair damage caused by infestation or infection by wood-destroying pests or organisms found, including leaking shower stalls and replacing of tiles removed for repairs, and all work to correct conditions that causes such infestation or infection shall be done at the expense of Seller.

Funds for work to be performed shall be held in escrow and disbursed upon receipt of written Certification as provided in Business and Professions Code 8519(b) that the property "is now free of evidence of active infestation or infection".

Buyer agrees that any work to correct conditions usually deemed likely to lead to infestation or infection by wood-destroying pests or organisms, but where no evidence of existing infestation or infection is found with respect to such conditions, is NOT the responsibility of the Seller, and that such work shall be done only if requested by Buyer and then at the expense of Buyer.

If inspection of inaccessible areas is recommended by the report, Buyer has the option of accepting and approving the report or requesting further inspection be made at the Buyer's expense. If further inspection is made and infestation, infection, or damage is found, repair of such damage and all work to correct conditions that caused such infestation or infection and the cost of entry and closing of the inaccessible areas shall be at the expense of Seller. If no infestation, infection, or damage is found, the cost of entry and closing of the inaccessible areas shall be at the expense of Buyer. Other _____

Buyer's Initials _____ Seller's Initials _____

F. SMOKE DETECTOR: Approved smoke detector(s) shall be installed as required by law, at the expense of ☐ Buyer, ☐ Seller.

Buyer's Initials _____ Seller's Initials _____

G. FLOOD HAZARD AREA DISCLOSURE: The subject property is situated in a "Special Flood Hazard area" as set forth on a Federal Emergency Management Agency (FEMA) "Flood Insurance Rate Map (FIRM) or "Flood Hazard Boundary Map" (FHBM). The law provides that, as a condition of obtaining financing on most structures located in a "Special Flood Hazard Area," lenders require flood insurance where the property or its attachments are security for a loan.

The extent of coverage and the cost may vary. For further information consult the lender or insurance carrier. No representation or recommendation is made by the Seller and the Brokers in this transaction as to the legal effect or economic consequences of the National Flood Insurance Program and related legislation.

Buyer and Seller acknowledge receipt of copy of this page, which constitutes Page 3 of _____ Pages.

Buyer's Initials (_____) (_____)   Seller's Initials (_____) (_____)

OFFICE USE ONLY
Reviewed by Broker or Designee _____
Date _____

MB-E6-MB/1

REAL ESTATE PURCHASE CONTRACT AND RECEIPT FOR DEPOSIT (DLF-14 PAGE 3)

Subject Property Address _____

Buyer's Initials   **Seller's Initials**

____ / ____   ____ / ____   **H. SPECIAL STUDIES ZONE DISCLOSURE:** The subject property is situated in a Special Studies Zone as designated under Sections 2621-2625, inclusive, of the California Public Resources Code; and, as such, the construction or development on this property of any structure for human occupancy may be subject to, the findings of a geologic report prepared by a geologist registered in the State of California, unless such report is waived by the City or County under the terms of that act.

California Public Resources Code §2621.5 excludes structures in existence prior to May 4, 1975; California Public Resources Code §2621.6 excludes wood frame dwellings not exceeding two (2) stories in height and mobile homes over eight (8) feet in width; California Public Resources Code §2621.7 excludes conversion of existing apartment houses into condominiums; California Public Resources Code §2621.8 excludes alterations and additions under 50% of value of the structure from the Special Studies Zone Act.

Buyer is allowed _____ calendar days from date of Seller's acceptance to make further inquiries at appropriate governmental agencies concerning the use of the subject property under the terms of the Special Studies Zone Act and local building, zoning, fire, health and safety codes. When such inquiries disclose conditions or information unsatisfactory to the Buyer, which the Seller is unwilling or unable to correct, Buyer may cancel this agreement. BUYER'S FAILURE TO NOTIFY SELLER SHALL CONCLUSIVELY BE CONSIDERED APPROVAL.

Buyer's Initials   **Seller's Initials**

____ / ____   ____ / ____   **I. ENERGY CONSERVATION RETROFIT:** If local ordinance requires that the property be brought in compliance with minimum energy Conservation Standards as a condition of sale or transfer, ☐ Buyer, ☐ Seller shall comply with and pay for these requirements. Where permitted by law, Seller may, if obligated hereunder, satisfy the obligation by authorizing escrow to credit Buyer with sufficient funds to cover the cost of such retrofit.

J. HOME PROTECTION PLAN: Buyer and Seller have been informed that Home Protection Plans are available. Such plans may provide additional protection and benefit to a Seller or Buyer. California Association of Realtors' and the Broker(s) in this transaction do not endorse or approve any particular company or program.

Buyer's Initials   **Seller's Initials**

____ / ____   ____ / ____   ☐ Buyer, ☐ Seller to pay for a Home Protection Plan to be issued by _____ company, at a cost not to exceed $ _____ .

Buyer's Initials   **Seller's Initials**

____ / ____   ____ / ____   Buyer and Seller elect not to purchase a Home Protection Plan.

Buyer's Initials   **Seller's Initials**

____ / ____   ____ / ____   **K. CONDOMINIUM / P.U.D.:** The subject of this transaction is a condominium / planned unit development (P.U.D.) designated as unit _____ and _____ parking space(s) and an undivided _____ interest in all community areas, and _____ . The current monthly assessment charge by the homeowner's association (or other governing body(s)) is $ _____ . As soon as practicable, Seller shall provide Buyer with copies of covenants, conditions and restrictions, articles of incorporation, by-laws, current rules and regulations, most current financial statements, and any other documents as required by law. Seller shall disclose in writing any known pending special assessment, claims, or litigation to Buyer. Buyer shall be allowed _____ calendar days from receipt to review these documents. If such documents disclose conditions of information unsatisfactory to Buyer, Buyer may cancel this agreement. BUYER'S FAILURE TO NOTIFY SELLER SHALL CONCLUSIVELY BE CONSIDERED APPROVAL.

Buyer's Initials   **Seller's Initials**

____ / ____   ____ / ____   **L. OTHER TERMS AND CONDITIONS:** _____
_____
_____

21. **OFFER:** This constitutes an offer to purchase the described property. Unless acceptance is signed by Seller and the signed copy delivered in person or by mail to Buyer, or to _____ who is authorized to receive it, in person or by mail at the address below, within _____ calendar days of the date hereof, this offer shall be deemed revoked and the deposit shall be returned. Buyer acknowledges receipt of a copy hereof.

22. **AMENDMENTS: This agreement may not be amended, modified, altered or changed in any respect whatsoever except by a further agreement in writing executed by Buyer and Seller.**

REAL ESTATE BROKER _____   BUYER _____

By _____   BUYER _____
Address _____   Address _____
Telephone _____   Telephone _____

ACCEPTANCE

The undersigned Seller accepts and agrees to sell the property on the above terms and conditions. Seller has employed _____
_____
as Broker(s) and agrees to pay compensation for services as follows: _____
Payable; (a) On recordation of the deed or other evidence of title, or (b) if completion of sale is prevented by default of Seller, upon Seller's default, or (c) if completion of sale is prevented by default of Buyer, only if and when Seller collects damages from Buyer, by suit or otherwise, and then in an amount not less than one-half of the damages recovered, but not to exceed the above fee, after first deducting title and escrow expenses and the expenses of collection, if any. Seller shall execute and deliver an escrow instruction irrevocably assigning the compensation for services in an amount equal to the compensation agreed to above. In any action between Broker and Seller arising out of this agreement, the prevailing party shall be entitled to reasonable attorney's fees and costs. The undersigned acknowledges receipt of a copy and authorizes Broker(s) to deliver a signed copy to Buyer.

Dated _____ Telephone _____   SELLER _____ _____

Address _____   SELLER _____

Real Estate Broker(s) agree to the foregoing. Broker _____ By _____ Date _____
Broker _____ By _____ Date _____

OFFICE USE ONLY
Page 4 of _____ Pages.   Reviewed by Broker or Designee _____
                              Date _____

MB-E6-MB/1

REAL ESTATE PURCHASE CONTRACT AND RECEIPT FOR DEPOSIT (DLF-14 PAGE 4)

Understanding the New Form

Let us analyze the basic points outlined in this document to better understand it.

Introduction. The introductory material includes the place where the buyer signs the offer. Avoid abbreviations in the date. Also detail:

1. full name of persons involved;

2. deposit and purchase price, stated in figures and written out;

3. the type of deposit agreed; and

4. an accurate description of the property in sufficient detail.

If the listing agreement calls for a minimum deposit, that amount should be obtained and noted on the form. If the check is to be postdated, you should obtain the seller's authorization to hold the check until the indicated date.

Financing clause. Only the most common forms of financing can be covered in preprinted text. If creative financing or seller-backed financing is involved, additional terms can be included in the blank spaces provided. Point K is very important in that the buyer is obligated to be diligent in applying for financing and can be given a time frame in which financing should be obtained. If the seller does not receive written notification from the buyer within the time specified, either party may cancel the contract.

Occupancy clause. If property is a one- to four-unit building and the buyer is to live in one of the units, then mark this section accordingly. It will facilitate proof in any controversy over disposition of the deposit, particularly in the case of liquidated damages (#10 on contract).

Supplements clause. Appropriate boxes should be checked and corresponding form(s) attached.

Escrow clause. Insert the name of the proposed escrow holder, dates for delivery of preliminary and final escrow instructions and terms of escrow fee payment.

Title clause. This constitutes a reasonable compromise between the seller's legitimate concern about providing an additional "escape" for the buyer and the need to protect the buyer from an unknowing acceptance of unexpected "clouds" and restrictions on the title.

Prorations clause. As in the old form, write out the proration terms to be completed in escrow.

Possession clause. Several options are listed. New to the form is space for reference to an "occupancy agreement after sale."

Vesting clause (#8). Indicates the manner in which title should be vested. This is a legal decision and the buyer should be encouraged to seek legal advice.

Multiple listing service clause (#9). This clause authorizes the broker participant in MLS to report the sale, price, terms and financing for use by authorized board members.

Liquidated damages clause (#10). By initialing this clause, the buyer and seller can limit the amount of damages in the event of buyer default. Although this was contained in the old form, this is an area that often is neglected. If the buyer initials the box and the seller does not, the contract may be unenforceable.

Arbitration clause (#11). The parties may use arbitration procedure to resolve disputes about the disposition of the buyer's deposit in case of default.

Attorney's fees clause (#12). This means that in the event of litigation the "loser pays."

Keys clause (#13). This new paragraph is included to alert the seller of the obligation to provide the buyer with all available keys.

Personal property clause (#14). Any items of personal property that may be included in the purchase price should be listed here.

Fixtures clause (#15). Wording is *new.* The most common fixtures are included. Careful questioning of the parties helps avoid disputes in this area.

Structural modification clause (#16). This new paragraph obligates the seller to comply with Civil Code Section 1134.5, effective July 1, 1985. As soon as practical before the transfer of title, a statement should be gotten from the seller for delivery to the buyer.

Tax withholding clause (#17). The inspiration for this new clause is the Internal Revenue Code sections 1445 and 897 and the Treasury Department regulation. Unless the exemptions apply, every buyer of U.S. real property is obligated to withhold ten percent of the gross sales price from the seller's proceeds.

Entire contract clause (#18). Slightly expanded from the old form, this clause includes the "time is of the essence" provision, indicating that the performance of any act under the agreement has a completion deadline unless extended in writing.

Captions (#19). This merely states that the captions in the above clauses are for convenience and reference purposes only and are not intended to be part of the contract.

Additional terms and conditions (#20). Designated by letters A through L, these are optional clauses not effective unless initialed by all buyers and sellers.

Offer clause (#21). This spells out that this is an offer to purchase the designated property with deadlines for both acceptance by the seller or revocation by the buyer.

Amendments clause (#22). Modifying, altering or changing the contract except by a further agreement in writing executed by both buyer and seller is prohibited.

Acceptance (#23). When signed by the seller, this form becomes a binding contract. If either party defaults after this step has been taken, a penalty is inflicted on the defaulter.

■ **Note:** Each page of the form must be initialed by both seller and buyer.

■ **Note:** The real estate transaction is consummated on the proper completion of this form. Because few, if any, salespeople or brokers know *all* the answers pertaining to the legal interpretation of this form, use extreme caution in giving advice that might have legal consequences.

If you need further information, a guide to the proper completion of the deposit receipt form is provided in *Successful Real Estate Sales Agreements* by Erik Jorgensen, Axion Press, San Francisco, California.

Presenting an Offer

An axiom to follow when presenting an offer is, "Prepare before you present." Actually, the word *present* is a misnomer. "Negotiate" better describes the job you face when you take an offer to the sellers.

Prepare the Buyer To Compromise

Preparing the buyer to compromise requires empathy. Put yourself in the buyer's shoes. Ask yourself, "If I were the buyer, what would I be willing to give up?" Begin this presentation by picking an amenity that is not essential to everyday living, such as a shop, a sewing room or a darkroom. Some questions you could ask in preparing the buyer to compromise are:

- If you had to give up something, what is the feature you need least, the one you would least like to pay for?

- To get all the features you have named in the home you are looking for, would you be willing to increase your initial investment or your monthly payments?

Analyze from the Seller's Point of View

Professional negotiators know beforehand what they are prepared to do. They have examined both their side's and the other side's position on possible areas of compromise and trade-off. They know what they are willing to concede and what they expect in return. Presenting the buyer's offer in a real estate transaction means being prepared to negotiate. To do this, you need accurate assumptions about the seller's needs and receptivity.

Such questions as these should be resolved before proceeding with your negotiations:

1. Is the purchase offer within negotiating probability?

2. How does the offer compare with the competitive market analysis that has been prepared? How did the seller react to it?

3. What are the financing terms of the offer and how do they affect the seller's projected net?

4. What are the payoff or assumption terms of the seller's present financing in relation to the offer to purchase?

5. How quickly can the escrow be closed?

6. Does the buyer want personal property included and will the seller be willing to sell it?

7. How long has the property been on the market and how anxious is the owner to sell?

8. Do the buyer and seller have any common characteristics, such as marital status, children, retirement, business success, love of beauty?

9. Is the transaction free of contingencies?

10. Are there any other possible objections you have failed to consider? If so, devise a logical answer to each objection, countering the objection with a benefit to the seller.

Present the Purchase Agreement   If you have done your homework well, you are prepared to negotiate.

■   **Note: Caution:** Do not look on presenting the offer as a game you are going to play with the seller, a matching of wits, where you, the salesperson, win and the seller loses. Rather, the salesperson should be a neutral party, interested in seeing that both the buyer and the seller come out with gains.

Buyers often are unaccustomed to business negotiation, so care must be taken to set the stage properly and establish a degree of mutual trust. To do this, have your appointment with the seller made by someone other than yourself. Try to have all parties to the transaction present at the same time. Pick a time when the principals can give sufficient time to your proposal. The place of presentation also is important.

Insofar as possible, eliminate distraction during the negotiation. Carefully arrange seating so you are facing the principals involved. This enables you to watch their expressions and observe their nonverbal signals, such as nods, glances, frowns or shrugs.

Present each principal with a copy of the purchase offer. Take a few moments to build your case and, above all, create a receptive negotiating atmosphere. You must control the negotiation, which means directing the conversational flow. This allows for a proper sequence in presenting data, which will make the offer clearer to the seller.

Do not monopolize the conversation, but ask questions and allow meaningful interruptions.

Keep in mind that the offer is a package. Present the whole package before discussing the parts. This prevents the seller from picking on individual elements. Present the buyer's financial qualifications. This anticipates a question that is naturally in the seller's mind. A strong buyer will improve your negotiating position.

A major problem in presentation is that agents often only hit the highlights. The entire offer must be read with the seller and then reread in reverse order. The seller must be taken through it point-by-point, ending with the price.

Closing Techniques with the Seller

Just as certain techniques should be used in obtaining the offer from the buyer, so closing techniques are necessary in getting an acceptance of the buyer's offer from the seller.

Desire for solution. Many times the seller has a pressing need for a solution to a problem. The goal then is to make any financial sacrifice insignificant in relation to the benefit of an immediate solution.

Fear of loss. In a fear-of-loss close, the sellers are made to feel that if they do not complete the transaction with this buyer, another buyer may not offer nearly so much. In other words, encourage the seller to accept a sure thing now, rather than speculate on the risk of future gain.

Narrative close. A narrative close for the seller has the same purpose as for the buyer: "It happened to someone else. It might also happen to you."

Positive choice. As with the buyer, the seller is given a choice between two things. For example: "Would you like me to see if I can obtain a close by expediting the loan or will a 60-day period be satisfactory?"

Minimize the difference. The goal of minimizing the difference is to make the difference—the unattained portion—appear ridiculously small in relation to the whole.

Communication barriers. Unless care is exercised in negotiations, a psychological wall may be built between the buyer and the seller. Figure 7.6 shows the bricks of a psychological wall between two principals.

Obtaining a Counteroffer

Licensees may be plagued with some of the following problems:

1. proposed wording that is unacceptable to the seller;

2. changes in the amount or terms in loans;

3. changes in date of possession;

4. limitations on the liability for termite damage, repairs, etc.;

5. exclusions of personal property items to be included in the package; and

6. limitation of time required for buyer to obtain financing.

**Figure 7.6
A Psychological
Wall**

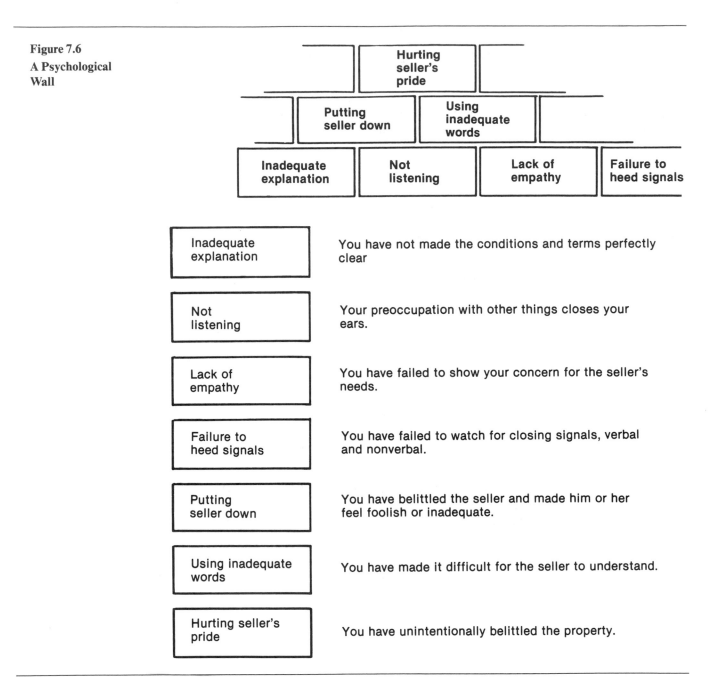

When all other efforts have failed in obtaining acceptance of the offer in its present form, always get a **counteroffer.** If the seller is unwilling to accept the buyer's offer as written, the writer of the offer must make the appropriate corrections in the acceptance clause and draw the counteroffer on an addendum to the contract. Very short and simple counteroffers may be written on the back of the contract. In either event, a change in the acceptance clause is necessary. The clause might read "as amended on the attached addendum" or "as amended on the reverse side hereof."

Acceptance of an offer must be unqualified; a qualified acceptance must be considered as a new offer or a counteroffer. In legal effect, any changes reject the original offer and bar its later acceptance.

Follow-through   Because the individuals involved in the closing of a transaction may miss certain details and errors may creep in, it is your job to check frequently to uncover small problems before they become big ones. Check frequently to see if everything is moving according to schedule. Keep all parties fully informed of all events and conclusions. Remember, referrals depend on good follow-through.

Summary

This chapter has discussed techniques in completing the sale, including watching for buying signals, overcoming objections and attempting trial closes.

You can overcome objections in a number of ways: Welcome all objections; concede before answering; rephrase as a question; meet objections halfway; and forestall objections. Respond to questions by asking questions.

In closing the sale, use the assumptive close, positive choice close, inducement close, fear of loss close or narrative close.

Licensees should understand each clause in the deposit receipt form. The focus of presenting and selling the offer contained in the deposit receipt is on negotiation. Successful negotiation requires understanding the buyer's and seller's positions and avoiding the possible barriers to communication of the offer, as well as handling counteroffers.

Questions

1. There are numerous advantages to owning a home. Which of the following is *not* one of these?

   a. security
   b. desire for profit or gain
   c. liquidity of investment
   d. comfort and convenience

2. When we speak of things the prospect does not want in making a sale, it is called:

   a. negative motivation.
   b. buyer's motivation.
   c. motivation without want.
   d. positive motivation.

3. If the buyer says "Don't you think the price is a little too high?" the alert salesperson may even consider it as:

   a. an objection.
   b. a buying signal.
   c. a point not worth considering.
   d. the response of a crank.

4. There are certain basic closing techniques. The ones that most nearly fit this category are:

   a. positive choice close.
   b. pay as you go technique.
   c. inducement technique.
   d. both a and c

5. The printed portion of the real estate purchase contract and receipt for deposit makes provision for:

   a. restrictions, rights and conditions of record.
   b. proration of property taxes and assessments.
   c. discount points.
   d. none of the above

6. Which of the following is *not* an effective technique for overcoming objections?

   a. Welcome all objections.
   b. Tell customers they are wrong and then prove it.
   c. Meet all objections halfway.
   d. Turn the objections into questions.

7. Which of the following might be considered a buying signal?

   a. actions of the customer
   b. an objection to a particular point
   c. a change in facial expression
   d. all of the above

8. Assume that the seller accepted an offer within the designated time limit. While the broker was notifying the buyers by telephone of the acceptance, the buyers revoked their offer. Under these conditions:

   a. the buyers cannot be held to the contract.
   b. the buyers would lose the deposit.
   c. the sellers could sue for performance.
   d. both b and c are correct

9. Which of these techniques is not used in presenting the offer?

   a. watch for buying signals
   b. use cold canvass method
   c. overcome resistance
   d. appeal to buying motives

10. When purchasing a home, a person should be aware of the disadvantages in so doing. Which of these reasons is considered to be such?

    a. restricted mobility
    b. risk
    c. both a and b
    d. neither a nor b

11. As we consider sensory appeals in selling real property, consideration is given to:

    a. sense of sound.
    b. sense of taste.
    c. sense of touch.
    d. all of the above

12. Typical objections that might arise in obtaining an offer might be:

    a. the water pressure is too low.
    b. I cannot buy until I sell.
    c. I cannot get occupancy soon enough.
    d. all of the above

13. Which one of these is *not* included in the positive approach to closing a sale?

    a. overeagerness to sell
    b. asking leading question
    c. getting agreement throughout sale
    d. ask for the order

14. In what document is the term "time is of the essence" included?

    a. option
    b. deposit receipt
    c. exclusive-right-to-sell listing
    d. grant deed

15. Which of the following might necessitate a counteroffer before acceptance can be had?

    a. changes in amount or terms of loan
    b. changes in date of possession
    c. limitation of time required for buyer to obtain financing
    d. all of the above

16. If the sellers and the buyers had placed their initials in the space provided in clause 12 and there is a default by the buyers:

    a. the buyers could demand the return of their deposit.
    b. the broker would be entitled to a full commission.
    c. the sellers would be entitled to retain the deposit.
    d. none of the above

17. If, on default of the buyer, the seller collects damages, the broker is entitled to one-half of the amount after the deduction of:

    a. expenses of collection.
    b. escrow expenses.
    c. title expenses.
    d. all of the above

18. In a conflict between reason and emotion, you can generally assume that:

    a. logic makes people reason.
    b. emotion makes people act.
    c. buyers buy what they want rather than what they need.
    d. all of the above

19. Which of the following statements is (are) related to the term "buying signals"?

    a. They are like green traffic lights.
    b. The buyer says, "I'm ready to talk terms if you are."
    c. both a and b
    d. neither a nor b

20. The technique of overcoming objections includes all of the following techniques *except:*

    a. welcome objections.
    b. meet objections halfway.
    c. ignore objections.
    d. concede before answering.

8

Escrow and Title Insurance

Chapter Preview

This chapter explains the last major step in the real estate sales transaction, the escrow. The discussion includes a comprehensive definition of the term, as well as identification of the parties included in an escrow—the buyer, seller, escrow officer and lender—and describes the duties and responsibilities of each.

The chapter points out those that may act as escrow agents, including escrow companies, which must be licensed by the Commissioner of Corporations. Others that may act as escrow agents but need not be licensed under the escrow licensing law are banks, savings and loan associations, attorneys, title and insurance companies and real estate brokers.

The legal requirements of the escrow officer are enumerated, along with the steps in the procedure for processing a transaction, from the opening to the closing of escrow.

The importance of title insurance also is explained, as well as the procedure followed and the risks covered under both standard and extended policies.

Terms To Look For

ALTA policy
Beneficiary statement
Closing costs
CLTA policy
Credit
Debit
Deed of reconveyance
Escrow
Escrow instructions
Extended policy
Impound account
Proration
Reconveyance
Settlement sheet
Standard policy
Title insurance
Trust fund

Escrow	The word *escrow* is derived from the French word *escroue,* meaning scroll or roll of writing. An owner of real property would execute an instrument in the form of a deed, conveying land to another party on the completion of certain conditions. This instrument, the *escroue,* was given to a third person with instructions that it would take effect as a deed on the performance of an act or the occurrence of an event, such as payment of a designated sum of money. The term was taken into English as **escrow,** meaning "a deed, a bond, money or a piece of property held in trust by a third party, to be turned over to the grantee only on fulfillment of a condition."

What Is an Escrow?	Escrow is the last step in a property transaction. The California Financial Code defines escrow as follows:

> Escrow means any transaction wherein one person for the purpose of affecting the sale, transfer, encumbering or leasing of real or personal property to another person, delivers any written instrument, money, evidence of title to real or personal property or other things of value to a third person to be held by such third person until the happening of a specified event. The performance is then to be delivered by such third person to a grantee, grantor, promisor, obligee, obligor, bailee, or bailor or any agent or employee of any of the latter.

This definition has been changed somewhat and the activities of an escrow agent have been expanded considerably. In brief, an escrow agent is an impartial third party who receives and disburses documents, money and papers from every party involved in a transaction, such as a sale of real estate.

Escrow Requirements	When a sum of money is offered by the buyer to the seller and the seller's acceptance is transmitted to the buyer, a binding contract is formed. This is the first requirement for a sales escrow. Escrow is created on the conditional delivery of transfer instruments and monies to a third party.

Although escrows are not required by law in California, they nevertheless have become an almost indispensable mechanism in this state to protect the parties involved in exchanges, leases, sales of securities, loans, mobile home sales and, primarily, real property sales.

Escrow Responsibility	The escrow agent holds all money and documents while the title is cleared. When it is determined that the title is clear, procedures are agreed on by the buyer and seller, and the deed and the monies involved are disbursed to the appropriate parties concurrently. (See figure 8.1.)

**Figure 8.1
Escrow**

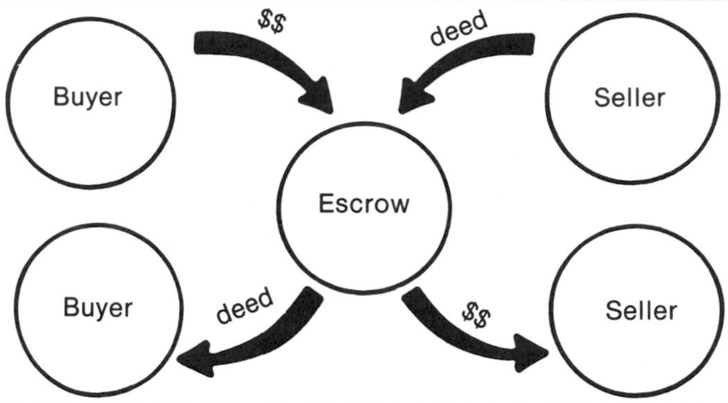

Parties to an Escrow

Buyers

Buyers who have made a contract to purchase real property understandably do not want to part with their money until they are sure that the seller's deed will convey clear title. When buyers have performed in full (paid the purchase price), they are entitled to a deed transferring title, subject only to encumbrances agreed on by both parties. While the title search is being conducted, the buyers' monies are held in escrow. In the event of death, incompetency or bankruptcy of sellers in the period between a purchase offer's acceptance and transfer of title from seller to buyer, buyers may be put to extra expense in order to clear the title.[1]

Sellers

Although sellers may have made a firm contract to sell their real property, they do not want to give up their title until they are certain of getting their money. They therefore retain legal title to the property as security until they have the money in hand. The sellers' legal title usually is transferred by deed. The title is placed in escrow until the buyer has produced the full purchase price of the property. If a seller dies before a transaction has been completed, the seller's right to the unpaid part of the purchase price passes to his or her heirs.

Lenders

Once committed to lending the money to buyers to complete a purchase price, lenders, like buyers, do not want to commit funds without assurance that titles to the properties in question are free and clear. Therefore, impartial third parties (escrow agents) will hold money, deeds and other documents until clear titles have been confirmed. Thereafter, it is the escrow agents' responsibility to see that the proper disbursements are made.

Escrow Agents

In California, all escrow companies must be corporations and, as such, be licensed by the California Commissioner of Corporations. Individuals cannot be licensed under the escrow law, but certain organizations and individuals are permitted to act as escrow agents. They are:

[1] *California Department of Real Estate Reference Book,* 1984-1985 edition, p. 166.

- banks;

- attorneys;

- brokers;

- title and trust companies; and

- savings and loan associations.

In northern California, the majority of the escrow transactions are handled by title insurance companies, which usually process the escrow and issue the title insurance policy together. In southern California, escrow companies handle the majority of escrow transactions, with a title company issuing the title insurance separately. Brokers may act as escrow agents only in transactions in which they represent the buyer or the seller or both. They may not act as escrow agents for any other broker or for individuals acting without a broker.

Escrow funds held by a broker must be placed in a special trust account, subject to a periodic inspection by the Commissioner of Corporations and, at the broker's own expense, subject to an independent annual audit. Brokers may not advertise that they have an escrow department unless they specify in the advertisement that such services are offered only in connection with their own real estate brokerage business.

Requirements for escrow licensure. Any corporation applying for an escrow license under the Escrow Act must meet the following qualifications:

- be financially solvent;

- furnish a surety bond for $10,000;

- arrange for the bonding of responsible employees;

- set up a trust fund for all monies deposited in escrow;

- keep accurate records, subject to audit at any time by the Commissioner of Corporations and the Department of Real Estate; and

- submit to an independent audit annually at its own expense.

Laws governing escrow. California law stipulates that an *individual* may not be licensed as an escrow holder or agent. The license must be held by a duly organized corporation for the express purpose of conducting an escrow business.

No escrow licensee may disseminate misleading or deceptive statements referring to its supervision by the state of California. A licensee also is prohibited from describing either orally or in writing any transaction that is not included under the definition of escrow in the California Financial Code.

Licensed escrow agents are prohibited by law from paying referral fees to anyone except a regular employee of their own escrow company. Escrow licensees are prohibited by law from soliciting or accepting escrow instructions or amended or supplemental instructions containing any blanks to be filled in after the instructions are signed. Furthermore, escrow licensees may not permit any person to make addition to, deletion from or alteration of an escrow instruction unless it is signed or initialed by all signers of the original instructions.

The escrow holder is at first the agent of both parties. When conditions are performed, he or she usually becomes the agent of each. To the *grantor,* the escrow holder delivers the deed. To the *grantee,* the escrow holder pays over the purchase price.[2]

Table 8.1 summarizes legal requirements pertaining to the actions of escrow officers.

Table 8.1
Legal Requirements for Escrow Officers

Officers Must:	Officers May Not:
1. Act according to issued written instructions.	1. Make a transaction for another officer.
2. Act as a neutral party at all times.	2. Negotiate with the parties separately.
3. Hold monies deposited by parties until disbursed.	3. Suggest that terms or provisions be inserted in the escrow.
4. Follow escrow instructions in every detail.	4. Act as a collection agency to get a client to furnish funds.
5. Give to parties only that information that concerns them.	5. Notify parties that they have not ordered a certain document that may be necessary to close an escrow.
6. Make sure that escrow does not close with an unverified check.	

Advantages of an Escrow

If you decide to buy a television set, you make your purchase from an appliance store. You pay for it by giving cash or adding it to your credit account. Rarely would you give a second thought as to whether or not the store has a right to sell the set to you. You probably give no thought at all to whether or not you need written evidence of your right to own the appliance. It is a simple sales transaction.

Not so with the sale of real property; the procedure is much more complicated. The seller could sign a simple deed of conveyance and deliver it to the buyer in exchange for the purchase price. However, neither the buyer nor the seller should agree to such an arrangement, because:

1. Title to the property may be encumbered. The buyer needs someone to make a title search to clear the title.

2. An accurate description of the property is necessary for legal purposes.

3. The seller and the buyer need an experienced person to prepare the instrument of conveyance for their signatures.

4. The buyer and the seller need assurance that their instructions have been carried out and that deeds will be delivered and any monies transferred only when all terms of the contract have been met.

There are distinct advantages to escrow and the use of a neutral third party in the transaction.

[2]*California Department of Real Estate Reference Book,* 1984-1985 edition, p. 168.

1. Escrow provides a custodian of papers, instructions, funds and documents until the transaction is closed.

2. It makes possible the handling of accounting details in a professional manner.

3. It assures the validity of a binding contract between participating parties.

4. It is of value to the buyers, assuring them that their monies will not be transferred until the title is cleared.

5. It is of value to the sellers, assuring them that the monies have been paid and all other terms and conditions have been met.

Escrow Procedures

When a transaction will be closed in escrow, certain procedures must be followed to fulfill the legal requirements for escrow procedures. The broker needs to provide certain information to the escrow agent. Buyers and sellers must be aware of the responsibilities each must assume in the escrow procedure.

Materials Needed

Brokers should take this information to the escrow agent:

1. Information on the buyer and the seller, including:

   - full names;

   - addresses;

   - telephone numbers;

   - ZIP codes; and

   - marital status of the parties.

2. Information on all brokers and salespeople involved in the transaction, including names, addresses, ZIP codes and telephone numbers.

3. Current loan information on the property:

   - names and addresses of all lenders involved;

   - approximate remaining balances on loans, if they are to be paid off;

   - accurate balances, if they are to be assumed or taken subject to; and

   - loan account numbers (these will make the escrow officer's job much easier).

4. Fire insurance policy that may be assumed or paid off.

5. Termite report.

6. Amount of deposit to be held in escrow.

7. Personal property (such as furnishings) included in sale, if any.

8. Closing date.

9. Current tax bills and most recent title policy, if available.

10. If the transaction involves income property, this additional information is needed:

   - a list of tenants and addresses;

   - cleaning and/or security deposits posted by each tenant;

   - copies of rental agreements or leases; and

   - list of current rents and rental due dates.

Opening the Escrow   The steps in opening an escrow may vary between the northern and southern parts of California. In either case, however, the general order is:

1. The broker usually opens the escrow after obtaining a completed deposit receipt signed by all concerned parties.

2. The real estate broker prepares the escrow instructions or requests the escrow agent to do so.

3. Prepared escrow instructions are signed by all parties to the contract. (In southern California, a single set of instructions, called "bilateral escrow instructions," is signed by the buyer and seller.)

4. The escrow agent orders a title search from a title company, which sends its report to escrow. (In northern California, the escrow agent is likely to be an employee of the title company that will do the search.)

5. The real estate broker either prepares a deed or has the escrow agent prepare one.

6. Buyers' and sellers' instructions, along with the deed and the buyers' deposit, are sent to escrow.

Escrow instructions are the written directions from the principals to the impartial third party, the escrow agent, to do all the necessary acts to carry out the escrow agreement of the principals. All principals in the escrow agreement (buyers, sellers, lenders, borrowers) sign identical instructions that fully set out the understanding of the parties to the transactions. They deliver the signed instructions to the escrow agent. The instructions should be drawn and signed soon after escrow procedures are opened, to clear up everyone's intent.

Escrow instructions. Communities vary in their escrow procedures. However, a title or escrow company uses preprinted forms for instructions, while a bank or other authorized agent more often issues instructions by letter.

Use of an instruction sheet. As the buyer and seller meet to open escrow, instructions are agreed on and entered on basic forms or worksheets. Sample buyer and seller instruction sheets are shown as Figures 8.2 and 8.3.

Figure 8.2
Buyer's Instructions

BUYER'S INSTRUCTIONS
FOUNDERS TITLE COMPANY

I Office _____

Phone No. _____   Escrow Officer _____

Property Address _____   Escrow No. _____

_____   Date _____

The undersigned hand you herewith:

Title Company is authorized and instructed to fill in dates on Note as follows: Interest to commence _____

First payment due _____   Final payment due _____

You are authorized to deliver or record all of said documents and disburse all funds deposited in this escrow for my account, in accordance with the instructions herein, and the below statement, when you can cause to be issued a policy of Title Insurance. Unless otherwise instructed in writing concerning the type of policy to be issued, you are to issue a Standard Form CLTA Policy in the amount of $ _____ , showing record title to the property described in your report under the above number to be vested of record in;

Subject to the printed provisions, exceptions and stipulations in said policy and subject to:

1. Taxes for fiscal year 19____ 19_____
2. Exceptions numbered _____of the above preliminary title report dated_____and

As of _____ prorate on the basis of a 30 day month: ( ) Taxes (Based on the most recent tax bill available);( ) Assessments; ( ) Fire insurance premiums (if acceptable to buyer); ( ) Interest on existing loan; ( ) Mortgage insurance; ( ) Rents; ( ) Homeowners Assoc. Dues. ( ) Credit existing loan trust funds, if any, to seller. ( ) _____

BUYER'S STATEMENT	CHARGES	CREDITS
01		01
02		02
03		03
04		04
05		05
06		06
07		07
08		08
09		09
10		10
11		11
12		12
13		13
14		14
15		15
16		16
17		17
18		18
19		19
20		20
21		21
22		22
23		23
24		24
25		25
26		26
27		27
28		28
29		29

These instructions shall remain in full force and effect until rescinded in writing. See reverse hereof for additional escrow provisions, which are incorporated herein and hereby approved. The undersigned agree to pay any balance for fees, costs or shortage due in connection with these instructions.

It is agreed and understood that this document and agreement shall be the whole and only agreement between the parties hereto with regard to the instructions and the obligations of the title company named herein, in connection with this escrow, and shall supersede and cancel any prior instructions. You are specifically directed to follow these instructions only, and you shall have no responsibility to follow the terms of any prior agreements entered into between the parties herein. In the event suit is brought by any party to this escrow, or any other party, as against each other, or others, including the title company, claiming any right they may have as against each other or against the title company, then in that event, the parties hereto agree to indemnify title company against any attorney's fee and cost incurred.

Buyer _____   Buyer _____

Buyer _____   Buyer _____

Address _____

_____

By: _____ Date: _____   Phone _____

FTG-3044

Figure 8.3
Seller's Instructions

SELLER'S INSTRUCTIONS
FOUNDERS TITLE COMPANY

I Office _____
  Phone No. _____   Escrow Officer _____
  Property Address _____   Escrow No. _____
  _____   Date _____
  The undersigned hand you herewith:

  You are authorized to deliver or record all of said documents and disburse all funds deposited in this escrow for my account, in accordance with the instructions herein, and the statement included herein, when you can cause to be issued a policy of Title Insurance in the amount of $ _____insuring property described in your report under the above number to be vested as instructed by buyer.
  Obtain Note and _____ Deed of Trust from buyer to seller for $_____ naming Payee and Beneficiary as_____
  _____
  _____
  _____, said Note shall be payable $ _____ or more per_____ including interest at _____% per annum.
  Interest to start: _____ . The first payment shall be due_____
  Due in full:_____

  Unless otherwise instructed in writing concerning the type of policy to be issued, you are to issue a Standard Form CLTA Policy to Seller showing said Deed of Trust subject to the exceptions in your Preliminary Report which are to be shown in Buyer's Title Insurance Policy.
  As of _____ prorate on the basis of a 30 day month: ( ) Taxes (Based on the most recent tax bill available); ( ) Assessments;
  ( ) Fire Insurance premiums (if acceptable to buyer); ( ) Interest on existing loan; ( ) Mortgage insurance; ( ) Rents; ( ) Homeowners Assoc. Dues.
  ( ) Credit existing loan trust funds, if any, to seller. ( )

  SELLER'S STATEMENT   **CHARGES**   **CREDITS**

  These instructions shall remain in full force and effect until rescinded in writing. See reverse hereof for additional escrow provisions, which are incorporated herein and hereby approved. The undersigned certifies that there are no encumbrances or liens affecting said property other than as shown on the above mentioned report. The undersigned agree to pay any balance for fees, costs or shortage due in connection with these instructions.
  It is agreed and understood that this document and agreement shall be the whole and only agreement between the parties hereto with regard to the instructions and the obligations of the title company named herein, in connection with this escrow, and shall supersede and cancel any prior instructions. You are specifically directed to follow these instructions only, and you shall have no responsibility to follow the terms of any prior agreements entered into between the parties herein. In the event suit is brought by any party to this escrow, or any other party, as against each other, or others, including the title company, claiming any right they may have as against each other or against the title company, then in that event, the parties hereto agree to indemnify title company against any attorney's fee and cost incurred.

  Seller _____   Seller_____

  Seller _____   Seller_____

                                                      Address_____

  Received **FOUNDERS TITLE COMPANY**

  By: _____ Date:_____   Phone _____
  FTG-3045

Closing Escrow   When the escrow agent has fulfilled all instructions from buyer, seller and lender, the remainder of the purchase price has been produced and a deed has been signed, the escrow arrangements are complete. The basic steps in closing escrow are as follows:

1. A statement showing the condition of the indebtedness and the unpaid balance of the loan is requested from the beneficiary, the lender.

2. When the escrow agent receives all the funds, documents and instructions necessary to close the escrow, he or she then makes any necessary adjustments and prorations on a settlement sheet.

3. All instruments pertinent to the transaction are then sent to the title insurance company for recording. At this point, time becomes important.

4. The title search runs right up to the last minute of the escrow recording to ensure that nothing has been inserted in the record. If no changes have taken place, the deed and other instruments are recorded on the following morning at 8 A.M. Thus, a title policy can be issued with the assurance that no intervening matters of record against the real property have occurred since the last search.

5. On the day the deed is recorded, the escrow agent disburses funds to the parties according to their signed instructions.

6. The escrow agent presents closing statements to the parties who should receive them. Once these have been approved, the escrow agent records the necessary papers with the county.

7. The title insurance company endeavors to issue a policy of title insurance on the day of recordation.

8. Shortly thereafter, the recorded deed is sent to the escrow agent for forwarding to the buyer.

Terms Used in Escrow Transactions

Impound account. For the protection of the lender, when a real estate loan is made, monthly payments for taxes and fire insurance may be required. The lender estimates needed funds for taxes and insurance, which vary from year to year. A deposit equal to one month's taxes or more may be required. These funds are placed in a special **trust fund** called an **impound account.** When the sale of the property is made and the loan is paid off, the seller is entitled to the unused portion of the impound account.

Beneficiary statement. If an existing loan is to be paid or assumed by the buyer, the escrow agent will obtain a **beneficiary statement** showing the exact balance due from the one holding the deed of trust, so that the buyer can receive the proper amount of credit.

Reconveyance. If the seller has a loan that is not being assumed by the buyer, the loan must be paid off to clear the title. The seller instructs the escrow agent to pay off the loan, for which the buyer receives a **deed of reconveyance.** A reconveyance fee is charged the seller for this service. The sum due the lender is entered in the seller's escrow instructions as an estimate. The total figure will not be known until the final computations are made by the lender at the time of closing.

Closing costs. The sum that the seller and buyer have to pay beyond the purchase price is called the **closing costs.** Closing costs consist of fees charged for the mortgage loan, title insurance, escrow services, reconveyances, recording of documents, and transfer tax, among others. The amount will vary, depending on the particular locale involved and the price of the property. Figure 8.4 shows a sample from the *seller's* standpoint, but this varies regionally. Costs also will vary from area to area, and from institution to institution within an area. Some costs change with fluctuations in the economy. Figure 8.5 lists those items for which the *buyer* is responsible.

As indicated in these charts, certain costs are customarily charged to the buyer; others to the seller. However, the two parties may agree to share some of these. Adapt this division of charges to your area. For actual fees, obtain copies of fee schedules from an escrow or title company in your area.

Figure 8.4
Closing Costs
Customarily
Paid by the Seller

Legal Closing

1. Owner's Title Policy
2. Escrow Services
3. Drawing Deed
4. Drawing Reconveyance
5. Notary Fees
6. Recording Reconveyance
7. Documentary transfer tax (providing County has adopted this tax), @ 55¢ for each $500 or fractional part thereof. Check your local area for differences in rates and requirements for transfer taxes.
8. Other agreed charges

Financial Closing

1. Mortgage discounts (points)
2. Appraisal charge for advance commitment
3. Termite report or structural repair (if any needed)
4. Interest on existing loan from last monthly payment to closing date
5. Beneficiary Statement (balance of existing loan)
6. Loan Payoff (1st Trust Deed and/or any junior trust deed)
7. Prepayment penalty
8. Other agreed charges
9. Escrow fees in VA transactions

Adjustments Between Seller and Buyer (depend on closing or other date agreed upon)

1. Pay any tax arrears in full
2. Pay any improvement assessment arrears (assessment may have to be paid in full)
3. Pay any other liens or judgments necessary to pass clear title
4. Pay broker's commission
5. Reimburse buyer for prepaid rents and deposits and adjust taxes, insurance, and interest as required
6. Occupancy adjustments

Source: *California Department of Real Estate Reference Book,* 1981-1982 edition, p. 517.

Figure 8.5
Closing Costs
Customarily
Paid by the Buyer

Legal Closing

1. Standard or Owner's Policy (in counties other than those named in footnote)
2. ALTA policy and inspection fee, if ordered
3. Escrow services
4. Drawing second mortgage (if used)
5. Notary fee
6. Recording deed
7. Other agreed charges

Financial Closing

1. Loan origination fee
2. Appraisal fee
3. Credit report
4. Drawing up note(s) and trust deed(s)
5. Notary fees
6. Recording trust deed
7. Tax agency fee
8. Termite inspection fee (if agreed upon)
9. Interest on new loan (from date of closing until first monthly payment due)
10. Assumption fee
11. Other agreed charges
12. New fire insurance premium 1 year prepaid, if applicable

Adjustments between Buyer and Seller (depend on closing date or other date agreed upon)

1. Reimburse seller for prepaid taxes
2. Reimburse seller for prepaid insurance
3. Reimburse seller for prepaid improvement assessment
4. Reimburse seller for prepaid impounds (in case buyer is assuming an existing loan)
5. Other
6. Other occupancy adjustments

Reserves (impounds)—limitations by RESPA.

1. Reserve to lender to meet next tax payment
2. Reserve to lender to meet next insurance payment (1 year)
3. Reserve to lender to meet FHA insurance premium

Variations:

(1) Any variation from custom in closing a transaction should be agreed upon in advance. Sometimes through sheer bargaining power, one party can demand to be relieved of all or some of the customary charges and offsets generally assessed. The financial aspects of each transaction differ and should always be negotiated by the parties.
(2) Accruals: Unless agreed upon in advance, interest bearing debts are accrued up to date of settlement, and constitute a charge against the seller.

Source: *California Department of Real Estate Reference Book,* 1981-1982 edition, p. 518.

Prorations

The adjustment and distribution of costs to be shared by buyer and seller is called **proration.** Costs that are typically prorated include interest, taxes and insurance, and, in the event income property is involved, prepaid rents. Costs are prorated in escrow as of the closing of escrow or an agreed-on date. The mathematical computations used in prorations will be explained later in the text.

Property taxes. Property taxes are levied annually (July 1 to June 30 is the tax year) and paid in two installments. Taxes usually require proration. If, for example, the seller had paid the first installment of a given year's taxes but completed the sale before that tax period was over, he or she would receive a credit for the remainder of that period's taxes. If, on the other hand, the seller retained the property through part of the second tax period but had not yet paid taxes for that period, the amount due would be prorated between seller and buyer, with the seller having to pay for the portion of the tax period during which he or she still owned the property.

Insurance. Fire insurance is normally paid for one year in advance. If the buyer assumes a fire insurance policy that has not yet expired, the seller is entitled to a prorated refund of the unused premium.

Interest. If a loan of record is being taken over by the new buyer, interest would be prorated between buyer and seller.

Rents. Prepaid rents will be prorated in cases involving income-producing properties.

Closing Statements

Procedure for Closing Statements

Closing statements do not follow usual bookkeeping formulas. In a normal accounting situation, such as balancing a checkbook, all the credits (deposits to the account) are added. Then all the debits (checks written) are added and deducted from the credits and the remainder is the balance.

At a closing, a separate statement is issued for both the buyer and the seller. Each **settlement sheet** will include **debits** (amounts owed) and **credits** (amounts entitled to receive). In contrast to usual accounting procedures, on the seller's settlement sheet, all the credits to the seller are added (selling price of the property, prorations, etc.). Any debits owed by the seller are then added and deducted from the credits. The difference then is written as a cash credit (usually) to the seller, and the escrow forwards a check for this amount at the close of escrow.

On the buyer's settlement sheet, the buyer is charged (debited) with the purchase price of the property. The loans the buyer has obtained are credited to him or her. Cash is credited, prorations may be debited or credited (as the case warrants) and escrow fees and closing costs are debited. The difference between the total debits and credits usually is called for in cash by the escrow agent. The cash payment into escrow becomes an additional credit and forces the account to balance. Because of the forced balances, the totals on the buyer's and seller's statements will be different from each other and from the purchase price.

Example of a Closing Statement

A typical situation involving an escrow closing statement may assist you in understanding the allocation of costs.

Mr. and Mrs. Allen are purchasing a single-family residence from Mr. and Mrs. Baxter. The property is located in 15 Tract 6 in the Via Pedro Estates in Newport Beach, California. The purchase price is $150,000. Terms are $30,000 cash, with the seller carrying back a first trust deed for the balance. The close of escrow is October 1, 1986. The purchaser is to assume the first trust deed payable at $820 per month, including interest at 9.5 percent. The seller has paid the interest up to September 1, 1986. Taxes for the year were $1,200 and have not been paid.

The purchaser is to assume a one-year fire insurance policy with a prepaid premium of $360 and a beginning date of June 1, 1986. The parties agreed that escrow expenses of $410 would be divided equally and the standard title insurance policy of $350 would be paid by the sellers. The sellers also are to pay the broker's commission of five percent of the sales price.

The closing statements for this transaction are as follows:

Seller's Statement

Debit		Credit	
First trust deed	$120,000	Selling price	$150,000
Commission	7,500	Prepaid insurance	120
Property taxes	300		
Title insurance	350		
Escrow	205		
Interest	950		
Subtotal	$129,305		
Cash to seller	20,815		
Total	$150,120	Total	$150,120

Buyer's Statement

Debit		Credit	
Purchase price	$150,000	First trust deed assumed	$120,000
Escrow	205	Accrued interest	950
Prepaid insurance	120	Property taxes	300
		Subtotal	$121,250
		Final payment	29,075
Total	$150,325	Total	$150,325

Broker's Added Responsibility

Despite the care taken in escrow, mistakes can be made. The real estate broker's final duties are to meet with the buyers or sellers and explain the closing statement, to help them understand all charges and credits on the statement and to verify that they have received the correct amount from escrow or paid the correct amount into escrow.

Escrow is complete when:

1. The escrow agent sends the deed and deeds of trust to the recorder's office to be recorded. This offers protection of the title to the buyer and of the lien to the lender.

2. The escrow agent sends the closing statements to the seller and buyer showing the disbursement of funds.

3. The escrow agent forwards the title policy insuring the buyer of marketable title, except for certain items; the agent sends the original copy to the buyer.

Title Insurance

Title insurance insures the ownership of real property (land, buildings and minerals below the surface) against any encumbrances and other items that may cloud the title. These are primarily claims that might be made by a third party against the property. Buyers are assured that a thorough search has been made of all public records affecting the property being purchased and that they have a marketable title.

Title insurance is paid for once, at the time title passes from one owner to another, and it remains in effect until the property is sold again, at which time title passes to the new owner. If a property owner dies, title insurance continues to protect his or her heirs.

Both the lender and the buyer should have title insurance; the buyer to ensure clear title and thus protect his or her investment and the lender to protect his or her interest in the property.

The three basic types of policies are standard, extended coverage and American Land Title Association (ALTA) loan policy.

Standard Policy

The policy usually used by the buyer is known as a CLTA policy (California Land Title Association). This policy, usually paid for by the seller, is called a **standard policy.** It insures the owner for the amount of the purchase price against the following risks:

1. risks of record; and

2. off-record risks not disclosed in a search of public record, including forged deeds, impersonation and lack of capacity of the parties.

A standard policy does not insure against:

1. defects in the title known to the insured at the time the policy was issued but not disclosed to the insurance company;

2. unrecorded easements and liens;

3. rights of possession not shown by the record but ascertainable by physical inspection of the land or by survey;

4. mining claims, patent reservations and claims on water rights; and

5. zoning ordinance.

A sample CLTA policy is shown in Figure 8.6.

Figure 8.6
Sample CLTA Title
Insurance Policy

 **TICOR TITLE INSURANCE**   **Policy of Title Insurance**

SUBJECT TO SCHEDULE B AND THE CONDITIONS AND STIPULATIONS HEREOF, TICOR TITLE INSURANCE COMPANY OF CALIFORNIA, a California corporation, herein called the Company, insures the insured, as of Date of Policy shown in Schedule A, against loss or damage, not exceeding the amount of insurance stated in Schedule A, and costs, attorneys' fees and expenses which the Company may become obligated to pay hereunder, sustained or incurred by said insured by reason of:

1. Title to the estate or interest described in Schedule A being vested other than as stated therein;

2. Any defect in or lien or encumbrance on such title;

3. Unmarketability of such title; or

4. Any lack of the ordinary right of an abutting owner for access to at least one physically open street or highway if the land, in fact, abuts upon one or more such streets or highways;

and in addition, as to an insured lender only;

5. Invalidity of the lien of the insured mortgage upon said estate or interest except to the extent that such invalidity, or claim thereof, arises out of the transaction evidenced by the insured mortgage and is based upon

    a. usury, or
    b. any consumer credit protection or truth in lending law;

6. Priority of any lien or encumbrance over the lien of the insured mortgage, said mortgage being shown in Schedule B in the order of its priority; or

7. Invalidity of any assignment of the insured mortgage, provided such assignment is shown in Schedule B.

SAMPLE FORM

TICOR TITLE INSURANCE COMPANY OF CALIFORNIA

By _Gerald L. Ippel_   President

Attest _Eiichi E. Everlach_   Secretary

TO 1012 CA (5-86) California Land Title Association Standard Coverage Policy – 1973 (Amended 12-6-85 and 2-20-86)   CAT NO NN00240

Source: Ticor

Figure 8.6 (continued)

Schedule B Part I

1. Taxes or assessments which are not shown as existing liens by the records of any taxing authority that levies taxes or assessments on real property or by the public records.

Proceedings by a public agency which may result in taxes or assessments, or notices of such proceedings, whether or not shown by the records of such agency or by the public records.

2. Any facts, rights, interests or claims which are not shown by the public records but which could be ascertained by an inspection of the land or by making inquiry of persons in possession thereof.

3. Easements, liens or encumbrances, or claims thereof, which are not shown by the public records.

4. Discrepancies, conflicts in boundary lines, shortage in area, encroachments, or any other facts which a correct survey would disclose, and which are not shown by the public records.

5. (a) Unpatented mining claims; (b) reservations or exceptions in patents or in Acts authorizing the issuance thereof; (c) water rights, claims or title to water, whether or not the matters excepted under (a), (b), or (c) are shown by the public records.

6. Any right, title, interest, estate or easement in land beyond the lines of the area specifically described or referred to in Schedule C, or in abutting streets, roads, avenues, alleys, lanes, ways or waterways, but nothing in this paragraph shall modify or limit the extent to which the ordinary right of an abutting owner for access to a physically open street or highway is insured by this policy.

7. Any law, ordinance or governmental regulation (including but not limited to building and zoning ordinances) restricting or regulating or prohibiting the occupancy, use or enjoyment of the land, or regulating the character, dimensions or location of any improvement now or hereafter erected on the land, or prohibiting a separation in ownership or a change in the dimensions or area of the land or any parcel of which the land is or was a part, whether or not shown by the public records at Date of Policy, or the effect of any violation of any such law, ordinance or governmental regulation, whether or not shown by the public records at Date of Policy.

8. Rights of eminent domian or governmental rights of police power unless notice of the exercise of such rights appears in the public records.

9. Defects, liens, encumbrances, adverse claims, or other matters (a) whether or not shown by the public records at Date of Policy, but created, suffered, assumed or agreed to by the insured claimant; (b) not shown by the public records and not otherwise excluded from coverage but known to the insured claimant either at Date of Policy or at the date such claimant acquired an estate or interest insured by this policy or acquired the insured mortgage and not disclosed in writing by the insured claimant to the Company prior to the date such insured claimant became an insured hereunder; (c) resulting in no loss or damage to the insured claimant; (d) attaching or created subsequent to Date of Policy; or (e) resulting in loss or damage which would not have been sustained if the insured claimant had been a purchaser or encumbrancer for value without knowledge.

10. Any facts, rights, interests or claims which are not shown by the public records but which could be ascertained by making inquiry of the lessors in the lease or leases described or referred in Schedule A.

11. The effect of any failure to comply with the terms, covenants and conditions of the lease or leases described or referred to in Schedule A.

Conditions and Stipulations

1. Definition of Terms

The following terms when used in this policy mean:

(a) "insured": the insured named in Schedule A, and, subject to any rights or defenses the Company may have had against the named insured, those who succeed to the interest of such insured by operation of law as distinguished from purchase including, but not limited to, heirs, distributees, devisees, survivors, personal representatives, next of kin, or corporate or fiduciary successors. The term "insured" also includes (i) the owner of the indebtedness secured by the insured mortgage and each successor in ownership of such indebtedness (reserving, however, all rights and defenses as to any such successor who acquires the indebtedness by operation of law as described in the first sentence of this subparagraph (a) that the Company would have had against the successor's transferor), and further includes (ii) any governmental agency or instrumentality which is an insurer or guarantor under an insurance contract or guaranty insuring or guaranteeing said indebtedness, or any part thereof, whether named as an insured herein or not, and (iii) the parties designated in paragraph 2(a) of these Conditions and Stipulations.

(b) "insured claimant": an insured claiming loss or damage hereunder.

(c) "insured lender": the owner of an insured mortgage.

(d) "insured mortgage": a mortgage shown in Schedule B, the owner of which is named as an insured in Schedule A.

(e) "knowledge": actual knowledge, not constructive knowledge or notice which may be imputed to an insured by reason of any public records.

(f) "land": the land described specifically or by reference in Schedule C, and improvements affixed thereto which by law constitute real property; provided, however, the term "land" does not include any area excluded by paragraph 6 of Part I of Schedule B of this Policy.

(g) "mortgage": mortgage, deed of trust, trust deed, or other security instrument.

(h) "public records": those records which by law impart constructive notice of matters relating to the land.

(Conditions and Stipulations Continued on the Inside of the Last Page of This Policy)

Figure 8.6 (continued)

(Conditions and Stipulations Continued from Reverse Side of Policy Face)

2. (a) Continuation of Insurance after Acquisition of Title by Insured Lender

If this policy insures the owner of the indebtedness secured by the insured mortgage, this policy shall continue in force as of Date of Policy in favor of such insured who acquires all or any part of said estate or interest in the land described in Schedule C by foreclosure, trustee's sale, conveyance in lieu of foreclosure, or other legal manner which discharges the lien of the insured mortgage, and if such insured is a corporation, its transferee of the estate or interest so acquired, provided the transferee is the parent or wholly owned subsidiary of such insured; and in favor of any governmental agency or instrumentality which acquires all or any part of the estate or interest pursuant to a contract of insurance or guaranty insuring or guaranteeing the indebtedness secured by the insured mortgage. After any such acquisition the amount of insurance hereunder, exclusive of costs, attorneys' fees and expenses which the Company may be obligated to pay, shall not exceed the least of:

(i) the amount of insurance stated in Schedule A;

(ii) the amount of the unpaid principal of the indebtedness plus interest thereon, as determined under paragraph 6(a) (iii) hereof, expenses of foreclosure and amounts advanced to protect the lien of the insured mortgage and secured by said insured mortgage at the time of acquisition of such estate or interest in the land; or

(iii) the amount paid by any governmental agency or instrumentality, if such agency or instrumentality is the insured claimant, in acquisition of such estate or interest in satisfaction of its insurance contract or guaranty.

(b) Continuation of Insurance after Conveyance of Title

The coverage of this policy shall continue in force as of Date of Policy, in favor of an insured so long as such insured retains an estate or interest in the land, or owns an indebtedness secured by a purchase money mortgage given by a purchaser from such insured, or so long as such insured shall have liability by reason of covenants of warranty made by such insured in any transfer or conveyance of such estate or interest; provided, however, this policy shall not continue in force in favor of any purchaser from such insured of either said estate or interest or the indebtedness secured by a purchase money mortgage given to such insured.

3. Defense and Prosecution of Actions—Notice of Claim to be Given by an Insured Claimant

(a) The Company, at its own cost and without undue delay, shall provide for the defense of an insured in litigation to the extent that such litigation involves an alleged defect, lien, encumbrance or other matter insured against by this policy.

(b) The insured shall notify the Company promptly in writing (i) in case of any litigation as set forth in (a) above, (ii) in case knowledge shall come to an insured hereunder of any claim of title or interest which is adverse to the title to the estate or interest or the lien of the insured mortgage, as insured, and which might cause loss or damage for which the Company may be liable by virtue of this policy, or (iii) if title to the estate or interest or the lien of the insured mortgage, as insured, is rejected as unmarketable. If such prompt notice shall not be given to the Company, then as to such insured all liability of the Company shall cease and terminate in regard to the matter or matters for which such prompt notice is required; provided, however, that failure to notify shall in no case prejudice the rights of any such insured under this policy unless the Company shall be prejudiced by such failure and then only to the extent of such prejudice.

(c) The Company shall have the right at its own cost to institute and without undue delay prosecute any action or proceeding or to do any other act which in its opinion may be necessary or desirable to establish the title to the estate or interest or the lien of the insured mortgage, as insured; and the Company may take any appropriate action, whether or not it shall be liable under the terms of this policy, and shall not thereby concede liability or waive any provision of this policy.

(d) Whenever the Company shall have brought any action or interposed a defense as required or permitted by the provisions of this policy, the Company may pursue any such litigation to final determination by a court of competent jurisdiction and expressly reserves the right, in its sole discretion, to appeal from any adverse judgment or order.

(e) In all cases where this policy permits or requires the Company to prosecute or provide for the defense of any action or proceeding, the insured hereunder shall secure to the Company the right to so prosecute or provide defense in such action or proceeding, and all appeals therein, and permit the Company to use, at its option, the name of such insured for such purpose. Whenever requested by the Company, such insured shall give the Company, at the Company's expense, all reasonable aid (1) in any such action or proceeding in effecting settlement, securing evidence, obtaining witnesses, or prosecuting or defending such action or proceeding, and (2) in any other act which in the opinion of the Company may be necessary or desirable to establish the title to the estate or interest or the lien of the insured mortgage, as insured, including but not limited to executing corrective or other documents.

4. Proof of Loss or Damage—Limitation of Action

In addition to the notices required under paragraph 3(b) of these Conditions and Stipulations, a proof of loss or damage, signed and sworn to by the insured claimant shall be furnished to the Company within 90 days after the insured claimant shall ascertain or determine the facts giving rise to such loss or damage. Such proof of loss or damage shall describe the defect in, or lien or encumbrance on the title, or other matter insured against by this policy which constitutes the basis of loss or damage, and, when appropriate, state the basis of calculating the amount of such loss or damage.

Should such proof of loss or damage fail to state facts sufficient to enable the Company to determine its liability hereunder, insured claimant, at the written request of the Company, shall furnish such additional information as may reasonably be necessary to make such determination.

No right of action shall accrue to insured claimant until 30 days after such proof of loss or damage shall have been furnished. Failure to furnish such proof of loss or damage shall terminate any liability of the Company under this policy as to such loss or damage.

5. Options to Pay or Otherwise Settle Claims and Options to Purchase Indebtedness

The Company shall have the option to pay or otherwise settle for or in the name of an insured claimant any claim insured against, or to terminate all liability and obligations of the Company hereunder by paying or tendering payment of the amount of insurance under this policy together with any costs, attorneys' fees and expenses incurred up to the time of such payment or tender of payment by the insured claimant and authorized by the Company. In case loss or damage is claimed under this policy by the owner of the indebtedness secured by the insured mortgage, the Company shall have the further option to purchase such indebtedness for the amount owing thereon together with all costs, attorneys' fees and expenses which the Company is obligated to pay. If the Company offers to purchase said indebtedness as herein provided, the owner of such indebtedness shall transfer and assign said indebtedness and the mortgage and any collateral securing the same to the Company upon payment therefor as herein provided. Upon such offer being made by the Company, all liability and obligations of the Company hereunder to the owner of the indebtedness secured by said insured mortgage, other than the obligation to purchase said indebtedness pursuant to this paragraph, are terminated.

6. Determination and Payment of Loss

(a) The liability of the Company under this policy shall in no case exceed the least of:

(i) the actual loss of the insured claimant; or

(ii) the amount of insurance stated in Schedule A, or, if applicable, the amount of insurance as defined in paragraph 2(a) hereof; or

(iii) if this policy insures the owner of the indebtedness secured by the insured mortgage, and provided said owner is the insured claimant, the amount of the unpaid principal of said indebtedness, plus interest thereon, provided such amount shall not include any additional principal indebtedness created subsequent to Date of Policy, except as to amounts advanced to protect the lien of the insured mortgage and secured thereby.

(b) The Company will pay, in addition to any loss insured against by this policy, all costs imposed upon an insured in litigation carried on by the Company for such insured, and all costs, attorneys' fees and expenses in litigation carried on by such insured with the written authorization of the Company.

(c) When the amount of loss or damage has been definitely fixed in accordance with the conditions of this policy, the loss or damage shall be payable within 30 days thereafter.

7. Limitation of Liability

No claim shall arise or be maintainable under this policy (a) if the Company, after having received notice of an alleged defect, lien or encumbrance insured against hereunder, by litigation or otherwise, removes such defect, lien or encumbrance or establishes the title, or the lien of the insured mortgage, as insured, within a reasonable time after receipt of such notice; (b) in the event of litigation until there has been a final determination by a court of competent jurisdiction, and disposition of all appeals therefrom, adverse to the title or to the lien of the insured mortgage, as insured, as provided in paragraph 3 hereof; or (c) for liability voluntarily admitted or assumed by an insured without prior written consent of the Company.

(Conditions and Stipulations Continued and Concluded on Reverse Side of This Page)

SAMPLE FORM

Figure 8.6 (continued)

(Conditions and Stipulations Continued and Concluded from Reverse Side of This Page)

8. Reduction of Insurance—Termination of Liability

All payments under this policy, except payment made for costs, attorneys' fees and expenses, shall reduce the amount of the insurance pro tanto; provided, however, if the owner of the indebtedness secured by the insured mortgage is an insured hereunder, then such payments, prior to the acquisition of title to said estate or interest as provided in paragraph 2(a) of these Conditions and Stipulations, shall not reduce pro tanto the amount of the insurance afforded hereunder as to any such insured, except to the extent that such payments reduce the amount of the indebtedness secured by such mortgage.

Payment in full by any person or voluntary satisfaction or release of the insured mortgage shall terminate all liability of the Company to an insured owner of the indebtedness secured by the insured mortgage, except as provided in paragraph 2(a) hereof.

9. Liability Noncumulative

It is expressly understood that the amount of insurance under this policy as to the insured owner of the estate or interest covered by this policy, shall be reduced by any amount the Company may pay under any policy insuring (a) a mortgage shown or referred to in Schedule B hereof which is a lien on the estate or interest covered by this policy, or (b) a mortgage hereafter executed by an insured which is a charge or lien on the estate or interest described or referred to in Schedule A, and the amount so paid shall be deemed a payment under this policy. The Company shall have the option to apply to the payment of any such mortgage any amount that otherwise would be payable hereunder to the insured owner of the estate or interest covered by this policy and the amount so paid shall be deemed a payment under this policy to said insured owner.

The provisions of this paragraph 9 shall not apply to an owner of the indebtedness secured by the insured mortgage, unless such insured acquires title to said estate or interest in satisfaction of said indebtedness or any part thereof.

10. Subrogation Upon Payment or Settlement

Whenever the Company shall have paid or settled a claim under this policy, all right of subrogation shall vest in the Company unaffected by any act of the insured claimant, except that the owner of the indebtedness secured by the insured mortgage may release or substitute the personal liability of any debtor or guarantor, or extend or otherwise modify the terms of payment, or release a portion of the estate or interest from the lien of the insured mortgage, or release any collateral security for the indebtedness, provided such act occurs prior to receipt by such insured of notice of any claim of title or interest adverse to the title to the estate or interest or the priority of the lien of the insured mortgage and does not result in any loss of

priority of the lien of the insured mortgage. The Company shall be subrogated to and be entitled to all rights and remedies which such insured claimant would have had against any person or property in respect to such claim had this policy not been issued, and the Company is hereby authorized and empowered to sue, compromise or settle in its name or in the name of the insured to the full extent of the loss sustained by the Company. If requested by the Company, the insured shall execute any and all documents to evidence the within subrogation. If the payment does not cover the loss of such insured claimant, the Company shall be subrogated to such rights and remedies in the proportion which said payment bears to the amount of said loss, but such subrogation shall be in subordination to an insured mortgage. If loss should result from any act of such insured claimant, such act shall not void this policy, but the Company, in that event, shall as to such insured claimant be required to pay only that part of any losses insured against hereunder which shall exceed the amount, if any, lost to the Company by reason of the impairment of the right of subrogation.

11. Liability Limited to this Policy

This instrument together with all endorsements and other instruments, if any, attached hereto by the Company is the entire policy and contract between the insured and the Company. Any claim of loss or damage, whether or not based on negligence, and which arises out of the status of the lien of the insured mortgage or of the title to the estate or interest covered hereby, or any action asserting such claim, shall be restricted to the provisions and Conditions and Stipulations of this policy.

No amendment of or endorsement to this policy can be made except by writing endorsed hereon or attached hereto signed by either the President, a Vice President, the Secretary, an Assistant Secretary, or validating officer or authorized signatory of the Company.

No payment shall be made without producing this policy for endorsement of such payment unless the policy be lost or destroyed, in which case proof of such loss or destruction shall be furnished to the satisfaction of the Company.

12. Notices, Where Sent

All notices required to be given the Company and any statement in writing required to be furnished the Company shall be addressed to its Principal Office: Claims Department, 6300 Wilshire Boulevard, P.O. Box 92792, Los Angeles, California 90009.

13. THE PREMIUM SPECIFIED IN SCHEDULE A IS THE ENTIRE CHARGE FOR TITLE SEARCH, TITLE EXAMINATION AND TITLE INSURANCE.

Figure 8.6 (continued)

CAT. NO. NN00645
TO 1961 A (6-83) California Land Title Association Standard Coverage Policy-1973 or American Land Title Association Owners Policy Form B-1970

Schedule A

Policy No.:	Date of Policy:
Amount of Insurance: $	Premium: $

1. Name of Insured:

2. The estate or interest referred to herein is at Date of Policy vested in:

SAMPLE FORM

3. The estate or interest in the land described in Schedule C and which is covered by this policy is a fee.

Figure 8.6 (continued)

CAT. NO. NN00866
TO 1991 B (1-84) California Land Title Association Standard Coverage Policy - 1973

Schedule B

This policy does not insure against loss or damage, nor against costs, attorneys' fees or expenses, any or all of which arise by reason of the following:

Part I

All matters set forth in paragraphs numbered 1 (one) to 11 (eleven) inclusive on the inside cover sheet of this policy under the heading of Schedule B Part I.

Part II

SAMPLE FORM

Figure 8.6 (continued)

CAT. NO. NN00525
TO 1866 C (1-84) American Land Title Association Loan Policy-1970 with ALTA Endorsement Form 1 Coverage or American Land Title Association Owner's Policy Form B-1970 or California Land Title Association Standard Coverage Policy—1973

Schedule C

The land referred to herein is described as follows:

SAMPLE FORM

Extended Coverage Policies

An **extended policy** covers all risks that are covered by the standard policy, plus some risks that the standard policy does not cover. These include defects that might not be disclosed by a physical inspection of the property, such as unrecorded easements and liens or rights in possession. Buyers may purchase this policy at an increased premium.

ALTA Policy

An **ALTA policy** is an extended coverage policy and can be purchased only for the benefit of the *lender.* It insures that the lender has a valid and enforceable lien, subject only to the exclusions from coverage noted in the exception schedule of the policy. It insures the lender for the amount of the loan, not the purchase price of the property. Figure 8.7 shows a sample ALTA loan policy.

Figure 8.7
Sample ALTA
Loan Policy

TICOR TITLE INSURANCE   **Policy of Title Insurance**

SUBJECT TO THE EXCLUSIONS FROM COVERAGE, THE EXCEPTIONS CONTAINED IN SCHEDULE B AND THE PROVISIONS OF THE CONDITIONS AND STIPULATIONS HEREOF, TICOR TITLE INSURANCE COMPANY (a Stock Company), a California corporation, herein called the Company, insures, as of Date of Policy shown in Schedule A, against loss or damage, not exceeding the amount of insurance stated in Schedule A, and costs, attorneys' fees and expenses which the Company may become obligated to pay hereunder, sustained or incurred by the insured by reason of:

1. Title to the estate or interest described in Schedule A being vested otherwise than as stated therein,

2. Any defect in or lien or encumbrance on such title,

3. Lack of a right of access to and from the land,

4. Unmarketability of such title,

5. The invalidity or unenforceability of the lien of the insured mortgage upon said estate or interest except to the extent that such invalidity or unenforceability, or claim thereof, arises out of the transaction evidenced by the insured mortgage and is based upon

      a. usury, or
      b. any consumer credit protection or truth in lending law,

6. The priority of any lien or encumbrance over the lien of the insured mortgage,

7. Any statutory lien for labor or material which now has gained or hereafter may gain priority over the lien of the insured mortgage, except any such lien arising from an improvement on the land contracted for and commenced subsequent to Date of Policy not financed in whole or in part by proceeds of the indebtedness secured by the insured mortgage which at Date of Policy the insured has advanced or is obligated to advance, or

8. The invalidity or unenforceability of any assignment, shown in Schedule A, of the insured mortgage or the failure of said assignment to vest title to the insured mortgage in the named insured assignee free and clear of all liens.

This policy shall not be valid or binding until countersigned below by a validating signatory of the Company

SAMPLE FORM
TICOR TITLE INSURANCE COMPANY

By _Gerald L. Ippel_   President

Attest _Erich E. Everlach_   Secretary

Countersigned,

By _____
          Validating Signatory

TO 2609 (11-84) American Land Title Association Loan Policy 1970 (Amended 10/17/70 and 10/17/84)   CAT NO NN01185

Source: Ticor

Figure 8.7 (continued)

Schedule of Exclusions from Coverage

The following matters are expressly excluded from the coverage of this policy:

1. (a) Governmental police power.

(b) Any law, ordinance or governmental regulation relating to environmental protection.

(c) Any law, ordinance or governmental regulation (including but not limited to building and zoning ordinances) restricting or regulating or prohibiting the occupancy, use or enjoyment of the land, or regulating the character, dimensions or location of any improvement now or hereafter erected on the land, or prohibiting a separation in ownership or a change in the dimensions or area of the land or any parcel of which the land is or was a part.

(d) The effect of any violation of the matters excluded under (a), (b) or (c) above, unless notice of a defect, lien or encumbrance resulting from a violation has been recorded at Date of Policy in those records in which under state statutes deeds, mortgages, lis pendens, liens or other title encumbrances must be recorded in order to impart constructive notice to purchasers of the land for value and without knowledge; provided, however, that without limitation, such records shall not be construed to include records in any of the offices of federal, state or local environmental protection, zoning, building, health or public safety authorities.

2. Rights of eminent domain unless notice of the exercise of such rights appears in the public records at Date of Policy.

3. Defects, liens, encumbrances, adverse claims, or other matters (a) created, suffered, assumed or agreed to by the insured claimant; (b) not known to the Company and not shown by the public records but known to the insured claimant either at Date of Policy or at the date such claimant acquired an estate or interest insured by this policy or acquired the insured mortgage and not disclosed in writing by the insured claimant to the Company prior to the date such insured claimant became an insured hereunder; (c) resulting in no loss or damage to the insured claimant; (d) attaching or created subsequent to Date of Policy (except to the extent insurance is afforded herein as to any statutory lien for labor or material).

4. Unenforceability of the lien of the insured mortgage because of failure of the insured at Date of Policy or any subsequent owner of the indebtedness to comply with applicable "doing business" laws of the state in which the land is situated.

SAMPLE FORM Conditions and Stipulations

1. Definition of Terms

The following terms when used in this policy mean:

(a) "insured": the insured named in Schedule A. The term "insured" also includes (i) the owner of the indebtedness secured by the insured mortgage and each successor in ownership of such indebtedness (reserving, however, all rights and defenses as to any such successor who acquires the indebtedness by operation of law as distinguished from purchase including, but not limited to, heirs, distributees, devisees, survivors, personal representatives, next of kin or corporate or fiduciary successors that the Company would have had against the successor's transferor), and further includes (ii) any governmental agency or instrumentality which is an insurer or guarantor under an insurance contract or guaranty insuring or guaranteeing said indebtedness, or any part thereof, whether named as an insured herein or not, and (iii) the parties designated in paragraph 2 (a) of these Conditions and Stipulations.

(b) "insured claimant": an insured claiming loss or damage hereunder.

(c) "knowledge": actual knowledge, not constructive knowledge or notice which may be imputed to an insured by reason of any public records.

(d) "land": the land described, specifically or by reference in Schedule A, and improvements affixed thereto which by law constitute real property, provided, however, the term "land" does not include any property beyond the lines of the area specifically described or referred to in Schedule A, nor any right, title, interest, estate or easement in abutting streets, roads, avenues, alleys, lanes, ways or waterways, but nothing herein shall modify or limit the extent to which a right of access to and from the land is insured by this policy.

(e) "mortgage": mortgage, deed of trust, trust deed, or other security instrument.

(f) "public records": those records which by law impart constructive notice of matters relating to said land.

2. Continuation of Insurance after Acquisition of Title

(a) This policy shall continue in force as of Date of Policy in favor of an insured who acquires all or any part of the estate or interest in the land described in Schedule A by foreclosure, trustee's sale, conveyance in lieu of foreclosure, or other legal manner which discharges the lien of the insured mortgage, and if the insured is a corporation, its transferee of the estate or interest so acquired, provided the transferee is the parent or wholly owned subsidiary of the insured, and in favor of any governmental agency or instrumentality which acquires all or any part of the estate or interest pursuant to a contract of insurance or guaranty insuring or guaranteeing the indebtedness secured by the insured mortgage, provided that the amount of insurance hereunder after such acquisition, exclusive of costs, attorneys' fees and expenses which the Company may become obligated to pay, shall not exceed the least of:

(i) the amount of insurance stated in Schedule A,

(ii) the amount of the unpaid principal of the indebtedness as defined in paragraph 8 hereof, plus interest thereon, expenses of foreclosure and amounts advanced to protect the lien of the insured mortgage and secured by said

insured mortgage at the time of acquisition of such estate or interest in the land, or

(iii) the amount paid by any governmental agency or instrumentality, if such agency or instrumentality is the insured claimant, in the acquisition of such estate or interest in satisfaction of its insurance contract or guaranty.

(b) Continuation of Insurance after Conveyance of Title

The coverage of this policy shall continue in force as of Date of Policy in favor of an insured so long as such insured retains an estate or interest in the land, or holds an indebtedness secured by a purchase money mortgage given by a purchaser from such insured, or so long as such insured shall have liability by reason of covenants of warranty made by such insured in any transfer or conveyance of such estate or interest; provided, however, this policy shall not continue in force in favor of any purchaser from such insured of either said estate or interest or the indebtedness secured by a purchase money mortgage given to such insured.

3. Defense and Prosecution of Actions — Notice of Claim to be Given by an Insured Claimant

(a) The Company, at its own cost and without undue delay, shall provide for the defense of an insured in all litigation consisting of actions or proceedings commenced against such insured, or defenses, restraining orders or injunctions interposed against a foreclosure of the insured mortgage or a defense interposed against an insured in an action to enforce a contract for a sale of the indebtedness secured by the insured mortgage, or a sale of the estate or interest in said land, to the extent that such litigation is founded upon an alleged defect, lien, encumbrance, or other matter insured against by this policy.

(b) The insured shall notify the Company promptly in writing (i) in case any action or proceeding is begun or defense or restraining order or injunction is interposed as set forth in (a) above, (ii) in case knowledge shall come to an insured hereunder of any claim of title or interest which is adverse to the title to the estate or interest or the lien of the insured mortgage, as insured, and which might cause loss or damage for which the Company may be liable by virtue of this policy, or (iii) if title to the estate or interest or the lien of the insured mortgage, as insured, is rejected as unmarketable. If such prompt notice shall not be given to the Company, then as to such insured all liability of the Company shall cease and terminate in regard to the matter or matters for which such prompt notice is required; provided, however, that failure to notify shall in no case prejudice the rights of any such insured under this policy unless the Company shall be prejudiced by such failure and then only to the extent of such prejudice.

(c) The Company shall have the right at its own cost to institute and without undue delay prosecute any action or proceeding or to do any other act which in its opinion may be necessary or desirable to establish the title to the estate or interest or the lien of the insured mortgage, as insured, and the Company may take any appropriate action under the terms of this policy, whether or not it shall be liable thereunder, and shall not thereby concede liability or waive any provision of this policy.

(Conditions and Stipulations Continued and Concluded on Last Page of This Policy)

Figure 8.7 (continued)

(Conditions and Stipulations Continued and Concluded from Reverse Side of Policy Face)

(d) Whenever the Company shall have brought any action or interposed a defense as required or permitted by the provisions of this policy, the Company may pursue any such litigation to final determination by a court of competent jurisdiction and expressly reserves the right, in its sole discretion, to appeal from any adverse judgment or order.

(e) In all cases where this policy permits or requires the Company to prosecute or provide for the defense of any action or proceeding, the insured hereunder shall secure to the Company the right to so prosecute or provide defense in such action or proceeding, and all appeals therein, and permit the Company to use, at its option, the name of such insured for such purpose. Whenever requested by the Company, such insured shall give the Company all reasonable aid in any such action or proceeding, in effecting settlement, securing evidence, obtaining witnesses, or prosecuting or defending such action or proceeding, and the Company shall reimburse such insured for any expense so incurred.

4. Notice of Loss — Limitation of Action

In addition to the notices required under paragraph 3 (b) of these Conditions and Stipulations, a statement in writing of any loss or damage for which it is claimed the Company is liable under this policy shall be furnished to the Company within 90 days after such loss or damage shall have been determined and no right of action shall accrue to an insured claimant until 30 days after such statement shall have been furnished. Failure to furnish such statement of loss or damage shall terminate any liability of the Company under this policy as to such loss or damage.

5. Options to Pay or Otherwise Settle Claims

The Company shall have the option to pay or otherwise settle for or in the name of an insured claimant any claim insured against or to terminate all liability and obligations of the Company hereunder by paying or tendering payment of the amount of insurance under this policy together with any costs, attorneys' fees and expenses incurred up to the time of such payment or tender of payment by the insured claimant and authorized by the Company. In case loss or damage is claimed under this policy by an insured, the Company shall have the further option to purchase such indebtedness for the amount owing thereon together with all costs, attorneys' fees and expenses which the Company is obligated hereunder to pay. If the Company offers to purchase said indebtedness as herein provided, the owner of such indebtedness shall transfer and assign said indebtedness and the mortgage and any collateral securing the same to the Company upon payment therefor as herein provided.

6. Determination and Payment of Loss

(a) The liability of the Company under this policy shall in no case exceed the least of:

(i) the actual loss of the insured claimant, or

(ii) the amount of insurance stated in Schedule A, or, if applicable, the amount of insurance as defined in paragraph 2 (a) hereof, or

(iii) the amount of the indebtedness secured by the insured mortgage as determined under paragraph 8 hereof, at the time the loss or damage insured against hereunder occurs, together with interest thereon.

(b) The Company will pay, in addition to any loss insured against by this policy, all costs imposed upon an insured in litigation carried on by the Company for such insured, and all costs, attorneys' fees and expenses in litigation carried on by such insured with the written authorization of the Company.

(c) When liability has been definitely fixed in accordance with the conditions of this policy, the loss or damage shall be payable within 30 days thereafter.

7. Limitation of Liability

No claim shall arise or be maintainable under this policy

(a) if the Company, after having received notice of an alleged defect, lien or encumbrance insured against hereunder, by litigation or otherwise, removes such defect, lien or encumbrance or establishes the title, or the lien of the insured mortgage, as insured, within a reasonable time after receipt of such notice,

(b) in the event of litigation until there has been a final determination by a court of competent jurisdiction, and disposition of all appeals therefrom, adverse to the title or to the lien of the insured mortgage, as insured, as provided in paragraph 3 hereof, or

(c) for liability voluntarily assumed by an insured in settling any claim or suit without prior written consent of the Company.

8. Reduction of Liability

(a) All payments under this policy, except payments made for costs, attorneys' fees and expenses, shall reduce the amount of the insurance pro tanto, provided, however, such payments, prior to the acquisition of title to said estate or interest as provided in paragraph 2 (a) of these Conditions and Stipulations, shall not reduce pro tanto the amount of the insurance afforded hereunder except to the extent that such payments reduce the amount of the indebtedness secured by the insured mortgage.

Payment in full by any person or voluntary satisfaction or release of the insured mortgage shall terminate all liability of the Company except as provided in paragraph 2 (a) hereof.

(b) The liability of the Company shall not be increased by additional principal indebtedness created subsequent to Date of Policy, except as to amounts advanced to protect the lien of the insured mortgage and secured thereby. No payment shall be made without producing this policy for endorsement of such payment unless the policy be lost or destroyed, in which case proof of loss or destruction shall be furnished to the satisfaction of the Company.

9. Liability Noncumulative

If the insured acquires title to the estate or interest in satisfaction of the indebtedness secured by the insured mortgage, or any part thereof, it is expressly understood that the amount of insurance under this policy shall be reduced by any amount the Company may pay under any policy insuring a mortgage hereafter executed by an insured which is a charge or lien on the estate or interest described or referred to in Schedule A, and the amount so paid shall be deemed a payment under this policy.

10. Subrogation upon Payment or Settlement

Whenever the Company shall have settled a claim under this policy, all right of subrogation shall vest in the Company unaffected by any act of the insured claimant, except that the owner of the indebtedness secured by the insured mortgage may release or substitute the personal liability of any debtor or guarantor, or extend or otherwise modify the terms of payment, or release a portion of the estate or interest from the lien of the insured mortgage, or release any collateral security for the indebtedness, provided such act occurs prior to receipt by the insured of notice of any claim of title or interest adverse to the title to the estate or interest or the priority of the lien of the insured mortgage and does not result in any loss of priority of the lien of the insured mortgage. The Company shall be subrogated to and be entitled to all rights and remedies which such insured claimant would have had against any person or property in respect to such claim had this policy not been issued, and if requested by the Company, such insured claimant shall transfer to the Company all rights and remedies against any person or property necessary in order to perfect such right of subrogation and shall permit the Company to use the name of such insured claimant in any transaction or litigation involving such rights or remedies. If the payment does not cover the loss of such insured claimant, the Company shall be subrogated to such rights and remedies in the proportion which said payment bears to the amount of said loss, but such subrogation shall be in subordination to the insured mortgage. If loss of priority should result from any act of such insured claimant, such act shall not void this policy, but the Company, in that event, shall be required to pay only that part of any losses insured against hereunder which shall exceed the amount, if any, lost to the Company by reason of the impairment of the right of subrogation.

11. Liability Limited to this Policy

This instrument together with all endorsements and other instruments, if any, attached hereto by the Company is the entire policy and contract between the insured and the Company. Any claim of loss or damage, whether or not based on negligence, and which arises out of the status of the lien of the insured mortgage or of the title to the estate or interest covered hereby or any action asserting such claim, shall be restricted to the provisions and conditions and stipulations of this policy. No amendment of or endorsement to this policy can be made except by writing endorsed hereon or attached hereto signed by either the President, a Vice President, the Secretary, an Assistant Secretary, or validating officer or authorized signatory of the Company.

12. Notices, Where Sent

All notices required to be given the Company and any statement in writing required to be furnished the Company shall include the number of this policy and shall be addressed to its Principal Office, Claims Department, 6300 Wilshire Boulevard, P.O. Box 92792, Los Angeles, California 90009.

SAMPLE FORM

Figure 8.7 (continued)

CAT. NO. NN00338
TO 1448.1 (6-83) American Land Title Association Loan Policy

Schedule A

No.

Date of Policy:

Amount of Insurance:

$

1. Name of Insured:

2. The title to the Fee Simple estate in said land is at the date hereof vested in:

3. The mortgage and assignments, if any, covered by this policy are described as follows:

SAMPLE FORM

4. The land referred to in this policy is located in the County of
    State of   and described as follows:

THIS POLICY IS VALID ONLY IF SCHEDULE B IS ATTACHED

Figure 8.7 (continued)

CAT. NO. NN00848
TO 2131 (1-84) American Land Title Association Single Form Policy · 1970 or Loan Policy · 1970

Schedule B

No.

Part I

This policy does not insure against loss or damage by reason of the following:

SAMPLE FORM

Part II
In addition to the matters set forth in Part I of this Schedule, the title to the estate or interest in the land described or referred to in Schedule A is subject to the following matters, if any be shown, but the Company insures that such matters are subordinate to the lien or charge of the insured mortgage upon said estate or interest.

Summary   This chapter defined an escrow officer as an impartial third party used as a depository for all paperwork and monies needed to complete a sales transaction. The parties to escrow are the buyer, the seller and, in some cases, the lender and the escrow officer. Escrow officers can be banks, trust companies, savings and loan associations, insurance companies, attorneys, escrow companies (corporations licensed by the Commissioner of Corporations) and brokers. Brokers have to be an agent of the buyer or the seller to act as escrow agents. California law regulates the activities of escrow officers and their operation.

The procedures for opening, administering and closing an escrow include preparing needed materials, preparing instructions to the escrow agent, calculating prorations, determining fees charged, completing settlement sheets and closing statements and disbursing funds.

The granting of *title insurance* is important. The coverage varies as to whether a policy is standard or extended. Lenders may buy ALTA policies, which provide extended coverage.

Questions

1. All the following preparations are essential in an escrow transaction *except:*
   a. the seller's acceptance of an offer transmitted to buyer.
   b. a binding contract formed between buyer and seller.
   c. a sales commission paid to broker.
   d. conditional delivery of transfer instruments to third party.

2. Which of these must be licensed by the Corporations Commissioner to act as an escrow agent?
   a. independent escrow companies
   b. real estate brokers, if they handle escrows in which they also are the agent
   c. title insurance companies
   d. attorneys at law

3. When a buyer and a seller utilize an escrow agent as a stakeholder, that escrow can only be terminated by:
   a. full performance.
   b. mutual cancellation.
   c. revocation by a party.
   d. any of the above

4. Regarding property tax prorations, which of the following is true?
   a. credit the buyer for taxes he or she has to pay
   b. credit the seller for taxes he or she has paid beyond the escrow date
   c. debit the seller for next year's taxes
   d. any of the above

5. In closing escrow all the following take place *except:*
   a. All pertinent instruments are sent to the title insurance company for recording.
   b. The broker is reimbursed for his or her commission.
   c. Prorations and adjustments are entered on the settlement sheet.
   d. A beneficiary statement is requested from the lender.

6. Which of these statements is *not true* regarding escrow instructions?
   a. They are written instructions from principals to the escrow officer.
   b. Escrow agents can alter instructions if they wish.
   c. Escrow agents can do no more or no less than they are instructed to do.
   d. Instructions must be agreed on by all parties.

7. Which type of title insurance protects against all risks?
   a. extended coverage policy
   b. standard policy
   c. ALTA policy
   d. none of the above

8. The steps in opening an escrow will vary. However, which of these steps are always followed?
   a. Buyers' and sellers' instructions are signed and sent to escrow.
   b. Escrow orders a title search.
   c. All monies are sent to escrow.
   d. All steps are followed.

9. If there is a difference between escrow instructions and the purchase agreement on an important item, the licensee should:
   a. insert in the escrow instructions that all agreements are cancelled and only escrow instructions prevail.
   b. insert in escrow instructions a statement referring to the purchase agreement and stating that escrow instructions take precedence.
   c. amend the purchase agreement to correspond to the escrow instructions.
   d. none of the above

10. Which of these statements would be considered correct? Escrow can be completed or terminated:

    a. by mutual agreement of the parties to escrow.
    b. by the broker advising the escrow holder to cancel the escrow.
    c. when all terms of the escrow instructions have been complied with.
    d. both a and c

11. Escrows are opened for the protection of the:

    a. property.
    b. buyer and seller.
    c. escrow holder.
    d. licensee.

12. If you look through the public records, you will be apt to find:

    a. known existing claims against real estate.
    b. recorded claims against real estate.
    c. valid claims against real estate.
    d. all of the above

13. Proration is one of the responsibilities of the escrow holder. Which of the following expenses is *never* prorated?

    a. real property
    b. commission paid on the sale
    c. prepaid rent
    d. prepaid insurance

14. Which of the following applies to the term "impound account"?

    a. a trust fund for the protection of lender
    b. a sum used to pay borrowers' taxes and insurance
    c. the account will vary from year to year
    d. all statements describe the term

15. Customs in closing a transaction differ in northern and southern California in that:

    a. escrow companies are employed to handle escrows in the south.
    b. title companies are employed to handle escrows in the north.
    c. both a and b
    d. neither a nor b

16. A standard coverage title insurance policy insures against all of the following items *except:*

    a. forgery.
    b. incapacity of parties.
    c. patent reservations.
    d. impersonation.

17. Although real estate brokers do not come under the jurisdiction of the escrow licensing law, they may act as escrow agents:

    a. in another broker's transaction.
    b. if they are the agent of either a buyer or seller.
    c. for another person, covering the other person's transaction.
    d. any of the above

18. Which of the following is covered by an extended but not a standard policy of title insurance?

    a. encroachments
    b. recorded trust deeds
    c. homestead exemptions
    d. tax liens

19. The standard policy of title insurance protects against:

    a. forgery.
    b. incompetence of parties.
    c. anything in the records.
    d. all of the above

20. Brokers can act as escrow agents when they:

    a. are licensed by the Real Estate Commissioner.
    b. are in possession of assets totaling $1,000,000.
    c. represent either the buyer or seller in the transaction.
    d. none of the above

9

Real Property Financing

Chapter Preview   To properly counsel and assist his or her customers, a broker needs a working knowledge of real estate financing. This chapter contains a brief discussion of the money market in California, including a detailed explanation of the steps to take to obtain real estate financing. The discussion includes the best sources for obtaining funds, the instruments used and the types of loans available under given circumstances. The chapter concludes by covering the laws and regulations affecting various types of real estate financing.

Terms To Look For

Acceleration clause	Land contract
Alienation clause	Maker
Blank endorsement	Mortgage Loan Brokerage Law
Cal Vet	Negotiable instrument
Capacity	Noninstitutional lenders
Capital	Partially amortized note
Character	Payee
Conventional loan	Personal defenses
Co-signer	Prepayment penalty
Discount rate	Promissory note
Fair Credit Reporting Act	Qualified endorsement
Fed	Real defenses
Federal Home Loan Bank	Restrictive endorsement
FHA	Special endorsement
FHLMC	Straight note
FNMA	Subordination clause
Fully amortized note	Trust deed
GNMA	VA
Holder in due course	Wraparound mortgage
Institutional lenders	

Sources of Funds: Money Markets

Almost everyone is at some time a user, a buyer or a seller of real estate. On the average, in this country, a person spends approximately 20 percent of his or her lifetime income on some form of real estate, either as rental or purchase, as an investment or as a residence. Because real estate is the largest purchase most people make in their lifetimes, few are prepared to pay cash. Thus, the completion of most real estate sales will depend on funds available in the money market at the time of the transaction.

Because most buyers are unable or unwilling to pay cash for real property, long-term financing in the form of a mortgage loan is necessary. Understanding the use of real estate mortgage money requires an understanding of the sources of these funds. Money to finance real estate purchases is available through two primary money market areas: directly, from someone who has saved this money, or indirectly, from a lending institution that loans money deposited in customers' accounts. You should be constantly aware of the status of the money market in your area, including policies of lenders, interest rates, points and lending costs. Lenders can be generally divided into two groups: **institutional lenders** and noninstitutional lenders.

Institutional Lenders

There are three major types of institutional lenders: commercial banks, savings and loan associations and insurance companies (see Figure 9.1).

**Figure 9.1
Institutional Lenders**

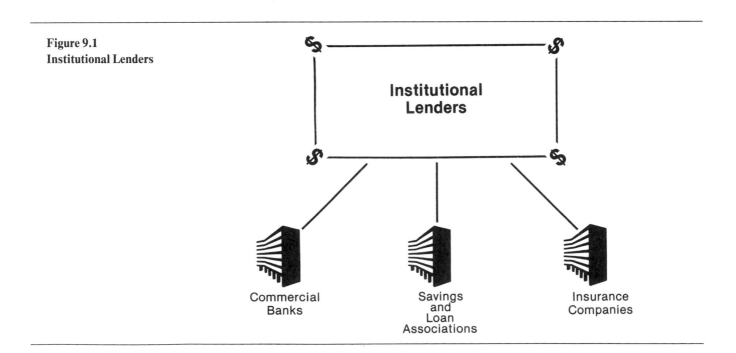

Commercial banks. Commercial banks are familiarly known as the "department stores" of financial institutions because of the variety of operations in which they are engaged. A principal activity of commercial banks is lending money.

In California, banks are either federally chartered or state chartered and they are regulated by federal and state laws, respectively. They tend to favor short-term loans and they follow relatively conservative appraisal and lending practices. Their real estate loans generally are limited to 80 percent of the appraised value of the property, with a term of 25 to 30 years for prime property. Interest rates in banks fluctuate but are traditionally on the low side. Loan fees typically average $50 to $100. Banks are quite versatile in the type of loans they may consider, but they seldom allow secondary financing.

Commercial banks in California distribute their real estate loans as follows:

- approximately 60 percent conventional loans;

- approximately 35 percent FHA loans; and

- approximately five percent VA loans.

Federal Reserve system. The supply and cost of money available from banks and savings and loans is governed by the Federal Reserve bank system (known as the **Fed**). The Federal Reserve system is composed of 12 Federal Reserve districts, each served by a Federal Reserve bank, often called a "banker's bank."

The Fed is empowered to regulate the availability of money for mortgages and other loans in three ways: establishing reserve requirements for member banks, through open market operations and by establishing discount rates.

1. *Reserves*—Each member bank is required to hold in reserve certain funds, the amount of which is set by the Fed. These funds cannot be loaned, thus reducing the money supply in the mortgage market.

2. *Open market operations*—The Fed is allowed to buy and sell government securities. When the Fed buys securities, the sellers have money to put in member banks. This increases the money supply by increasing bank reserves beyond reserve requirements, freeing individual banks to make more loans. When the Fed sells government securities, individual banks' reserves decrease, which in turn decreases their capacity to grant loans.

3. *Establishing discount rates*—To prevent their reserves from being depleted, banks may borrow from the Fed. The interest rate the Fed charges banks for this money is called the **discount rate.** Raising the discount rate leads banks to cover their costs by charging borrowers higher interest rates. This generally discourages the public's desire for loans.

Savings and loan associations. Savings and loan associations account for more home loans than any other institution. S & Ls, as they are familiarly referred to, are state chartered as well as federally chartered and are under the administration of the **Federal Home Loan Bank** system. The Federal Home Loan Bank board governs the operation of all member savings and loan associations, much as the Fed does with banks, by providing a reserve credit system, or "banker's bank," for its members.

Savings and loan associations prefer making home loans rather than loans for other purposes. The rate of interest on such loans varies but is considered relatively high. The traditional term of such loans has been 30 years. S & Ls usually charge a loan fee of one to five percent of the loan amount and generally they charge a prepayment penalty. They are allowed to loan up to 95 percent of the property's appraised value, although an 80 percent loan-to-value ratio is most usual.

■ Savings and loans have begun to emphasize a variety of differently structured loans as a result of the economic climate of the 1970s. Adjustable rate mortgages, known as ARMS, are one of the most popular types. An ARM has a floating or fluctuating interest rate to permit lenders to adjust to changes in inflation and the cost of money.

In California, savings and loan associations distribute their loans as follows:

• Approximately 95 percent are conventional loans.

• Approximately three percent are VA-guaranteed loans.

• Approximately two percent are FHA-insured loans.

Life insurance companies. The lending policies of life insurance companies are governed by the laws of the state in which the company is chartered, the laws of the state in which the loan originates, the policies of management and the availability of loan funds.

Insurance companies supply most of the loans on properties for which large loans are required (commercial properties, shopping centers, industrial properties and hotels). In California, they make loans for up to 75 percent of the property's market value. Company policy usually limits the loan period to not more than from 25 to 30 years. Insurance companies' interest rates often are lower than those of banks or savings and loan institutions. Generally, these loans seldom have due-on-sale clauses.

In California, insurance companies distribute their loans as follows:

1. Approximately 50 percent are FHA and VA loans.

2. Approximately 30 percent are for commercial income development properties.

3. Approximately 20 percent are on higher priced, new or recently built houses.

Noninstitutional Lenders

Noninstitutional lenders that make real estate loans include private individuals, mortgage companies and real estate investment trusts (see Figure 9.2).

Private individuals. As lenders, private individuals do not follow uniform lending practices; in general, they are not subject to national or state licensing laws or the requirements of other regulatory bodies. For this reason, they can take greater risks in their investments.

Generally, private individuals do not use technical credit analysis procedures adopted by institutional lenders. As a result, they make many loans that would be turned down by institutional lenders.

Private individuals make more month-to-month mortgage loans than any other class of mortgages. They issue by far the largest number of junior mortgage loans. They take greater risks by accepting extremely high loan-to-value ratios and their interest rates tend to be correspondingly higher. Most of their loans are conventional loans, usually with a maximum term of ten years, the maturity of most ranging from five to ten years.

Figure 9.2
Noninstitutional
Lenders

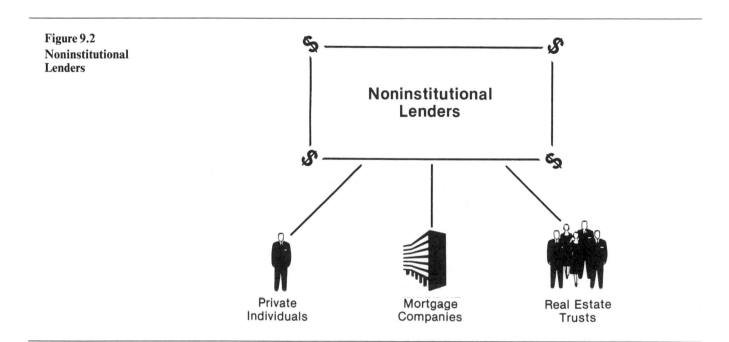

Mortgage companies. Mortgage companies operate for the most part as mortgage loan correspondents of life insurance companies, mutual savings banks (mainly operating in the northeastern states), pension funds and other financial institutions. They may furnish mortgage loans to these institutions from only one metropolitan area or from one state or sometimes from several states.

Because many have sizable funds of their own, mortgage companies not only engage in lending activities but also are involved in other business operations, such as property rentals, leases, property management and insurance. They are free of such confining lending limitations as are placed on institutional lenders. They are active in construction lending and deal predominantly in mortgages readily salable in the secondary market. Mortgage companies generally restrict their conventional loans to selected residential and business risks and to loans in price ranges suitable to the needs of investment firms that compose the secondary market.

Real Estate Investment Trust. The Real Estate Investment Trust was created in 1960 to encourage small investors to pool their resources with others to raise venture capital for real estate transactions. To qualify as a real estate investment trust, there must be at least 100 investors and 90 percent of the real estate investment trust's income must be distributed annually to its investors.

Pension funds. At one time pension funds primarily invested in stocks. However, they now are becoming a more important factor in the mortgage market. They prefer to lend on large projects.

Credit unions. Many credit unions offer funds for first and second deeds of trust. The amount available for first loans is quite small, typically $10,000 to $15,000. They are a good source of secondary financing.

Government Agencies and the Secondary Mortgage Market

Three agencies, the Federal National Mortgage Association, the Government National Mortgage Association and the Federal Home Loan Mortgage Corporation, are responsible for creating and establishing a viable secondary mortgage market. Through their operations, there is a national securities market for the sale of real estate debt instruments by the originators to second owners. Selling the loans frees capital to create more real estate mortgages. The secondary market also minimizes the effects of regional cycles and redistributes the funds from cash-rich areas to cash-poor ones.

Federal National Mortgage Association

The Federal National Mortgage Association (**FNMA**), familiarly known as "Fannie Mae," was established to stimulate the secondary mortgage market by buying FHA-insured and VA-guaranteed mortgages made by private lenders. Fannie Mae has evolved into a private, profit-oriented corporation that markets its own securities and handles a variety of real estate loans. These loans are purchased at a discount and then sold to other private lenders or investors. Stabilizing the market gives lenders a sense of security and encourages them to make more loans.

Government National Mortgage Association

"Ginnie Mae," the Government National Mortgage Association (**GNMA**), is a wholly government-owned agency. Higher-risk—but important—programs, such as urban renewal, low-income housing and other special-purpose government-backed programs, are financed through this agency. Ginnie Mae's participation in the secondary mortgage market is through its mortgage-backed securities programs. Qualified mortgage originators and approved dealers can get additional capital for mortgages by pooling a group of homogeneous existing loans and pledging them as collateral. Ginnie Mae guarantees that holders of these securities will get timely principal and interest payments.

Federal Home Loan Mortgage Corporation

Nicknamed "Freddie Mac," the Federal Home Loan Mortgage Corporation (**FHLMC**) was founded with money provided by the 12 Federal Home Loan Banks when new mortgage loans could not be made because money was flowing out of the S & Ls. Freddie Mac was able to create needed funds by floating its own securities, backed by its pool of mortgages and guaranteed by Ginnie Mae. This gave S & Ls a secondary market for selling their conventional mortgages. Freddie Mac buys loans that have been closed within one year prior to the sale to Freddie Mac at specified discount rates.

Figure 9.3
The Financing
Process

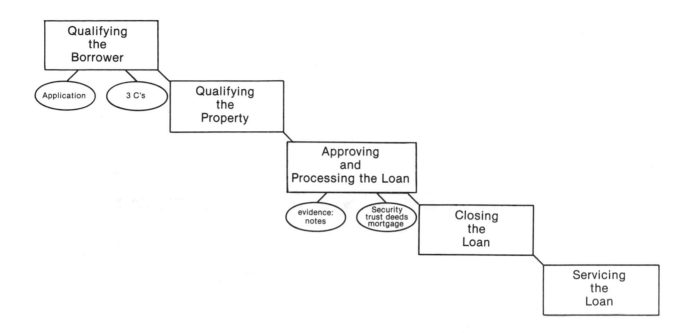

The Financing Process

The basic steps for obtaining real estate financing are much the same with any type of lender. Figure 9.3 illustrates the five-step financing process described here. The steps are: (1) qualifying the buyer, (2) qualifying the property, (3) approving and processing the loan, (4) closing the loan and (5) servicing the loan.

Qualifying the Borrower

Lenders will first ask that prospective borrowers complete an application form. Most applications are similar to the one in Figure 9.4, which asks for the borrower's employment record, credit references and a financial statement of assets and liabilities. To verify the accuracy of the information, the loan officer will check with past employers, request verification of deposits from the bank(s) and talk with references. The loan officer also may request a Dun & Bradstreet report (in cases of commercial loans) and a credit report by an outside agency, so there is no question of the borrower's ability to repay the loan.

In addition, most lenders use the following three Cs as a screening device to determine that the borrower meets the lender's qualifications: character, capacity and capital.

**Figure 9.4
Application Form**

RESIDENTIAL LOAN APPLICATION

| MORTGAGE APPLIED FOR | ☐ Conventional ☐ FHA ☐ VA | Amount $____ | Interest Rate ____% | No. of Months ____ | Monthly Payment Principal & Interest $____ | Escrow/Impounds (to be collected monthly) ☐ Taxes ☐ Hazard Ins. ☐ Mtg. Ins. ☐ ____ |

Prepayment Option   "IN ACCORDANCE WITH PROMISSORY NOTE OR ASSUMPTION AGREEMENT."

SUBJECT PROPERTY

| Property Street Address | City | County | State | Zip | No. Units |

Legal Description (Attach description if necessary)   Year Built

Purpose of Loan: ☐ Purchase ☐ Construction-Permanent ☐ Construction ☐ Refinance ☐ Other (Explain)

| Complete this line if Construction-Permanent or Construction Loan ➡ | Lot Value Data | Original Cost | Present Value (a) | Cost of Imps. (b) | Total (a + b) | ENTER TOTAL AS PURCHASE PRICE IN DETAILS OF PURCHASE. |
| | Year Acquired ____ $____ | $____ | $____ | $____ | $____ | |

Complete this line if a Refinance Loan   Purpose of Refinance   Describe Improvements [ ] made   [ ] to be made

| Year Acquired | Original Cost | Amt. Existing Liens | | | | Cost: $____ |
| | $____ | $____ | | | | |

Title Will Be Held In What Name(s)   Manner In Which Title Will Be Held

Source of Down Payment and Settlement Charges

This application is designed to be completed by the borrower(s) with the lender's assistance. The Co-Borrower Section and all other Co-Borrower questions must be completed and the appropriate box(es) checked if ☐ another person will be jointly obligated with the Borrower on the loan, or ☐ the Borrower is relying on income from alimony, child support or separate maintenance or on the income or assets of another person as a basis for repayment of the loan, or ☐ the Borrower is married and resides, or the property is located, in a community property state.

BORROWER				CO-BORROWER			
Name		Age	School Yrs ____	Name		Age	School Yrs ____
Present Address No. Years ____ ☐ Own ☐ Rent				Present Address No. Years ____ ☐ Own ☐ Rent			
Street				Street			
City/State/Zip				City/State/Zip			
Former address if less than 2 years at present address				Former address if less than 2 years at present address			
Street				Street			
City/State/Zip				City/State/Zip			
Years at former address ☐ Own ☐ Rent				Years at former address ☐ Own ☐ Rent			
Marital Status ☐ Married ☐ Separated ☐ Unmarried (incl. single, divorced, widowed)		DEPENDENTS OTHER THAN LISTED BY CO BORROWER NO AGES		Marital Status ☐ Married ☐ Separated ☐ Unmarried (incl. single, divorced, widowed)		DEPENDENTS OTHER THAN LISTED BY BORROWER NO AGES	
Name and Address of Employer		Years employed in this line of work or profession? ____ years Years on this job ____ ☐ Self Employed*		Name and Address of Employer		Years employed in this line of work or profession? ____ years Years on this job ____ ☐ Self Employed*	
Position/Title	Type of Business			Position/Title	Type of Business		
Social Security Number***	Home Phone	Business Phone		Social Security Number***	Home Phone	Business Phone	

GROSS MONTHLY INCOME				MONTHLY HOUSING EXPENSE**			DETAILS OF PURCHASE	
Item	Borrower	Co-Borrower	Total		PRESENT	PROPOSED	Do Not Complete If Refinance	
Base Empl. Income	$	$	$	Rent	$		a. Purchase Price	$
Overtime				First Mortgage (P&I)		$	b. Total Closing Costs (Est.)	
Bonuses				Other Financing (P&I)			c. Prepaid Escrows (Est.)	
Commissions				Hazard Insurance			d. Total (a + b + c)	$
Dividends/Interest				Real Estate Taxes			e. Amount This Mortgage	( )
Net Rental Income				Mortgage Insurance			f. Other Financing	( )
Other† (Before completing, see notice under Describe Other Income below.)				Homeowner Assn. Dues			g. Other Equity	( )
				Other:			h. Amount of Cash Deposit	( )
				Total Monthly Pmt.	$	$	i. Closing Costs Paid by Seller	( )
				Utilities			j. Cash Reqd. For Closing (Est.)	$
Total	$	$	$	Total	$	$		

DESCRIBE OTHER INCOME			
➡ B—Borrower C—Co-Borrower	NOTICE: † Alimony, child support, or separate maintenance income need not be revealed if the Borrower or Co-Borrower does not choose to have it considered as a basis for repaying this loan.		Monthly Amount $

IF EMPLOYED IN CURRENT POSITION FOR LESS THAN TWO YEARS COMPLETE THE FOLLOWING						
B/C	Previous Employer/School	City/State	Type of Business	Position/Title	Dates From/To	Monthly Income
						$

THESE QUESTIONS APPLY TO BOTH BORROWER AND CO-BORROWER

If a "yes" answer is given to a question in this column, explain on an attached sheet.	Borrower Yes or No	Co-Borrower Yes or No	If applicable, explain Other Financing or Other Equity (provide addendum if more space is needed).
Have you any outstanding judgments? in the last 7 years, have you been declared bankrupt?	____	____	
Have you had property foreclosed upon or given title or deed in lieu thereof?	____	____	
Are you a co-maker or endorser on a note?	____	____	
Are you a party in a law suit?	____	____	
Are you obligated to pay alimony, child support, or separate maintenance?	____	____	
Is any part of the down payment borrowed?	____	____	

*FHLMC/FNMA require business credit report, signed Federal Income Tax returns for last two years, and, if available, audited Profit and Loss Statements plus balance sheet for same period.

**All Present Monthly Housing Expenses of Borrower and Co-Borrower should be listed on a combined basis.

***Neither FHLMC nor FNMA requires this information.

FHLMC 65 REV. 8/78
FORM 1751, 9/78   FNMA 1003 Rev. 8/78

Figure 9.4
Application Form
(continued)

This Statement and any applicable supporting schedules may be completed jointly by both married and unmarried co-borrowers if their assets and liabilities are sufficiently joined so that the Statement can be meaningfully and fairly presented on a combined basis; otherwise separate Statements and Schedules are required (FHLMC 65A/FNMA 1003A). If the co-borrower section was completed about a spouse, this statement and supporting schedules must be completed about that spouse also. ☐ Completed Jointly   ☐ Not Completed Jointly

ASSETS		LIABILITIES AND PLEDGED ASSETS			
Indicate by (*) those liabilities or pledged assets which will be satisfied upon sale of real estate owned or upon refinancing of subject property.					
Description	Cash or Market Value	Creditors' Name, Address and Account Number	Acct. Name if Not Borrower's	Mo. Pmt. and Mos. left to pay	Unpaid Balance
Cash Deposit Toward Purchase Held By	$	Installment Debts (include "revolving" charge accts)		$ Pmt./Mos. /	$
Checking and Savings Accounts (Show Names of Institutions/Acct. Nos.)				/	
				/	
				/	
Stocks and Bonds (No./Description)				/	
				/	
Life Insurance Net Cash Value Face Amount ($)		Other Debts Including Stock Pledges		/	
SUBTOTAL LIQUID ASSETS	$				
Real Estate Owned (Enter Market Value from Schedule of Real Estate Owned)		Real Estate Loans			
Vested Interest in Retirement Fund					
Net Worth of Business Owned (ATTACH FINANCIAL STATEMENT)					
Automobiles (Make and Year)		Automobile Loans			
Furniture and Personal Property		Alimony, Child Support and Separate Maintenance Payments Owed To			
Other Assets (Itemize)					
		TOTAL MONTHLY PAYMENTS		$	
TOTAL ASSETS	A $	NET WORTH (A minus B) $		TOTAL LIABILITIES	B $

SCHEDULE OF REAL ESTATE OWNED (If Additional Properties Owned Attach Separate Schedule)

Address of Property (Indicate S if Sold, PS if Pending Sale or R if Rental being held for income)		Type of Property	Present Market Value	Amount of Mortgages & Liens	Gross Rental Income	Mortgage Payments	Taxes, Ins. Maintenance and Misc.	Net Rental Income
			$	$	$	$	$	$
TOTALS →			$	$	$	$	$	$

LIST PREVIOUS CREDIT REFERENCES

B Borrower C Co-Borrower	Creditor's Name and Address	Account Number	Purpose	Highest Balance	Date Paid
				$	

List any additional names under which credit has previously been received _____

AGREEMENT   The undersigned applies for the loan indicated in this application to be secured by a first mortgage or deed of trust on the property described herein, and represents that the property will not be used for any illegal or restricted purpose, and that all statements made in this application are true and are made for the purpose of obtaining the loan. Verification may be obtained from any source named in this application. The original or a copy of this application will be retained by the lender, even if the loan is not granted. The undersigned ☐ intend or ☐ do not intend to occupy the property as their primary residence

I/we fully understand that it is a federal crime punishable by fine or imprisonment, or both, to knowingly make any false statements concerning any of the above facts as applicable under the provisions of Title 18, United States Code, Section 1014.

_____ Date _____   _____ Date _____
Borrower's Signature   Co-Borrower's Signature

INFORMATION FOR GOVERNMENT MONITORING PURPOSES

The following information is requested by the Federal Government if this loan is related to a dwelling, in order to monitor the lender's compliance with equal credit opportunity and fair housing laws. You are not required to furnish this information, but are encouraged to do so. The law provides that a lender may neither discriminate on the basis of this information, nor on whether you choose to furnish it. However, if you choose not to furnish it, under Federal regulations this lender is required to note race and sex on the basis of visual observation or surname. If you do not wish to furnish the above information, please initial below.

BORROWER: I do not wish to furnish this information (initials)_____	CO-BORROWER: I do not wish to furnish this information (initials)_____
RACE/ ☐ American Indian, Alaskan Native ☐ Asian, Pacific Islander	RACE/ ☐ American Indian, Alaskan Native ☐ Asian, Pacific Islander
NATIONAL ☐ Black ☐ Hispanic ☐ White SEX: ☐ Female	NATIONAL ☐ Black ☐ Hispanic ☐ White SEX: ☐ Female
ORIGIN ☐ Other (specify) _____ ☐ Male	ORIGIN ☐ Other (specify) _____ ☐ Male

FOR LENDER'S USE ONLY

(FNMA REQUIREMENT ONLY) This application was taken by ☐ face to face interview ☐ by mail ☐ by telephone

_____   _____
(Interviewer)   Name of Employer of Interviewer

FOR CONSTRUCTION LOANS ONLY:
SUBJECT PROPERTY ☐ IS NOT ☐ IS OR WILL BE COVERED BY A CONSTRUCTION WARRANTY.
INSURANCE IS _____ COVERAGE FROM _____ TO _____

FHLMC 65 Rev. 8/78   REVERSE   FNMA 1003 Rev. 8/78

Character. With regard to prospective borrowers' **character,** lenders consider their attitude toward financial obligations as evidenced by their track record of borrowing and repaying loans. Lenders also try to ascertain whether borrowers are honest in their dealings.

Capacity. In considering borrowers' **capacity,** lenders want to know their ability to repay the debt. Capacity is strengthened by an occupation that assures a steady income. The level of present debts and obligations also is a factor; too much debt may prevent a borrower from discharging a new obligation. A rule of thumb is that loan payments, taxes, insurance and other fixed charges for residential real estate should not exceed 33 percent of the buyer's gross monthly income.

Capital. To evaluate borrowers' capital needs, lenders consider their net worth. Lenders have established desirable ratios of expenses, such as the ratio of monthly income to monthly payments for shelter. Ratios from 5 to 1 to as much as 7 or 8 to 1 are established, depending on the amount of the loan.

A rule of thumb used by the Federal Housing Authority (as well as many, if not most, real estate professionals) to determine a prospective borrower's financial ability to pay is that monthly income less monthly debt payments should be from two and one-half to three times the monthly installment payment, including principal, interest, mortgage insurance, hazard insurance, real estate taxes and special assessments or bonds.

The following example illustrates. If the monthly payment (including principal, interest, insurance and taxes) is $900, the monthly income of the borrower should be at least in the range of

$$\$900 \times 2\frac{1}{2} = \$2,250$$
$$\$900 \times 3 = \$2,700$$

Lending institutions sometimes take overtime wages into consideration. Other lenders under such circumstances will consider both spouses' wages in computing the gross income of the borrower, even if only one spouse is applying for the loan. Occasionally a lender will request a **co-signer** to strengthen the borrower's application. A co-signer is a person with additional capital who agrees to share liability for the loan.

Qualifying the Property

After the loan is granted, the lender will have to rely for a long time on the status of the security for the loan. For this reason, lenders consider it important to qualify the property as well as the borrower.

Because the underlying security for almost every property loan is the property itself, lenders require a careful valuation of the property. The value will depend on the property's location, age, architecture, physical condition, zoning, floor plan and general appearance. The lender will have an appraisal done by the financial institution's appraiser or by an outside fee appraiser. (The appraisal process is discussed in Chapter 13.) Brokers who are familiar with lending policies of loan companies are in a good position to make accurate and helpful estimates.

Approving and Processing the Loan

Processing involves drawing up loan papers, preparing disclosure forms regarding loan fees and issuing instructions for the escrow and title companies. Loan papers include the **promissory note** (the evidence of the debt) and the security instruments (the **trust deed** or mortgage). These instruments will be described in greater detail in the next section.

Closing the Loan

Closing the loan involves signing all the loan papers and preparing the closing statements. First-time buyers, especially, often are confused by the various fees involved. Real estate licensees play a vital role in making this transition period smooth. Ways to do this were discussed in Chapter 8.

Servicing the Loan

After the title has been transferred and the escrow closed, the loan servicing portion of the transaction begins. This refers to the record-keeping process once the loan has been placed. Many lenders do their own servicing, while others use outside sources. The goal of loan servicing is to see that the lender makes the expected yield on the loan, keeping the cost of the entire package at a minimum.

Real Estate Financing Instruments

Promissory Notes

Lending institutions ask people who want to borrow money for the purchase of real estate to sign promissory notes, which are evidence of the debt and specify the terms of repayment. The borrower is called the maker of the note or the payor. The lender is called the payee or the holder.

There are three main types of notes: straight notes, partially amortized notes and fully amortized notes.

Straight note. A straight note calls for the payment of interest only during the term of the note. For example, if Sally Shrewd borrowed $20,000 at 12 percent interest on a straight note for ten years, she would pay $2,400 per year in interest. She would make no payments on the principal each month. Consequently, she is not reducing the balance of the loan. After ten years, when the note is due, she still owes $20,000, even though she paid $2,400 interest each year.

Partially amortized note. An amortized note calls for the payment of both principal and interest during the term of the loan. The monthly interest is high at first and declines over the term of the loan. The monthly payment on the principal is low at the outset and increases over the term of the loan. A partially amortized note is not fully paid off when the note falls due, giving rise to a substantially larger final payment, known as a balloon payment. A balloon payment usually is at least twice as large as the previous payments.

Fully amortized note. The only difference between a fully amortized note and a partially amortized note is that in a fully amortized note the entire loan is fully paid off at the due date. There are no balloon payments. Most real estate first loans are fully amortized loans. A second deed of trust usually has a balloon payment.

Negotiable Instruments

A promissory note is said to be a **negotiable instrument**, freely transferable in business. When properly prepared, promissory notes are accepted virtually as the equivalent of cash.

For an instrument to be regarded as negotiable, it must meet the following requirements specified in the Uniform Commercial Code:

1. It must be an unconditional promise.

2. It must be in writing.

3. It must be made by one person to another.

4. It must be signed by the maker.

5. It must be a promise to pay on demand or at a fixed or determinable future time.

6. It must contain a sum certain in money.

7. It must be made to order or to bearer.

Holder in Due Course

A **holder in due course** is a person who has taken a negotiable instrument under the following conditions:

1. It is complete and regular on its face.

2. The person becomes the holder before the negotiable instrument is due and without notice of any previous dishonor.

3. The person takes it in good faith and for a valuable consideration.

4. At the time the instrument is negotiated to the holder, he or she has no knowledge of any infirmity in the title of the negotiator.

A holder in due course who acquires a promissory note may obtain greater rights than the original payee.

Provisions of Notes

Personal defenses. A does not have to pay B, but must pay C if:

1. The maker was fraudulently induced by the payee to sign the note.

2. The payee failed to perform or give consideration in exchange for the maker's promissory note.

Real defenses. A does not have to pay B or C if:

1. The note was forged.

2. The amount of the note was raised.

3. The maker did not have legal capacity.

4. The instrument is illegal.

Endorsements. If a note is made payable "to bearer," it can be transferred by simple delivery. If the note is made payable "to the order of" a named person, that person must order the maker to pay the transferee by endorsing the instrument.

There are four basic types of endorsements:

- **blank endorsement**—The holder simply signs his or her name, transferring the note to whoever possesses it.

- **special endorsement**—The endorser writes "Pay to order of" a specified person.

- **restrictive endorsement**—The endorser restricts the use of the note, for example, by endorsing a check "For deposit only."

- **qualified endorsement**—If the endorser adds the words "without recourse" to the endorsement and the maker refuses to pay, the endorser will not be held liable.

Trust Deed or Mortgage

Lenders require borrowers of money for the purchase of real estate to give security for the note. **Trust deeds** (also called deeds of trust) and mortgages are instruments used as security devices. The deed of trust is preferred by lenders and is the instrument generally used in California. However, because many of your buyers are likely to have come from other parts of the United States, you should understand the differences between the two instruments.

These instruments differ in the following areas:

- parties;

- title;

- statute of limitations;

- remedy;

- redemption; and

- deficiency judgment.

Table 9.1 describes the nature of these differences.

Clauses in Trust Deeds and Notes

Acceleration clause. An **acceleration clause** stipulates that on the happening of a certain event, the entire balance of the loan becomes due and payable. Events that trigger an acceleration clause include the borrower's delinquency in paying taxes, loan payments or insurance.

Alienation clause. An **alienation clause** is a special type of acceleration clause that specifies that the entire loan balance is payable if the property is sold or the ownership interest is transferred. The *Tucker Lassen Savings and Loan Association* case and the *Wellenkamp* case have altered the courts' decisions somewhat, putting an added burden on the lender to prove that allowing assumption of an existing loan would be economically detrimental to the lender's interest. FHA and VA loans may not contain alienation clauses.

Prepayment penalty clause. A lock-in clause, called a **prepayment penalty** clause, assesses a penalty to a borrower who repays a loan before its due date. Most loans allow the borrower to prepay without penalty. FHA and VA loans have no prepayment penalty provisions.

Table 9.1
Comparison Between
Trust Deed
and Mortgage

Area Being Compared	Trust Deed	Mortgage Contract
Statute of limitations	Rights of creditors to foreclose against property are not ended when statute has run out on note, because trustee holds title and can still sell to pay off debt	Mortgage note and contract both outlaw four years from due date; no relief; monies involved not collectible
Parties involved	Trustor—borrower	Mortgagor—borrower
	Beneficiary—lender	Mortgagee—lender
	Trustee—neutral third party	
Title during loan term	Rests in trustee	Rests in mortgagor
Foreclosure	Court action or trustee's sale	Court action only
Owner's rights of redemption	If foreclosure by court action—same as for a mortgage	Before decree of foreclosure: Owner may redeem any time by bringing payments current
	Trustee's Sale—notice of default: Owner may reinstate by bringing payments current within three months	
	Notice of sale posted: Owner may redeem only by paying entire note in full	After decree of foreclosure and sale: Owner has one year "Equity of Redemption"; must pay note in full to redeem
	Sale final—no redemption	
Lender's rights	If foreclosure by court action—same as for mortgage	Possible deficiency judgment
	Trustee's sale—no deficiency judgment	
Receipt for payment	Deed of reconveyance recorded	Satisfaction of mortgage—recorded

Subordination clause. A **subordination clause** provides that the loan may be subordinated in priority of payment to an anticipated future lien. For example, a mortgage loan created to finance the sale of vacant land to a developer would probably include a subordination clause granting the developer an opportunity to secure new financing to construct houses on a portion of the already encumbered land. Since the construction lender for the houses would insist on being in *first lien* position, the existing mortgage given to buy the land would have to be subordinated on those specific portions to be financed with construction mortgages. The land mortgages would then be in a *junior lien* position to the first mortgagee on those specific parcels on which houses were to be built.

The wording used to establish this type of subordination could be "The mortgagee shall, upon written request from the mortgagor, subordinate the lien of this mortgage on the lot or lots specified in order of release, to the lien of a new construction loan or loans from a recognized lending institution."[1]

[1]Sirota, David, *Essentials of Real Estate Finance,* 4th Edition (Chicago: Longman Group USA Inc., 1986), p. 136.

Types of Loans

Real estate financing has become quite confusing in light of the economic environment of the past few years. While the majority of one- to four-family dwellings still are financed by conventional loans, the choice of a loan is no longer a foregone conclusion. Buyers and sellers both need to know what is currently available, which loan best suits their requirements and even where to go for financing. With retailers like Sears getting into the real estate business and real estate firms allying themselves with financial institutions, even the players are changing every day. Real estate licensees are in an ideal position to be the primary information resource of sellers and buyers.

Whether buyers choose a conventional loan or one of the alternative instruments, they should use the following categories to compare lenders:

1. loan-to-value ratio;

2. interest rate;

3. loan fees required; and

4. prepayment penalties.

Conventional Loans

A **conventional loan** is any loan that is not backed by the government.

The advantages of conventional over government-backed loans are that conventional loans involve less red tape and shorter processing time. Government loans do not have equivalent flexibility. In addition, sellers are not required to pay discount points. Buyers can obtain a larger loan amount, and, because there are more sources for conventional loans, borrowers have the option of choosing a fixed or a variable interest rate.

Disadvantages of conventional loans in comparison to government-backed loans include higher down payments and prepayment penalties. Furthermore, loans are not assumable and private mortgage insurance must be purchased.

**Government
Participation Loans**

There are three types of government-backed loans: FHA-insured loans, VA-guaranteed loans and Cal Vet loans. These types of loans are compared in Table 9.2.

Federal Housing Administration. The purposes of the Federal Housing Administration (**FHA**) are stated in its preamble: "Encourage improvement in housing standards and conditions to provide a system of mutual mortgage insurance and for other purposes."

There are two divisions under which this protection is granted: Title I and Title II. Section 203 (b) of Title II accounts for most loans for one- to four-family residences. In general, the following types of loans are available:

Table 9.2
Government Home
Loan Programs

	FHA	GI (VA)	Cal-Vet
Who is eligible?	Anyone who qualifies	U.S. vets	California vets only, born or living in California when inducted
Who makes the loans?	Approved lending institutions	Approved lending institutions	State bonds
Interest rates	May be negotiated	Set by VA	Interest rate is variable Increased periodically
What is maximum you can pay for a home?	No limit	Not over appraisal (CRV)	Cannot exceed the Cal-Vet appraisal
Maximum loan allowed	1 unit $90,000 2 units $101,300 3 units $122,650 4 units $142,650	No money down, maximum, $110,000 Jumbo loan, $135,000	Single-family, $75,000 Farm, $200,000
Term	Usually 30 years	Usually 30 years	Usually 25 years
Down payment	3% of first $25,000* 5% of excess up to appraisal plus all amount over appraisal	None required	House—3% on homes costing $35,000 or less; 5% on homes costing over $35,000
Secondary financing	Not allowed at time of sale, but can be placed later	Not allowed at time of sale, but can be placed later	Yes—but the 1st and 3rd cannot exceed 90% of the Cal-Vet appraisal
Prepayment penalty	None	None	2% if paid within 2 yr.

*FHA has numerous plans. These figures represent the popular "normal" 203b FHA transaction, with which the public is most familiar.

- Title I—loans for modernization, repairs or alterations on existing homes; and

- Title II—loans for purchase or construction of residential structures.

Veterans Administration. The Servicemen's Readjustment Act of 1944 (GI Bill) was intended to assist veterans in making the necessary readjustments to civilian life, particularly in the acquisition of homes. The Veterans Administration (**VA**) does not make loans, but it guarantees a portion of the loan. As of 1980 the maximum guarantee on a loan was $27,500 or 60 percent of the loan amount, whichever is the lesser amount. VA loans may be used for the following purposes:

1. to buy or build a home or business property;

2. to purchase a farm or farm equipment;

3. to alter, repair or improve real estate;

4. to purchase a mobile home; and

5. to refinance existing mortgage loans for dwellings owned and occupied by veterans.

To qualify for a VA-guaranteed loan, an individual must have had 181 days of service. The property is checked by an appraiser approved by the Veteran's Administration.

Cal Vet loans. Under the **Cal Vet** loan program (the California Farm and Home Purchase Program), California veterans can acquire suitable farm or home property at a low financing cost. The State of California actually lends the money rather than guaranteeing payment. The property is acquired under land contract, with the state retaining title to the property until the final payment is made.

The state advances the required funds with the money raised by state bond issues. The state's ability to make Cal Vet loans depends on the availability of bond money. The property purchased must meet minimum acceptable standards set by the California Department of Veterans' Affairs.

Other Types of Mortgages and Trust Deeds

Open-end trust deed. An open-end trust deed allows the borrower to receive additional loan money using the same trust deed or mortgage as security.

Blanket trust deed. With a blanket trust deed, the borrower uses more than one parcel of property as security. This type of document should contain a release clause, which would allow the reconveyance of part of the property on repayment of a portion of the loan.

Wraparound mortgage. A **wraparound mortgage** also is called an *all-inclusive trust deed*. There are times when it is almost impossible for borrowers to refinance an existing loan on investment real estate to raise additional capital. By using a wraparound mortgage, the existing loan is not disturbed, but the new lender assumes the payment of the existing mortgage while giving the borrower a new, increased loan at a higher rate of interest.

Builders often use this type of financing when selling newly constructed homes. To expedite the sale of property listed with them, brokers occasionally loan back their own personal funds. The loan must represent the existing value and set terms the borrower can meet.

Hard money second mortgages. In some instances, a third party advances cash to bridge the gap between the down payment plus the new or existing loan and the sales price. This is called a hard money second mortgage. The rates usually are higher, together with fees, which are not present on created paper.

Other Types of Financing

It may be possible for would-be borrowers to hypothecate (make property security for a debt without giving up possession of the property) existing bank accounts, stocks and bonds, automobiles, coin collections or anything else that has value as security for a loan. Another possibility is to exchange all or a portion of an equity for another equity. Small syndicates might be formed to enable several people to purchase property together. This will entail a smaller outlay of cash from each participant. The surrender value of a life insurance policy might provide financial help.

Real property sales contract. A real property sales contract also is known as a land contract, agreement of sale contract or conditional sales contract. If a potential buyer is unable to make an adequate down payment, the seller may sell the property under a real property sales contract. In this type of transaction, the buyer will not gain title to the property until the terms of the contract have been met.

Advantages to the buyer are:

1. Little or no down payment is required.
2. The buyer can receive quick possession of the property.
3. Buyers with little or no savings can start acquiring an estate with this type of transaction.

Disadvantages to the buyer are:

1. Lending institutions will consider this type of equity as poor collateral.
2. After the buyer has performed the contract in full, the seller may be unable to deliver clear title.
3. If the seller should be adjudicated bankrupt or should die, proving title may involve expensive litigation and may be time-consuming.
4. The terms may not allow the buyer to assign or transfer his or her interest.
5. Because the buyer holds title to the property until the content is fulfilled, he or she only holds an equitable title.

Advantages to the seller are:

1. The seller retains title to the property, relinquishing only possession.
2. The seller may eliminate the purchaser's interest in the event of default.

Disadvantages to the seller are:

1. The buyer may subject the title to a mechanic's or other lien.
2. If the buyer defaults, clearing the title may be costly as well as time-consuming for the seller.
3. The seller's interest in the contract is less salable.
4. If the buyer records the transaction, it automatically creates a "cloud on the title."

The law prohibits the seller from putting anything in the contract denying the buyer the right to record the contract.

Loan assumptions. When the seller still owes money on the property, he or she can endeavor to get a buyer to assume the original loan. When a loan is assumed, the original borrower (the seller) is relieved of primary responsibility. If the buyer chooses to purchase "subject to" the existing loan, the original borrower still is responsible for the loan. If foreclosure occurs and there is a deficiency, the original borrower must formally assume the loan.

Foreclosure

What happens in the event the borrower fails to keep up payments on the loan or fails to fulfill other requirements of the loan contract?

Steps in the Sale in the Event of a Default

The beneficiary under a deed of trust has a choice of foreclosing through the courts or by trustee's sale. Foreclosure through the courts is used only when the lender thinks the property will bring too little at the trustee's sale to cover the balance of the mortgage. In that event, the lender could obtain a deficiency judgment against the trustor to recover the difference. Remember, if a deficiency judgment is used, the redemption is the same as for a mortgage—one year. Certain types of loans are not subject to deficiency judgments. Purchase-money loans on dwellings of up to four units are the most common exception.

In a foreclosure by trustee's sale, the beneficiary notifies the trustee that the borrower (or trustor) is in default. The trustee records a notice of default and sends a copy to the borrower. This begins a three-month reinstatement period. During this period, the reinstatement of the borrower can take place if he or she pays any back payments plus any foreclosure costs. After three months, the trustee posts a notice of sale on the property and advertises the sale in a newspaper of general circulation once a week for three weeks. During the three-week publishing period, the borrower must pay the entire amount of the loan plus penalties and fees to redeem his or her property.

After the trustee has advertised the sale for three weeks, the property is sold to the highest bidder for cash. The trustee's fees, which are nominal, are paid first. The beneficiary is then paid; if there is any money remaining, it goes to the trustor. When the power of sale is used in a trustee's sale, no deficiency judgment is possible.

Loan Payoff

If the security for the loan is a trust deed and the total indebtedness is paid off, the trustee confers the title back to the trustor by means of a reconveyance deed. If the security for the loan is a mortgage and it is paid off, a satisfaction of mortgage is recorded.

Regulation of Real Estate Financing

Because this is a real estate practice text, all references to the regulations in real estate financing will, of necessity, be brief. For further information relating to this subject, consult a real estate finance book.

Truth-in-Lending Act

The Truth-in-Lending Act (Regulation Z) is a key portion of the federal Consumer Credit Protection Act passed in 1969. The Truth-in-Lending Act applies to banks, savings and loan associations, credit unions, consumer finance companies and residential mortgage brokers.

The act itself is a disclosure act requiring that lenders reveal to customers how much they are being charged for credit. This must be expressed in terms of an annual percentage rate. The act allows the customer to make credit cost comparisons between various credit sources, so as to avoid use of credit.

The act gives individuals seeking credit a right of rescission of the contract. This means that under certain circumstances a customer has the right to cancel a credit transaction up until midnight of the third day after signing. This right of rescission may involve a lien on the customer's residence (other than a purchase-money first mortgage loan).

The Federal Trade Commission, which enforces the act, has published a booklet, "What You Ought to Know About Truth in Lending." To get a copy, write to: Truth in Lending, Federal Trade Commission, Box 36005, San Francisco, CA 94102.

Real Estate Settlement Procedures Act

The regulations contained in the Real Estate Settlement Procedures Act apply only to first loans on one- to four-unit residential properties. This act is another disclosure act. A lender must furnish the buyer within three days of the date of the loan application an itemized list of all the closing costs that will be encountered in escrow. This must be a good-faith estimate to every person requiring credit. Each charge for each settlement service the buyer is likely to incur must be expressed as a dollar amount or range. The lender also must furnish a copy of a special information booklet prepared by the Secretary of the Department of Housing and Urban Development (HUD). It must be delivered or placed in the mail to the applicant no later than three business days after the application is received.

Fair Credit Reporting Act

The **Fair Credit Reporting Act** affects credit reporting agencies and users of credit information. If a loan is rejected because of information disclosed in a credit report, the borrower must be notified. The borrower then can proceed to obtain the following information from the reporting credit agency:

1. all the information it has in its file on the buyer;

2. the sources of the information; and

3. all the creditors that have been furnished reports by the credit agency within the past six months.

Mortgage Loan Brokerage Law

According to the Mortgage Loan Brokerage Law, a person who acts for compensation in negotiating a new loan is required to be licensed as a real estate broker or salesperson. Real estate brokers who negotiate mortgage loans under the Mortgage Loan Brokerage Law are limited in the amount that they may charge as a commission for arranging the loan and for costs and expenses of making the loan. Loans on first trust deeds of $20,000 or more or second trust deeds of $10,000 or more do not come within the purview of the law, but commissions and expenses are negotiable between the broker and the buyer.

Commission maximums under the law are as follows:

• first trust deeds (less than $20,000)—five percent of the principal if less than three years; ten percent if three years or more; and

• second trust deeds (less than $10,000)—five percent of the principal if less than two years; ten percent if at least two years but less than three years; 15 percent if three years or more.

If the loan comes under the purview of the law, expenses of making the loan, appraisal fees, escrow fees, title charges, notary fees, recording fees and credit investigation fees cannot exceed five percent of the principal amount of the loan; however, if five percent of the loan is less than $195, the broker may charge up to that amount. Regardless of the size of the loan, the buyer (borrower) cannot be charged more than $375 for costs and expenses; in no event may the maximum be charged if it exceeds the actual costs and expenses incurred.

**Real Property
Securities
Dealer's Law**

Under the Real Property Securities Dealer's Law, real property securities are defined as:

1. deeds of trust sold under an investment contract where the dealer guarantees the deed of trust in one of several ways or makes an advance to or on behalf of the investor;

2. one in a series of promotional notes;

3. a sales contract; and

4. an out-of-state subdivision.

A real property securities dealer is a person who:

1. guarantees a loan or yield by agreeing to make the payments, advance the payments or repurchase the loan.

2. in servicing a loan, makes payments with funds other than the obligor's.

3. accepts funds for a continual reinvestment plan in **real property securities**.

4. accepts funds and indicates a return from real property sales contracts or notes that is greater than the rate specified on the contracts or notes.

5. arranges the sale of **promotional notes** secured by real property. A promotional note is a promissory note on real estate prior to the first sale as a means of financing the purchase or improvements. The note may become subordinate to a later loan. Promotional notes do not include loans over three years or construction loans with obligatory advances.

6. arranges the sale of one in a series of real property sales contracts in a subdivision pertaining to separate properties all of which are executed by the same party(ies) as owner(s).

7. sells out-of-state subdivision property in California.

Every person who acts as a real property securities dealer must have a real estate license endorsed as a real properties security dealer and must post a $5,000 bond.[2]

---

[2]Pivar, William H., *California Real Estate Law* (Chicago: Real Estate Education Company, 1987), pp. 37–38.

Summary   This chapter included a brief description of the money market, including an explanation of the Federal Reserve system and how that body regulates the flow of money in the mortgage market through adjusting reserve requirements in member banks, buying and selling of securities on the open market, and establishing discount rates with member banks.

The steps needed in a loan transaction include qualifying the borrower, qualifying the property, selecting a lender and determining the type of loan—conventional or government-backed.

To aid understanding of the financing available under special situations, the chapter included a table showing the difference between trust deeds and mortgages and the steps involved in the completion of a loan contract or in case of default in a contract. Another table described the characteristics of FHA-insured, VA-guaranteed and Cal-Vet loans.

A number of important laws affect real estate financing: the Truth-in-Lending Law, Real Estate Settlement Procedures Act, Fair Credit Reporting Act, Mortgage Loan Brokerage Law and Real Property Securities Law.

Questions

1. Which of the following would be classified as an institutional lender?

    a. insurance company
    b. commercial bank
    c. savings and loan association
    d. all of the above

2. The Federal Reserve controls the money supply by which of the following means?

    a. prime rate
    b. buying and selling government securities
    c. through taxation
    d. all of the above

3. A mortgage company is considered:

    a. a noninstitutional lender.
    b. an institutional lender.
    c. both an institutional and a noninstitutional lender.
    d. none of the above

4. "Ginnie Mae" stands for:

    a. Government National Mortgage Association.
    b. Government Mortgages.
    c. Government Institute of National Mortgages.
    d. none of the above

5. A "trust deed" is the same as a:

    a. mortgage.
    b. real estate property sales contract.
    c. promissory note.
    d. none of the above

6. If a trust deed is paid off, the trustor should get a:

    a. deficiency judgment.
    b. new trust deed.
    c. deed of reconveyance.
    d. beneficiary statement.

7. If the borrower is trying to qualify for $1,000 payment (including principal, interest, taxes and insurance), the borrower should earn approximately _____ per month.

    a. $1,500
    b. $3,000
    c. $4,500
    d. $5,000

8. Usually the lenders will want to qualify:

    a. the borrower.
    b. the property.
    c. both the property and the borrower.
    d. none of the above

9. In using a trust deed the lender is called a:

    a. beneficiary.
    b. trustor.
    c. mortgagor.
    d. all of the above

10. A client borrows $10,000 at 11 percent for five years on a straight note. How much will the client pay in five years (including both principal and interest)?

    a. $10,000
    b. $11,100
    c. $15,000
    d. $15,500

11. If a note is made payable "to the order of," then the note can be transferred by:

    a. delivery.
    b. endorsement.
    c. either delivery or endorsement.
    d. none of the above

12. When comparing lenders, the borrower should compare:

    a. loan-to-value ratios.
    b. prepayment penalties.
    c. interest rates.
    d. all of the above

13. A nongovernment loan is called a:
    a. private loan.
    b. noninstitutional loan.
    c. conventional loan.
    d. institutional loan.

14. Which of the following is correct regarding FHA loans?
    a. The only FHA loan is a 203b loan.
    b. FHA has no graduated payment loans.
    c. FHA loans cannot be used in combination with VA loans.
    d. none of the above

15. When using an FHA loan, the maximum number of units that can be purchased is:
    a. one.
    b. two.
    c. three.
    d. four.

16. A blanket trust deed is best defined as a loan that:
    a. uses more than one parcel of property as security.
    b. uses more than one loan to cover one property.
    c. uses only installment contracts to finance more than one property.
    d. none of the above

17. A common name for an all-inclusive trust deed is:
    a. an installment sale.
    b. a wraparound mortgage.
    c. an exchange.
    d. a land contract.

18. Using a land contract, the buyer will receive:
    a. equitable title.
    b. legal title.
    c. partial title.
    d. no title.

19. "Subject to" is the same as:
    a. definancing.
    b. a loan assumption.
    c. exchanging.
    d. none of the above

20. Regulation Z is called the:
    a. Borrower's Protection Act.
    b. Seller's Protections Act.
    c. Truth-in-Lending Act.
    d. none of the above

Taxation of Real Property Ownership

Chapter Preview

Because taxes play an important role in nearly every real estate transaction, knowledge of various taxes involved and the manner in which they affect property values is extremely helpful. This chapter covers the areas of taxation that most affect property ownership. They are real property taxes, special assessments and income taxes. Each of these areas will be explored, including assessments, appraisals, exemptions, advantages and disadvantages, deferments and payments.

Terms To Look For

ACRS
Adjusted basis
Ad valorem tax
Basis
Boot
Depreciable basis
Depreciation
Homeowner's exemption
Installment sale
Original basis
Points
Property taxes
Reassessment event
Recurring costs
Renter's Relief Provisions
Sale-leaseback
Senior citizen's property tax assistance
Special assessments
Tax-deferred exchange
Veteran's exemption

Real Property Taxes

Real property taxes are **ad valorem taxes.** *Ad valorem* is a Latin expression meaning "according to value." Real estate tax rates are a percentage of the property's value. The concept is not new; throughout history people's wealth was largely determined by the amount of real property they owned. Landowners almost always have been taxed on the basis of their property holdings.

The levying of real property taxes profoundly affects the real estate market. If taxes are high, potential customers may hesitate to involve themselves with such an expense by purchasing property. On the positive side, revenues from property taxes are a vital source of government income on the local level, enabling local government to provide for the health, education, safety and welfare of the citizenry.

Real Property Tax Calendar

A basic understanding of real property taxes in California begins with knowing the chronological order for processing real property taxes. This is illustrated in the real property tax calendar in Figure 10.1.

Proposition 13

Real property taxation in California was abruptly changed in June of 1978 with the passage of an amendment to the California State Constitution known as Proposition 13 (the Jarvis/Gann initiative). Among other changes, the initiative limited the amount of property tax to one percent of the "full cash value" of the property as of the tax year 1975–76. Each subsequent year, the tax collector may add a two percent annual inflationary factor plus an additional sum of from 0.20 to 0.25 percent to pay for voter-approved bonded indebtedness.

To summarize, under Proposition 13:

1. A limit has been placed on the amount of taxes that local governments can collect.

2. Any increase in a property's assessed value now is restricted to the time of a reassessment event.

As of the November 1986 general election and the passage of Proposition 62, new or increased taxes for special purposes require approval by two-thirds of the voters. General taxes for general governmental purposes require approval by two-thirds of the legislative body of the local government or district *and* a majority of voters. Local taxes already in effect and imposed after August 1, 1985, must be ratified by a majority of voters.

Assessment Procedures

Assessed value. In accordance with Proposition 13 and related laws and state regulations, real property is appraised as of March 1, 1975, the lien date for the 1975–1976 tax year or at the time of a subsequent reassessment event. According to the *Department of Real Estate Reference Book* (p. 481, A-D), "property is reassessed (revalued) if a *reassessment event* occurs; that is, if the property is sold, further improved (by an addition, for instance), or newly constructed." The county tax assessor uses the full cash value thus determined as the assessed value of the property. Formerly, assessed value was 25 percent of full cash value, with the result that a tax rate of $4 per $100 of assessed value would be applied to effect a one percent overall tax rate.

**Figure 10.1
Real Property Tax
Calendar**

January	February	March
	Feb. 1: Second installment of taxes due.	March 1: Taxes for the next year become a lien on property.

April	May	June
April 10: Second installment of taxes becomes delinquent at 5:00 p.m. April 15: Homeowner's exemption must be filed.		June 8: Delinquency list is published. June 30: "Book sale" is held. June 30: Tax year ends.

July	August	September
July 1: Tax year begins.		Sept. 1: Tax rates are determined.

October	November	December
	Nov. 1: First installment of taxes due.	Dec. 10: First installment of taxes becomes delinquent at 5:00 p.m.

Billing. If taxes are to be paid through a lending agency, the state sends a tax bill to that agency and a copy of it to the owner. The owner's copy states that it is for information only. If the owner is to pay the taxes, the original bill is sent directly to the owner for payment. The tax bill includes special assessments. Unpaid taxes become delinquent and a penalty is charged even if the taxpayer never received a notice of taxes due. It is the taxpayer's responsibility to make sure that tax payment deadlines are met.

Special assessments. Cities, counties and special districts may, by a two-thirds vote of the electors of the district, impose special taxes on such districts. These **special assessments** are levied for specific local improvements, such as streets, sewers, irrigation, drainage, flood control and special lighting.

This voter-approved bond indebtedness varies from county to county and within each county. For assessment purposes, the land usually is appraised separately from the building. The building value usually is determined by a residence cost handbook or rules covering unit-cost prices and rates of depreciation.

Typical tax bill. The contents of a typical tax bill include:

1. an identifying parcel number, with reference to the map page and property number or other description;

2. a breakdown between land assessments and improvement assessments;

3. the full cash value as of March 1, 1975, or as of the date of a subsequent reassessment event;

4. the assessed value upon which special assessments are computed;

5. breakdown of the bonded indebtedness or special assessments;

6. the full amount of the tax; and

7. itemization or perhaps separate payment cards with the full tax equally divided into first and second installments.

Change in ownership statement. Any person acquiring an interest in property subject to local taxation must notify the county recorder or assessor by filing a change in ownership statement within 45 days of the date of recording or, if the transfer is not recorded, within 45 days of the date of transfer.

Exemptions

Some of the numerous properties that are assessed are partially or wholly tax exempt. For example, most nonprofit charitable organizations, many churches, all governments and several nonprofit educational institutions are entirely exempt. Other relief is available in various forms for homeowners, veterans, senior citizens and renters.

Proposition 58, approved by voters in the general election of November 1986 provides that the terms "purchase" and "change of ownership," for purposes of property tax reassessment, do *not* include transfers of real property between spouses and transfers of a principal residence and the first $1 million of other real property between parents and children. Voters also approved Proposition 60, which authorizes the legislature (if it chooses) to allow persons over age 55 who sell their residence and buy or build another within two years *in the same county* to transfer the old residence's assessed value to the new residence.

Homeowner's exemption. Each residential property that is owner occupied on the lien date of March 1 receives an annual tax **homeowner's** exemption of $7,000 from assessed value. The homeowner needs to apply only once for this homeowner's exemption if there is no change from year to year in the ownership of and residency on the property. A homeowner must have been the owner of record on or before March 1 and have actually occupied the property to claim this exemption for the upcoming tax year beginning July 1. A homeowner is allowed only one exemption at a time. Once this exemption has been filed, it remains in effect until terminated. The assessor must be notified of a termination, or an escape assessment plus 25 percent penalty may be made.

Veteran's exemption. California war veterans may receive a $4,000 **veteran's exemption** on the full value of their homes. Veterans may not claim this exemption if their total property owned, whether taxable or exempt, has a value of $5,000 or more ($10,000 if owned by husband and wife). One-fourth of the assessed value of real property and the full value of other property is used in computing total property value, which maintains their proportionate values. An individual may not claim both the veteran's and homeowner's exemptions on the same property.

A veteran who is blind, crippled in two or more limbs or totally disabled because of an injury received during military service is entitled to a greater exemption.

Senior Citizen's Property Tax Assistance

Another form of relief is **senior citizen's property tax assistance.** A homeowner who is at least 62 years old as of January 1 and has a total household income of $12,000 or less may be eligible for a special state-assisted rebate on real property tax. Persons of any age who are blind or totally disabled and meet the income requirement also are eligible. The amount of the tax rebate is determined by the Franchise Tax Board.

The State of California also has made it possible for a qualified person aged 62 or over to postpone payment of his or her real estate taxes for an indefinite period of time. To qualify, a person must have at least a 20 percent equity in the property and earn not more than $24,000 annually ($34,000 in 1983). If approved, the state places a lien against the property and charges interest on the postponed account. Payments are deferred until the homeowner sells the property, dies or no longer qualifies. The tax plus the interest would then be covered.

California Renter's Relief Provisions

Through the state **Renter's Relief Provisions,** California residents who are paying rent on property that is not exempt from property tax and who are occupying this property as their principal residence are entitled to a tax deduction of up to $137 from their state income tax liabilities. As of 1986, $60 is allowed for a single person; $68.50 for a married person filing a separate return; $99 for a joint custody head of household; and $137 for married persons filing a joint return, a head of household and a qualifying widow(er) with a dependent child.

Income Taxes

In this day and age income taxes play an important role in real estate owners' decisions, from buying or selling their personal residences to decisions involving the most exotic real investment properties. Because the tax laws are ever changing, it is important for the real estate agent to stay abreast of them. Some basic tax definitions and calculations stay the same from law change to law change. We will begin with the concept of depreciation.

Depreciation

The two most obvious and important characteristics of real estate investments are income and expenses. Real estate is one of those assets that also benefits from a special accounting device for a special kind of expense called **depreciation.**

Depreciation is a method of accounting for the wear that results from the *use* of a capital good. A capital good, such as a piece of equipment or a building, does not last forever. As it is used, it wears out or becomes obsolete; at some point the owner must replace it or substantially repair it. Depreciation is used to reflect this replacement cost. The main reasons depreciation is allowed are to encourage home ownership and investment in real estate and to reflect, in accounting terms, the real costs of property ownership.

In this text we mainly will discuss the federal tax. The State of California has its own tax law, which differs from the federal tax law. This will be discussed further in the next section.

We use a recovery system instead of depreciation, but the word depreciation has been around so long that the term *depreciation* still is used. The federal law uses the Accelerated Cost Recovery System (ACRS), so-called because property is assigned a useful life over which it is depreciated that may have no relationship to its actual utility.

For depreciation purposes real estate can be divided into two categories: (1) residential property and (2) nonresidential property. Residential property is where people live, e.g., a single-family residence, fourplexes and multiunit apartments. Nonresidential property is property that is not residential in nature (industrial, commercial, office buildings and other similar types of properties). Since January 1, 1987, all real property must use the straight-line method of depreciation. Residential rental property must generally use a useful life of 27.5 years. Nonresidential property must generally use a useful life of 31.5 years.

If the real estate agent were to look in the past, he or she would find that the IRS has changed the useful life many times. Not only the useful life but the ways that property may be depreciated may be important in a transaction. (See Table 10.1 for further information.)

Basis

In preparing to explore the tax implications of investment properties, it is necessary to understand the concept of **basis.** You should know how to compute the original basis, depreciable basis and adjusted basis correctly. The **original basis** (OB) is used to determine the depreciable basis and adjusted basis. The **depreciable basis** (DB) is used to determine the amount of allowable depreciation. The **adjusted basis,** which changes as time progresses, is required to calculate the gain on the disposition of a property.

Table 10.1
Real Property
Depreciation
Methods Chart

DATE PROPERTY PLACED IN SERVICE	METHODS AVAILABLE	USEFUL LIFE	IRS TABLES REQUIRED
BEFORE JAN. 1, 1981	STRAIGHT LINE	NEGOTI-	NO
	125% DECLINING BALANCE	ABLE	NO
	150% DECLINING BALANCE	20 TO	NO
	200% DECLINING BALANCE	40 YRS	NO
	SUM-OF-THE-YEARS'-DIGITS		NO
JAN. 1, 1981 TO MAR. 15, 1984	ACRS	15	YES
	ACRS (low income housing)	15	YES
	ALTERNATE ACRS (S/L)	15, 35, 45	NO
MAR. 16, 1984 TO JUNE 22, 1984	ACRS	18	YES
	ACRS (low income housing)	15	YES
	ALTERNATE ACRS (S/L)	18	YES
	ALTERNATE ACRS (S/L)	35, 45	NO
JUNE 23, 1984 TO MAY 8, 1985	ACRS	18	YES
	ACRS (low income housing)	15	YES
	ACRS (outside the U.S.)	35	YES
	ALTERNATE ACRS (S/L)	18, 35, 45	YES
	S/L (outside the U.S.)	35	YES
MAY 9, 1985 TO DEC. 31, 1986	ACRS	19	YES
	ACRS (low income housing)	15	YES
	ACRS (outside the U.S.)	35	YES
	ALTERNATE ACRS (S/L)	19, 35, 45	YES
	S/L (outside the U.S.)	35	YES
JAN. 1, 1987 TO PRESENT	RESIDENTIAL (S/L only)	27.5, 40	YES
	NONRESIDENTIAL (S/L only)	31.5, 40	YES

Original Basis

The original basis of a property is the sum of its purchase price and the buying expenses on acquisition. When a client first purchases a property, the escrow statement will include the purchase price (sales price) and a listing of other costs and expenses. These amounts can be classified into four basic groups: (1) purchase price (PP), (2) operating expenses (OE), (3) buying expenses (BE) and (4) nondeductible items (ND).

The purchase price. The PP is the amount the buyer is willing to pay for the property and the seller is willing to accept in payment for the property. On the escrow statement, the PP usually is on the top line and is called total consideration. Generally, the PP is financed in some manner. These loans do *not* affect the basis. Furthermore, if one takes out a new loan, refinances or takes a second mortgage, these loans do not increase the basis.

Operating expenses. Operating expenses (usually **recurring costs** such as interest, insurance and taxes) are written off against the income produced by the property. **Points** (loan origination fees) are nonrecurring interest costs that are amortized over the life of the loan; they are not operating expenses.

Buying expenses. Buying expenses are defined as nonrecurring escrow costs (excluding points to obtain a loan). The BE are added to the PP, making up the OB. Points are never added to the basis.

$$OB = PP + BE$$

Depreciable Basis

The DB is defined as the OB multiplied by the percentage of improvements to land (% I):

An alternative formula is the OB less the land value

$$DB = OB \times \%I$$
$$DB = OB - LV$$

Determination of the Depreciable Basis

Investment real estate is composed of two items, the land and the structure; only the structure can be depreciated. Because land is not depreciable, its value must be subtracted from the total original basis to arrive at the depreciable basis, the improvements.

Once the percentage of improvements (%I) is found, it is simple to determine the depreciable basis (DB):

$$DB = OB \times \%I$$

Three methods for determining the percentage of improvements are the assessed value method, the appraisal method and the contract method.

Assessed value method. The county assessor's property tax statement now lists the full cash value of the land and the improvements. The value of the improvements for depreciation purposes is thus the assessor's determination of the part of the purchase price that represents the value of the improvements.

Example: Lilli Depre purchased a property for $100,000 and received the following tax bill from the county assessor's office:

Assessed Value:	
Land	$ 30,000
Improvements	70,000
Total	$100,000

The improvements give Ms. Depre a depreciable basis of $70,000.

Appraisal method. The property owner may secure the services of a professional appraiser to appraise the building and land. Sometimes the appraisal method will give a more or a less favorable ratio than the assessed method. The taxpayer should compare the ratios from the two methods to verify which is more advantageous.

Contract method. One other method of determining the percentage of improvements is the contract method. With this method, the buyer and the seller determine the relative values of the improvements and land and designate these values in the contract, deposit receipt or escrow instructions. Note that the determination must be at arm's length and reasonable. Before using this method, it is strongly suggested that the agent get professional help.

Date property placed into service. The taxpayer must first determine when the property was placed into service. Placed into service means the first day the property can be used. For example, if the property is a rental and escrow closed on January 2 of this year, many would think this is the first day of service. However, if the property needs repairs before it can be rented, the first day of service is the day all the repairs are made and the property is ready to rent. If the taxpayer procrastinates until August 1 to finish the repairs, then the first day the property could be rented would be August 1 and that would be the first day of service.

Adjusted Basis

The adjusted basis (AB) of a property is the amount that the client has invested in the property for tax purposes. In other words, the AB is equal to OB, plus improvements (IMP), less all depreciation (D) taken:

$$AB = OB + IMP - D$$

It is extremely important that the homeowner or investor understand the relationship between the basis and the final sales price of the property, because basis is the beginning point for calculating the amount of gain or loss on the sale. Calculation of the basis is affected by how the property originally was acquired.

- *Basis by purchase* is the price paid for the property, as described above.
- *Basis by gift* is the donor's (gift giver's) adjusted basis plus the gift tax paid, not to exceed the fair-market value at the time of the gift.
- *Basis by inheritance* generally is the fair-market value at time of death.

Computing Gain

The basis is the beginning point for computing the gain or loss on the sale, but numerous adjustments to the basis will always be made during the ownership period. Some of the costs that increase the basis are: title insurance, appraisal fees, legal fees, cost of capital improvements, and sales costs on disposition. Accrued (past) depreciation is deducted from the basis. The result is the adjusted basis.

The gain (or loss) is the difference between the adjusted basis and the sales price. An example may clarify this.

$ 80,000	original basis
+ 800	applicable closing costs
+ 3,000	capital improvements
+ 4,000	sales costs
$ 87,800	
− 12,500	accumulated depreciation
$ 75,300	adjusted cost basis
$100,000	sales price
− 75,300	adjusted cost basis
$ 24,700	total gain

Depreciation for Federal and State Income Tax Purposes

The State of California has not followed federal tax law on depreciation. California taxpayers generally must choose one of three methods: straight-line, declining-balance or sum-of-the-years'-digits depreciation. Under each method, the annual depreciation amount is the depreciation percentage multiplied by the depreciable basis. Table 10.2 shows the methods for calculating depreciation percentage and depreciable basis. The method of depreciation that can be used under specific circumstances depends on regulations set up by the Franchise Tax Board (FTB).

For federal tax purposes, as mentioned earlier, the straight-line method now is used over a useful life of 27.5 years for residential rental property and 31.5 years for nonresidential property.

Table 10.2

Depreciation Method	Depreciation Percentage	Depreciable Basis
Straight-line	$1.00 \div$ No. of years	Same each year
Declining-balance	$1.25 \times$ No. of years* $1.50 \times$ No. of years* $2.00 \times$ No. of years*	Reduce by previous year's depreciation
Sum-of-the-years'-digits	Year $\times$ Sum-of-the-years'-digits †	Same each year

*Percentage remains constant each year.
†Percentage changes each year.

Methods of Depreciation

When determining the depreciation allowance, use the *CALM* method.

1. determine the *C*ost or basis of the property;

2. determine the *A*llocation between land and improvements;

3. determine the *L*ife of the property; and

4. determine the *M*ethod used.

Straight-line method. With this method an equal amount is deducted each year based on the projected useful life of the property. For example, a property improvement with a 50-year life will depreciate at the rate of two percent per year (100% ÷ 50 = 2% per year). This amount is charged against the taxpayer's income as an expense. The straight-line method affords the greatest amount of depreciation in the later years of the property's useful life.

Declining-balance method. There are three basic declining-balance methods: 200 percent, 150 percent and 125 percent. Each may be used only in specific instances as directed by the California Internal Revenue Service.

When computing declining-balance depreciation, compute the straight-line amount for the property involved, then multiply this figure (1) by two for the 200 percent method, (2) by one and one-half for the 150 percent method or (3) by one and one-fourth for the 125 percent method. This method does not exactly correspond to the table, though they are algebraically equivalent. Each year when the depreciation amount is computed, subtract this amount from the original value. This is the new depreciable basis to be multiplied by the depreciation percentage. The percent will remain the same each year, but the base will change; hence the term "declining balance." For example:

Compute the depreciation on a $100,000 property improvement with an estimated life of 50 years, using the 200 percent declining-balance method.

Step 1: 100% ÷ 50 = 2% per year straight line
Step 2: 2 × 2% = 4% per year declining balance
Step 3: First year: 4% × $100,000 = $4,000.00 depreciated
                         −   4,000
         Second year: 4% × $ 96,000 = $3,840.00 depreciated
                         −   3,840
         Third year: 4% × $ 92,160 = $3,686.40 depreciated

The 200 percent declining-balance method gives the greatest amount of depreciation in the first year of the property's life.

Sum-of-the-years'-digits method. The sum-of-the-years'-digits method and the declining-balance method are referred to as accelerated methods. In computing sum-of-the-years'-digits depreciation, a different fraction or percentage will be used each year, but the depreciable basis remains the same.

The first step is to calculate the sum of the digits of the years of the property's life. For example, for an item valued at $3,000 with a life of five years, the sum-of-the-years'-digits is:

$$1 + 2 + 3 + 4 + 5 = 15$$

To find the depreciation percentage, use the sum, 15, as the denominator of a fraction. The denominator will remain the same each year and each year's numerator will be the remaining years of the property's life. The depreciation amount will be largest in the first year and be reduced each year, as follows:

First year	5/15 × $3,000 = $1,000
Second year:	4/15 × $3,000 = 800
Third year:	3/15 × $3,000 = 600
Fourth year:	2/15 × $3,000 = 400
Fifth year:	1/15 × $3,000 = 200
	Total depreciation = $3,000

The useful life of real property might be as much as 40 to 50 years. The following formula will assist you in easily determining the denominator of the fraction to be used in your calculations.

$$\text{Sum-of-the-years'-digits} = \frac{\text{Number of years} \times (\text{Number of years} + 1)}{2}$$

To use the sum-of-the-years'-digits method to compute the accrual depreciation for the first three years of a $100,000 parcel or real property improvements with a useful life of 40 years, substitute in the given formula:

$$\frac{40 \times (40 + 1)}{2} = 820$$

Then calculate the depreciation amount:

First year: $40/820 \times \$100,000 = \$4,878$
Second year: $39/820 \times \$100,000 = \$4,756$
Third year: $38/820 \times \$100,000 = \$4,634$

Problem:

Compute the first year's depreciation under each of the three methods we have just discussed for a property having a basis of $800,000, with a land value of $200,000 and no salvage value (remaining value after being fully depreciated). The useful life of the improvements is 27.5 years and the 200 percent declining balance is applicable.

With a useful life of 27.5 years, depreciation is 3.636 percent per year. Depreciation on improvements having a basis of $600,000 is thus 3.636 percent of $600,000, or $21,816 in the first (and every) year.

Under the double-declining-balance method, the first year's depreciation is $21,816 multiplied by two, or $43,632. Depreciation in subsequent years is less.

Under the sum-of-the-years'-digits method, a fraction with a numerator of 27.5 (the number of years remaining in the useful life of the property) and denominator of 395.5 (the sum of the numbers representing the years of life of the property) is multiplied by the property's basis. Thus, the first year's depreciation using this method is 27.5/395.5 multiplied by $600,000, or $41,700. Depreciation in subsequent years is less.

ACRS Method

Recovery period. Recoverable property is all personal or real property that can be depreciated (cost recovered) under the Accelerated Cost Recovery System (**ACRS**). ACRS puts all revocable property into one of five class life categories. The recovery period simply is based on the property's category. We will use property being depreciated over 19 years, except low-income housing, which can be depreciated over 15 years.

Recovery tables. The IRS publishes tables that show what percentage of the property's value may be depreciated in each year of the recovery period. Table 10.3 is the ACRS table for real property placed into service after May 8, 1985. The first column shows the recovery year and the other columns contain the recovery percentages, based on the month in which the property was placed in service (i.e., January is 1, February is 2, and so on).

The first-year percentages in these tables are based on the number of months remaining in the first year that the property is placed in service. If the property is purchased in April, then use the percentages under the fourth column for the next 20 years. The chart goes to 20 years to handle the partial year, at the end of the 19-year term. Note that almost half of the property's value will be recovered in the first six years.

Mr. I. Want purchased a property for $300,000 and escrow closed on September 2 of 1986. He wished to recover the property using ACRS and the land value is estimated at $100,000, thus making his recoverable basis $200,000. He will use the ACRS table for Real Estate for 19 years. The recovery for the next six years is computed as follows:

Year 1	$ 5,400	($200,000 times 2.7%)
Year 2	18,000	($200,000 times 9.0%)
Year 3	16,200	($200,000 times 8.1%)
Year 4	14,800	($200,000 times 7.4%)
Year 5	13,400	($200,000 times 6.7%)
Year 6	12,200	($200,000 times 6.1%)
Total	$80,000	

Table 10.3
ACRS Table for Real Estate (except low-income housing)

19-YEAR TABLES

YEAR	1	2	3	4	5	6	7	8	9	10	11	12
1	8.8	8.1	7.3	6.5	5.8	5.0	4.2	3.5	2.7	1.9	1.1	0.4
2	8.4	8.5	8.5	8.6	8.7	8.8	8.8	8.9	9.0	9.0	9.1	9.2
3	7.6	7.7	7.7	7.8	7.9	7.9	8.0	8.1	8.1	8.2	8.3	8.3
4	6.9	7.0	7.0	7.1	7.1	7.2	7.3	7.3	7.4	7.4	7.5	7.6
5	6.3	6.3	6.4	6.4	6.5	6.5	6.6	6.6	6.7	6.8	6.8	6.9
6	5.7	5.7	5.8	5.9	5.9	5.9	6.0	6.0	6.1	6.1	6.2	6.2
7	5.2	5.2	5.3	5.3	5.3	5.4	5.4	5.5	5.5	5.6	5.6	5.6
8	4.7	4.7	4.8	4.8	4.8	4.9	4.9	5.0	5.0	5.1	5.1	5.1
9	4.2	4.3	4.3	4.4	4.4	4.5	4.5	4.5	4.5	4.6	4.6	4.7
10	4.2	4.2	4.2	4.2	4.2	4.2	4.2	4.2	4.2	4.2	4.2	4.2
11	4.2	4.2	4.2	4.2	4.2	4.2	4.2	4.2	4.2	4.2	4.2	4.2
12	4.2	4.2	4.2	4.2	4.2	4.2	4.2	4.2	4.2	4.2	4.2	4.2
13	4.2	4.2	4.2	4.2	4.2	4.2	4.2	4.2	4.2	4.2	4.2	4.2
14	4.2	4.2	4.2	4.2	4.2	4.2	4.2	4.2	4.2	4.2	4.2	4.2
15	4.2	4.2	4.2	4.2	4.2	4.2	4.2	4.2	4.2	4.2	4.2	4.2
16	4.2	4.2	4.2	4.2	4.2	4.2	4.2	4.2	4.2	4.2	4.2	4.2
17	4.2	4.2	4.2	4.2	4.2	4.2	4.2	4.2	4.2	4.2	4.2	4.2
18	4.2	4.2	4.2	4.2	4.2	4.2	4.2	4.2	4.2	4.2	4.2	4.2
19	4.2	4.2	4.2	4.2	4.2	4.2	4.2	4.2	4.2	4.2	4.2	4.2
20	0.2	0.5	0.9	1.2	1.6	1.9	2.3	2.6	3.0	3.3	3.7	4.0

Alternate ACRS (straight-line). A taxpayer may elect to use straight-line recovery instead of accelerated depreciation. The election to use the straight-line method can be made on a case-by-case basis, but once it is made it cannot be revoked unless permission is granted by the IRS Commissioner. A taxpayer who chooses the optional straight-line method may choose one of three different recovery periods for real property: 19 years, 35 years or 45 years (for low-income housing, the choice is 15, 35 or 45 years). Table 10.4 shows a recovery table for 19-year alternate ACRS.

Tax-deferred Exchange

Under Internal Revenue Code Section 1031, gain or loss is not recognized under a properly structured real estate exchange. To qualify, property must be

Table 10.4
Straight-line Table
for Real Estate
(except low-income
housing)

19-YEAR TABLES

YEAR	1	2	3	4	5	6	7	8	9	10	11	12
1	5.0	4.6	4.2	3.7	3.3	2.9	2.4	2.0	1.5	1.1	0.7	0.2
2	5.3	5.3	5.3	5.3	5.3	5.3	5.3	5.3	5.3	5.3	5.3	5.3
3	5.3	5.3	5.3	5.3	5.3	5.3	5.3	5.3	5.3	5.3	5.3	5.3
4	5.3	5.3	5.3	5.3	5.3	5.3	5.3	5.3	5.3	5.3	5.3	5.3
5	5.3	5.3	5.3	5.3	5.3	5.3	5.3	5.3	5.3	5.3	5.3	5.3
6	5.3	5.3	5.3	5.3	5.3	5.3	5.3	5.3	5.3	5.3	5.3	5.3
7	5.3	5.3	5.3	5.3	5.3	5.3	5.3	5.3	5.3	5.3	5.3	5.3
8	5.3	5.3	5.3	5.3	5.3	5.3	5.3	5.3	5.3	5.3	5.3	5.3
9	5.3	5.3	5.3	5.3	5.3	5.3	5.3	5.3	5.3	5.3	5.3	5.3
10	5.3	5.3	5.3	5.3	5.3	5.3	5.3	5.3	5.3	5.3	5.3	5.3
11	5.3	5.3	5.3	5.3	5.3	5.3	5.3	5.3	5.3	5.3	5.3	5.3
12	5.3	5.3	5.3	5.3	5.3	5.3	5.3	5.3	5.3	5.3	5.3	5.3
13	5.3	5.3	5.3	5.3	5.3	5.3	5.3	5.3	5.3	5.3	5.3	5.3
14	5.2	5.2	5.2	5.2	5.2	5.2	5.2	5.2	5.2	5.2	5.2	5.2
15	5.2	5.2	5.2	5.2	5.2	5.2	5.2	5.2	5.2	5.2	5.2	5.2
16	5.2	5.2	5.2	5.2	5.2	5.2	5.2	5.2	5.2	5.2	5.2	5.2
17	5.2	5.2	5.2	5.2	5.2	5.2	5.2	5.2	5.2	5.2	5.2	5.2
18	5.2	5.2	5.2	5.2	5.2	5.2	5.2	5.2	5.2	5.2	5.2	5.2
19	5.2	5.2	5.2	5.2	5.2	5.2	5.2	5.2	5.2	5.2	5.2	5.2
20	0.2	0.6	1.0	1.5	1.9	2.3	2.8	3.2	3.7	4.1	4.5	5.0

exchanged for other like-kind property, which is real estate meeting certain specific requirements. Although this is often referred to as a "tax-free" exchange, the gain is merely deferred. Through a **tax-deferred exchange,** the gain is deferred until the new property is sold. Because exchanges can be extremely complex, this text will not go into detail. A special taxation and exchange course is offered by most California community colleges.

Like-kind properties. To qualify for tax deferral, the exchange must involve a transfer of like-for-like property. Like-kind property exchanges include:

- investment property *for* investment property;

- property held for production of income *for* property held for production of income; and

- property used in a trade or business *for* property used in a trade or business.

The size or worth of the properties does not defeat the "like for like" requirement. For example, a six-unit apartment house of ten units selling for $300,000 or a store selling for $130,000.

Boot. If the values of the properties being exchanged differ, the exchanger of the lower value property may give additional consideration called **boot.** Boot may be cash, a note or other property. If boot is given, a loss is not recognized and a gain becomes taxable at the time of the exchange to the extent of the value of the boot received. Thus, boot always is taxable in an exchange.

A simple exchange involving boot may be described as follows:

Property X	Property Y
$ 80,000 adjusted basis of property	$100,000 adjusted basis of property
$ 20,000 boot	
$100,000 exchange	$100,000 exchange

The owner of Y will have to count $20,000 boot received as ordinary income for income tax purposes in the year received.

It is especially important when boot is involved in an exchange that the person giving boot and the person receiving boot be identified. For example, property owner A exchanges a six-unit apartment house complex with a depreciated cost basis of $120,000 and $4,000 cash for property owner B's fourplex worth $124,000. Although owner B's gain is $7,000, only a portion of this gain, $4,000 (the amount of boot), is recognized and taxable at the time of the exchange. The remaining $3,000 of gain is not recognized at this time but is postponed by increasing the cost basis of the new property to only $121,000. On resale of the fourplex, the remaining $3,000 of the former gain is then taxable.

Mortgage relief. A transfer in which property is subject to mortgage indebtedness is more complicated. If one of the parties involved in an exchange reduces his or her loan liability, that party receives mortgage relief and may be subject to tax liability. In other words, if one property is mortgaged, gain becomes taxable at the time of the exchange to the extent of the relief of the taxpayer from such indebtedness, regardless of any personal liability. In the event that both properties are mortgaged, which is a common occurrence, the difference between the mortgages is considered subject to immediate tax, to the extent of the gain. For example:

Owner A		Owner B	
$100,000	adjusted basis	$100,000	adjusted basis
− 80,000	first trust deed	− 75,000	first trust deed
$ 20,000	difference	$ 25,000	difference

If A trades to B, B will receive $5,000 in boot to equalize the equities in the form of $5,000 in mortgage relief. This will result in a tax liability to B.

Installment Sales

Because of the inflationary appreciation of real property, owners who purchased their homes in the past ten years may hesitate to sell now because the increased value of their homes makes them subject to significant taxes. If they paid their income tax on the full gain on the sale in one year, their tax would be so large that it would discourage investments in real estate.

By using an **installment sale,** the investor can spread the tax gain over two or more years. The following guidelines concern the use of the installment method of reporting deferred-payment sales:

1. The total tax to be paid in any one year may be reduced by spreading the payment amount, and thus the gain, over two or more tax years.

2. The seller pays tax in future years with cheaper, inflated dollars.

3. The seller does not pay the entire tax until after receiving the entire amount of the purchase price.

4. A provision of the prior law stating that no more than 30 percent of the sales could be received in the taxable year of the sale to qualify for installment sales treatment has been eliminated, but all depreciation recapture income is fully recognized in the year of sale, whether or not the principal is received in that year.

5. The installment sales method is automatic unless the taxpayer elects *not* to have the installment sale treatment apply.

Sale-Leaseback

Buyers and sellers can derive tax advantages through an arrangement in which property is sold with provisions for the seller to continue occupancy as a lessee. This form of transaction is called a **sale-leaseback,** *purchase-lease, sale-lease, lease-purchase* and *leaseback.* All these terms have the same meaning.

With a sale-leaseback, seller-lessees gain the advantages of getting property exactly suited to their needs without tying up working capital in fixed assets. Often more capital can be raised than by borrowing. In addition, because leases are not considered long-term liabilities, rent is totally tax deductible. Frequently, writing off total lease payments is better than depreciation, for the land portion of property cannot be depreciated. Often only the land is leased and sold back. Rent on land is a deductible expense, while improvements can be written off with depreciation deductions. If the lease term is longer than a mortgage term would be (for example, 99 years versus 25 years), the balance sheet looks better and credit is enhanced, because sellers can pay for their capital in the form of rent over a long period with constantly inflating dollars.

For companies working under government contracts that pay them cost plus a fixed fee, rent is an allowable expense item, but mortgage interest is not. This is why many aircraft, electronic and other defense plants are leased rather than owned.

Buyer-lessors gain the advantage of obtaining a long-term carefree investment and appreciation in the value of the property. Usually the yield on a sale and leaseback is higher than on a mortgage.

The lease payments will pay off the original investment, and the lessor still will have title to the property. The investment will not be paid off prematurely (as mortgages often are through refinancing), so the investor will not have to go out seeking another good investment to replace the one prematurely paid off. In addition, the lease terms often give the lessor a claim against other assets of the lease in the event of a default, which is better security protection than a trust deed affords. Finally, a transaction usually requires a large amount of money. It costs the investor no more to service one large loan than it does for many small mortgages.

Summary

The taxes affecting the ownership of real property are real property taxes, special assessments and income taxes.

The chapter described the method of assessing real property taxes and special assessments, along with a description of Proposition 13 and special exemptions that are allowed.

Property ownership has some tax advantages for the homeowner as well as the income investor, including deductions for depreciation and other expenses. Other benefits involve tax-deferred exchanges, installment-sales provisions and sale-leaseback transactions. The next chapter will discuss benefits to homeowners in greater depth.

Questions

1. Real property tax is considered:
   a. a progressive tax.
   b. an ad valorem tax.
   c. a flat tax.
   d. none of the above

2. For California property tax, the tax year begins:
   a. in February.
   b. on March 1.
   c. on July 1.
   d. on November 1.

3. The California Homeowners Tax Exemption is a deduction of _____ from the assessed value.
   a. $1,000
   b. $1,750
   c. $4,000
   d. $7,000

4. California law requires that all property be taxed proportionally to its:
   a. market value.
   b. loan value.
   c. book value.
   d. size.

5. On March 1, property tax liability becomes:
   a. due.
   b. subject to exemption.
   c. a lien on the property.
   d. delinquent if first installment is unpaid.

6. Which of the following transactions will cause a reassessment of real property?
   a. creation of a live estate
   b. traditional sale
   c. refinancing
   d. all of the above

7. A property tax limitation was effected by which of the following enactments?
   a. California gift tax
   b. Jarvis-Gann Amendment
   c. California Property Tax Reduction Act
   d. all of the above

8. Which of the following properties would have the shortest useful life?
   a. office building
   b. multiunit apartment building
   c. warehouse
   d. none of the above

9. The adjusted basis is increased by:
   a. loans added to the property.
   b. depreciation.
   c. capital improvements.
   d. all of the above

10. Which of the following are (is) not depreciable?
    a. orange trees
    b. parking lots
    c. land
    d. all of the above

11. A useful life of a theater is:
    a. 27.5 years.
    b. 31.5 years.
    c. both a and b
    d. none of the above

12. If an investor purchases an investment property, when does depreciation begin?
    a. at the close of escrow
    b. on the first day available for rent
    c. any time the purchaser wishes
    d. There is no ruling on this issue.

13. For California income tax, the taxpayer:
    a. may use ACRS.
    b. may use the ACRS optional straight-line method.
    c. must use the new ACRS rules.
    d. none of the above

14. An investor purchases a property for $500,000 and buying cost of $10,000. The original basis is:
    a. $500,000.
    b. $510,000.
    c. $520,000.
    d. none of the above

15. The original basis is defined as:
    a. the purchase price plus the buying costs.
    b. the purchase price plus the selling costs.
    c. the sales price plus the buying costs.
    d. none of the above

16. The original basis is needed to find:
    a. the depreciable basis.
    b. the adjusted basis.
    c. both a and b
    d. none of the above

17. The gain is found by:
    a. subtracting the selling costs and adjusted basis from the sales price.
    b. adding the sales price plus the adjusted basis plus the selling costs.
    c. adding the sales price plus the adjusted basis minus the selling costs.
    d. none of the above

18. Your client purchased a property for $450,000, with buying costs of $5,000, and paid $6,000 in points on the new loan. The client has held the property for the past four years and sold it this year for $600,000. During the four-year period the client took $80,000 in depreciation. What is the client's adjusted basis at the time of sale?
    a. $320,000
    b. $375,000
    c. $435,000
    d. $515,000

19. An investor purchases a property with an original basis of $600,000 including both land and improvements. The tax bill shows a land value at $150,000 and improvements at a value of $450,000. What is the depreciable basis?
    a. $112,500
    b. $150,000
    c. $450,000
    d. $600,000

20. A home buyer bought a new home for personal use for $100,000, including buying expenses. The tax bill shows the building at 60 percent of value and the land at 40 percent. What is the buyer's depreciable basis?
    a. $40,000
    b. $60,000
    c. $100,000
    d. none of the above

11

Tax Implications of Home Ownership

Chapter Preview   This chapter describes the difference between a sale and an exchange of a client's primary personal residence. The agent must learn what qualifies as a home and what does not. Also important are the tax implications of the sale of a home, including the once-in-a-lifetime $125,000 exclusion. This chapter is extremely important to those who work with residential homeowners because it explains the nature of and limitations on homeowners benefits.

The information in this chapter will not qualify readers to be tax preparers. It is merely intended to enable agents to talk intelligently with clients about the client's tax position with regard to home ownership.

Terms To Look For   **Buy-up rule**
Deferred gain
Excluded gain
Home improvements
No-choice rule
$125,000 exclusion
Original basis
Primary personal residence
Realized gain
Recognized gain
Replacement rule

The laws and tax rules that govern the tax treatment of a personal residence differ from rules applicable to investment properties. The objectives of these tax rules are to permit families to own homes and expanding families to move up to larger (and more costly) housing without being penalized.

Definition of a Home	Real estate that constitutes a taxpayer's personal residence receives special tax treatment. A principal residence may include any one of the following:

- single-family house;
- houseboat;
- mobile home;
- motor home;
- trailer;
- condominium; and
- cooperative housing.

The location of a taxpayer's home may be anywhere. It may be in any state, territory or foreign country.

Primary or Secondary Residence	A taxpayer may have only one principal residence at a time. The following statement defines a **primary personal residence** (principal residence).

■ In general a primary personal (or principal) residence is the dwelling in which a taxpayer lives and which the taxpayer occupies most of the time.

The term personal residence is generally understood to refer to the taxpayer's primary residence; that is, the place occupied more often than any other. All other residences are termed secondary residences. One secondary residence will receive favorable income tax treatment, but unlike a primary residence, a secondary residence does not qualify for Section 1034 treatment, which will be discussed later.

Land	The term residence not only includes the improvements but also the land (Rev. Rul. 56 420, 1956 2 CB 519). However, vacant land cannot be considered a personal residence. When a principal residence is located on a large tract of land, the question arises as to just how much of the land is included with the principal residence. There is no clear-cut answer to this question, but the courts have established that it is determined based on the use and the intent of the taxpayer rather than on the amount of land involved.

Acquiring a Home	There are several ways in which a home may be acquired. A taxpayer may purchase a home from the current owner. Or a person may build his or her own home, inherit a home or receive one as a gift. Each of these has its own tax implications.
Buying	Usually the purchaser of a home will pay from one to two percent of the purchase price of the home in buying costs. These costs are found on the escrow closing settlement statement (see Figure 11.1 following) and may be classified into three categories:

1. write-off itemized deductions;

2. buying expenses added to basis; and

3. nondeductible expenses.

Itemized deductions include real estate taxes, mortgage interest and points (loan origination fees) in the year paid. These are written off on the taxpayer's schedule A.

Buying expenses are usually the nonrecurring closing costs. Some examples are appraisal fees, credit report, escrow fees, termite inspection, notary fees, recording fees and title insurance.

Nondeductible items are the closing costs that are neither a write-off nor a buying expense. These include impound accounts, homeowner's insurance and certain origination fees paid to obtain FHA or VA loans. Loan origination fees on FHA or VA loans do *not* qualify as interest; they are considered to be a form of service charge (Rev. Rul. 67297; Rev. Rul. 6865).

Original Basis

Of particular interest to the buyer of a home is the **original basis** (OB)—purchase price plus allowable costs—of the residence. Someday the homeowner will want to dispose of the home, and the higher the basis, the lower the gain, and the lower the taxes. The OB is equal to the purchase price (PP) plus the buying expenses (BE).

$$OB = PP + BE$$

Example: Figure 11.2 is an escrow statement for Mr. Realrich. The loan is a conventional loan. What can he deduct this year on his tax return? How much will be added to the basis? How much is his original basis?

Figure 11.1
Escrow Chart

Escrow Item	Amount
Deductions:	
Taxes	$ 100
Interest	250
Points conventional loan	620
Total Deductions	$ 970
Buying Expenses:	
Recording of trust deed	$ 3
Appraisal fee	75
Escrow fee	197
Handling of beneficiary papers	50
Total Buying Expenses	$ 325
Calculation of Original Basis:	
Purchase price	$85,000
Buying expenses	325
	$85,325

Figure 11.2
Buyer's Escrow
Statement

Escrow Statement

NAME: Realrich

ITEMS	DEBIT	CREDIT
Total Consideration	85,000	
First Trust Deed in Favor of: GotU Mortgage		62,000
Second Trust Deed in Favor of:		
Deposit		25,000
Paid Outside of Escrow		

ADJUSTMENTS

					DEBIT	CREDIT
Taxes	$ 340	for 1 yr.	from 7/1	to 10/5	100	
Interest on	$62,000	at 9.75%	from 10/1	to 10/15	250	
Interest on	$	at %	from	to		
Insurance	Prem. $150		from 10/9	to 10/15	150	
Rents						

DISBURSEMENTS

	DEBIT
Policy of Title Insurance	
ALTA Loan Title Insurance	
Title Company's Sub-escrow Fee	
Recording Deed	3
Recording Trust Deed	
Recording Reconveyance	
Documentary Transfer Stamps	
Tax Service	
Termite	
Commission	
Principal of Loan Paid to:	
Interest on at % from to	
Loan Prepayment Charges	
Loan Company-Service Charge	
Principal of Loan Paid to:	
Interest on at % from to	
Loan Prepayment charges	
New Loan Origination or Discount Fee at 1% Paid to:	620
Credit Report	
Appraisal Fee	75
Impound Account:	480
:	
Interest on $ at % from to	

ESCROW CHARGES

	DEBIT	CREDIT
Escrow Fee	197	
Loan Escrow Fee		
Preparing Deed		
Preparing Trust Deed		
Handling Beneficiary Papers	50	
Balance: due you for which our check is enclosed	75	
Totals	87,000	87,000

(Please Retain This Statement for Income Tax Purposes)

Building

For taxpayers who build their own home, their basis would be the total cost of building the home. This would include cost of the land, legal fees, permits, architectural fees, materials, and so on.

> **Example:** Five years ago Ms. Doit decided to build her own personal residence, and she purchased the land for $20,000. This year she paid $3,000 for permits and plans. Materials cost her $77,000. Ms. Doit's basis in her new home is the total of these expenses, or $100,000.

Inheriting

For the taxpayer who inherits a home, the basis would be the fair-market value at the time of the decedent's death. This is called the stepped-up basis. An alternative valuation date can be used, but it is beyond the scope of this text. However, the agent should be aware that this other method exists.

> **Example:** Mr. Passaway died and left his home to his son. His basis in the home was $10,000, but at the time of death it had a fair-market value of $150,000. The son's basis in the home is $150,000.

Receiving a Home as a Gift

The basis on gifted property is determined by the following formula:

$$NB = AB + \frac{FMV - AB}{FMV} \times GT$$

In the above formula *NB* is the donee's new basis, *AB* is the donor's adjusted basis, *FMV* is the fair-market value, and *GT* is the gift tax paid by the donor.

> **Example:** Mr. Hardwork gives his daughter a home. His adjusted basis in the home was $40,000, and at the time of gift the fair-market value of the home was $100,000. He paid a gift tax of $15,000.

1. Fair-market value (*FMV*)	*$100,000*
2. Donor's adjusted basis (*AB*)	*40,000*
3. Net increase in value (line 1 − line 2)	*60,000*
4. Percentage increase in value (line 3 ÷ line 1)	*60%*
5. Gift tax paid (*GT*)	*15,000*
6. Gift tax due to net increase in value (line 4 × line 5)	*9,000*
7. Donee's new basis (line 2 + line 6)	*49,000*

Tax Benefits

Income Tax Write-offs during Home Ownership

Homeowners are eligible for certain income tax write-offs, while they own their home. To be eligible for these tax deductions, taxpayers must be the legal owner or equitable owner of the home.

The general rule:

> For income tax purposes, ownership transfers at the time that the title is transferred (a deed given) or when the buyer is given the rights of possession (the benefits and burdens of ownership), whichever occurs first.

■ Note: When the property is purchased on a land contract, the owner has equitable title.

During ownership, owners may write off real estate taxes and mortgage interest in the year they are paid. Note that paying monies into an impound account is not the same as paying them to the agency to whom they are owed. Money paid into an impound account is not deductible. Only the money paid from the impound account to the proper authority can be deducted.

Interest

The amount of interest is normally provided by the lender on the year-end loan statement. A common exception is when the loan is a junior loan being carried back by the seller or a private lender. Both the buyer and the seller (if carrying back a note on the sale) need to know how much interest is being paid each year. The seller must declare the interest as income and the buyer can write off the interest on his or her tax return. Under California Civil Code, Div. III, Part 4, Title XIV, Ch. 2, sections 2956–2967 (Full Loan Disclosure), it is up to the arranger of the credit (usually the buyer's agent) to disclose all material facts. An amortization table certainly would be a material fact of a loan.

After a few years in a home, the homeowner's equity will usually increase (equity build-up and appreciation). At this time the homeowner might want to pull some of his or her equity by refinancing. Whether the loan is a new one or a second loan on the property, the transaction will get the same tax treatment if it is for the homeowner's principal residence. What the homeowner must be aware of in deciding how much money he or she should refinance the property for is that the interest on the loan amount over the purchase price plus home improvements is not deductible as home interest. There are two exceptions: if the money is used (1) for education or (2) for medical purposes.

> **Example:** Mr. Bior purchased a home five years ago for $100,000 and procured an $80,000 first trust deed. The FMV of the property today is $150,000 and the $80,000 loan is now paid down to $75,000. He now wants to pull out his equity and takes out a new first for $125,000. He may write off the interest on the first $100,000. On the next $25,000 the interest may not be deducted, unless it was spent on medical expenses or education.

A homeowner can not only deduct the interest on his principal residence but he or she can also deduct the interest on a secondary residence. For a property to qualify as a secondary residence the taxpayer must use it part of the year as his or her residence. Interest on outstanding debt on a secondary residence is fully deductible to the extent that the debt does not exceed the purchase price plus improvements or the FMV, whichever is the lesser.

Points

Points on the refinancing of a home must be amortized over the life of the loan. There is one exception: if the loan is used to make home improvements, then the points may be written off in the year they are paid.

Home Improvements

Systematically recording amounts spent for home improvements and retaining any and all receipts are of great importance to the homeowner. Unfortunately, they are often neglected. Many homeowners are completely unaware of the ultimate tax implications of the home improvements or capital improvements that are added to their properties through the years. These improvements may be added to the homeowner's basis, making the adjusted basis greater and reducing the gain at the time of sale. The adjusted basis (AB) is equal to the original basis (OB) plus home improvements (HI).

$$AB = OB + HI$$

There is a great deal of misunderstanding as to what items are classified as home improvements. The IRS defines improvements differently for homes than it does for rental property. Some examples of home improvements:

- electric wiring (new, replacement, rearrangement);
- floors;
- heating units;
- partitions (including removal);
- pipes and drainage (including replacement);
- roof (new or reshingling over old shingles);
- walls (plastering, strengthening);
- room additions;
- patios;
- pools;
- fencing;
- landscaping (trees, shrubbery, grass seed, etc.); and
- sprinkler systems.

Maintenance items are *not* home improvements. Some examples are:

- painting;
- papering;
- carpeting;
- drapes;
- furniture; and
- replacement of built-in appliances (stoves, ovens, dishwashers, etc.).

> **Example:** Mr. Overbuild purchased a home for $125,000 with buying expenses of $2,000. He has owned it for five years. During that time he has put in drapes ($1,400), a patio ($5,000), a fence ($2,000) and new plumbing ($1,000). The original basis is $127,000 ($125,000 + $2,000). Total home improvements are $8,000 ($5,000 + $2,000 + $1,000). The $1,400 for drapes is not a home improvement. The adjusted basis is $135,000 ($127,000 original basis + $8,000 home improvements).

Disposition

Homeowners may dispose of their homes in a variety of ways. Disposition may entail one of the following types of transactions:

1. sale (IRC 1034);

2. exchange (IRC 1034);

3. condemnation (IRC 1033); or

4. repossession (IRC 1038).

This chapter examines only the sale and exchange of the principal residence.

The selling escrow statement lists a number of expenses. The expenses are write-offs (deductions), selling expenses or nondeductible expenses. The mortgage interest and real estate taxes are deductions. Selling expenses, however, are not deductions; they are used to reduce the gain. When sellers pay points for a buyer's loan, the points are not considered to be interest but, rather, a selling expense. These selling expenses are used to determine gain over basis.

> **Example:** Mr. Sails shows you his escrow statement (Figure 11.3). He has the following selling expenses:
>
> SELLING EXPENSES:
>
> | | |
> |---|---:|
> | Policy of Title Insurance | $ 400 |
> | Recording Reconveyance | 3 |
> | Documentary Stamps | 165 |
> | Tax Service | 25 |
> | Commission | 7,500 |
> | Termite Report | 25 |
> | Loan Company Service Charge | 25 |
> | Escrow Fee | 300 |
> | Preparing Deed | 15 |
> | Handling Beneficiary Papers | 25 |
> | Total selling expenses | $8,483 |

Sale of a Home

The gain on the sale of a residence is a capital gain. To calculate this gain, taxpayers need three pieces of information: (1) the sales price, (2) the adjusted basis and (3) the selling expenses. The buyer, seller and market conditions will determine the sales price.

Figure 11.3
Seller's Escrow
Statement

ESCROW STATEMENT

NAME: Mr. Sails

ITEMS	DEBIT	CREDIT
Total Consideration		150,000
First Trust Deed in Favor of:		
Second Trust Deed in Favor of:		
Deposit		
Paid Outside of Escrow		

ADJUSTMENTS

						DEBIT	CREDIT
Taxes	$ 400	for 6 mos.	from 7/1	to 9/30		200	
Interest on	$	at	%	from	to		
Interest on	$	at	%	from	to		
Insurance	Prem. $			from	to		
Rents							

DISBURSEMENTS

ITEMS	DEBIT	CREDIT
Policy of Title Insurance	400	
ALTA Loan Title Insurance		
Title Company's Sub-escrow Fee		
Recording Deed		
Recording Trust Deed		
Recording Reconveyance	3	
Documentary Transfer Stamps	165	
Tax Service	25	
Termite	25	
Commission	7,500	
Principal of Loan Paid to: The Money Mart	50,000	
Interest on $50,000 at 12% from 9/1 to 9/30	500	
Loan Prepayment charges		
Loan Company-Service Charge	25	
Principal of Loan Paid to:		
Interest on at % from to		
Loan Prepayment charges		
New Loan Origination or Discount Fee at % Paid to:		
Credit Report		
Appraisal Fee		
Impound Account:		
:		
Interest on $ at % from to		

ESCROW CHARGES

ITEMS	DEBIT	CREDIT
Escrow Fee	300	
Loan Escrow Fee		
Preparing Deed	15	
Preparing Trust Deed		
Handling Beneficiary Papers	25	
Balance: due you for which our check is enclosed	90,817	
Totals	150,000	150,000

(Please Retain This Statement for Income Tax Purposes)

Gain on Sale

This information is used to compute gain as in the following equation.

$$G = SP - SE - AB$$

G is the gain (realized gain), *SP* is the sales price, *SE* is the selling expenses, and *AB* is the adjusted basis.

Types of gain. The gain on the sale of a capital asset—including a residence—may be placed into one of the following categories.

1. **Realized gain** (loss)—When a home is sold, a gain or loss is virtually always realized; in other words, there usually is a potential taxable event.

2. **Recognized gain**—The part of the realized gain on which income tax must be paid is called recognized gain. Losses on a personal residence cannot be recognized; that is, they may not be written off.

3. **Deferred gain**—The part of the realized gain that may be postponed from recognition is deferred gain; the taxpayer may postpone paying it.

4. **Excluded gain**—The part of the realized gain on which there is no tax obligation is the excluded gain. Excluded gain can be used with a personal residence only if the taxpayer qualifies for the $125,000 exclusion discussed later in the chapter.

In other words, a realized gain includes the other three categories:

Realized Gain = Recognized Gain + Deferred Gain + Excluded Gain

When a gain is realized, a part may be recognized, a part may be deferred and a part may be excluded. The important point is: *Taxes are paid only on the recognized gain.* In a sale of a home, all realized gain must be recognized (the taxpayer must pay taxes on all the gain). However, if a new principal residence is purchased or the property is exchanged, all or some of the realized gain may be deferred. Furthermore, if the client is 55 years of age or older, then he or she may be able to exclude up to $125,000 of the realized gain, subject to certain conditions cited later in this chapter. In some cases, all of these events may apply to the same transaction.

Examples: Two examples of how to determine gain follow.

1. Ms. Sailor sold her home for $150,000. She is 45 years old and does not plan to buy another home. It cost her $12,000 in selling costs, and, at the time of sale, her adjusted basis was $68,000. Her realized gain is determined with these calculations.

Sales price	$150,000	Net sales price	$138,000
Selling costs	– 12,000	Adjusted basis	– 68,000
Net sales price	$138,000	Realized gain	$ 70,000

Since this is a sale, all of the realized gain must be recognized:

Realized Gain = Recognized Gain + Deferred Gain + Excluded Gain
$70,000   = $70,000   +   zero   +   zero

Examples continued:

2. Mr. O'Dam sold his home for $125,000; at the time of sale the adjusted basis of the home was $120,000. It cost Mr. O'Dam $10,000 in selling expenses. His realized gain is, in reality, a realized loss of $5,000, which cannot be recognized:

Sales price	$125,000	Net sales price	$115,000
Selling costs	− 10,000	Adjusted basis	−120,000
Net sales price	$115,000	Realized loss	($ 5,000)

Capital Gains

All homes will be considered capital assets. Therefore, any gain on a home will be taxed at the applicable tax rates.

Example: Mr. Holmes sells his home and has a $50,000 gain. This gain puts Mr. Holmes in the 28 percent tax bracket, and he will pay $14,000 ($50,000 × .28) on the gain.

To avoid capital gains tax penalties on families trying to buy larger homes, IRS rules (Section 1034) allow the deferral of taxes when a new principal residence of equal or greater value is purchased. Real estate agents must realize that most times when clients buy or sell their homes, the clients are actually involved in a *tax-deferred transaction,* not just a simple purchase or sale. Agents are not only dealing with real estate law, but they are also involved in a transaction that has important tax considerations.

Two rules must be followed in qualifying for a Section 1034 transaction: (1) the replacement rule and (2) the buy-up rule. If a taxpayer qualifies under these two rules for a 1034 exchange, the taxpayer must treat the transaction as a tax-deferred event. This fact is sometimes called the no-choice rule.

Replacement Rule

Homeowners may be able to defer payment of taxes on the capital gains that occur on the sale of their residences by purchasing replacement residences within a certain time span (see Figure 11.4).

■ A replacement residence must be *purchased* and *occupied* within a 24-month period before or after the sale of the old residence.

Figure 11.4
Replacement Rule

	Date of Sale	
	of Old Residence	
Before		After

_____ X _____

24 Months   24 Months

Notice that the residence must be purchased *and* occupied. Too often, all that is stressed is that another residence must be purchased, and occupancy is never mentioned.

Purchase Before Sale

A person who purchases a new home before selling the currently owned home has two years in which to sell the old home. For example, if Mr. Presail purchased a new home on January 1 this year, he has until December 31 of the next year to sell his old home. Homeowners who buy new homes but have not sold their old homes usually have two house payments to make. To cover their costs, they may rent either the old or the new residences until the old homes are sold. Collecting rents does not destroy the property's classification as a personal residence, because it is considered a temporary rental. IRS Regulation 1.1034(c)(3)(i) states the following:

> The mere fact that the property is, or has been, rented is not determinative that such property is not used by the taxpayer as his principal residence.

While this regulation may make it seem obvious that owners should be able to rent out one of their homes and still qualify for a Section 1034 exchange, it is not so easily done. The IRS does not always agree with taxpayers if the taxpayers do not follow correct procedures. Homeowners should get professional tax help in this area. The following are some general areas of concern that come into consideration:

1. Whether or not the property is listed through a local real-estate agent for sale (at fair-market value), whether rented or not.

2. Whether or not the lease is month-to-month, for no more than 90 days at a time. The lease should also give the landlord the right to show the property (especially the interior) for sale.

3. Whether or not the property is sold within a short time. Any increase in the sales price asked for in the broker's listing should be accompanied by correspondence from the broker substantiating that the increased price is reasonable and reflects the change in the market. In general it is best not to increase the sales price.

4. Whether or not the taxpayer can prove, by consulting an independent real estate broker, that renting the property pending sale is a good marketing technique.

5. Whether or not the taxpayer can establish that the rental of the old residence was motivated by financial needs; that is, the rental income was needed to help make the two monthly payments necessitated by the move.

The answers to these questions determine the best action to take. Before taking specific action, the taxpayer should consult with a tax advisor and the Internal Revenue Service.

Purchase After Sale

Taxpayers who sell their old homes have two years in which to purchase a replacement home. For example, Ms. Post sold her old residence on January 1 of this year. She has until December 31 of the following year to purchase and occupy a new home.

Taxpayers should remember the importance of the date of occupancy. For Ms. Post, in the preceding example, the two-year period ends on December 31. Assume that she purchases a replacement and escrow closes on December 27, just in time. However, the contract says "COE+5" (meaning the seller elects to stay in the property those five days), and Ms. Post does not move in until January 2. She does not have a Section 1034 exchange.

Actual cases that illustrate the importance of the date of occupancy are: (1) A taxpayer was ready to move into his new home, and a fire destroyed it. The Section 1034 exchange was disallowed (Rev. Rul. 75438, 19752 CB 334). (2) A taxpayer became too ill to move in, and by the time he recovered the time period had elapsed. The Tax Court ruled there was no Section 1034 exchange (*Bazzell,* TC Memo 1967101).

Sale and Construction

Taxpayers have 24 months after the sale of their old residence to start building a new home and complete it. They may occupy the newly built residence from 24 months before to 24 months after sale of the old residence to qualify for a Section 1034 exchange. There is no additional extension beyond this 24-month period.

Buy-up Rule

The second requirement to qualify for the Section 1034 exchange is that taxpayers must "buy-even" or "buy-up." This stipulation is called the buy-up rule.

■ The cost of the replacement residence must equal or exceed the adjusted sales price of the old residence.

Cost of replacement residence. For this rule, the cost of the replacement residence consists of the purchase price of the new residence, the buying costs and any additional construction, reconstruction or capital improvements that are made within two years after the sale of the old residence. (Reg. 1.10341 [c][4]).

For example, Mr. Biup sold his residence on January 1 of this year. The adjusted sales price was $150,000. In February of the same year he purchased a replacement residence for $120,000 plus buying costs of $3,000. In December of the same year, he added a pool for $20,000. In November of the following year, he installed a new fence for $7,000). Therefore, his total replacement cost was $150,000 ($120,000 + $3,000 + $20,000 + $7,000). The taxpayer has met the obligations of the buy-up rule.

Adjusted sales price. The adjusted sales price (*ASP*) is equal to the sales price (*SP*) minus the selling expense (*SE*) minus the fixing-up expense (*FE*). Fixing-up expenses are decorating and repair expenses incurred only to assist in the sale of the old property. They are not ordinarily deductible in figuring the adjusted basis of the old residence. Fix-up expenses must have been incurred for work performed within 90 days before the contract to sell was signed, and must have been paid not later than 30 days after the sale.

$$ASP = SP - SE - FE$$

For example, Ms. Decor sold her home for $100,000; selling costs were $8,000, and it cost her $12,000 to decorate her home for sale (fix-up expenses). She did this decorating within 90 days before the contract to sell, and the bills were paid promptly. If Ms. Decor's adjusted basis was $52,000, then it is a simple matter to calculate her gain and adjusted sales price.

Sales price	$100,000
Selling costs	– 8,000
Net sales price	$ 92,000
Net sales price	$ 92,000
Adjusted basis	– 52,000
Realized gain	$ 40,000
Net sales price	$ 92,000
Fixing up expenses	– 12,000
Adjusted sales price	$ 80,000

Reinvestment of Equity

It is *not* necessary to reinvest the money received from the sale of an old residence in the new replacement residence. The proceeds can be disposed of in any manner that the client desires. That is, it can be reinvested, banked or spent.

For example, GI Joe sold his home for $100,000 and had a $70,000 gain. He bought a new home on a VA "no-no" (no money down, and no closing costs; the seller pays the closing costs) for $100,000. He did all this within one month. Therefore he qualified for a Section 1034 tax deferral and deferred recognition of the $70,000 gain. He is at liberty to dispose of the equity dollars in any way he desires.

The No-Choice Rule

Taxpayers whose transactions meet the two requirements for a Section 1034 exchange *must* defer the capital gain. They have no choice. *That is,* they may not elect to pay the taxes.

Computations

For taxpayers who buy and sell a personal residence and purchase a replacement within the 24-month period, the tax deferment benefits that are allowed fall into three categories. These three categories are defined by the relationship between the adjusted basis and adjusted sales price of the old residence and the purchase price of the new residence (see Figure 11.5).

1. When the purchase price is less than the adjusted basis (same as a sale), all of the gain must be recognized. This is called a total *buydown* or sale.

2. When the amount of the purchase price is between the adjusted basis and adjusted sales price, there is a partial tax-deferred exchange. If the new residence purchase price is less than the adjusted sales price, the gain is recognized to the extent of the difference. The remainder of the gain, the difference between purchase price and adjusted basis, is deferred. This is called a *buydown*.

3. When the purchase price is equal to or greater than the adjusted price, it is totally tax-deferred exchange. All of the gain must be deferred. This is called a *buy-up*.

Figure 11.5
Tax Deferment
Categories

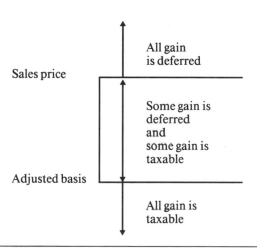

Basis

When a taxpayer completes a tax-deferred exchange, the basis of the new property is not the purchase price. Rather, it is the purchase price minus any deferred gain. This will be illustrated in the examples that follow.

Tax forms. Computations concerning Section 1034 transactions are reported on IRS Form 2119.

Capital gains holding period. In an exchange the holding period is carried forward from the old home and added to that of the new home.

> **Example:** Mr. Trade bought his first home and owned it for three months. Next, he sold it and bought a replacement (an exchange) and owned it for four months. Finally, he sold the second residence. The gain on the sale is a long-term capital gain, because the length of time that he owned both homes totals seven months (more than six months). It should be noted that only one exchange may be done in a two-year period; this will be discussed later.

A total buydown. Mr. Down sold his old home for $100,000; at the time of the sale the adjusted basis was $52,000. The selling costs were $8,000, and there were no fixing-up expenses. He moved to Sandy, Arizona, and purchased a mobile home a month later for $50,000, including buying costs. He has a total buydown on the sale.

Sales price	$100,000
Selling costs	– 8,000
Net sales price	$ 92,000
Net sales price	$ 92,000
Adjusted basis	– 52,000
Realized gain	$ 40,000
Net sales price	$ 92,000
Fixing up expenses	–0–
Adjusted sales price	$ 92,000

Since the new purchase price ($50,000) was less than the adjusted basis ($52,000), the entire gain of $40,000 is taxable. Notice that Mr. Down's new basis is the price he paid for the new property.

A buydown. Mr. Parshall sold his old home for $100,000, with selling expenses of $8,000. His adjusted basis at the time of sale was $52,000, and there were no fixing-up expenses. He purchased a new home in Palmdale, California, for $82,000, including closing cost, a month later. He has a partial buydown.

Sales price	$100,000
Selling costs	– 8,000
Net sales price	$ 92,000
Net sales price	$ 92,000
Adjusted basis	– 52,000
Realized gain	$ 40,000
Net sales price	$92,000
Fixing-up expenses	–0–
Adjusted sales price	$ 92,000
Adjusted sales price	$ 92,000
Cost of new residence	– 82,000
(may not be less than zero)	
Recognized gain	$ 10,000
Realized gain	$ 40,000
Recognized gain	– 10,000
Deferred gain	$ 30,000
Cost of new residence	$ 82,000
Deferred gain	– 30,000
New basis	$ 52,000

The new purchase price ($82,000) is more than the adjusted basis ($52,000) and less than the adjusted sales price ($92,000). So part of the gain is taxable and the remainder is deferred. Notice that the deferred gain reduces the new basis.

A buy-up. Ms. Ups sold her old home for $100,000, with selling costs of $8,000. Her adjusted basis at the time of sale was $52,000, and there were no fixing-up expenses. She purchased a new home a month later for $130,000. She has bought up.

Sales price	$100,000
Selling costs	– 8,000
Net sales price	$ 92,000
Net sales price	$ 92,000
Adjusted basis	– 52,000
Realized gain	$ 40,000
Net sales price	$ 92,000
Fixing-up expenses	–0–
Adjusted sales price	$ 92,000
Adjusted sales price	$ 92,000
Cost of new residence	–130,000
(may be less than zero)	
Recognized gain	–0–
Realized gain	$ 40,000
Recognized gain	–0–
Deferred gain	$ 40,000
Cost of new residence	$130,000
Deferred gain	– 40,000
New basis	$ 90,000

The new purchase price is greater than the adjusted sales price; therefore, no gain has to be recognized. The new basis is $90,000. So if Ms. Ups were to sell the property for $130,000 the day after the close of escrow, her gain would be $40,000.

Tax Issues

Several areas of the IRS Code and federal and state laws are tricky. An understanding of these peculiarities can save consumers a great deal of consternation as well as tax dollars.

The Buy-Sell Trap

If two (or more) purchases of principal residences have occurred within the 24-month rule, which of these is treated as the replacement residence? As logic would indicate, the last one purchased is the replacement residence. Therefore, if there is a capital gain on an intermediate home, it must be recognized. Since the taxpayer is obligated to "skip over" the immediate transaction, some call this rule the hopscotch rule. The Internal Revenue Code [IRC 1034 (C) (4)] states:

If the taxpayer, during the period described in subsection (a) purchases more than one residence which is used by him as his principal residence at some time within 24 months after the date of the sale of the old residence, only the last of such residences so used by him after the date of such sale shall constitute the new residence.

One exception. Current law permits one exception to the hopscotch rule: If within 24 months after selling his or her principal residence on which gain has been deferred a taxpayer relocates for employment purposes, the taxpayer will be permitted a tax-deferred rollover of the gain from the sale of the intermediate residence if he or she otherwise qualifies under Section 1034.

The intent of this rule is to protect taxpayers who have multiple rollovers within a 24-month period because of changes in work location. When taxpayers qualify, the gain on the intermediate transactions is also deferred. To qualify, a taxpayer:

1. may be an employee or self-employed, and the sale must be in connection with a new principal place of work; and

2. must satisfy the two qualifications required for eligibility for moving expenses: that is, (1) the new job must be at least 35 miles farther from the old residence than the old job was and (2) the taxpayer must work at least 39 weeks at the new job if an employee or at least 78 weeks if self-employed.

Section 1031 exchange. A personal residence also qualifies for a tax-free exchange under Section 1031 of the Internal Revenue Code, as described in Chapter 10. It is important here to remember that if boot is received by one of the parties, its value will be taxed. Otherwise, the homeowner's basis in the new property is the same as the basis in the old property.

Once-in-a-Lifetime $125,000 Exclusion

Taxpayers may elect to take advantage of the **$125,000 exclusion** on the realized gain on the sale or exchange of their principal residence if they meet the new following qualifications:

1. The taxpayer must be 55 years old or older on the date of sale. If a married couple elects the $125,000 exclusion, only one of them has to be 55.

2. The taxpayer must have owned and occupied his or her principal residence for a total of at least three years. This three-year period can be spread out over the five years that immediately preceded the sale. The taxpayer may not add on a holding period from any prior residences unless the previous residence was involuntarily converted (through fire, condemnation, etc.) and replaced with the one being sold.

If taxpayers elect this exclusion, they do not pay tax on any gain from the sale or exchange of their residence, up to $125,000. Any gain over $125,000 would be subject to taxation.

Limitations on the Exclusion

A taxpayer or spouse who has made an election of the $125,000 exclusion may no longer make this election for any subsequent sale or exchange of a personal residence. If one spouse qualifies for and uses the $125,000 exclusion, then both are treated as having used it. For married taxpayers who file separate returns, the maximum exclusion is $62,500 on each separate return. If a married couple makes an election and are subsequently divorced, then no further elections are available to *either* of them or to *their new spouses,* should they remarry. Therefore, this election is called a once-in-a-lifetime exclusion.

Computing a "Minimum Purchase Price"

If a taxpayer has realized gain in excess of $125,000, and the taxpayer wishes to purchase a replacement residence of a sufficient price to defer the remainder of the gain, the minimum purchase price to accomplish this goal must be determined. To accomplish this, the cost of the new residence must be at least equal to the adjusted sales price of the old residence, less the $125,000 exclusion. Hence:

Adjusted Sales Price − $125,000 = Minimum Purchase Price of the New Residence

For example, Mr. Show sold his home for $250,000 and incurred selling costs of $25,000. There were no fixing-up expenses. The adjusted basis at the time of the sale was $50,000. Mr. Show qualifies for the $125,000 exclusion. His gain is $175,000. Since his gain is greater than $125,000, he wants to defer the $50,000 above the exclusion. What should be the minimum purchase price of the property he buys?

$$ASP = SP - SE - FE$$
$$= \$250,000 - \$25,000 - 0$$
$$= \$225,000$$

Subtracting the $125,000 exclusion gives the minimum purchase price:

$$\$225,000 - \$125,000 = \$100,000$$

Summary

The reader should have come to the realization that when a person is selling his or her home, that person could be involved with a tax-deferred (1034) transaction or a 1031 exchange. There are special requirements. For example, if a seller purchased a residence within two years before the sale of a home or purchases a new personal residence within two years after the sale of a home, a 1034 exchange is involved, and gain must be deferred to the extent allowable. The agent must understand what the buyer or seller is trying to accomplish.

Questions

1. A personal residence can be which of the following?
   a. single-family home
   b. houseboat
   c. mobile home
   d. all of the above

2. A buyer of a home in the year of purchase can write off:
   a. all the escrow cost.
   b. taxes.
   c. title insurance.
   d. recordation fees.

3. For tax purposes a sale occurs when:
   a. title is passed.
   b. possession is given.
   c. both a and b
   d. none of the above

4. Which Internal Revenue Code Section explains the deferral of tax on the sale of a personal residence?
   a. 1031
   b. 1034
   c. 1043
   d. none of the above

5. In dealing with the sale or exchange of a personal residence, which types of gain could you deal with?
   a. excluded gain
   b. recognized gain
   c. deferred gain
   d. all of the above

6. Your client sells his or her home for $100,000, selling costs of $8,000, and has an adjusted basis of $42,000. What is your client's realized gain?
   a. $50,000
   b. $58,000
   c. $92,000
   d. $100,000

7. If Mr. Looser has a $15,000 loss on his principal residence, how much can he deduct on his tax return?
   a. $–0–
   b. $6,000
   c. $7,500
   d. $15,000

8. Which of the following would qualify for the replacement rule?
   a. You purchase a new home and then sell the old within two years.
   b. You purchase a new home, occupy it, and then sell the old within two years.
   c. both a and b
   d. none of the above

9. Which of the following would exclude the necessity of occupying a house to qualify for a 1034 exchange?
   a. illness
   b. property destroyed by fire
   c. both a and b
   d. none of the above

10. The cost of the replacement residence must equal or exceed the:
    a. sales price of the old.
    b. adjusted sales price of the old.
    c. adjusted basis of the old.
    d. fair market value of the old.

11. If a home qualifies for a 1034 exchange, then the gain:
    a. can be deferred.
    b. can be recognized.
    c. must be recognized.
    d. must be deferred.

12. If the purchase price of the new home is less than the purchase price of the old, then you will have a:
    a. total buydown.
    b. partial buydown.
    c. total buy-up.
    d. partial buy-up.

13. The tax form to report a sale or exchange of a personal residence is a:

    a. 2106.
    b. 2119.
    c. 2219.
    d. 2911.

14. The holding period of the old property:

    a. is not counted toward the new property.
    b. only half the time is added to the new property.
    c. is added on to new property.
    d. none of the above

15. Your client exchanges his home (valued at $100,000) for another home (valued at $125,000). The gain on the old home is $50,000. What is his new basis?

    a. can't tell
    b. $125,000
    c. $100,000
    d. $75,000

16. A home owner can do _____ 1034 exchanges in a two-year period.

    a. one
    b. two
    c. an unlimited number of
    d. none of the above

17. If a client has owned and lived in his or her home for the last three years, and is 55 or over, then the client may exclude:

    a. $0
    b. $62,500
    c. $100,000
    d. $125,000

18. Ms. Petersen sold a home four years ago and took a $60,000 exclusion. She purchased another and has lived in it the last three years of the five-year period. She now has a $125,000 gain in the new home. How much can she exclude?

    a. $0
    b. $65,000
    c. $100,000
    d. $125,000

19. A person can do a 1034 exchange on:

    a. a personal primary (principal) residence.
    b. a personal secondary residence.
    c. both a and b
    d. none of the above

20. The adjusted basis of a personal residence is:

    a. purchase price + buying expenses + improvements − depreciation.
    b. purchase price + buying expenses + improvements.
    c. purchase price + buying expenses − depreciation.
    d. purchase price + buying expenses.

12

Investment Analysis

Chapter Preview   Most people try to save a portion of their income for future investment. They understand that their money will work harder for them if it is invested prudently. An investment is the allocation of funds for income or for profit. The primary reasons for investments are the potential for income and profit from the sale of the investment.[1] This chapter explains that each type of investment has advantages and disadvantages that can be viewed in terms of the investment's risk, liquidity, management, and appreciation. The two external factors influencing investments are taxes and inflation.

Various types of investments are discussed, with special emphasis on such real estate investments as single-family dwellings, apartment houses, office buildings, shopping centers, industrial properties and special-use properties. Other specialized subjects covered are the importance of record keeping, the use of leverage, and pyramiding.

Terms To Look For   **Appreciation**
Industrial property
Inflation
Leverage
Liquidity
Pyramiding
Rent controls
Risk
Special-use property

---

[1]The information in this chapter relies heavily on the *California Real Estate Practice Instructor's Guide,* published by the California Community Colleges.

Reasons for Investing

Investment income can take the form of interest, dividends or rents. The profit that is made when the investment is sold comes from appreciation, that is, an increase in value. There are many different types of investments, each with advantages and disadvantages. Some people invest their money in saving accounts, life insurance or stocks and bonds. Others invest their money in real estate. Whichever form their investments take, investors are primarily concerned with the *income* to be received and the potential *profit* to be made when the investment is sold.[2]

Even though an investor is concerned primarily with the monetary returns from an investment, he or she also buys to satisfy other desires, such as survival, security, greed, comfort and pride. When selling real estate investments, keep in mind that you are selling the benefits that owning property will bring. You are not selling investment property as such; you are selling:

- a college education for a son or daughter;

- an assurance of a comfortable retirement;

- freedom from financial worry;

- a secure future;

- an extended trip abroad; or

- a new automobile, a swimming pool, an addition to a home or other goods bought with investment income.[3]

Evaluating Investments

When considering investments, how can a prospective investor find out if the investment is likely to be a wise one? There are two kinds of factors to consider: internal factors and external factors. Internal factors are those imposed by the nature of the investment itself. External factors are imposed on the investment by outside forces.

Internal Factors

The four internal factors that influence all types of investments are shown in Figure 12.1. They are risk, liquidity, management and appreciation.

Risk. Every investment should return the initial amount invested plus a profit. But there is always the chance that an investment won't return the amount invested, much less a profit. This element of chance is called the investment's **risk.**

An investment's risk is directly proportional to its expected return. The higher the expected rate of return, the greater the risk. The risk involved with savings accounts, life insurance and bonds is considered low. Although there is a higher degree of risk in real estate investments, the returns in the current economy have been favorable.

[2]*California Real Estate Practice Instructor's Guide*, p. 12-1.
[3]*California Real Estate Practice Instructor's Guide*, p. 12-2.

Figure 12.1
Internal Factors
Used in Evaluating
Investments

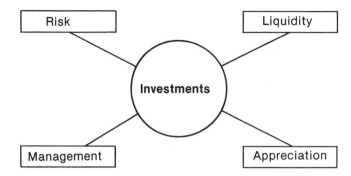

The licensee will come to realize that different investors will probably wish to take different risks. For example, a young person may purchase with a small down payment, expecting to use the available depreciation schedule and let his or her equity accumulate. A senior citizen might make a larger down payment and be interested primarily in income, not depreciation, because his or her peak earning years are over. A high-income investor may think little of the added burden if a property must be carried (held at a loss) for several months before becoming profitable. Risk must be matched to the individual investor's ability to supply added cash if necessary.[4]

Liquidity. The term **liquidity** refers to the ability of the investment to be converted readily into cash. Savings accounts, life insurance and stocks and bonds have high liquidity, meaning that investors can convert them into cash easily and quickly.

Real estate is less liquid than these other types of investments. However, at the right price, real estate in today's market will sell at a handsome profit in a reasonable period of time. If additional cash is needed in an emergency, sufficient equity in the property will allow refinancing for this purpose. The liquidity of a real estate investment depends upon three factors:

1. how quickly it can be sold;

2. how quickly and easily a loan can be placed against the equity; and

3. the location of the property.

Thus, the liquidity of real estate will vary from property to property. Investors should be able to sell well-located property on a distress sale basis within a short period of time, say, 30 days. And, if the same property has a measurable equity (30

[4]*California Real Estate Practice Instructor's Guide*, p. 12-2.

percent to 40 percent real equity), the investor should be able to obtain a loan against equity in slightly less than 30 days.[5]

Raw land far from an urban center might well be considered illiquid. A popularly priced family home, close to schools and shopping centers, might be considered liquid. However, real estate ranks low as a liquid investment. Costs of sales are high, and the sale of real estate is difficult compared with sales of some other investments because of legal requirements involved in property transfer. An old saying brings this out: "If we transferred title to shoes as we do to real estate, we might all go barefoot."

Management. All investments require management. Although the cost of management is negligible on savings accounts and insurance, it is nonetheless present, and the net return on the investment is reduced somewhat.

Management plays a relatively large role in real estate. Even if an owner does his or her own managing and charges nothing to the cost of management in an expense statement, there still is the cost of the owner's time because he or she could be working someplace else for compensation. When dealing with larger properties, professional management is usually required to make the investment "pay off."[6]

Appreciation. In most cases, investors hope to sell the investment for more than they originally paid for it. Consequently, **appreciation** is an extremely important factor affecting investment.

Investments such as savings accounts, bonds and insurance generally have no appreciation value. Even though interest may have accumulated, the dollar amount of the capital investment remains the same.

External Factors Two external factors that influence investments are taxes and **inflation.**

Inflation. Inflation takes its toll of fixed-income investments, such as saving accounts, stocks, annuities and bonds. The investor will receive a stipulated interest rate regardless of the effect of inflation.

On the other hand, investments in real estate generally are considered a fine hedge against inflation. However, an important point to recognize is that because of its slow marketability, legal restrictions and lack of standardization, real estate usually remains behind the economic market.[7] For example, real properties don't always increase in value during periods of inflation, because they are often subject to long-term leases at fixed rents. Also, since rent is payable in dollars, and dollar income may not be increased under certain leases, this type of investment may have a poor degree of inflation protection.

Nevertheless, some rents (for example, apartment house rents) increase under normal inflationary conditions. Also, buyers are willing to accept lower returns on real estate investments in times of inflation because they realize the returns will increase when leases are renewed. Then, too, real estate is a tangible asset, desired when money starts to lose its value.

[5]*California Real Estate Practice Instructor's Guide,* pp. 12-2 and 12-3.
[6]*California Real Estate Practice Instructor's Guide,* p. 12-3.
[7]*California Real Estate Practice Instructor's Guide,* p. 12-9.

Taxes. It is important that the agent understand the real estate investment as a tax shelter. The first step is to calculate the taxable income from the investment. This is done by determining the gross income and then subtracting the operating expenses, the interest on the mortgages and the depreciation. The interest deduction cannot exceed the gross income.

Example:	Gross Rents		$20,000
	Operating Expenses:		
	Advertising	$ 20	
	Insurance	1,000	
	Interest	12,000	
	Repairs & Maintenance	2,300	
	Taxes	1,500	
	Utilities	180	
	Total Operating Expenses		17,000
	Depreciation		2,000
	Taxable Income		$ 1,000

■ *Note:* Since the $15,000 interest does not exceed the $20,000 gross income, the entire amount of interest may be deducted.

We notice in the above example that we had a positive taxable income, and this income would be treated like wages and added to the client's tax return. On the other hand, if this were a loss, it would be necessary to determine if the property owner were actively engaged in the management of the property. If the owner were not actively engaged in the management of his/her property then the loss would be considered passive. The loss could only be written off against passive income (interest, dividends or similar passive income). Wages or earned income are not considered passive income.

However, if the property owner were actively engaged in the management of his or her property, then the owner could write off the loss up to a limit of $25,000 for all properties on his or her tax return. This maximum write-off of $25,000 is limited to the owner's adjusted gross income (AGI). If the AGI is $100,000 or less, the owner may get up to the $25,000 limitation as a deduction; however, if the AGI is greater than $100,000, then for every $2 increase in AGI the limitation is reduced by $1. Therefore, if the AGI is $150,000 or more, there is no deduction.

> **Example:** Mr. Writoff's losses from rental properties in whose management he was actively engaged were $35,000. He is limited to a $25,000 deduction. His AGI on his tax return for the year was $120,000; therefore, his $25,000 limitation would be reduced by $10,000 ($120,000−$100,000 = $20,000 ÷ 2). The maximum rental loss that may be deducted by Mr. Writoff for the year is $15,000 ($25,000−$10,000).

Investment loss to be written off against salary and other income will be phased out over the next five years. Table 12.1 shows the phase-out over the next five years.

Table 12.1
Five-year Phase-out

YEAR	PERCENTAGE THAT MAY BE WRITTEN OFF
1987	65%
1988	40%
1989	20%
1990	10%
1991 and after	0%

Tax law changes. Because tax laws are constantly changing, seeking the advice of a tax advisor is strongly recommended. Investors who use a tax advisor should be prepared to ask the following questions:

1. How much depreciation may I claim? What will the impact be?

2. How much interest may be charged on mortgage loans?

3. How can the expenses of the organization be treated?

4. What items may be treated as capital gain?

5. How do I divide the investment amount between land and improvements?

6. What opportunities are there for tax-deferred liability?[8]

Keep in mind that federal income tax considerations may not be the only requirements to consider when handling a property. State laws, license fees, franchise taxes and sales taxes are also important.

Sources of tax information. For further general information in determining the tax status of real property investments, you may wish to do research on your own. One important source is professional journals, such as *The Appraisal Journal, The Real Estate Review, The Property Management Journal* and *The NAR Journal.* The Internal Revenue Service publishes a free booklet entitled "Current Laws and Rules." Libraries carry federal income tax services. Major accounting, management consulting and securities dealers, as well as local, state and national real estate associations, hold periodic seminars.[9]

Residential Real Estate Investment

A real estate investment might be defined as a commitment of funds by an individual with a view to preserving capital, minimizing risk and earning a profit. In other words, it is a commitment of discretionary income—money over and above that needed for securing necessities. Real estate investments generally are worthwhile since most real estate will increase in value over a period of years.

[8]*California Real Estate Practice Instructor's Guide,* pp. 12-7 and 12-8.
[9]*California Real Estate Practice Instructor's Guide,* p. 12-8.

Real estate investment involves many kinds of property. Every licensee need not become an expert in all areas, but a general knowledge of the major areas will improve a licensee's skills and abilities in handling real estate investments. (Because full semester courses in real estate investment are available through most community colleges, this chapter serves only as an introduction to the subject.) This section describes the advantages and disadvantages of some types of residential investment property.

Single Units

Some advantages of single-unit residential properties as investments are:

1. There is a greater choice in the market.

2. They are much easier to manage.

3. Resale chances are excellent, increasing the liquidity of the investment.

4. Tenants usually pay for utilities and upkeep.

5. Home prices have a history of rapid appreciation.

Some disadvantages of this type of investment are:

1. During a vacancy 100 percent of the monthly rent is lost.

2. Such properties are usually self-managed, and many investors are not equipped to do so.

3. The cost of household repairs is constantly rising.

4. If investors own more than one such unit, chances are that the units are scattered, necessitating greater expenditure of time and money.[10]

Two- to Four-unit Properties

The advantages of two- to four-unit residential properties include:

1. This type of property is usually found in most communities.

2. They are small enough to be managed by one owner.

3. The tenants usually pay the utilities and handle the maintenance.

4. This size investment is quite popular.

5. There is more privacy for tenants than in larger apartments, so vacancies are filled relatively fast.

6. They possess a higher loan-to-value ratio, so they usually offer greater leverage.

The disadvantages include:

1. There are fewer investment units of this size because of high land costs.

2. It is necessary to set aside reserves for replacement of drapes, carpets and appliances.

3. The landlord usually pays for water, outside lights and often a laundry room.

[10]*California Real Estate Practice Instructor's Guide*, p. 12-4.

4. Repair costs are higher per unit than for a larger apartment house.[11]

Apartment Houses   Apartment houses have a number of advantages:

1. They are in constant demand.

2. They have proved to be a safe investment over the years.

3. Management of several units is concentrated in one location.

4. Resident managers may be utilized, relieving the owner of the responsibility for showing units, maintaining grounds and collecting rents. (State law requires a resident manager for an apartment house that contains 16 or more units.)

5. Operation costs are less per unit.

6. They provide an excellent tax shelter.

7. Write-offs can be utilized on carpets, drapes and appliances.

Some disadvantages are:

1. Maintenance costs are usually high.

2. Reserves need to be set up for replacements.

3. Sale at a sacrifice may become necessary.

4. Building value may decrease due to encroachment of industrial buildings.

5. Sale of building might become difficult or impossible due to decreasing rents, high vacancy factors, loss from bad debts and difficulty of financing.

6. There may be rent correction problems and increasing legal fees due to new laws.[12]

Apartment houses are generally defined as multiunit residential dwellings that accommodate more than four families in individual, self-contained units. Of the residential investments, apartment houses constitute the largest component within the real estate investment field. This is not surprising, considering that in many California cities, 30 to 75 percent of the housing units are larger than one- to four-family houses—in other words, apartment housing.

Over a period of years, the desire to invest in apartment houses has increased. This has become apparent to builders, who have switched from building standard family units to garden apartments, condominiums, high-rise apartments and townhouse rental developments. Demand has increased for apartment units that can be shared by two or more singles.

Rent-earning Capacity   Since investors are buying the future productivity of the buildings in which they are investing, they should be sure to analyze the present and future rent-earning capacity of the properties. In making these analyses investors should carefully note that past income statements are not necessarily prognosticators for future earnings. It

---

[11]*California Real Estate Practice Instructor's Guide*, p. 12-5.
[12]*California Real Estate Practice Instructor's Guide*, p. 12-5.

Figure 12.2
Apartment Checklist

Position in Market:

☐ Can this apartment fit into this market?
☐ Will the proposed rent schedule meet the area competition?
☐ Are the individual units comparable in size to the competition?
☐ Are operational costs rather stable?
☐ Are services offered to tenants competitively?
☐ Will the investment be financially operable with the type of tenants involved?
☐ Are established vacancy rates favorable?

Location:

☐ Are reliable tenants available in the area?
☐ Is the property in the directional growth of the community?
☐ Are such services as shopping, transportation, schools and churches available?
☐ Is the area plagued by nuisances?
☐ Is the property accessible to public and private transportation?
☐ Is the apartment building located in an attractive, improving rental market area?
☐ Is the area properly zoned and under other code restrictions?
☐ Are the property taxes and other assessments reasonable?

Physical Condition:

☐ Are assessed land values within reason?
☐ Is the building size adequate, with sufficient expansion room?
☐ Is the appearance of the building and the area appealing?
☐ Are there signs of deterioration, such as poor soil, poor drainage or deferred maintenance?
☐ Is there sufficient parking for tenants and guests?
☐ Is there easy access to surrounding streets?

Improvements:

☐ Is there an available record of past rents and expenses?
☐ Is the economic age ahead of the actual age?
☐ Does the interior permit proper functional use of the available space?
☐ Can improvements be economically modernized, improved or rehabilitated?
☐ Is adequate financing readily available?

has been said that past income statements are only vague shadows of future results and, like all shadows, can easily become distorted.

If certain investors' apartments are fully rented while those of adjacent apartment houses have vacancies, they may reason that they are charging less than they should for their apartments. They must analyze the price structure of the units, just as any other business would analyze the price structure of its products. Further analysis might reveal that each apartment varied considerably in its earning capacity, due to sizes of rooms, view provided, room layout, adequacy of baths, location in the building (e.g., a corner unit) or presence of a porch or terrace.[13]

[13]*California Real Estate Practice Instructor's Guide,* p. 12-6.

Rent Controls   Operating procedures pertaining to apartment house investments have at times
                           been curtailed by government controls. The foremost of these is rent controls,
                           which may be applied from time to time by government agencies.

                           Rent control has caused such serious setbacks in some areas that construction of
                           new apartment houses has been curtailed. Landlord-tenant relationships pertain-
                           ing to rent control have grown increasingly hostile.[14]

Analyzing Real   Four basic questions used in appraising potential investment property are:
Estate Investments

                               1. How does it fit into the present and future market?

Figure 12.3
Shopping Center   *Position in Market:*
Checklist   ☐ Are past building vacancies no more than five percent?
                           ☐ Are competitive sales activity records readily available?
                           ☐ Is the trading area showing definite signs of improving?
                           ☐ Is the "buying power" in the area sufficient to support a shopping center?
                           ☐ How do the types and locations of competing centers compare?
                           ☐ Are the lease terms acceptable in this area?

                           Location:
                           ☐ What is the potential market (customers who have adequate transportation to the area)?
                           ☐ Is the center in the directional growth of the community?
                           ☐ Is the population in the area on the increase?
                           ☐ Are the income and shopping habits of families in the area conducive to the financing
                              of the center?
                           ☐ What is the competitive impact of other centers?
                           ☐ Will employment conditions lend stability to the area?
                           ☐ Will the area in any way be affected by present or projected freeways or public
                              transportation?
                           ☐ Are the spending patterns of the targeted customers representative of the area?

                           Physical Condition:
                           ☐ Is the site readily available to both public and private transportation?
                           ☐ Will the size and shape of the area permit possible expansion?
                           ☐ Are all required utilities readily available?
                           ☐ Will the ground drainage and other soil conditions permit future buildings?
                           ☐ Is there sufficient access for service and delivery vehicles?

                           Improvements:
                           ☐ Can the available space adequately accommodate changing store uses?
                           ☐ Is the lighting for the entire area adequate?
                           ☐ Is there sufficient room for parking now and in the event of future expansion?
                           ☐ Do present tenants comply with controlled use of signs?
                           ☐ Is sufficient lighting, heating or air-conditioning provided?
                           ☐ Do customers have ready access to the stores?

---

[14]*California Real Estate Practice Instructor's Guide*, p. 12-6.

2. Is it in a proper location?

3. What is its physical condition?

4. Are the building's improvements acceptable?[15]

Examples of five checklists are given that will help you determine the value of various types of investments and what you might need to do to make an investment more worthwhile. The types of property covered are apartments (Fig. 12.2), shopping centers (Fig. 12.3), office buildings (Fig. 12.4), industrial property (Figure 12.5) and special-use property (Fig. 12.6).

Figure 12.4
Office Building Checklist

Position in Market:

☐ Has a detailed survey of the needs for office space been conducted?
☐ What kinds of businesses will require office space, and what type of space will they need?
☐ What kinds of office buildings are now serving the area?
☐ Has an adequate inventory of competitive office buildings been conducted?
☐ What kinds of services do the tenants require?
☐ Will the local business area support proposed office buildings?

Location:

☐ Will local ordinances and regulations permit the planned type of office building?
☐ Is the proposed location the most favorable in the area?
☐ Is the proposed development accessible to adequate public and private transportation?
☐ What characteristics of the area might attract office buildings?
☐ Are property taxes and assessment rates reasonable?

Physical Condition:

☐ Can the ground properly support the building?
☐ Can property be changed to meet new property restrictions?
☐ Are parking facilities sufficient for now and in the future?
☐ Is the size and shape of the building project conducive to possible expansion?
☐ Are the needed facilities adequate?
☐ Is the site readily accessible to public and private transportation?
☐ Are you fully knowledgeable concerning public and private land-use restrictions?

Improvements:

☐ Is the appearance of the building appealing to clients and customers?
☐ Is a report readily available on all present tenants, lease terms and vacancies?
☐ Is the economic age of the building ahead of the actual age?
☐ Have you availed yourself of professional help in determining rental capacities and interior-use arrangements?
☐ Are facilities, including plumbing, lighting, heating, air-conditioning and elevator service, adequate and well maintained?

---

[15]*California Real Estate Practice Instructor's Guide,* p. 12-6.

Figure 12.5
Industrial Property
Checklist

Position in Market:

☐ Is information on competing projects readily available?

☐ Is there appropriate needed land to support the development?

☐ Can the project be supported by the level of activity in the area?

☐ Are other activities related to the project strong and improving?

☐ Are the project leasing terms competitive in the area?

Location:

☐ Is the area zoned for industrial use?

☐ Are industrial activities showing signs of improvement and growth?

☐ Are needed raw materials, labor and markets readily available?

☐ Will attendant economic activity in the area properly support the project?

☐ Are needed materials, labor and equipment easily obtainable by potential tenants?

☐ Will the local area accept industrial activities?

☐ Is housing adequate for potential workers?

☐ Is union activity in the area favorable to both sides?

Physical Condition:

☐ Is the site readily accessible to all manner of transportation?

☐ Will the ground support proposed developments?

☐ Are the size, shape and topography of the land conducive to efficient industrial layouts?

☐ Is possible expansion on the present site within reason?

☐ Are all needed utilities readily available?

☐ Is there adequate fire and police protection in the area?

☐ Is the area relatively free from hazards and nuisances?

Improvements:

☐ Is there adequate space for such operating activities as warehousing and storage?

☐ Are facilities for docking sufficient?

☐ Is there room for possible expansion?

☐ Can changing use requirements be economically accommodated?

☐ Are buildings well lighted, ventilated, heated and cooled as required?

☐ Is the building layout proper for producing efficient industrial activity?

Figure 12.6
Special-use Property
Checklist (pharmacies,
nursing homes, tennis
courts, bowling alleys,
etc.)

Position in Market:

☐ Will local activities support the proposed project?

☐ Will the market provide users and clients with appropriate facilities?

☐ Will local markets provide sufficient clientele?

☐ Is the project feasible for this market?

☐ Will the project satisfy all portions of the market?

Location:

☐ Do local planning restrictions and codes permit the intended use of the property?

☐ Is the project location in the directional growth of the community?

☐ Are taxes and assessments economically feasible and reasonable?

☐ Is the location readily accessible to future clients?

Physical Condition:

☐ Will the ground support the development now and in the future?

☐ Will the location permit growth of the project in the future?

☐ Is there sufficient police and fire protection in the area?

☐ Are the size and shape of the land conducive to the development of this particular type of project?

☐ Is the area comparatively free from hazards, pollution and annoyances?

☐ Are sufficient necessary utilities readily available?

☐ Is there adequate parking for now and in the future?

☐ Is the site of the project readily accessible to public and private transportation?

Improvements:

☐ Is the area appropriate for the intended project?

☐ Do(es) the building(s) housing the project have expansion potential?

☐ Can facilities be adapted economically to other uses?

☐ Is it financially feasible to construct new facilities, should the occasion warrant this?

☐ Are the heating, lighting and ventilating facilities adequate?

Record Keeping

A vital part of real estate investment activity is keeping accurate records. Taxpayers should avail themselves of every advantage allowed under the law to keep their taxes as low as possible. (This does not mean tax evasion.) To make proper deductions, taxpayers must keep records and be able to produce them to verify each step taken. Examples of necessary records follow.

1. When property is purchased, records must be kept of price, legal fees, title insurance, surveys and commissions.

2. When property is held for investment, records must be kept of cost of maintenance, management expenses, operational expenses and expenses for preservation and upkeep.

3. When capital improvements are made, records must be kept, so that the cost of the improvements can be added to the property's basis.[16]

■ **Note:** A separate bank account and system of record keeping should be maintained for each piece of property.

Leverage. Leverage is the use of borrowed money to finance most of an investment. As applied to the purchase of real property, it allows the investor to purchase property with a minimum dollar investment. It is investing someone else's money, using a small amount of your own money (equity capital) and a large amount of someone else's money (borrowed capital). Leverage can be extremely advantageous if the property increases in value.

[16]*California Real Estate Practice Instructor's Guide*, p. 12-8.

For example, assume that Lisa Lever purchased a duplex for $200,000 and sold it later for $280,000. If she had paid cash for the duplex, she would have realized an $80,000 gain, or a return on her investment of 40 percent:

$280,000 resale price
−200,000 original purchase price
$ 80,000 gain

$ 80,000 divided by $200,000 = 40 percent

Actually, however, Lisa was able to get a $150,000 real estate loan. She only needed to invest $50,000 as a down payment. When she sold the property for $280,000 and paid off the $150,000 loan, she had a $130,000 gain, or a return on her investment of 260 percent.

$280,000	purchase price	$280,000	resale
−150,000	loan	−150,000	loan payoff
$ 50,000	down payment (investment)	$130,000	gain

Note that these percentages are computed prior to income tax payments, interest payments and other closing costs.

If property is declining in value, leverage can work in reverse. For example, if Dan Depreciate purchased property at $100,000 cash and resold it in a declining market for $90,000, the net loss would be $10,000, or ten percent. If Dan had used leverage with a cash outlay of $10,000 and a loan for the balance:

$90,000 resale price
−90,000 loan
　　-0-　gain (100 percent loss on the investment)

Obviously, investors should exercise caution in the use of leverage.

Pyramiding

As with leverage, pyramiding uses other people's money to increase your profit potential. In pyramiding the investor, instead of paying cash, keeps trading up to properties that offer greater profit. When using pyramiding, investors should endeavor to select property that will furnish sufficient income to pay all expenses related to owning the property and at the same time provide a profit.

Investors who make use of pyramiding never sell for cash but try to trade their property for another property in which they see an opportunity for higher profit. As the income-producing possibilities of their property increase, the investors are building a "pyramid of equity."

Pyramiding is successful only when property values are increasing, so follow these steps:

1. Diversify your investments by property type as well as by area.

2. Structure your financing so that refinancing is possible without extensive time delays and finance costs.

3. Keep abreast of market trends, so that you can get out while values are still moving up rapidly.

4. Be careful to secure properties on terms and prices that meet your goals.[17]

---

[17]*California Real Estate Practice Instructor's Guide*, pp. 12-9 and 12-10.

Summary

This chapter started by explaining that investors look for income and profit. They evaluate investments based on internal factors that include risk, liquidity, management and appreciation. Investors must also take into account the external factors of taxes and inflation.

Real estate investments may involve residential property, commercial property, industrial property or special-use property. Advantages and disadvantages of residential real estate investments were listed. Checklists were provided for use in analyzing residential and other investment opportunities according to (1) their position in the market, (2) proper location, (3) physical condition and (4) acceptable improvements.

The chapter concluded by noting that investors must keep complete records. They may wish to take advantage of leverage and pyramiding.

Questions

1. Two main reasons for investing are:
   a. profit and liquidity.
   b. profit and income.
   c. income and liquidity.
   d. liquidity and appreciation.

2. When a person buys an investment, he or she is buying:
   a. a retirement program.
   b. a college education.
   c. a secure future.
   d. all of the above

3. The greater the risk, the
   a. greater the return.
   b. less the return.
   c. less the profit.
   d. less the loss.

4. The liquidity of a real estate investment is measured by:
   a. how quickly it can be sold.
   b. the location of the property.
   c. how quickly a loan can be put on the property.
   d. all of the above

5. One reason for investing in real estate is:
   a. it is a hedge against inflation.
   b. it requires little management.
   c. it is very liquid.
   d. none of the above

6. The maximum that a taxpayer can write off as rental loss against earned income is:
   a. $25,000.
   b. $100,000.
   c. $150,000.
   d. none of the above

7. Investing requires a commitment of:
   a. funds.
   b. time.
   c. risk.
   d. all of the above

8. An advantage of investing in a single family residence is:
   a. there is no management.
   b. there are no vacancy factors.
   c. it is usually easier to sell than units.
   d. all of the above

9. An advantage of investing in units is:
   a. they are always in constant demand.
   b. the convenience of managing several units in one location.
   c. the operation cost is less per unit.
   d. all of the above

10. Which of the following discourages investment in rentals?
    a. rent control
    b. inflation
    c. taxes
    d. all of the above

11. Which of the following would you use in appraising a potential real estate investment?
    a. its location
    b. its physical condition
    c. its fit into present and future market conditions
    d. all of the above

12. Records must be kept on:
    a. purchase price.
    b. improvements.
    c. operational expenses.
    d. all of the above

13. Leveraging is the ability:
    a. to put down a large down payment.
    b. to get a large loan.
    c. to set up a large reserve account.
    d. none of the above

14. Pyramiding can be best described as:
    a. using other people's money to increase your profit potential.
    b. using taxes to your advantage.
    c. getting the best management for the property.
    d. none of the above

15. Which of the following is considered a feature of "position in the market"?

   a. stable operational costs
   b. area plagued by nuisances
   c. location of the property
   d. all of the above

16. Investment income can take the form of:

   a. rents.
   b. dividends.
   c. interest.
   d. all of the above

17. Internal factors of evaluating an investment are:

   a. liquidity and management.
   b. risk and taxes.
   c. appreciation and taxes.
   d. inflation and liquidity.

18. To make a profit, an investor hopes his property will:

   a. have liquidity.
   b. have appreciation.
   c. have risk.
   d. have no management.

19. An external factor of real estate would be:

   a. inflation.
   b. taxes.
   c. both a and b
   d. none of the above

20. A change in the tax law can affect the _____ of an investment.

   a. location
   b. management
   c. gain
   d. none of the above

13

Real Property Appraisal

Chapter Preview

One of the essential real estate activities is appraisal. Brokers and salespeople constantly get questions from clients about the worth, a fair price, a fair rental, a fair basis for trade or a proper amount of insurance coverage for a given piece of property.

This chapter deals with the subject of appraisal, the forces that influence value and the principles on which the determination of value is built. The three most frequently used appraisal forms are included.

Three methods are used to obtain a property appraisal: the cost approach, the income or capitalization approach and the comparative market approach. The advantages and disadvantages of each method are explored as they apply to various appraisal situations.

The chapter concludes with a discussion of the causes of depreciation and the methods used in computing allowable depreciation for appraisal purposes.

Terms To Look For

Accrual depreciation	Principle of balance
Appraisal	Principle of change
Capitalization rate	Principle of competition
Cost approach	Principle of conformity
Cubic foot method	Principle of consistent use
Demand	Principle of highest and best use
Depth tables	Principle of progression
Directional growth	Principle of regression
Economic obsolescence	Principle of supply and demand
Functional obsolescence	Plottage
Gross monthly multiplier	Quantity survey method
Income (capitalization) approach	Short form report
Letter form report	Sinking fund method
Market comparison approach	Square foot method
Market value	Unit-in-place method
Narrative report	Utility value
Principle of anticipation	Value

An **appraisal** is an *estimate* or an *opinion* of the value of a piece of property on a given date. Because it is an estimate, the accuracy of the appraisal depends on the experience, background and know-how of the party doing the appraising.

Value

There are different types of **value,** but appraisal is primarily concerned with **market value.** Market value is the price that a willing buyer will pay a willing seller for a given piece of property in an open market, assuming that both parties are knowledgeable about the full uses of the property, the buyer is not obligated to buy and the seller is not obligated to sell.

It is important to distinguish the market value of a property from its *cost* and *price.*

- Cost represents a measure of past money, labor, material or sacrifices of some kind in producing the property.

- Price is what one pays for property, regardless of pressure, motive or discernment of the seller or buyer.

Creation of Value

There are four basic elements that create value: demand, utility, scarcity and transferability.

Demand. The influence of **demand** arises not only from existing desire for a product. The desire for a product can often be stimulated with advertising, and it must always be supported by purchasing power.

Utility. Utility assumes that the property is useful. **Utility value** is related to an appraisal concept known as the "highest and best use," which means the use that will give the greatest net return over a period of years.

Scarcity. In economics, the values of goods are determined by their **scarcity** or abundance, meaning that their value increases as their availability decreases, assuming the elements of utility, demand and transferability are also present.

Transferability. The value of a good also comes from its **transferability.** While real estate cannot itself be moved around, it is transferable insofar as the use and ownership of the property are concerned.

Forces Influencing Value

Four major forces create, maintain, modify or destroy value and affect cost and price to some degree. These are physical, social, economic and political forces (see Figure 13.1).

Physical forces. Physical forces affecting value include quality of conveniences; availability of schools; proximity to shopping areas, public transportation, churches; homogeneity of land use; types of physical hazards; quality of climate; and size and shape of the lot.

Social forces. Social ideals and trends affecting value include population growth and decline; marriage, birth, divorce, and death rates; attitudes toward education and recreation; and other standards and preferences of the community.

Figure 13.1
Forces That
Influence Value

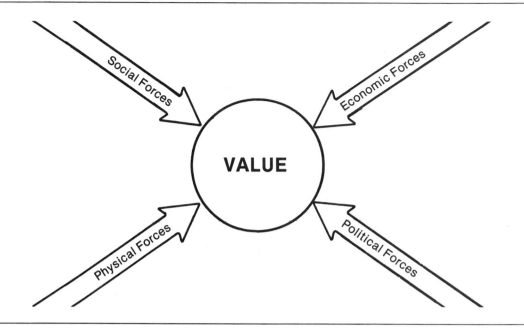

Economic forces. Economic forces affecting value include natural resources, including location, quantity and quality; industrial and commercial trends; employment trends; wage levels; price levels; interest rates and availability of money; price levels; and tax loads.

Political forces. Political and governmental regulations that affect value include building codes, zoning laws, public health measures, fire regulations, government-guaranteed loans, government housing, and credit controls.

Other Physical Factors Influencing Value

Location. A leading economist was once asked to name the three most important factors influencing value of real estate. His answer was, "Location, location, location." It is generally agreed that there is a great amount of truth in this reply, assuming that the improvements on the land constitute the highest and best use of the property.

Directional growth. Each city has a planning commission whose responsibility it is to construct a master plan of the proposed growth of the city. The value of the property will be based in part on whether or not it lies in the **directional growth** of the community, that is, the direction in which the city tends to expand. A smaller urban area tends to grow into a larger metropolitan area.

Utility. Utility refers to the use that can be made of the land. It involves the property's capacity to produce at its highest and best use.

Size. The square footage of a property is less important than its size in terms of width and depth. A wide, shallow plot is usually worth more than a narrow, deep lot.

Shape. A regularly shaped parcel can be developed more advantageously than an irregularly shaped parcel.

Thoroughfare conditions. The value of property facing a street will be affected by the traffic congestion, the width of the street and the condition of the pavement.

Exposure. The best location for a commercial business, such as a shoe store, a department store or a furniture store, is the south or west side or the southwest intersection, because pedestrians prefer the shady side of the street.

Plottage or assemblage. The value of a given number of parcels of land can be increased when several parcels are brought under one ownership, as opposed to the same number of parcels under separate ownership. This procedure, called **plottage** or assemblage, makes it possible to gain a higher utility for the same amount of land.

Character of the soil. When buildings are to be constructed on a piece of land, the compaction of the soil may affect construction costs significantly. When rural land is considered for the production of crops, or the land in residential areas for beautification, the type and condition of the topsoil affect the value of the property.

Principles of Valuation

The appraisal principles discussed in this section will help you understand the nature of value.

Principle of change. Individual properties, neighborhoods and cities are constantly changing. All properties pass through three stages: (1) integration, a period of development during which property values increase; (2) equilibrium, a static stage in which property reaches a maximum value due to diminishing demand; and (3) disintegration, a period in which properties decline or decay and values decrease.

Principle of regression. The principle of regression states that in a neighborhood of differing values, the value of a higher-priced home will seek the value level of lower-priced homes. For example, assume that the average home in a new tract is worth $70,000, and Owner *A* has a home built for $90,000. A year later the average tract home sells for $75,000. Owner *A*'s home will probably sell for $80,000. If a more expensive home is built among less expensive homes, its value will tend to be lowered.

Principle of progression. The principle of progression is the opposite of regression. It contends that the value of a lower-priced home in an area of predominantly higher-priced homes will increase in value. The value of the lower-priced home will seek the value level of the more valuable homes.

Principle of highest and best use. The highest and best use is the one that will produce the greatest *net* return over a given period of time. Assume that a duplex is situated on a lot zoned for four units. Do you think that is representative of the highest and best use?

Principle of anticipation. The principle of anticipation suggests that some factor in the future will affect value beneficially. For example, a new rapid transit stop near a commercial area would add value due to an increase in benefits to the property.

Principle of supply and demand. When a commodity is scarce and the demand is high, its value increases. When there is an abundance of a commodity and a weak demand, its value tends to drop. Demand for real estate is affected by such factors as high or low interest rates and high or low taxes.

Principle of conformity. Appraisers point out that maximum values are achieved in areas where there is a great deal of similarity in properties. As a general rule, the architectural styles, age, and condition of the homes should be similar. Likewise, it is beneficial if the residents are homogeneous, or closely related in their economic, social and educational backgrounds.

Principle of consistent use. Underimproved structures on land are not unusual. When a triplex is situated on a lot zoned for 12 units, the triplex cannot increase the value of the land. Assume that the land would be valued at $60,000 if there were no improvements. The income from the triplex might justify a value of $45,000. A buyer would probably pay $60,000 for the property less the cost of demolition of the triplex if he or she planned to build 12 units.

Principle of competition. The possibility of good profits attracts competition. Excess profits will attract excess competition that, in many instances, destroys profits because the supply and demand relationship is adversely affected.

Principle of balance. The principle of balance is also referred to as the principle of contribution or the principle of increasing and decreasing returns. The principle contends that the balance of the four factors of production determines value. The four production factors are land, labor, capital and management. Greater value, or increasing returns, can be achieved by introducing more of each of the four factors—up to a certain point. If any of the four factors are increased beyond that point, it will result in decreasing, or diminishing, returns.

Uses of Appraisal

Estimates of value are needed and used in transferring property ownership, making real estate loans, carrying out condemnation actions, determining real property taxation and insuring real estate (see Figure 13.2).

Think of appraisal as a tool for the practitioner first—the lender second. By investing $100 in appraisal at the time of listing, the seller or the agent has invested in making the sale of the property much easier.

Transfer of Property Ownership

An appraisal assists buyers and sellers in arriving at a fair sales price. The seller needs an appraisal to list property correctly. A valuation is also necessary for distribution of estate properties among heirs.

Whether a broker, sales associate or appraiser should perform the appraisal will depend on the experience of those involved and the complexity of the property. A good time to have the appraisal done is before listing the property.

Real Estate Financing

An appraisal is made when property is pledged as security for mortgage loans. Lenders require an appraisal to protect themselves.

Condemnation Actions

A government body using the power of eminent domain must compensate property owners fairly. Therefore, properties under condemnation need to be evaluated at fair-market value.

Figure 13.2
Uses of Appraisal

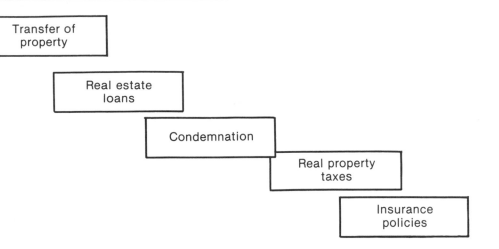

Real Property Taxes   Governments also need appraisals for property tax purposes. Properties subject to gift or inheritance taxes must be evaluated. Income-producing properties must be appraised to establish the basis for computing depreciation.

Insurance Policies   Appraisals are important in insuring properties for homeowners' insurance and fire insurance. The valuations are useful in settling claims when property is destroyed.

Appraisal Reports   Appraisal reports include a final value conclusion, the date of the valuation, market data, and an adequate description of the property. When this information is put in writing it protects the appraiser and the client.

The three principal types of reports are the letter form, short form and narrative form (see Figure 13.3).

Letter Form   The **letter form report** is a letter that contains a brief description of the property, the type of value sought, the purpose served by the appraisal, the date of the value estimate, the value conclusion and the appraiser's signature.

Short Form   The **short form report** is normally used by lending institutions. It consists of simple check sheets to be filled in by the appraisers.

Narrative Form   The **narrative report** is the most comprehensive and extensive report form. It includes all pertinent information about the area and the property, along with reasons and computations for the value conclusion. It also includes maps, photographs, charts and plot plans.

Figure 13.3
Types of Appraisal
Reports

Letter
Form

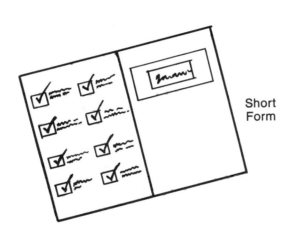

Short
Form

Narrative
Form

Methods of
Appraisal

The effectiveness and importance of each method of appraisal vary with the type of property appraised, the purpose of the appraisal, the complexity of the property and the availability of reliable data. Each approach to appraisal is used independently to arrive at a reasonable estimate of value. The final step in arriving at a final estimate of value is to reconcile the projected values and assign appropriate weights to each according to its merits.

Final estimates must give consideration to applicable data on physical, social, political and economic trends. Three approaches to consider in making a market value estimate are the cost approach, comparative market approach and income (capitalization) approach (See Figure 13.4).

1. The **cost approach** considers the value of the land, assumed vacant, added to the depreciated replacement cost of the improvements. It is sometimes called the "sticks and stones" method.

2. In the **comparative market approach,** recent sales and listings of similar properties in the area are analyzed to form an opinion of value.

3. With the **income (capitalization) approach,** the property's estimated potential income is capitalized into value, after allowance has been made for operating expenses. Most knowledgeable appraisers will use all three methods of appraising, and will rely on no single method to compute a reliable estimate.[1]

Cost Approach

The cost approach to appraisal, often referred to as the replacement cost approach, estimates what the property would cost to replace in today's dollars. The cost approach tends to set an upper limit on the value of property because a buyer will not usually pay more for a property than it would cost to replace it. There are four basic methods or means of calculating the cost estimate: the square foot method, the cubic foot method, the quantity survey method and the unit-in-place method.

Square foot method. For the **square foot method,** the dimensions of the house are measured from outside walls and the square feet of floor area are calculated. The total cost is divided by the number of square feet. This is the most frequently used method in California. Because the cost per square foot in the garage is much less, areas of garage and house are computed separately. Uncompleted or shell structures are usually computed at one-half the value of completed areas.

Cubic foot method. The **cubic foot method** is similar to the square foot method except that three dimensions are used; in other words, the cubic foot contents of the building are used. This method is used in industrial estimating or in areas where rooms with ten-foot ceilings are common.

Quantity survey method. The **quantity survey method** takes into account a detailed cost estimate of all labor and material used in the building. Even though it is expensive and time-consuming, this method is used by building contractors and professional estimators because it gives accuracy in computations. It also includes such indirect costs as overhead, insurance and profits.

Unit-in-place method. To use the **unit-in-place method** involves computing the actual cost of units in the building as they are installed. Units refer to such individual items as roofing, flooring, heating systems, glass window areas and the like. The method requires specialized knowledge in each of these areas, so it is seldom used by appraisers. When using this method of appraisal, cost figures can be obtained from local contractors and appraisers or by consulting certain cost guide publications.

Steps in the cost approach. Regardless of the method of estimating costs, there are basically four steps in the cost approach to appraisal.

1. Estimate the value of the land without improvements.

2. Determine the current replacement cost of existing improvements.

---

[1] *California Department of Real Estate Reference Book,* 1984-1985 edition, p. 442.

Figure 13.4
Appraisal Methods

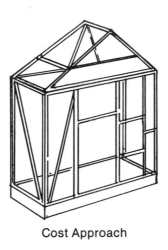

Cost Approach

Comparative Market Approach .

Income (Capitalization) Approach

3. Determine and subtract accrued depreciation from the replacement cost. (Accrued depreciation refers to the difference between the cost of replacement as of the date of the appraisal and the present appraised value.)

4. Add the value of the land to the depreciated cost of the improvement. The answer is the total estimated value of the entire property using the cost approach.

For example, a 40-foot by 60-foot house with a 25-foot by 25-foot garage is to be appraised. Improvements are ten years old and had an expected life of 50 years when the house was built. The lot is worth $25,000 today. If the cost to replace the home is $40 per square foot and the garage is $20 per square foot, what is the value of the property, using the square foot method (See Figure 13.5)?

Figure 13.5

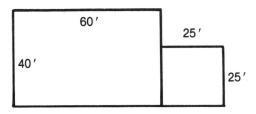

House   = 40′ × 60′ = 2,400 sq. ft. × $40/sq. ft. = $96,000
Garage = 25′ × 25′ =   625 sq. ft. × $20/sq. ft. = +12,500
Total cost of improvements $108,500

Less depreciation (for 10 years of
50-year life)   −21,700
                                                    86,800
Add land value   +25,000
Appraisal total $111,800

Depreciation is difficult if not impossible to compute accurately, especially if the effective age is maintained and improvements are updated.

Advantages. The advantages of the cost method of appraisal are:

1. It usually establishes an upper limit of value, as people will not ordinarily pay more for property than it would cost to replace it.

2. It is particularly adaptable to appraising newly built improvements. The less the amount of depreciation that has occurred, the more accurate the estimate.

3. It is the appropriate method for appraising service-type properties, such as public schools, city halls and libraries.

4. It provides a method for adjusting fire and homeowner's insurance claims.

Disadvantages. Disadvantages of the cost method of appraisal are:

1. The construction costs do not take into account the *amenities* of a property (things of benefit or beauty that increase the value of the property).

2. It is difficult to estimate the replacement cost of older improvements.

3. Accurate costs of individual replacement items are difficult to estimate.

4. Accrued depreciation is difficult to measure.

Comparative Market Approach

The comparative market approach to appraisal is most useful in estimating the value of single-family residences and vacant land. It is widely used by real estate licensees and appraisers because of its reliability and relative simplicity. This method takes into consideration the amenities or pleasing features of properties.

Adjustments are influenced by:

1. *Time of sale*—If the property to be appraised was sold within the last year or so, the value of comparable properties should be adjusted to meet inflationary trends.

2. *Location of property*—The quality of the neighborhood will have a decided effect on the extent to which adjustments will affect the comparisons.

3. *Physical characteristics*—Some of the physical characteristics that are used in making value adjustments are:

   - view from the lot;

   - larger parcel;

   - architectural style;

   - number of rooms;

   - number of baths;

   - square footage;

   - off-street parking for recreational vehicles or boats; and

   - outdoor living areas, such as swimming pools, patios and landscaping.

Sources of data. Licensees can obtain data from a variety of sources. Among these are:

- appraiser's own files;

- public records (county assessor's office keeps a record of all sales transactions recorded in the county);

- recorder's office (for the date of recording of any deed);

- multiple-listing offices, other appraisers or brokers; or

- classified ads and listings.

Steps in the comparative market approach. The procedure for the comparative market approach has three steps:

1. Gather data concerning the sales price on three or more similar properties (having sold recently) in the same geographical area. Properties are more competitive than comparable when first placed on the market.

2. Set up a chart that indicates the items that can be adjusted in comparison with the subject property.

3. Examine and weigh points of difference and similarity to ascertain a probable price at which the subject property could have been sold as of the date of the appraisal. For example: The market appreciates ten percent per year. Any adjustments for difference plus or minus, better or poorer, is $1,000.

Advantages. The advantages of the comparative market approach are:

1. It is most frequently used for home valuation by appraisers.

2. It is the most reliable approach for appraising homes.

3. It is the easiest to compute and apply.

Disadvantages. Some disadvantages of the comparative market approach are:

1. It is difficult at times to locate sufficient comparable recent sales in the area.

2. It is sometimes difficult to make precise adjustments.

3. Financing frequently influences the final selling price.

Income (Capitalization) Approach

The income approach is primarily concerned with the present worth of future benefits that may be derived from the property. It is particularly important in the valuation of income-producing property.

This method is a little more complex and should not be used by an inexperienced broker or appraiser. It involves accurate estimates of: (1) gross income and (2) expenses of operation. It also involves the selection of the capitalization rate and determination of the period of time over which the net income is to be capitalized.

Steps in the income approach. To use the income approach, follow these steps:

1. Estimate the gross scheduled income—100 percent of the income the property is capable of producing.

2. Deduct the annual allowance for a vacancy factor or collection loss. This amount is called effective, or operating, gross income.

3. Deduct the estimated probable fixed and operating expenses. Operating expenses include such items as:

   - taxes;

   - insurance;

   - repairs;

   - management;

   - reserve for replacements;

   - maintenance; and

   - utilities.

4. Compute the net operating income.

5. Having selected a capitalization rate, capitalize the income by dividing the net income by the capitalization rate.

Capitalization rate. The **capitalization rate,** commonly called the cap rate, is the rate of return an investor might expect to receive on the purchase price if the property were free and clear of liens. The cap rate has the following characteristics:

- The greater the risk, the higher the cap rate.

- The higher the cap rate, the lower the value.

- The lower the cap rate, the higher the value.

To establish a cap rate, investors often check the rate against actual market action or develop their own, using the band-of-investment theory. This theory is merely a synthesis of mortgage and equity rates, as disclosed by market data. The rate is a weighted average, the weighting being for the percentages of the total value occupied by the mortgages and equity positions, or band of investments.

For example, if a buyer were to purchase a certain investment property, he or she would be required to make a deposit of 25 percent down. The owner expects to make an 18 percent return on the investment. A 50 percent first trust deed can be secured for ten percent and a new second can be procured for 25 percent of the purchase price at an interest rate of 12 percent. The cap rate is computed as follows:

First trust deed	$50\% \times 10\% =$	5.00%
Second trust deed	$25\% \times 12\% =$	3.00%
Equity (down payment)	$25\% \times 18\% =$	4.50%
Cap rate	100%	= 12.50%

Example of the income approach. Assume an appraiser is estimating the value of an apartment building using the data that follow:

Rent Schedule

Apt. 1:	$ 400 per month
Apt. 2:	450 per month
Apt. 3:	500 per month
Apt. 4:	400 per month
Total	$1,750 per month

Operating Expenses

Taxes	$1,500 per year
Insurance	400 per year
Managing cost	1,200 per year
Other expenses	600 per year
Average vacancy and uncollectibles	7%
Capitalization rate	15%

What is the value of the property?

Gross scheduled income ($1,750 × 12)	$21,000
Less vacancy factor (7% of income)	– 1,470
Effective gross income	$19,530
Less operating expenses	– 3,700
Net income	$15,830

$$\frac{\text{Net income}}{\text{Cap rate}} = \frac{\$15,830}{.15} = \$105,533 \text{ value of property}$$

Gross Monthly Multiplier

The **gross monthly multiplier** is a method of estimating the value of income property without using the cost approach or the income (capitalization) approach. Instead of being based on accurate measurements and facts, it is merely a "guesstimate" of the projected value of the property.

Gross monthly multipliers are ratios that state the relationship between monthly rental income and the sales price. By observing home sales in a neighborhood, an appraiser observes that homes with common characteristics tend to sell for some amount times their gross monthly rental.

The formula for this ballpark method is:

$$\frac{\text{Sales price}}{\text{Gross monthly rent}} = \text{Gross monthly multiplier}$$

When an appraiser uses this method to appraise a home, he or she uses the following formula:

$$\begin{array}{c}\text{Estimate of the home's}\\\text{monthly rental}\end{array} \times \begin{array}{c}\text{Gross monthly}\\\text{multiplier}\end{array} = \begin{array}{c}\text{Estimate of}\\\text{home's value}\end{array}$$

For example, if the gross monthly income of a property is $500, and a multiplier of 140 is the average for this type of property, the value would be estimated as:

$$\$500 \times 140 = \$70,000$$

Depreciation

Depreciation is an important factor in the appraisal of real property. Depreciation is defined, for appraisal purposes, as a loss in value from any cause.

Causes of Depreciation

The principal causes of reduced value of property are of three kinds: physical deterioration, functional obsolescence and economic and social obsolescence.

Physical deterioration. Sources of physical deterioration include:

1. wear and tear from use;

2. negligent care (deferred maintenance);

3. damage by damp rot, termites, etc.; and

4. severe changes in temperature.

Functional obsolescence. This type of depreciation results from:

1. poor architectural design and style;

2. lack of modern facilities;

3. out-of-date equipment;

4. changes in styles of construction;

5. changes in construction methods and materials; and

6. changes in utility demand.

Economic obsolescence. This type of depreciation results from:

1. misplacement of an improvement;

2. zoning and/or legislative restrictions; or

3. recession, unemployment, or other economic upheaval.

Accrual Depreciation

Accrual depreciation is usually used in accounting and is the amount or percentage reserved on the books of an owner to provide for the replacement of an asset. Accrual or future depreciation is the loss in value that has not yet occurred on income-producing property, but will come in the future. It is especially significant in the income method of appraisal. Depreciation in this instance is the provision for the recapture of the improvement value and can be accomplished in any one of several different ways.

One way is the **sinking fund method.** The sinking fund method includes a fixed annual depreciation deduction from income. These yearly deductions are placed in a special fund at compound interest. At the end of the building's useful life, these funds will offset the depreciated value of the structure.

Other Measures of Value

Depth Tables

Appraisers use **depth tables** to determine the value of a lot according to its depth. The *4-3-2-1 rule* adds value to a lot that is deeper than adjacent lots. The percentages that are used are shown in Figure 13.6.

**Figure 13.6
The 4-3-2-1
Rule**

1	10%
2	20%
3	30%
4	40%

Front

Front Foot Value   Front foot value is quoted as a number of dollars per front foot. It is derived by measuring the width of the lot bordering on the street. The deeper the lot, the greater the front foot value.

Square Foot Value   The value per square foot is determined by dividing the total value of a lot by its total area in square feet.

Summary

Appraisal is an *estimate* or an *opinion* of value, and *market value* is the price a willing seller will ask of a willing buyer in an open market. The basic elements that create value are *demand, utility, scarcity* and *transferability.* Emphasis is placed on those principles that affect the value of property, along with specific physical factors that influence property values.

Appraisal is used in five different situations: (1) transfer of property, (2) real estate loans, (3) condemnation proceedings (eminent domain), (4) assessing real property taxes and (5) insurance policies.

There are three methods of real estate appraisal—the cost approach, income approach and market data approach—each with advantages and disadvantages.

The causes of property depreciation are physical deterioration, economic obsolescence and functional obsolescence.

Questions

1. Which of the following forces affect value?
   a. economic
   b. social
   c. political
   d. all of the above

2. An appraisal is:
   a. a statement of market value.
   b. obtained from a civil engineer.
   c. prepared by an attorney.
   d. a formal written report.

3. Value is created by:
   a. cost.
   b. scarcity.
   c. taxation.
   d. all of the above

4. Which of the following is a physical factor affecting value?
   a. location
   b. utility
   c. size
   d. all of the above

5. When individual properties, neighborhoods and cities are constantly changing, this is called the principle of:
   a. regression.
   b. progression.
   c. change.
   d. none of the above

6. When a commodity is scarce and the demand is high, its value increases. This is called the principle of:
   a. anticipation.
   b. conformity.
   c. competition.
   d. none of the above

7. Demand for real estate is affected by:
   a. interest rates.
   b. management.
   c. liquidity.
   d. none of the above

8. The appraisal report may be in a:
   a. letter form.
   b. short form.
   c. narrative form.
   d. all of the above

9. The methods of appraising include:
   a. the cost approach.
   b. the evaluation approach.
   c. the gross divider approach.
   d. all of the above

10. Accurate square footage or cubic footage methods are most needed with the:
    a. comparative market approach.
    b. cost approach.
    c. income approach.
    d. income capitalization approach.

11. Which of the following is least important in determining the market value of a home?
    a. size of the lot
    b. original cost
    c. quality of construction
    d. location

12. The utility of a property is most affected by:
    a. interest rates.
    b. credit controls.
    c. building codes and restrictions.
    d. property taxes.

13. A disadvantage of the cost approach is:
    a. construction costs do not take the amenities into account.
    b. it establishes an upper limit of value.
    c. it cannot be used to appraise a new building.
    d. none of the above

14. The gross multiplier is defined as the:
    a. sale price divided by the monthly operating income.
    b. sale price divided by the gross monthly rent.
    c. net operating income divided by the sales price.
    d. none of the above

15. In appraising a home, which method is most frequently used?

    a. cost approach
    b. market approach
    c. income approach
    d. gross multiplier

16. The gross income of a property is $50,000 and the net operating income is $20,000. If the property has a value of $200,000, what is its cap rate?

    a. 4%
    b. 10%
    c. 25%
    d. none of the above

17. Front foot value is quoted as:

    a. the number of linear feet.
    b. a number of dollars per foot.
    c. the number of feet in a depth table.
    d. none of the above

18. If the going cap rate for an area is five percent and the net operating income of your client's property is $30,000, then the sales price would be:

    a. $150,000.
    b. $300,000.
    c. $600,000.
    d. none of the above

19. The cost approach results in the most accurate appraisal of:

    a. an old building
    b. a single-family residence
    c. a new building
    d. none of the above

20. Given the following diagram and information:

    $40 sq. ft. for the house
    $20 sq. ft. for the garage
    $40,000 for land
    property will last 50 years
    will depreciate for 20 years
    What is the appraised value?

    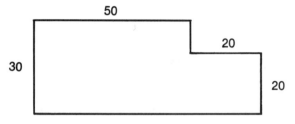

    a. $95,280
    b. $100,000
    c. $102,820
    d. none of the above

14

Organization and Administration of a Real Estate Office

Chapter Preview   This chapter presupposes that you either anticipate opening your own office or you are already supervising your own operation. A step-by-step procedure is used, starting with the very first decision you will have to make: choosing the legal form of ownership you will use. The chapter will point out the advantages and disadvantages of individual proprietorship, types of partnerships, and corporations.

The other requirements in developing and administering a real estate office will follow in this order: selecting a name, selecting a physical site, laying out office, budgeting, developing a policy manual, and recruiting and training personnel.

Terms To Look For

Attrition	**Franchisor**
Career nights	**General partnership**
Corporation	**Limited partnership**
DBA	**Office manager**
Fictitious name	**Policy**
Franchise	**Policy manual**
Franchisee	

Today the public places stricter demands on the real estate broker, there is stiffer competition in the field and overhead costs are increasing. For these reasons, a prospective entrepreneur needs to become acquainted with market surveys, long-range economic forecasts, cost analyses and the money market in general before opening his or her own office.

What motivates a licensee who has been a successful salesperson to relinquish that security for the role of a broker-owner? Some reasons are:

1. Some make the change because they think their growth is limited. They have convinced themselves that they have superior knowledge but have not received adequate compensation for their time and efforts.

2. Many feel that their special talents have been ignored.

3. Some strike out for themselves because of their independent spirit and drive to achieve in spite of the odds.

Regardless of your reasons, you may eventually be faced with the prospect of launching out on your own. Whether you are preparing to open your own office or already operate one, this discussion should prove helpful. A careful plan is indispensable if you would taste the fruits of success in your new endeavor.

Choosing a Legal Form of Ownership

The three basic forms of ownership most frequently found in the real estate business are: individual proprietorship, partnership and corporation.

Individual Proprietorship

The most frequently observed form of ownership is the individual proprietorship. There are both advantages and disadvantages in this form of ownership.

Advantages. Advantages of an individual proprietorship are:

1. You are your own boss.

2. Policies, procedures and specializations may be changed simply and quickly.

3. You don't have to split profits. *Jaxes --*

4. The business is easier to organize.

5. You can take action independently.

6. You have absolute control of the business.

Disadvantages. Some disadvantages include:

1. Outside capital is limited, necessitating the tying up of your own capital.

2. You must take total responsibility for all actions.

3. You will have to spend considerable time in office management.

4. Growth is limited by your financial resources. Do you have the capital or the line of credit to meet demands?

5. Your business continually needs upgrading. Do you have the ability and desire to do so?

6. It makes severe demands on your time.

7. Vacations are difficult to arrange because continuous personal attention is necessary.

8. Problems are sure to arise in case of illness.

9. Handling all specialized phases of a real estate brokerage operation is difficult.

10. Success is completely dependent on the ability of a single individual.

11. It is difficult to budget your time to service all levels.

12. You have unlimited legal liability.

Partnership

A partnership is an association of two or more individuals who carry on a continuing business for profit as co-owners. There are two categories of partnerships: general and limited.

The **general partnership** need not be in writing and the partners are jointly and severally liable for the debts of the partnership. The **limited partnership** must be in writing and the limited partners are liable only to the extent of their individual financial involvement. Note that a limited partnership must include a general partner, who bears the remaining liability.

Advantages. Some advantages of partnerships are:

1. Partners can pool their ideas, experience, finances and talents.

2. Each is relieved of constant supervision.

3. There are tax advantages over the corporate structure.

4. Shared funding increases possible increased capitalization.

5. Operational responsibilities are shared.

6. Two or more people share decision making and planning.

7. Each has more time to pursue other interests.

8. An increased scale of operations is possible, with greater stability.

Disadvantages. Partnerships also have disadvantages, including:

1. Each partner is responsible for the business actions and obligations of the others.

2. Partners must reconcile and adjust decisions to suit each other's ideas.

3. Creditors may seek each partner's personal assets to pay debts incurred by the partnership.

4. Partners share profits in accordance with and in proportion to the partnership agreements.

Corporation

The **corporation** has proved to be the least popular form of ownership in California real estate offices.

Advantages. The advantages of corporation ownership include:

1. Holders of stock are not liable for the debts of a corporation.

2. Almost unlimited capitalization potential is provided through the issuance of stock.

3. Individual stockholders are liable only to the extent of their investments.

4. Individuals may enter and leave the organization without appreciable effort.

5. Once a firm grows to a certain size, the corporate form offers distinct advantages.

Disadvantages. Some disadvantages are:

1. Organizing and forming a corporation is relatively complex and costly.

2. It is more difficult to obtain credit.

3. Creditors may not proceed against the stockholders to satisfy a debt beyond the corporation's ability to pay from its own assets.

4. It is more difficult to make decisions directly, due to the complexity of the organizational structure.

5. This type of organization is subject to higher taxation; the corporation's income is taxed to the corporation and any income paid in dividends is taxed to the stockholders.

S-Corporation -- treats comp. as if a partnership

Franchising

A **franchise** is a form of ownership that gives an individual real estate firm the right to use the name and operating procedures of a large parent company.

The parent company, known as the **franchisor,** neither owns nor operates the offices of the individual **franchisees.** The franchisees agree to pay a fee or a percentage of their offices' gross commissions for the right to use the franchisor's trade name and logo and receive such other services as may be contained in the franchise agreement. Some examples of such organizations are Red Carpet, Century 21, Real Estate Network and Herbert Hawkins Realtors.

Advantages. Some advantages of being a franchisee are:

1. Operating procedures are often better defined in offices of brokers who are members of a franchise system.

2. Marketing identification is made easier through the use of a readily identifiable trade name or trademark.

3. Large-scale advertising is readily available.

4. Franchisors provide assistance with administrative procedures.

5. Mass purchasing power is available for supplies and equipment.

6. Interagency cooperation is granted.

7. Fringe benefits, such as group insurance and retirement plans, are available.

Disadvantages. Some disadvantages of being a franchisee are:

1. The broker relinquishes the individual firm name in favor of the name of the parent organization.

2. Compliance with the franchise agreement requires initial expenses.

3. To continue under the contract will entail additional costs and payment of fees.

4. The franchisee relinquishes a degree of control to the franchisor.

5. Bookkeeping procedures may have to be installed that normally may not be required.

Selecting a Name

Some entrepreneurs like to use their own name as the company name. This decision may depend on the track record the broker has already established, that is, the way the broker is regarded by customers and clients. Does his or her name stand for fair play and honesty? Brokers should beware that they are not on an ego trip when they choose a name.

If a firm uses a name other than the name of the owner, it is said to be using a **fictitious name.** A "Fictitious Business Name Statement" must be filed with the county clerk in the county where the principal place of business is located.

The **DBA** ("doing business as") must be filed not later than 40 days from the beginning of business transactions. Within 30 days after the statement has been filed, it must be published for four successive weeks in a newspaper of general circulation in the county where it is filed. This is required to avoid duplication in the use of the name.

Caution: A Fictitious Business Name Statement expires at the end of five years unless it is purposely abandoned by filing a statement of abandonment prior to the expiration date.

Physical Site

Office location

Perhaps one of the most vital decisions that the broker must make in laying plans for his or her first office is selecting a location. The final decision will probably depend largely on whether the broker wants to engage in a general operation or specialize in a particular field.

For example, a broker who intends to specialize in commercial or industrial sales would be well advised to locate in the central business district. A broker who plans to devote his or her major activities to residential brokerage should look for a location in a suburban area. The office site should be selected only after a careful neighborhood survey, including an analysis of freeways and growth patterns, an analysis of land values and preparation of projections, charts and maps. Because most of the business transacted by the typical real estate office will be in the neighborhood where the office is located, brokers should locate in the area they feel they can best serve.

Other items to take into consideration are:

1. Plans for expansion must be given consideration and projected into the future.

2. Provision for adequate parking space must be made.

3. Pleasant surroundings should be sought after.

4. Especially for the residential broker, a dramatic office entrance is desirable.

5. An area that will draw walk-in business and where window displays can be used might be advantageous.

6. Offices strategically located in shopping centers draw much business.

7. The size of the operation will often dictate the specific location.

8. Some brokers recognize the value of location on or near a main highway.

Office Layout

The layout of the real estate office will depend largely on the size of the operation. The functional plan of the office should allow for:

- adequate floor space for each sales associate and secretary and for administrative personnel;

- desks for office personnel;

- a private office for the broker;

- a reception room or reception area;

- a closing or conference room; and

- a supply room or workroom.

Floor space for each employee. It will be difficult to determine with any degree of certainty the exact number of square feet to be allowed for each person. However, a rule of thumb is to allow anywhere from 50 to 300 square feet per employee. Because all sales associates are not in the office at the same time, the lower figure or somewhere in between might be adequate.

Desk space for office personnel. Studies have indicated that approximately 125 to 150 square feet of office space are required for each desk. Inasmuch as the desk is the employee's workbench, there should be a suitable surface for writing and processing information. Desks that are not uniform in size and appearance but are of assorted sizes and finishes will detract from the professional appearance of the office.

Above all, sales associates' desks need to be kept in a neat and uncluttered condition. This means avoiding unkempt and unemptied ashtrays, overflowing wastebaskets or anything that detracts from a businesslike atmosphere.

Private office for broker. Where possible, the office manager/broker should have a private office that allows a good view of the entire staff. The office may be used as a reference center, for private interviews and to provide space for small conferences. It does not have to be lavishly furnished, but it should be well-planned and well-arranged.

Reception room. The importance of the reception room is rather obvious. It will be the first introduction to your office. Above all, this room or space should be neat and clean, attractive in decor and comfortably furnished. If a receptionist is employed, he or she should be located here. There should be adequate seating. Current magazines and some of your own direct mail pieces for customers, clients and visitors to read will spark their interest.

Closing or conference room. A closing or conference room is extremely important. It is difficult to talk to customers in the main part of the office while others are moving about or talking on the phone. Confusion often reigns supreme and no one else is able to concentrate. When discussions and sales presentations are made in a noisy office, they are often unsuccessful. However, in the event that a special closing room cannot be provided, the broker's office might be used for the same purpose.

Supply room and workroom. Space needs to be provided for supplies and equipment needed by sales associates and office personnel. This storage will consist of needed files, paper, office supplies, maps and records. In addition to this, office equipment, such as duplicating machines, typewriters and photocopy machines, needs to be well located. Because of the noise and confusion that can arise from its operation, machine activity should be segregated from the sales floor.

Budgeting

In the past 20 years, office costs have steadily increased. Some of these costs are:

- salaries for staff personnel;
- advertising;
- occupancy expenses;
- telephone;
- sales manager's salary; and
- other business expenses, including supplies, equipment costs and utilities.

The proportion of the budget spent on each category will vary, depending on the size of the office, efficiency of operation, fluctuations in business activity, and the company's interest in residential, commercial or industrial activity.

Salaries

Salary expenses will depend on the number of salaried personnel employed by the company. This will often be the largest single expense of the company's operation. Salary expenses are consequently somewhat flexible, especially if the owner/broker assumes some of the extra duties. The broker should remember, however, that assuming routine tasks that could be handled by other personnel sometimes results in false economizing.

Secretarial employees. Regardless of the size of the company, the requirement for clerical help will always exist. The broker/owner, after a careful self-analysis, can determine how many hours he or she spends on office details that can be handled by less experienced salaried personnel. Avoid being tied down to routine tasks by employing secretarial, typing and reception personnel. A loyal and efficient secretary is worth his or her weight in gold. A secretary can free you to spend your time more productively.

Bookkeeper. In smaller offices the secretary may perform bookkeeping tasks. Even if you hire a bookkeeper, you should develop some simple forms that a secretary or bookkeeper can complete that will enable you to obtain and retain facts about income, expenses and production to assist you in making management decisions.

Office manager. Every real estate office has an **office manager,** even though much of the time it is the owner/broker who serves this purpose. Whether or not a specific person is hired for the job, the office manager's responsibilities include seeing that clerks, secretaries and receptionists perform efficiently and delegating responsibilities to staff, so that the workload is well distributed.

If a separate individual is hired, he or she should be a person of integrity, professional appearance, good judgment, flexibility and ability to get along with others. Above all, he or she must possess managerial skills, including the ability to plan, organize and control.

Sales manager. Whenever a real estate office has two or more salespeople, you will need a sales manager, in fact if not in name. The responsibilities of the sales manager usually include recruiting, selecting, training and discharging sales personnel. The sales manager may also assist in preparing budgets, advertising, preparing production schedules and reports, and assisting in the difficult task of cost control.

If the size of the company warrants such a position, the following characteristics best describe a sales manager: He or she has a knowledge of the product, company policy and the activities of competition. Because much of his or her work will involve a close association with company personnel, he or she must possess the qualities of patience, understanding, ability to delegate and ability to get along with people.

Advertising

The second largest expense is usually advertising. Not only does it account for a share of the company dollar but it is the most difficult to control. Included in this expense are display and classified newspaper advertising, radio and television time, brochures, signs, direct mail, and other miscellaneous advertising schemes.

Remember, you advertise to get results and to motivate people to come to your office for your services. The number of calls generated by the ad is not as important as the number of qualified buyers gleaned from those calls. There are at least two underlying facts to consider: (1) you advertise to satisfy your agents and to attract new agents and (2) you advertise to satisfy listed customers.

Operating Expenses

Costs entailed in actually operating the office rank high on the list of expenses incurred. These operating expenses include supplies, travel, legal and accounting services, multiple-listing fees, association dues, licenses, postage, insurance and printing, to name a few.

Telephone

The cost for telephone use is actually part of the operating expenses, but because of its significance it is treated separately. This item must be tightly controlled to balance the office budget. Answering services, radio phones and recording devices are included in this category.

Certainly, salespeople should be allowed free access to phones for business purposes, but personal calls and long-distance calls should be kept to a minimum.

Unnecessarily long conversations should be curtailed; they not only add to the office expense but may tie up available lines.

Occupancy

Included in the occupancy expenses are such items as rent or mortgage interest, depreciation, maintenance, janitorial services and heat, light and other utilities. This area covers perhaps the fifth largest expense category.

Net Profit

What is left of the company dollar represents the net profit realized by the company. There are two ways a company can increase its net profits:

1. Increase the gross volume of commissions.
2. Decrease the overhead expenses.

Policy Manual

A **policy** is a definite course of action, a principle, or a procedure to govern employee action. A **policy manual** is a written collection of policies to be used in the operation of a real estate office—the written constitution of your office.

There are four management functions: planning, organizing, directing and controlling. To implement and reinforce these functions, the broker establishing his or her own office should develop a policy manual.

Characteristics

Any policy manual should feature the following characteristics:

1. It must be concise and understandable.
2. It must be in writing.
3. It must set forth the policies and procedures, plans, practices and philosophy of the real estate office.
4. It must be firm, yet flexible enough to meet unexpected emergencies.
5. It must be developed according to individual needs and preferences.
6. It should be constantly changed, edited and revised.
7. It should be arranged alphabetically, one or two topics to a page.
8. It is sometimes developed as a result of negative experience; for example, a lost sale or an unhappy client.
9. Employees should be allowed to assist in its gradual development.

Items That Must Be Included

The size of the manual will depend on the needs and the size of the company. Regardless of size, the manual includes items needed to help avoid conflicts, problems and misunderstandings. Some of these items are:

- job descriptions;
- duties and responsibilities;

- employee qualifications;
- training program;
- methods and formulas for compensation;
- company benefits; and
- termination procedures.

The following items may also be included in the policy manual:

- accounting procedures for trust funds;
- sales and escrow procedures;
- open houses;
- follow-up on listings;
- office hours;
- allocation of floor time;
- handling grievances;
- MLS procedure;
- handling correspondence;
- use of the telephone;
- ordering and placement of signs;
- conducting sales meetings;
- methods of compensation;
- granting bonuses;
- applying for vacations;
- health and disability insurance;
- arbitration procedures; and
- necessary reports and recordkeeping.

Advantages. A policy manual has numerous advantages. It can:

1. save money and valuable time by eliminating repetitive instructions;
2. reduce training time for new recruits;
3. reduce possible litigation;
4. reduce errors, conflicts, problems and misunderstandings;
5. place responsibility and develop a cooperative attitude;
6. explain office position on important issues;
7. serve as a training manual and/or reference book;
8. induce company integrity and stability;

9. generate confidence in management and the company; and

10. define and explain management skills.

Disadvantages. A policy manual also has some disadvantages, including the following:

1. The cost of initial preparation may be high.

2. It is often so standardized that individual initiative is restrained.

3. It may take five to ten years to formulate sound policy.

Additional Suggestions

In using a policy manual, try following some of these additional suggestions:

1. Don't try to write it all at once.

2. Seek the staff's input, feedback and approval.

3. Use a looseleaf binder so changes, additions and deletions can be made.

4. Keep a copy readily available.

5. The opening line should state the beliefs, goals and philosophies of the company, including:

   • what is to be done;

   • why it is to be done;

   • how it is done; and

   • when it is to be done.

6. It can be used as a personnel tool.

   • Have recruits read it after an interview.

   • Use it for answers to routine questions, conserving the manager's time and energy.

   • It gives authority to arbitrate.

Recruiting and Training Personnel

The broker/owner needs to hire and keep competent personnel to be successful. This assignment is particularly difficult today because sales associates seem to drift from office to office or even in and out of the real estate business. The basic premise in this regard is as follows: one-third coming in, one-third going out.

Reasons for Recruitment

The sales manager or broker/manager must understand the reasons for recruitment to make his or her endeavors pay off.

Attrition. Managers can anticipate attrition through depletion of personnel due to natural reasons such as retirement, opening own office or moving. Recruitment replaces these people.

Competition. Recruitment is an important part of growing in size to meet competitive expansion.

Stability. Adding new associates assures the broker of survival in a fluctuating market.

Upgrade. Brokers need to improve the caliber of their personnel by attracting people who are, if possible, better than their present personnel. No service business can afford to remain at the same level each year.

Diversity. Brokers need to attract new personnel with diverse backgrounds, experience and spheres of influence to develop a good staff mixture.

Continuous process. Recruitment as a continuous process assures the broker/owner of an efficient, growing organization at all times. This will assure him or her success in obtaining a fair share of the market.

Sources of Personnel

Even though the demand for outstanding employees is greater than the supply, there is a reservoir of sales talent that can be tapped.

Present staff. A source of qualified personnel often overlooked is your present staff members. If the need seems justified, inducements in the form of awards, money, prizes and recognition may be offered.

Colleges and universities. Because of the increased educational requirements for licensees, colleges and universities are a good source. These potential recruits are often eager, pliable and adaptable.

Civic groups. Becoming an active member of a church, service club, community group or social group may enable you to become acquainted with possible recruits.

Pirating. Salespeople in other businesses may have become disillusioned or be interested in a change. They may already have the skills required for this demanding industry.

Career nights. Host **career nights.** Advertise an evening meeting open to the public. By using successful salespeople as speakers, you can explain the rewards of a real estate career, as well as the sacrifices necessary to succeed.

Referrals. Wide-awake managers will solicit referrals from their clientele. Often these centers of influence, such as attorneys, doctors, bankers and contacts at title companies, may make worthwhile referrals. Other sources peculiar to your interests and contacts should be explored and, when possible, utilized.

Selecting Personnel

As a result of your recruitment efforts, you will undoubtedly receive numerous applications. Some of these will be worthy of consideration and others will not. Your job will be to screen the applicants, to glean the best possible future employees. This can be done through carefully prepared application forms and initial interviews.

Interviewing. The initial interview should enable you to get acquainted with the applicant and disclose to him or her what your company has to offer. Prior to the interview, the application will have acquainted you with the applicant's employment record, education, health, character and other data.

The applicant will be interested in knowing what his or her chances for success are with your company, the advantages and disadvantages in real estate, and what your company policies are and how they will affect his or her operation. If he or she is a likely prospect, you will find yourself extolling the virtues of your company. Do not oversell your company; that could cause future problems.

Testing. You may wish to use testing procedures to determine the worth of an applicant. You may develop your own test or use tests available through local colleges and universities or special testing centers. Use an attitude test that will evaluate those traits considered important for success in real estate:

- self-discipline (persistence and self-control);
- perception (learning and adaptability);
- adjustment to job (cooperation and stability);
- awareness (sensitivity to others' reactions); and
- closing skills (enthusiasm and persuasiveness).

Caution: Testing gives information that supplements, but never replaces, the manager's judgment and observation.

Problems. Some offices encounter problems in the selection of personnel because they:

1. hire almost anyone who applies;
2. neglect to check the accuracy of application forms submitted;
3. are unaware of the personality, education and experience required for the job;
4. fail to secure adequate information about the applicant; and
5. do not inform the applicant what is expected of him or her.

The national estimated cost of selecting a sales associate who fails is $8,000 to $12,000.

Training

One of the principal responsibilities of the manager after recruitment and selection of personnel has taken place is the role of teacher and trainer. The potential production of a new employee is directly proportional to his or her orderly transition into your company.

Assign the new recruit a desk and explain office security, the telephone system, floor priority and so forth. Allow him or her to spend some time reading the policy manual and prepare to answer any questions he or she may have.

Encourage the other sales associates to welcome the recruits. A friendly reputation and an open-minded attitude on the part of other staff members will give recruits a feeling of acceptance and help them overcome fear of the unknown.

Approaches to training. Many brokers are not in a position to conduct formal education programs, but they cannot divorce themselves from this responsibility. Keep in mind that training helps the manager in the areas of communications, costs, efficiency, image, morale, supervision time and profit.

The main purpose of training and education is to induce some behavioral change. Remember that people learn:

- 84 percent by sight;

- 10 percent by hearing;

- 3 percent by smell;

- 2 percent by touch; and

- 1 percent by taste.

Strive to strengthen the recruits' behavior and good performance through recognition of positive achievement. Regardless of where or when the training may take place, encourage the new sales associate to take notes. Without adequate notes, people forget 50 percent in one hour, 75 percent in one day, and 90 percent in one week. The method of training that appears the best and most thorough is that of role-playing.

Additional education. California has a strong real estate education program offered in evening schools, community colleges, universities and private schools. New employees should be encouraged to enroll in such courses for basic and specialized training. Another source from which to receive educational experience is through local, state and national real estate boards, and through attendance at seminars, conferences and clinics.

All employees should be encouraged to use books and magazines to keep abreast of changes taking place in this dynamic field. *California Real Estate* magazine, published monthly by the California Association of REALTORS®, contains provocative articles on vital real estate topics. New legislative changes are reviewed and pertinent questions answered in the Real Estate Commissioner's column.

Summary

The chapter was based on the premise that you either intend opening your own office or are already operating an office. Based on this premise, a step-by-step process for developing and operating an office was detailed.

Questions

1. Which of the following is a legal way to own a business?

   a. corporation
   b. partnership
   c. individual proprietorship
   d. all of the above

2. The best way to own a real estate business is:

   a. individual proprietorship.
   b. corporation.
   c. partnership.
   d. no best way

3. An advantage of individual proprietorship is:

   a. unlimited capital.
   b. splitting the profits.
   c. business is easier to organize.
   d. none of the above

4. An advantage of a partnership is:

   a. pooling ideas and concepts.
   b. shared financing of the business.
   c. shared operational responsibility.
   d. all of the above

5. A disadvantage of a corporation is:

   a. you must take total responsibility for the company.
   b. it is more difficult to obtain credit.
   c. limited liability.
   d. all of the above

6. A parent company that grants to another company the right to use its name and do business in a prescribed manner is called:

   a. an individual proprietorship.
   b. a franchise.
   c. a corporation.
   d. a partnership.

7. DBA means:

   a. doing business anonymously.
   b. doing business as.
   c. doing business adversely.
   d. none of the above

8. A fictitious business name statement expires at the end of:

   a. one year.
   b. two years.
   c. five years.
   d. seven years.

9. The office layout should have:

   a. adequate floor space.
   b. a closing room.
   c. a supply room.
   d. all of the above

10. The largest cost of operating an office will be:

    a. commission.
    b. advertising.
    c. telephone.
    d. general expenses.

11. A book that defines courses of action, principles or procedures to govern employee behavior is called a:

    a. sales manual.
    b. policy manual.
    c. operations manual.
    d. none of the above

12. One of the main objectives in a manager's dealings with personnel is:

    a. recruiting and training.
    b. recruiting and selling.
    c. training and selling.
    d. none of the above

13. Which of the following is *not* a reason for recruiting?

    a. competition
    b. cutting costs
    c. upgrading
    d. stability

14. An advantage of franchising is:

    a. market identification.
    b. fringe benefits.
    c. large-scale advertising.
    d. all of the above

15. Which of the following is a reason for keeping accurate books for the business?

    a. management decisions
    b. only if you are a corporation
    c. both a and b
    d. none of the above

16. Which of the following items must be included in the policy manual?

    a. open houses
    b. MLS procedures
    c. sales and escrow procedures
    d. employee qualifications

17. Whose responsibility is it to see that an agent is properly trained?

    a. owners
    b. managers
    c. fellow agents
    d. none of the above

18. The main purpose of training is:

    a. to induce behavioral change.
    b. to help the agent get rich.
    c. both a and b
    d. none of the above

19. An important item in site selection is:

    a. providing for future expansion.
    b. selecting a site commensurate with the company's activity.
    c. obtaining a site with pleasant surroundings.
    d. all of the above

20. Which of the following can be used to increase a company's net profit?

    a. budgeting
    b. bookkeeping
    c. both a and b
    d. none of the above

15

Property Management and Leasing

Chapter Preview

A discussion of the subject of property management and leasing is essential for real estate licensees who may someday become involved in this highly specialized field. A greater understanding of this area includes an analysis of the importance and scope of the field of property management.

The analysis includes what it takes to be an efficient property manager, types of property managers and the duties and responsibilities of a person holding this title.

Special techniques of managing different types of property—such as residential property, condominiums, mobile homes, public housing and office buildings—will be discussed, along with types of leases and how they are handled. The chapter concludes with an overview of the legal rights and responsibilities of landlords and tenants.

Terms To Look For

Assignment
Civil Rights Act of 1968
Condominiums
CPM
Estate at sufferance
Estate at will
Estate for years
Estate from period to period
Gross lease
Industrialization
IREM
Lease-option
Lessee
Lessor
Management agreement
Mobile home
Net lease
Percentage lease
Periodic tenancy
Rent schedule
Resident manager
Rumford Fair Housing Act
Sale-leaseback
Sublease
Unlawful detainer
Unruh Civil Rights Act

**The Property
Management Field**

Property management is a specialized field of real estate that originated with the founding of the Institute of Real Estate Management in 1933. It has gained additional momentum of late and now involves real estate brokers in increasing numbers.

Catalysts for Growth

The big impetus came from three basic factors: industrialization, the invention of the steel frame and the elevator, and the advent of professionalism.

Industrialization. As a result of the Industrial Revolution, more and more people began to occupy residential and commercial space that they did not own. This **industrialization** necessitated a type of property management. In the early stages, however, property management primarily involved rent collecting.

Invention of steel frames and elevators. As a result of the Industrial Revolution, more and more buildings were expanded and new buildings were constructed. This growing size and number of buildings increased the complexity of managing them, necessitating the use of specialists in management.

Professionalism. The number of people involved in property management increased rapidly. However, because these managers lacked qualification and had limited knowledge and abilities, there were many business failures.

To slow down this trend and improve the professional standing of this management group, in 1933 approximately 100 companies met and formed the Institute of Real Estate Management (**IREM**). These companies certified that they:

1. would refrain from commingling funds that belonged to their clients with personal funds;

2. would bond all employees handling client funds; and

3. would disclose all fees, commissions or other payments received as a result of activity relating to the client's property.

This move, while it improved the situation, still left something to be desired. After several years, it was perceived that the companies as such were not meeting the standards set, mainly because the personnel in the various companies were constantly changing.

**Certified Property
Manager**

In 1938 the Institute changed its policy and developed the designation certified property manager (**CPM**) to certify individual managers rather than the companies that employed them. Then and today the Institute's certification requirements are designed to ensure that managers have the appropriate amount of general business and industry-specific experience necessary to maintain high standards within the profession. To earn the CPM designation, an individual must actively support the Institute's rules and regulations; be able to demonstrate honesty and integrity; meet minimum educational requirements; demonstrate the ability to manage real estate, including at least three years' experience in a responsible real estate management position; and be a member of a local real estate board or a member of the NATIONAL ASSOCIATION OF REALTORS®.

Real Estate Managers

Types of Real Estate Managers

There are three basic kinds of building managers: licensee/property managers, individual property managers and resident managers.

Licensee/property manager. A licensee/property manager is a licensee of a real estate office or agency that manages a number of properties for various owners. These persons may be members of the firm, spending their full time in management; they may be self-employed as managing agents; or individuals may be one of several managers in the management departments of large real estate companies.

Individual property manager. An individual property manager manages a single property for the owner and may or may not possess a real estate license. He or she is usually employed on a straight salary basis.

Resident manager. A **resident manager,** as the title implies, lives on the property and may be employed by a real estate agency or a managing agent. He or she is usually qualified for this assignment by previous management experience or by previous special training. The personality of this person is critical if he or she is to be successful. Specifically, five basic traits are vitally important:

1. the merchandising ability to *contact, show* and *close* the rental of a unit;
2. a high degree of self-confidence and willingness to take charge;
3. accuracy in handling money, checks, bank deposits and other bookkeeping duties;
4. awareness of and sensitivity to the events occurring on and around the property; and
5. orderliness and legibility in keeping records and meticulousness in filing, cataloguing and making reports.

State law requires that the resident manager of a property containing 16 units or more be a "responsible person."

Functions of a Property Manager

The author of the following statement is unknown, but the words give a splendid overview of the making of a property manager:

"The past is his experience, and with its valuable ramifications, he is helped immeasurably to mold the plans for his future. During his years of experience, he has built and sold houses, appraised property, dealt in long-term commercial and industrial leases, made many complicated and intricate transactions, bought and sold hotels—in short, has had a long experience with the public, including businessmen, husbands and wives, doctors and lawyers, engineers and financiers, yes, with gamblers, beggarmen and thieves, mothers-in-law, fanatics, the feebleminded, strong and weak characters of every type and description, politicians too, and with this experience has automatically been turned out a well-rounded, socially conscious, alert and aggressive person—in short, a skillful businessman, and when he has reached this point, he has automatically qualified for the job of property management."

Depending on the complexity of the property, the property manager's duties and responsibilities are many and varied. Inherent in these duties is the dual role of an administrator for the owner and an advocate for the resident.

The property manager's responsibility is to understand and communicate with both parties. The astute property manager is in an ideal position to represent both the owner and the resident with procedures that are fair and equitable. He or she should recognize that the owner wants a fair return on investment and that the resident wants decent housing and a reasonable value for the rent money.

Administrator for the owner. As the administrator for the owner, the property manager must recognize that the owner is primarily interested in two things:

1. the highest return from the property, realizing its highest and best use; and

2. enhancement of the physical value of the property.

Advocate for the tenant/resident. As the advocate for the tenant/resident, the property manager must recognize that residents are interested in the following:

1. the best value obtainable from their rental dollar; and

2. assurance that everything is being done for their own personal safety and protection and for that of their children, if any.

This means that property managers need to be involved in community affairs to understand the development of community safety measures, building restrictions and general welfare of the community.

Specific Duties of a Property Manager

Under the property management system, the owner is relieved of all executive functions, as well as all details connected with the operation or physical upkeep of the property.

A conscientious manager will realize that:

1. Renters need to know what is expected of them and what they can expect from the owner. (This should be stated in writing.)

2. Residents' questions should be handled properly and promptly.

3. If any request is denied, the manager should state why and avoid pointless arguing.

4. The owner, manager and employees should guard against the attitude that the tenants "out there" are all unreasonable. However, it would be disastrous to adopt the principle that the customer is always right. The resident is, of course, *always* entitled to fair and sympathetic treatment.

As an agent the property manager must show good faith and loyalty to his or her principal (the owner); perform his or her duties with skill, care and due diligence; fully disclose all pertinent facts; avoid commingling funds; and refrain from personal profits without the principal's full knowledge and consent.

State-defined responsibilities. In addition to the general responsibilities described, the Department of Real Estate has prepared a list of specific duties:

1. Establish the rental schedule that will bring the highest yield consistent with good economics.

2. Merchandise the space and collect the rents.

3. Create and supervise maintenance schedules and repairs.

4. Supervise all purchasing.

5. Develop a tenant/resident-relations policy.

6. Develop employee policies and supervise their operations.

7. Maintain proper records and make regular reports to the owner.

8. Qualify and investigate prospective tenants' credit.

9. Prepare and execute leases.

10. Prepare decorating specifications and secure estimates.

11. Hire, instruct and maintain satisfactory personnel to staff the building(s).

12. Audit and pay bills.

13. Advertise and publicize vacancies through selected media and broker lists.

14. Plan alterations and modernizing programs.

15. Inspect vacant space frequently.

16. Keep abreast of economic conditions and posted competitive market conditions.

17. Pay insurance premiums and taxes and recommend tax appeals when warranted.[1]

Basic responsibilities. The principal functions of a property manager can be summarized as six basic responsibilities:

1. marketing space by advertising and securing desirable tenants;

2. collecting rents;

3. handling tenant complaints and physically caring for the premises;

4. purchasing supplies and equipment and paying for repairs;

5. hiring needed employees and maintaining good public relations; and

6. keeping proper records and preparing required reports.

Establishing rent schedules. Rent levels are usually determined on the premise of scarcity and comparability of values in the area. To set up proper rent schedules, the manager must make a skilled and thorough analysis of the neighborhood. This analysis will include but not be limited to the following factors:

1. the character of the immediate neighborhood;

2. economic level and size of families;

3. trends in population growth and occupants per unit;

4. directional growth of community and expansion and growth of local industries;

[1] *California Department of Real Estate Reference Book,* 1984-85 edition, p. 673.

5. availability of transportation, recreation, shopping, churches and schools; and

6. the condition of the housing market vs. population growth trends.

The objective of the analysis is to set up a rental schedule commensurate with the findings. Rents should bring the maximum income consistent with good economy.

The objective of good property management is to achieve as nearly as possible one hundred percent occupancy without underpricing. Conducting surveys and establishing rental schedules are very important. Statistics show that uncollected rent is worse than a vacancy because the property suffers wear and tear from the occupant.

Professional Qualifications of a Property Manager

What kind of person is qualified to be not only a human relations specialist but a detail manager as well? Such a person must:

1. *Be a specialist in merchandising.* The property manager must be able to advertise and to sell prospective tenants on the merits of a building.

2. *Be a leasing expert.* Being well informed on all types of leases will assist a manager in determining the most beneficial lease for a particular client.

3. *Be an accounting specialist.* The law requires certain records to be kept and reports to be made.

4. *Have maintenance know-how.* Preventative and corrective maintenance will prevent expensive repairs at some future date.

5. *Be a purchasing supervisor.* The manager must keep up with all current technological advances in building. This will enable him or her to recommend needed replacements for obsolete installations.

6. *Be a credit specialist.* Credit ratings are extremely important. Knowing whether or not a tenant can live up to the terms of a lease is vitally important.

7. *Be an insurance advisor.* Understanding the various types of policies available and the extent of coverage can save both the owner and the tenant time and money.

8. *Be a tax interpreter.* A manager must be well versed in property taxes and their effect on the property he or she manages. He or she should be cognizant of the relationship of depreciation to the income and profit of the property.[2]

Types of Property Managed

The most common types of properties involving property management are office buildings, apartment buildings, commercial structures, residences, shopping centers, public buildings, recreation centers, hotels, motels, specialized factories, restaurants and theaters. Recently other properties have joined the list and are rapidly gaining in importance and popularity. These include:

- industrial parks;
- mobile home parks;
- miniwarehouses;

[2]Adapted from *California Department of Real Estate Reference Guide,* 1984-85 edition, pp. 672-673.

- marinas; and

- airports.

A few of these will be described further in this section.

Residential Properties

Residential properties are by far the most numerous of the properties subject to professional management. There are more than 70 million permanent housing units in the United States. A housing shortage, nationwide, has almost always been present. It would require 3 million new housing starts each year merely to replace end-of-the-line units.

Condominiums. Individual ownership of condominiums nearly always involves property management. Condominiums and cooperatives are similar from the standpoint of managing.

Mobile homes. Management of a mobile home park is a specialty field involving:

- park development;

- public amenities;

- utility sales; and

- pad leasing.

Residential Income Property

Residential property bought for investment is the most common property using professional management. Statistics indicate that multiple units account for approximately 30 percent of residential housing in the United States. That totals 21 million, with this breakdown:

1. Duplexes account for about 6 million (8 percent).

2. Triplex and fourplex units account for about 4 million (7 percent).

3. Complexes with five or more units account for about 11 million (15 percent).

Public housing. Ownership of public housing is becoming increasingly important to property management. The largest single landlord in the United States is the collective 3,500 public housing authorities. More than 1.5 million units are controlled by public housing authorities.

Office Buildings

Office buildings are the major commercial property. Office space requirements will continue to grow due to the increase in the number of people working in offices or similar commercial structures. The larger users of office space, such as banks, savings and loan associations, and insurance companies, often build for their own use but also provide a large excess of space for leasing purposes. Specialized offices, such as medical or legal offices, will have special problems.

Merchandising office space. The rental or lease of office space can be tied to the following criteria:

- appearance of surroundings;

- transportation facilities;
- prestige and image of area;
- proximity to clients;
- building appearance;
- lobby appearance;
- elevator appearance and condition;
- corridor appearance;
- office interiors;
- tenant services offered;
- management; and
- other tenants.

Advertising is an essential part of conducting an aggressive leasing campaign. Such publicity ideas as the following can be most helpful:

1. groundbreaking ceremonies;
2. brochures;
3. newspaper ads;
4. mailing lists of professional groups, including attorneys, doctors and CPAs;
5. personal solicitation;
6. use of model office; and
7. making technical data readily available, including floor plans, space available and space arrangements.

Maintenance. The manager of an office building must meet any maintenance or service problem unique to this type of operation. This job will include such activities as:

- servicing all operating equipment and public facilities, such as lobbies, lights and washrooms;
- maintaining elevators, which are indispensable in a high-rise;
- cleaning, usually done at night; and
- other routine maintenance, including window cleaning, waste removal, light-bulb replacement, heating, ventilation and air-conditioning.

Protection. Protection of the premises is a management function. It includes such vital items as:

- key control;
- guard employment;
- fire-prevention techniques;
- emergency evacuation plans;

- properly marked exits; and
- maintenance operations manual, showing list of all equipment with the vital information concerning each piece of equipment.

Management Agreement

It makes no difference whether the property involved is an office building, a residential property or a shopping center; the responsibilities assumed by the manager are so important that they warrant a written agreement. The management agreement formalizes the relationship between the owner and the manager and points out the rights and duties of each party. The forms used for this purpose may vary; but, regardless of the property involved, certain basic points must be included:

1. identification of the parties;
2. sufficient identification of the property;
3. the contract period, including the beginning and the termination dates;
4. management's and owner's responsibilities;
5. management fees—the amount, when it is to be paid and the manner of payment; and
6. provision for management accounting, including records to be kept and reports to be made.

Accounting Records

Although the number of bookkeeping records needed will depend on the type of property managed and the volume of business involved, the selection and maintenance of an adequate trust-fund accounting system is essential in property management, due to the "fiduciary" nature of the business.

Reasons for accounting records. There are a number of basic reasons for keeping orderly records in property management:

1. The law states that a separate record must be kept for each managed property.
2. The "fiduciary" relationship between the owner and the manager dictates a full disclosure.
3. Contractual relationships call for an accounting of all funds.
4. Records are needed for income tax purposes.
5. It may be necessary to satisfy third parties who have an interest in the property.
6. Accurate records serve as a control in evaluating income and expenses, analyzing costs and preparing budgets.
7. Records provide the broker with a source of information when inquiries are made or problems arise.

A sample accounting record is shown as Figure 15.1.

Trust ledger. Section 2830 of the Commissioner's Regulations requires that a trust ledger for property management accounts be established. As rents come in, they are posted to the owner's account. Also recorded in the trust ledger is the money paid out on behalf of the owner. This includes any repair costs, payments of encumbrances, or payments for utilities or commissions. These expenses are charged against the income of the property, and the manager sends a statement to the owner at the end of each month.

Figure 15.1
Sample Accounting
Record for a Property

SEPARATE RECORD FOR EACH PROPERTY MANAGED

Owner _____   Deposit _____

Address _____   Monthly Rent _____

Property _____   Commission _____

Tenant's Name _____   Leases _____

Units _____   Collection _____

Remarks _____   Management _____

Date	Received From or Paid To	Description	Receipt or Check Number	Amount Received	Date Deposited	Amount Disbursed	Balance

---

Leases

One of the responsibilities of a property manager involves leasing the property or acting as a consultant when drawing up the terms of the lease.

Leasehold Estates

A **leasehold estate** arises when an owner or a property manager acting as the owner's agent grants a tenant the right to occupy the owner's property for a specified period of time for a consideration. The owner is the **lessor** and the tenant is the **lessee.**

There are four basic types of leasehold estates based on the length and nature of their duration. These are the estate for years, the estate from period to period, the estate at sufferance and the estate at will. (see Figure 15.2).

Estate for years. An estate that continues for a definite fixed period of time is an **estate for years.** The lease may be for any specified length of time, even for less than a year, measured in days, weeks or months. This is the most common type of leasehold.

Figure 15.2
Leasehold Estates

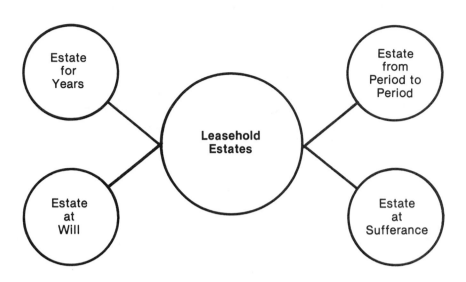

Estate from period to period. An estate from period to period is commonly called a **periodic tenancy.** The lease continues from period to period (either year to year, month to month or week to week), as designated.

Estate at sufferance. An **estate at sufferance** occurs when a tenant obtains possession of property legally but then remains on the property without the owner's consent after the expiration of the leasehold interest.

Estate at will. A lease that can be terminated without notice at any time by the lessor or lessee is an **estate at will** (not used in California).

Types of Leases

The three basic lease forms that the property manager will be expected to work with are the gross lease, net lease and percentage lease (see Figure 15.3).

Gross lease. Under a **gross lease,** the tenant pays a fixed rental and the owner pays all other expenses for the property.

Figure 15.3
Leases Used by
Property Managers

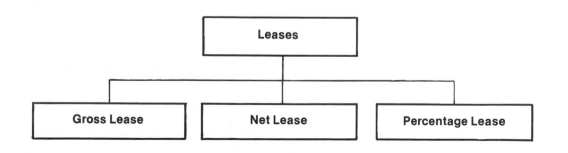

Net lease. Under the terms of a **net lease,** the tenant must pay, in addition to the stated rent, utilities, real estate taxes and other special assessments.

Percentage lease. A **percentage lease** usually provides for the payment of a fixed rental fee plus a percentage of the tenant's gross income in excess of a predetermined minimum amount. Table 15.1 shows typical percentages charged for different businesses having percentage leases. In determining the percent of gross sales that must be paid by the lessee, the greater the return from the property the lower the percentage lease. Example: 50 percent on a parking lot rental and two percent on a supermarket rental.

Table 15.1
Typical Percentages
Charged in the 1980s

Type of Business	Percent of Gross Sales
Grocery or supermarket	1–2
Discount store	1½–3
Laundromat	12–15
Shoe repair shop	10–15
Parking lot	40–50
Garage	40–50

Sales

Every business needs real estate—land, a building, physical facilities—but unless a company is in the real estate business, it does not want to tie up its money in real estate any more than is necessary. For example, a company that makes electronic components wants to be able to devote as much of its money as possible to things that will help it make the components more profitably. In other words, the company wants to spend as much of its money as possible as directly as possible on the business that it knows (electronic components), not on real estate, a business that it needs but does not necessarily know.

Sale-Leaseback

In recent years **sale-leasebacks** have become popular, especially with large companies. There are many variations, but here are two examples of how sale-leasebacks often work. A company that owns its own building wants money for expansion of its operations. Company management contacts an investor (either an individual or a group) and offers to sell the building. The company gets cash for expansion and a long-term lease for the space it needs. In the second example, a company needs a special type of building and cannot locate an appropriate facility. The company builds its own building, but it then needs cash to continue its current operations. It sells the building to an investor and then leases it back.

These are just examples, but the benefits to both parties should be clear. In both cases the companies obtain the physical facilities they need and also are in a position to devote more of their cash to doing what they do most profitably.

Lease-Option
Arrangement

With a **lease-option,** which is usually used when loans are not easily available, the purchaser leases the property desired with an option to purchase at a later date. Usually, a portion of the amount paid as rent will apply against the purchase price.

**Requirements of a
Valid Lease**

For a lease to be valid, it must:

1. contain the names of lessor and lessee and be signed by the *lessor;*

2. be in writing if for longer than one year;

3. contain an adequate description of the property;

4. show the amount of rent and the manner of payment;

5. be between parties who are capable of contracting;

6. state the duration of time the lease is to be in force; and

7. put any renewal provisions in boldface type.

**Cleaning and
Security Deposits**

A controversial item in leases and rental agreements is the security deposit. The security deposit functions as a form of insurance for the landlord in case the rental premises are left damaged or dirty. According to the law, the amount of security that may be demanded or received is limited to two months' rent in the case of unfurnished residential property and, for furnished residential property, an amount equal to three months' rent.

At the termination of the tenancy, the landlord is permitted to retain only that portion of the security deposit reasonably necessary to remedy tenant defaults. If the landlord must return any portion of the deposit to the tenant, the landlord must do so within two weeks after tenancy is terminated. If the landlord defaults on this obligation, the tenant may initiate legal action through an attorney or small claims court or file a complaint with the Consumer Protection Bureau or with the Legal Aid Office.

**Assignment vs.
Sublease**

Provided that the terms of the lease do not prohibit such activity, a tenant has the right to assign or sublet his or her interest in the property. Assignments and subleases are compared in Figure 15.4.

Assignment transfers the entire leasehold rights to a third party. The third party, the subassignee, pays his or her rent directly to the original lessor, thus legally eliminating the original lessee.

A **sublease** of property transfers only a part of the tenant's interest. The sublessee pays his or her rent to the original lessee who, in turn, is responsible to the lessor. The original lessee is said to have a "sandwich lease."

**Landlord-Tenant
Relationship**

A property manager must be ever aware of potential problems that might arise between the landlord and the tenant. The manager should be so versed in the law that mediating disputes, preventing altercations and providing definitive answers will present no difficulty.

Condition of rental unit. A tenant is entitled to housing commensurate with the standards set forth in the California Civil Code and the California Health and Safety Code. In the rental agreement, the tenant agrees to take over and return the rented property in good condition. It follows then that the landlord legally can hold the tenant responsible for any damages over and above normal wear and tear.

**Figure 15.4
Assignment and
Sublease**

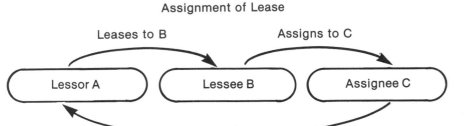

To protect both parties, the manager should prepare an inventory list.

Tenant's responsibilities. The California Civil Code states that the tenant is obligated to:

1. keep the living unit clean and sanitary;

2. dispose of garbage and other waste sanitarily;

3. use all utility fixtures properly, keeping them clean and sanitary;

4. avoid defacing or damaging property;

5. use property only for its intended use;

6. pay rent on time;

7. abide by rules and regulations;

8. give a 30-day notice when vacating;

9. return door and mailbox keys when vacating; and

10. leave the unit in a clean condition when vacating.

If a tenant does not comply with these regulations, the owner is relieved of his or her duties to maintain the property in a habitable condition.

Landlord's responsibilities. The California Health and Safety Code states that the landlord must provide the following:

1. hot and cold running water for every basin, tub or shower, maintaining all plumbing equipment in good working order;

2. light and ventilation for every habitable room;

3. heating equipment that is safe and adequate; and

4. a building that is in good condition, safe, watertight and rodent-proof.

If the owner neglects the responsibility to provide these services, the tenant has three options.

1. The tenant may abandon the property and not be held liable for back rents or an unfulfilled lease.

2. The tenant may refer the problem to a mediator, arbitrator or, in serious circumstances, the small claims court.

3. The tenant may notify the owner in writing of an emergency situation that must be taken care of. If the owner does not respond, the tenant may call in his or her own mechanics and offset the cost of repair with up to one month's rent on the next rent check. However, tenants may do this only twice in each year of tenancy.

Evictions and unlawful detainer. A landlord may evict a tenant and bring unlawful detainer action against him or her for failure to pay rent when due, violation of provisions contained in the lease or rental agreement, or failure to vacate the premises after termination of 30 days' written notice.

The process of removing a tenant is as follows:

1. The landlord serves the tenant with a three-day notice to quit the premises.

2. If the tenant fails to heed the notice, the landlord files an **unlawful detainer** action in court.

3. If the landlord wins, the court awards the landlord a judgment. The landlord then asks for a writ of possession authorizing the sheriff to evict the tenant.

4. The sheriff sends the tenant an eviction notice. If the tenant fails to leave, the sheriff then physically removes the tenant.

Small claims court. An individual may sue in small claims court anyone who owes him or her money. The maximum amount of the suit is $1,500. The procedure is simple and informal:

1. Determine the full legal name and address of the person(s) you are suing. This will help you decide where you must file your claim.

2. Visit the clerk of the small claims court and fill out the form after paying a $2 fee.

3. Arrange for the order to be served on the defendant (but not by yourself). The clerk will mail it for a $1.50 fee, or you may authorize someone to serve it personally.

4. While waiting for the trial, gather all important documents and have them ready. Contact all potential witnesses and arrange for them to come with you to the trial, or obtain a subpoena from the clerk for any witness who will not come voluntarily. If you need an interpreter, find out if one is available at small claims court; otherwise, bring your own.

5. Come to the court building early and ask the clerk where your case is being heard. When you get to the courtroom, check the calendar to see that your case is listed.

6. When your case is called, give your testimony, presenting only the facts. Be brief. Submit all papers and documents you think will help your case.

7. If you win, ask the defendant for the money awarded you in the judgment.

8. If you have difficulties in collecting your money, ask the clerk to assist you.

9. As plaintiff, you are not allowed to appeal if you lose (unless you must pay as the result of a counterclaim).

Illegal Housing Discrimination

State and federal housing laws prohibit housing discrimination in rentals, house sales and real estate services. An apartment manager should be familiar with the following state and federal fair housing laws.

Unruh Civil Rights Act. The State Civil Code Sections 51 and 52, known as the **Unruh Civil Rights Act,** prohibits discrimination in "all business establishments of every kind whatsoever." Court decisions have established that business establishments include dwellings of three units or more, tract developments and real estate brokerages.

Rumford Fair Housing Act. The State Health and Safety Code Sections 35700-35744 are known as the **Rumford Fair Housing Act.** This law prohibits discrimination in public and redevelopment housing; in apartments in structures of three or more units; and in transactions by real estate offices, builders, developers and lenders.

Civil Rights Act of 1968. The **Civil Rights Act of 1968** (Federal Fair Housing Section, 42 U.S. Code Sections 3601-3610) prohibits discrimination in the sale or rental of the following types of property: residential property containing five units or more; buildings with four units or less if the owner does not live in the building; and one-family houses sold or rented by the owner of more than three such houses. It also prohibits discrimination in all residential sales or rentals involving the services of a real estate broker, agent or salesperson and by mortgage or lending institutions.

Statute of 1966 (U.S. Code, Section 1982). The United States Supreme Court has determined that this law prohibits racial discrimination in the sale or rental of *any* kind of housing, regardless of whether the housing is covered under any other law.

Summary

This chapter discussed property management as a segment of the real estate industry. This discussion included the background and development of property management, along with the present activities, responsibilities and duties of a property manager. A property manager needs to be a human relations specialist with management know-how. He or she must be familiar with all types of property and the merchandising techniques necessary to make the enterprise pay off.

The chapter explained the different classifications of leases, as well as various leasing arrangements. Requirements for and terms of leases were discussed, including the legal rights and responsibilities of the landlord and the tenant. Related to rights and responsibilities are the laws prohibiting illegal housing discrimination.

Questions

1. A basic concept of IREM is:
   a. not to commingle funds.
   b. that the manager must be a full-time employee.
   c. both a and b
   d. none of the above

2. CPM stands for:
   a. certified public managers.
   b. certified property management.
   c. certified property managers.
   d. certified public management.

3. What is the difference between a resident manager and a property manager?
   a. They mean same thing.
   b. A resident manager is a licensed real estate agent.
   c. A property manager is a licensed real estate agent.
   d. all of the above

4. A duty of a property manager is:
   a. to supervise all purchasing.
   b. to collect rents.
   c. to keep records.
   d. all of the above

5. Rent schedules are set up on the premise of:
   a. scarcity.
   b. comparability of rents.
   c. both a and b
   d. none of the above

6. A good property manager should be able to do which of the following things?
   a. be a leasing expert
   b. be a credit specialist
   c. understand maintenance problems
   d. all of the above

7. What types of property are managed by property managers?
   a. all types
   b. only commercial
   c. only office buildings
   d. only industrial

8. The most numerous types of property managed by property managers are:
   a. commercial.
   b. residential.
   c. industrial.
   d. office buildings.

9. Accounting records must be kept:
   a. all together.
   b. for each property.
   c. but are not really necessary.
   d. none of the above

10. A lessor is the:
    a. landlord.
    b. tenant.
    c. property manager.
    d. none of the above

11. Which is a leasehold estate?
    a. from month to month
    b. from month to year
    c. from day to week
    d. all of the above

12. An estate for years continues:
    a. until the tenant dies.
    b. for a definite fixed period.
    c. from year to year.
    d. none of the above

13. An estate at sufferance is created when:
    a. the tenant gets sick.
    b. the lease is signed.
    c. a tenant stays after the expiration of the lease.
    d. all of the above

14. Which of the following is a type of lease?
    a. net lease
    b. percentage lease
    c. gross lease
    d. all of the above

15. In a gross lease the tenant pays:
    a. a fixed amount.
    b. a fixed amount plus a percentage of net profits.
    c. a percentage.
    d. none of the above

16. The expenses are usually paid by the _____ in a gross lease.
    a. lessee
    b. lessor
    c. lessee and lessor equally
    d. none of the above

17. In a sale-option agreement:
    a. the lessee leases the property until some later date, when he or she then may purchase it.
    b. the lessor leases the property back from the lessee.
    c. both a and b
    d. none of the above

18. When a security deposit is taken, the landlord may keep _____ at the end of the lease.
    a. all of it
    b. only that amount reasonably necessary to remedy tenant defaults
    c. half of it
    d. none of it

19. Assignment of a lease:
    a. is the same as a sublease.
    b. assigns the leasehold rights to a third party.
    c. both a and b
    d. none of the above

20. Which of the following laws protects against discrimination in businesses?
    a. Civil Rights Act of 1968
    b. Rumford Fair Housing Act
    c. Unruh Civil Rights Act
    d. none of the above

16

Specialties: Business Opportunities, Probate Sales, Insurance and Mobile Homes

Chapter Preview　　　The real estate business has many areas of specialization in which brokers often become involved. This chapter explores the legal requirements and techniques involved in the sale of business opportunities. This discussion also includes sales and use tax regulations and alcohol beverage control procedures.

Other specialties discussed in the chapter are probate sales and property and casualty insurance. The last part of the discussion is the regulation of mobile home sales.

Terms To Look For　　　**Alcohol Beverage Control Act**
Bulk sale
Bulk Sales Transfer Act
Business opportunity
Goodwill
Homeowners' insurance
Mobile home
Probate sales
Sales tax
Security agreement
Security interest
State Board of Equalization
Uniform Commercial Code
Workers' compensation insurance

Business Opportunities Sales	A law passed in 1966 eliminated the requirement for a special license to sell business opportunities. Today, any real estate licensee may legally negotiate the sale of a business opportunity.

What Is a Business Opportunity?

Real estate law defines the sale of a **business opportunity** as the sale or lease of a business, including the goodwill of an existing business. Typical business opportunity sales involve dry-cleaning establishments, Laundromats, restaurants, camera shops and clothing stores.

Real estate sales differ from business opportunities sales in a number of respects, hence the requirements for treating this subject separately. The sale of a business opportunity is the sale of *personal property.* As such, the transfer instrument is a bill of sale, not a deed, as in the sale of real property. The security is a security instrument rather than a trust deed or a mortgage. The sale of a business opportunity usually involves the separate sale and escrow of stock, fixtures and goodwill, while a real property transfer involves one basic transfer and one escrow. Business opportunities sales also involve the transfer of permits and licenses.

Required Knowledge

Before becoming involved as a broker of business opportunities, a broker needs specialized knowledge. This includes:

1. knowledge of the business being sold sufficient to form a valid opinion as to the worth and profitability of the business;

2. knowledge of accounting and the ability to analyze operating statements;

3. knowledge of norms and ratios that may apply to a particular business; and

4. knowledge of the laws and regulations governing the transfer of personal property.

Valuation of Business Opportunities

Step 1: Obtain data. One of the first steps in obtaining a salable business opportunity listing is for the licensee to obtain a copy of the business tax statements for the last three years. Through these statements, the licensee will be able to ascertain the trend in profits experienced by the business. These figures will be an excellent barometer for determining the rate of return the buyer can expect on the investment. If the seller is hesitant about furnishing such information, his or her profit-and-loss statements for the same period will supply similar data.

Step 2: Analyze data. The second step in the valuation process is to analyze the operating statements for present and future profit potential. In performing this function, the licensee should apply normal expense ratios to the following entries on the finance statements:

1. net worth and assets to liabilities;

2. current assets to current liabilities;

3. cash position;

4. stock turnover;

5. return on investment;

6. cost of sales; and

7. ratio of operating expenses to gross revenue.

Licensees who lack a sound knowledge of accounting should refer final analysis of operating statements and reports to an accountant.

Methods of valuation. Before a fair-market price for the business can be established, the result of the findings can be approached by one of two methods or by a combination of both.

One method involves capitalization value of the business. In other words, the value is based on the expectation of future profits and the return on the investment over the next few years. The buyer will want to know whether the rate of return on this business will be as great as the rate of return on some other investment. To determine this, the licensee will not only have to understand the potential of the business being analyzed but should also know the profit trends of other businesses. Good sources for such information are the publications of the U.S. Small Business Administration, Bank of America and National Cash Register Association. With this information at hand, the licensee can determine the capitalized value, that value that would bring future earnings at a specified rate.

Another method of valuing a business involves the appraisal of fixed assets and inventory. When this method is used, the appraisal usually includes not only the inventory of stock but also of sales and office supplies, fixtures, tools and equipment, and sometimes the real estate itself. It usually does not include such personal property as prepaid insurance, certain supplies, cash, accounts and notes receivable or any marketable securities.

The best valuation procedure is to combine the methods. Regardless of the method used, however, a study of authentic records should be made to determine an equitable selling price.

There is no magic formula for estimating an equitable, salable price of a business. These suggestions will be helpful and, if adhered to, will produce a ready, willing and able buyer as per the terms of the listing. The appraisal is only an estimate of value, and there will necessarily be differences of opinion. The appraisal of a business opportunity is exceptionally difficult due to the wide diversity in business. For this reason, brokers often specialize in certain areas, such as liquor stores, hotels or radio stations.

Goodwill. A business's **goodwill** is the expectation of continued and repeated patronage. Although the amount attributable to goodwill rarely exceeds the value of the physical stock, furniture, fixtures and equipment, it adds value to the business because of the owner's policies toward clients and customers. This value comes not only from advertising, merchandise and services but from the reputation that the business enjoys in its present location.

Determining the value of goodwill might be based on answers to these questions:

1. How long has the business been operating?

2. Does the location allow for increased volume in the future?

3. What is the nature of the competition?

4. Will the seller include the business name in the transaction?

5. Is the business properly suited to the location?

6. Will the seller agree not to compete within a certain geographical radius or within a fixed period of time?

Listings

As in real property transaction, the first step in a business opportunity transaction is the *listing,* which may be exclusive or nonexclusive.

The listing should include the following:

1. the general nature of the business;

2. the type of ownership;

3. the inventory and equipment (at least their general nature);

4. any liens on the inventory and/or the equipment;

5. the company's earnings record;

6. all expenses of the business (including utilities, insurance, taxes and wages);

7. the state of any existing lease;

8. the price and terms of the sale; and

9. the right to use the seller's business name.

Before preparing the listing agreement, the licensee should have on hand certain basic data concerning the business. A sample form for gathering this information is shown in Figure 16.1. The broker is responsible for the accuracy of the information in the listing agreement.

Other listing considerations are:

1. Is there an existing lease on the property? This item is vital and of the utmost importance for possible future success.

2. Will the seller or the seller's accountant or attorney cooperate in furnishing the broker with income and expense records, copies of leases, insurance policies, etc., so that the business can be properly evaluated?

3. The owner's motive for selling is important. If the business has not been particularly successful, the owner may have a tendency to alter financial statements to give a rosier picture. It is the responsibility of the broker to warn the seller against such fraudulent practices.

4. Financing is always an important factor. Is the licensee prepared to answer the following questions of the lending institution or to the buyer's satisfaction?

   • Are the profits satisfactory?

   • If not, what are the chances of increasing them?

   • Have profits been consistent over a period of years?

   • If the last year's profit was unusually high in comparison with previous years, why was it?

- What is the profit trend?

- Have profits been increasing consistently, or have they leveled off or started to decrease? Why?

5. Even if a business has not been successful, this does not mean that it would be a poor investment. Lack of success may have been due to poor management and the buyer may feel that better management can vastly improve the situation.

6. What are the strengths and weaknesses of the premises?

- Is the location suited to the business?

- Is desired pedestrian and/or vehicular traffic adequate?

Figure 16.1
Form for Gathering Listing Information

Business Name_____ Address_____

Date Bus. Established_____ Present Owner since_____

Hours Open_____ Day Closed_____

LEASE

Length_____ Date expires_____ Option?_____

Lessor Name_____ Phone_____ Address_____

Bldg. Size_____ Age_____ Construction_____ Air-Cond.?_____

Heat Type_____ Living Qtrs?_____ Lot Size_____

APPROXIMATE INCOME

Average Mo. Gross $_____ Average Yrly. Gross $_____

Average Mo. Net $_____ Average Yrly. Net $_____

APPROXIMATE MONTHLY EXPENSES

Rent_____ Lot Care_____ Utilities_____ Other_____

Labor_____ Repairs_____ Supplies_____

Miscel._____ License_____ Auto_____ Remarks_____

ESTIMATE VALUES

Furniture, Fixtures & Equipment $_____

Inventory $_____ Accountant Name_____

Business Price Including Inventory & Commission $_____

Terms_____

- Is parking available and sufficient?
- Can the store be seen, and do all signs conform to zoning ordinances?
- Is the square footage adequate for present and potential expansion?
- Do the premises conform to all zoning ordinances and building and safety codes?

7. What amounts and types of insurance are deemed necessary?

8. Are employee benefit plans and agreements being used? Are they adequate?

9. What about the hours of operation?

10. Is the business being operated within the laws applicable to that particular type of business?

Selling a Business Opportunity

When a buyer is found as per terms of the listing and before the sale is consummated, it is a good idea to take a physical inventory to assure that the value in the listing is correct. If by any chance the figure falls short of the stated amount, an adjustment will have to be made. The licensee should let sellers know that their books and records must be open for inspection after a deposit is received.

Seller's motives to sell. A seller's motives will vary with each individual business, but they might include one or more of the following:

- retirement;
- poor health;
- a move to another city;
- relocation and expansion;
- threat of bankruptcy; or
- a desire to quit business and work for others.

Buyer's motives to buy. A licensee must be cognizant of the special needs of the buyer, who relies on the licensee for advice. The buyer's motives will usually include one or more of the following:

- desire to be boss;
- desire for an opportunity to earn more;
- retirement to a second career;
- assertion of individuality;
- pursuit of a dream; or
- expansion of an existing ongoing business.

Licensee's responsibility to the buyer. The responsibility of a licensee toward the buyer in the sale of business opportunities is even greater than in standard real estate transactions. The licensee should ascertain whether or not the buyer's personality is compatible with the demands of the business contemplated. Remember, a buyer may be investing a lifetime's savings in a business on the prospect of future profit. In the hands of a buyer not adapted or adaptable to that business, a thriving business can become nearly worthless in a short period of time. Extreme care should be taken to make the potential risk known to the buyer.

Counseling a buyer. Before counseling a buyer, answer the following questions that cover the basic facts you should know about your prospect:

1. Has the buyer ever worked in a similar business?

2. Does the buyer have any prior business experience to show whether he or she can start a business and make it pay off?

3. How much money can the buyer invest?

4. Where can the balance of the money be obtained?

5. What kind of credit allowance can be expected from suppliers?

6. Has the buyer already consulted with an attorney, accountant or banker?

7. Will the broker be coordinating the purchase with them?

8. Is the buyer expecting an unreasonable net income from the business?

9. Is the buyer prepared to cover start-up costs, such as beginning inventory, deposits with utilities, licenses and permits, and advertising?

10. Can the buyer sustain unexpected losses or expenses, and for what period of time?

11. Will the current financial statements of the going business, together with the buyer's financial status, be adequate to obtain a direct loan from a bank or the Small Business Administration Loan Guaranty Plan?

Preparing the Offer of Purchase and Deposit Receipt   When the licensee and the buyer prepare the deposit receipt, certain contingencies must be carefully checked and included in the document to protect both the buyer and the broker. These include:

1. the amount of rent being paid;

2. if a lease exists, its terms and conditions and length;

3. the seller's legal right and ability to transfer the lease to the buyer;

4. the approval and inspection of all financing statements and records;

5. the inspection and approval of the inventory being transferred;

6. the transfer of various licenses; and

7. the ability to secure required permits.

Legal Requirements   Following the preparation of the offer and prior to the close of escrow, certain legal requirements must be met. The applicable laws are shown in Figure 16.2.

Figure 16.2
Laws Pertaining to the
Sale of Business
Opportunities

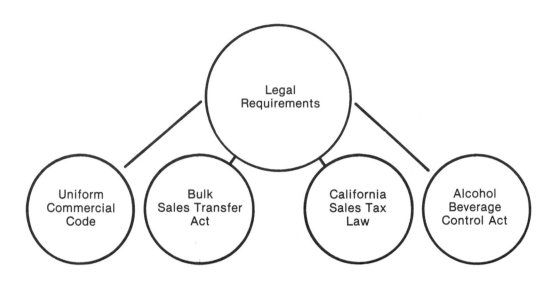

Uniform   For the purpose of regulating security transactions in personal property, the **Uni-**
Commercial   **form Commercial Code** was instituted.
Code

Security agreement. Under the Uniform Commercial Code, a borrower of money to purchase a business opportunity retains both title and possession but gives the lender a **security interest.** He or she executes a promissory note and a **security agreement.** The security agreement, formerly called a *chattel mortgage,* gives the lender a security interest in the personal property.

Financing statement. To protect the lender and give the public notice of the security interest, the debtor signs a financing statement. The statement is generally filed with the Secretary of State. The exception to this filing location is when the transaction involves consumer goods or farm equipment and farm products other than crops. This type of statement is filed with the county recorder in the county in which the debtor lives. The statement is effective for five years.

For further information concerning this type of transaction, a special booklet and forms can be obtained by writing to the California Secretary of State, Sacramento, CA 95808.

Bulk Sales   Division 6 of the Uniform Commercial Code is called the **Bulk Sales Transfer Act**
Transfer Act   and involves the bulk transfer of goods. A **bulk sale** is the transfer of goods making up a substantial portion of an inventory not ordinarily sold in the regular course of business.

The buyer in a bulk sale records the sale in the recorder's office of the county where the property is located at least 12 days before the transfer is to be consummated. The publication of the notice by the transferee is made in a newspaper of general circulation in the judicial district where the property is located at least 12 days prior to the date of the bulk transfer. The recording and publication allow the creditors to protect their rights before the assets are disposed of or encumbered.

Noncompliance with the requirements of Division 6 of the Uniform Commercial Code can render the transfer fraudulent and void against any creditors who hold claims based on transactions occurring before the bulk transfer.

California Sales Tax Provisions

A knowledge of the California sales tax law is of the utmost importance to licensees in the sale of business opportunities involving the sale of tangible personal property at retail. For the privilege of selling tangible personal property at retail, a 6.5 percent sales tax on gross receipts is imposed on all retailers. This includes local and state sales taxes. The seller of the business must take out a seller's permit when engaging in business and must post security for the collection of sales tax.

The buyer must obtain a clearance receipt, which will protect the buyer against successor's liability. In the absence of such a clearance receipt the buyer may be held liable if the seller has not remitted sales tax collected. The buyer must also obtain releases or subordination agreements covering sales tax liens against real or personal property.

The seller of a business must pay sales tax on the sale price of a business in proportion to the fair retail value of the tangible property involved.

Alcohol Beverage Control Act

A licensee who intends to become involved in the sale of business opportunities needs to become familiar with the legal controls involved in the sale and distribution of alcoholic beverages, especially the licenses and permits that are involved. These regulations are contained in the **Alcohol Beverage Control Act.**

Licenses. Licenses are issued to qualified adults, partnerships, fiduciaries and corporations for use at particular premises that have been approved by the department.[1] It is also within the jurisdiction of the department to deny a license for cause or to disapprove a location for cause. No employee of the department is authorized to give any applicant any assurance that a license will be granted nor can any applicant use any outside influence to obtain a license.[2]

The original on-sale or off-sale liquor license fee is $6,000. When a license is transferred, the purchase price or consideration that may be *paid* by a transferee or received by a transferor for that type of license issued after June 1, 1981, may not exceed $6,000. An exception to this rule is that when a license is transferred after a period of five years from the original date of issuance of the license, there is no restriction as to the purchase price.

Other restrictions. Brokers may not purchase licenses at a bankruptcy or trustee's sale, with the expectation of transfer to a nominee. The only person who may have an interest in an alcoholic beverage license is the person who is operating or intends

---

[1] *California Department of Real Estate Reference Book,* 1984-1985 edition, p. 710.
[2] Ibid., p. 711.

to operate the licensed business. The department may file a complaint against any broker who participates in the sale of a license against which disciplinary action is pending, if the agent fails to determine that fact and advise the purchaser.[3]

A copy of the Alcohol Beverage Control Act may be obtained from the nearest office of the Department of Alcohol Beverage Control. A licensee would be wise to obtain a copy of this law if he or she is going to be involved in the transfer of liquor business licenses.

Government Agencies Involved

In the transfer of a business opportunity, another of the responsibilities of the licensee to the prospective purchaser is to advise him or her of the governmental agencies (federal, state, and local) that must be contacted prior to opening the business. Such agencies are:

- *Internal Revenue Service* (to obtain employer identification number in connection with federal withholding taxes);
- **State Board of Equalization** (to obtain a sales tax permit);
- *State Department of Benefit Payments* (for state payroll tax withholding); and
- *State Department of Industrial Relations* (responsible for workers' compensation insurance).

Other agencies include the board of health, the Occupational Safety and Health Administration, police and fire departments, and various county and municipal agencies regarding licenses and permits.

Probate Sales

Probate is a legal process by which a superior court determines who will inherit the property of a deceased person and what the assets of the estate are. The estate of the deceased person is administered either by an executor named in the will or by an administrator appointed by the courts when a person dies without leaving a will (intestate). Either of these has similar powers, authorities and obligations under the jurisdiction of the court.

If during the probate proceedings it is necessary to dispose of the property by sale, open listings may be granted to interested brokers. The property may be sold by private or public **probate sale.** Usually a notice of intended sale is published in a newspaper of general circulation in the county in which the property is located.

Submitted Bids

After the first publication of the intention to sell, brokers may submit written bids to the clerk of the superior court where the property is located. The amount of the initial bid must be at least 90 percent of the inheritance tax appraisal of the property. All sealed bids are opened on the day of the sale and the highest *net* bid is accepted. However, this bid is subject to the approval of the court, and prior to this confirmation the judge may ask if there are any higher bids.

Any additional bids may be submitted by the broker on behalf of his or her client or by any other person present. Any new bid must be in the increased amount of ten

---

[3]*California Department of Real Estate Reference Book,* 1984-1985 edition, p. 712.

percent of the first $10,000 of the bid being considered plus 5 percent of the balance in excess of $10,000. Bids may continue until the court decides the amount to be the best and highest obtainable.

Broker's Commission

If a broker's bid is confirmed by the court, the court will usually order a full commission to be paid out of the proceeds of the sale. Even if the broker's original bid is overbid in the court, he or she is still entitled to one-half of the negotiated commission based on the original bid. Then if the broker submits the final and highest bid to the court, he or she will be awarded the remaining half of the commission based on the original bid.

In its order confirming the sale, the court will set forth the amount of commission to be paid and the division of the commission if more than one broker is to be paid.[4] Normal escrow procedures are used to complete the sales transaction in accordance with the terms and conditions approved by the courts.

Selling Insurance

The purpose of insurance is to shift the risk of a loss to a third party who is responsible for restoring the insured to his or her position before the loss. This is called *indemnifying* the insured for the loss.

It is quite common for larger real estate brokerage offices to represent insurance companies. It becomes a feed-in source of income to brokers, particularly for sales transactions originating in their offices.[5]

Requirements

A broker must be properly licensed as an insurance agent, and it is his or her responsibility to keep abreast of all changes relating to coverages, provisions, clauses and riders, so that mistakes can be avoided. In selling or managing property for a client a broker who carries an insurance license may act for the purchaser, seller or lender in placing insurance. However, as such, the broker is acting in a fiduciary capacity and is obligated to secure competitive rates.

Types of Insurance

There are a variety of insurance policies with which a broker/insurance agent must be familiar, particularly those that cover the risks of real property ownership. A single insurance company may have hundreds of insurance contracts, each of which can be changed by insurance endorsements. The following are brief descriptions of the major policies with which a homeowner should be concerned.

Fire insurance. Fire insurance is written to cover buildings and their contents, such as personal property, equipment and merchandise. The basis for any settlement of a loss is the actual cash value or the replacement cost less depreciation.

The insured should not expect to actually make money on an insured loss. The actual cash value is determined by deducting depreciation from current replacement cost (including any appreciation).

---

[4]*California Department of Real Estate Reference Book,* 1984-1985 edition, p. 214.
[5]Ibid., p. 582.

The amount of the insurance policy limits the company's obligation, and a loss will not be paid in excess of that amount. In other words, total destruction of the property does not necessarily mean that the insurance company will pay all of the loss. Most companies will suggest that a client insure for at least 80 percent of the true value of property. (This is considered 100 percent of the improvements, as the land will not be destroyed.) This means that if clients insure their properties for 80 percent of value, they will receive 100 percent of the value of the actual loss sustained. If they insure for less than this amount, the amounts for which they will be indemnified will be calculated on a pro rata basis.

For example, a home appraised at $100,000 is insured for 80 percent of that amount, or $80,000. In the event of a fire in which the loss is estimated at $20,000, the insured would receive the full amount based on this formula:

$$\frac{80}{80} \times \$20,000 = \$20,000$$

If the insured were to insure the same property for 60 percent of the value, the amount indemnified would be:

$$\frac{60}{80} \times \$20,000 = \$15,000$$

Multiperil homeowners' insurance. A **homeowners' insurance** policy is available to a homeowner as a composite package covering many different risks. The terms of coverage are often broader than would be provided in separate policies. It is a definite advantage to the homeowner to have several forms of insurance in one policy and from one insurance company.

There are many special features in homeowners' policies, and an increasing number of homeowners are converting to this coverage. The policies range from the lowest (Form HO-1) to the highest (Form HO-5) of all risks.

Multiple peril—business risks. Under this policy, an owner can obtain insurance on his or her building, equipment and stock against loss by fire and various additional perils, or on an all-risks basis, with business liability, employee dishonesty, boiler and machinery, burglary and robbery, and several other forms of coverage all in one policy.

Several insurance companies have introduced their own package policies, and there are a large number of plans from which to choose.

Workers' Compensation Insurance. All employers in California are subject to the Workmen's Compensation Act and must provide for the benefits required. **Workers' compensation insurance** including unlimited medical benefits for employees hurt on the job and payment of wages lost because of injury is offered by most property and casualty insurance companies.

One of the requirements for coverage under this plan is an employer-employee relationship. This determination in the case of the broker-salesperson relationship has caused a great deal of controversy. Does the broker-salesperson relationship have an employer-employee status, or is the salesperson considered to be an independent contractor? If the relationship is one of employer-employee, there should be workers' compensation insurance on the salesperson.

The Real Estate Commissioner is rather specific in interpreting this distinction. The following statements are from the *California Real Estate Reference Book:*

> An independent contractor is one who, in rendering services, exercises an independent employment or occupation and is responsible to the employer only as to the results of his/her work.

> For purposes of the Real Estate License Law—and this is of primary significance to a licensee—salespersons are *employees* of the broker as a matter of law and *cannot* be independent contractors.

> Questions relating to how other governmental agencies view the broker-salesperson relationship should be referred to those agencies. For purposes of Federal Income Taxes, Workmen's Compensation, Unemployment Insurance, or other matters outside the scope of the License Law, the relationship of the broker and the salesperson is a matter of fact.

Selling Mobile Homes

A **mobile home** is defined by the California Health and Safety Code as "a vehicle designed and equipped to contain not more than two dwelling units, to be used without permanent foundation. In the past, mobile homes were confused with trailers. The major difference is that trailers usually provide temporary housing only, while a mobile home is a permanent living unit. As a matter of fact, although they are still considered low-cost housing, mobile homes are now priced as high as $60,000 or even higher.

Rules and Regulations

The real estate agent must learn a whole new field of rules and regulations before venturing into mobile home sales. The pertinent Business and Professions Codes relating to Mobile Home Sales are Sections 10131.6, 10131.7 and 10177.2. Commissioner's Regulations dealing with the subject are Sections 2860, 2861, 2862 and 2863.

Licensees should also know the applicable provisions of other pertinent codes, including the Health and Safety Code, Commercial Code, Revenue and Taxation Code, Civil Code, Administrative Code, local zoning ordinances and the Truth-in-Lending Act.

One of the most recent laws seriously affecting mobile homes was recently approved. This law makes any mobile home that is sold on or after July 1, 1980, and is installed for occupancy as a residence subject to *local real property taxation,* rather than vehicle taxation.

Specific Legal Requirements

To list or sell a mobile home, a real estate licensee must comply with special aspects of the real estate law:

1. *New* mobile homes may not be sold by real estate licensees but only through mobile home dealers licensed by the Department of Housing and Community Development.

2. A real estate licensee can sell *used* mobile homes, provided they have been licensed for at least one year and are at least eight feet wide and 32 feet long.

3. The mobile home must be capable of being transported over a road. The hitch must be attached to the unit or stored underneath, and the axles must be attached to the frame.

4. The licensee is responsible for the proper completion and delivery of the title to the buyer.

5. Notification of transfer of ownership must be made within ten days of the date of the sale.

6. All fees must be paid to the Department of Housing and Community Development within 20 days of the sale date.

7. No concealment of a material fact or any other fraudulent act may be committed.

8. The buyer must be assured that the purchased mobile home may occupy a private lot for at least one year.

9. If the mobile home was manufactured after June 15, 1976, it must have a Department of Housing and Urban Development (HUD) tag guaranteeing its proper construction.

Business and Professions Code

Under the Business and Professions Code, real estate licensees may have their licenses suspended or revoked if they are found guilty of:

- failure to provide for delivery of proper certification of ownership of a mobile home;

- having knowingly participated in the purchase or sale of a stolen mobile home; or

- submitting a check, draft or money order to the Department of Housing and Community Development for payment of fees that is dishonored on presentation to the bank.

Financing Mobile Homes

Because mobile homes are essentially considered to be personal property in California, the method of encumbering the ownership is through the Certificate of Ownership (pink slip). Mobile homes can now be financed through FHA, VA and Cal Vet loans and, in addition, by loan associations and other real estate lenders. Most mobile home loans are amortized over a 15- to 20-year period. Interest rates on mobile home loans are usually higher than on conventional home loans.

Summary

This chapter explained the listing, evaluation and sale of business opportunities. To describe the legal requirements and responsibilities faced by the broker, a comparison was made between business opportunity sales and real property sales. A portion of the chapter was devoted to a better understanding of the seller's motives in selling a business and the buyer's motives for purchasing a business. Goodwill was explained, and those situations that determine the value of goodwill were explored.

The activities under the jurisdiction of the Uniform Commercial Code were included in the chapter. Laws introduced included the Bulk Sales Transfer Act, California sales tax law and the Alcohol Beverage Control Act. The discussion covered recording, advertising, sales tax liability and licensing. These activities involve numerous government agencies, including the Internal Revenue Service, State Board of Equalization, State Department of Industrial Relations, OSHA, and special county and municipal agencies.

The subject of probate sales was discussed, including submission of bids and broker's commissions.

The types of insurance that licensees could consider selling were treated, including fire insurance, workers' compensation, multiple peril—business risks and homeowners' insurance.

The chapter concluded with an explanation of the laws related to mobile home sales, including the transition from DMV-taxed homes to real property taxation.

Questions

1. The real estate agent, in a business opportunity sale, may sell which of the following?

   a. inventory
   b. personal property
   c. real property
   d. all of the above

2. A method of determining the sales price for a business is the:

   a. quick acid ratio test.
   b. turnover of accounts payable.
   c. capitalization value.
   d. all of the above

3. A business's goodwill is defined as:

   a. its resources.
   b. the expectation of continued patronage.
   c. both a and b
   d. none of the above

4. Which of the following would *not* be used in determining the goodwill of a business?

   a. single entry or double entry accounting system
   b. length of time the business has been in operation
   c. nature of competition
   d. the location of the business

5. The owner should have concern over which of the following items, when selling a business opportunity?

   a. financing
   b. cash method of accounting vs. accrual method of accounting
   c. both a and b
   d. none of the above

6. A "security agreement" is also called:

   a. a trust deed.
   b. a chattel mortgage.
   c. a promissory note.
   d. all of the above

7. Who records a bulk sale?

   a. seller
   b. buyer
   c. agent
   d. trustee

8. A bulk sale must be recorded at least _____ days before the sale (transfer of property).

   a. 7
   b. 10
   c. 12
   d. 30

9. Which of the following agencies might be involved in a sale of a business?

   a. Department of Real Estate
   b. Internal Revenue Service
   c. State Board of Equalization
   d. all of the above

10. Probate is defined as:

    a. the process of writing a will.
    b. a legal process by which the court determines the heirs.
    c. a process by which the oldest son determines the heirs.
    d. all of the above

11. When a person dies without a will, this is known as:

    a. dying intestate.
    b. dying in probate.
    c. both a and b
    d. none of the above

12. The purpose of insurance is:

    a. to make a profit.
    b. to maximize the loss.
    c. to shift the loss to a third party.
    d. none of the above

13. Which of the following regulations govern bulk sales transactions?

    a. Commissioner's Regulations
    b. Truth-in-Lending Law
    c. Uniform Commercial Code
    d. Real Estate Law

14. Which of the following types of loans can be placed on a mobile home?

    a. VA
    b. FHA
    c. conventional
    d. all of the above

15. A real estate agent may sell:

    a. a new mobile home.
    b. mobile homes more than a year old.
    c. both a and b
    d. none of the above

16. If a mobile home were purchased today, it would be taxed:

    a. by DMV.
    b. as personal property.
    c. both a and b
    d. none of the above

17. When hiring personnel to work in your business, you should always carry:

    a. life insurance.
    b. multiperil homeowners' insurance.
    c. health insurance.
    d. workers' compensation insurance.

18. A homeowner's multiperil insurance is designed:

    a. to cover multiple risks.
    b. to replace the entire building in case of fire.
    c. to cover fire and title insurance.
    d. none of the above

19. Which of the following agencies would be involved in a sale of a business opportunity?

    a. IRS
    b. State Board of Equalization
    c. both a and b
    d. none of the above

20. A business license may be issued to which of the following?

    a. corporation
    b. fiduciaries
    c. partnerships
    d. all of the above

Index